Quarterly National Accounts Manual
Concepts, Data Sources, and Compilation

By Adriaan M. Bloem, Robert J. Dippelsman, and Nils Ø. Mæhle

INTERNATIONAL MONETARY FUND
Washington DC
2001

Library of Congress Cataloging-in-Publication data

Bloem, Adriaan M.
    Manual for quarterly national accounts : concepts, data sources, and compilation /
by Adriaan M. Bloem, Robert J. Dippelsman, and Nils Ø. Mæhle. -- Washington, D.C. :
International Monetary Fund, 2001.
        p. : ill. ; cm.

    Includes bibliographical references.
    ISBN 1-58906-031-8

    1. National income – Accounting – Handbooks, manuals, etc. I. Dippelsman, Robert
J. II. Mæhle, Nils Øyvind. III. International Monetary Fund.
HC79.I5 B46 2001

Price: US$40.00

Please send orders to:
International Monetary Fund, Publication Services
700 19th Street, NW, Washington, DC 20431, U.S.A.
Telephone: (202) 623-7430   Telefax: (202) 623-7201
E-mail: publications@imf.org
Internet: http://www.imf.org

Although this manual has benefitted from comments from IMF
colleagues, it represents the views of the authors and not necessarily
those of the IMF.

Table of contents

Table of contents

Foreword

The recent financial crises taught us a number of important lessons. We were reminded that, for adjustment programs to be sustainable, there must be careful attention to institution-building, the social dimensions of structural change, and a country's political and cultural traditions. We have worked closely with other international organizations to develop standards and codes for sound monetary and fiscal policies, banking supervision, and economic data. Work in all of these areas helps to promote financial stability, and it helps countries take advantage of the enormous potential of private capital markets. In this context, it is important to develop instruments to improve the ability to detect sources of vulnerability and to propose timely corrective measures. One focus of the IMF's work in this area is on increasing the availability of key data.

The IMF has undertaken a range of activities in this regard. Significant among these is the development of two data initiatives, namely, the Special Data Dissemination Standard and the General Data Dissemination System. For both these initiatives it is important that international guidelines be available to help countries develop internationally comparable statistics. In several areas where international guidelines have been lacking or have become outdated, the IMF has undertaken to fill the gaps. One such area concerns quarterly national accounts, and I am very pleased to introduce the *Quarterly National Accounts Manual*, which has been drafted to help countries establish or strengthen quarterly national accounts that meet international standards. This manual takes its place alongside the other manuals prepared or being prepared in the IMF's Statistics Department, including the *Balance of Payments Manual*, the *Government Finance Statistics Manual*, and the *Monetary and Financial Statistics Manual*. Like these other manuals, this manual is fully consistent with the *System of National Accounts 1993*.

This manual is a direct result of technical assistance in support of the Special Data Dissemination Standard. It draws heavily from course material prepared for national accounts seminars for countries considering subscription to this Standard. The *Manual* has benefited from comments from country experts during these seminars and during an expert group meeting in June 2000, in which country experts and experts from other international organizations participated. I would like to thank all experts for their participation in the gestation process of this manual.

Quarterly national accounts data play a vital role in the development and monitoring of sound economic and financial programs. At this time, only a minority of Fund member countries have the benefit of a well-established system of quarterly national accounts, although their number is rapidly increasing. I hope that this trend continues and would like to commend the *Manual* to compilers as an important instrument in this work.

Horst Köhler
Managing Director
International Monetary Fund

Preface

This *Quarterly National Accounts Manual* was developed from materials prepared for seminars in Thailand (1997 and 1998) and Jordan (2000). Like the seminars, the *Manual* is aimed particularly at compilers who already have a knowledge of national accounting concepts and methods in an annual context and are in the process of introducing or improving a quarterly national accounts (QNA) system. As well, we believe it will be of interest to national accounts compilers generally and to sophisticated QNA users. QNA are an increasingly important specialty within national accounting. More and more countries are recognizing QNA as an essential tool for the management and analysis of the economy. The *Manual* aims to complement the *System of National Accounts 1993 (1993 SNA)*, which has only limited discussion of QNA, while retaining full consistency with that document.

Some general guidelines that emerge from this manual are the following:
- QNA should be built on a foundation of timely and accurate quarterly source data that directly cover a high proportion of the totals. Econometric methods and indirect behavioral relationships are not a substitute for data collection.
- QNA should be made consistent with their annual equivalents, partly for the convenience of users and partly— and more fundamentally—because the benchmarking process incorporates the information content of the annual data into the quarterly estimates.
- Revisions are needed to allow timely release of data and to allow incorporation of new data. Possible inconvenience of revisions can best be dealt with by openness about the process.
- QNA data should be presented as consistent time series.
- The potential scope of QNA is the whole of the *1993 SNA* sequence of accounts. Although gross domestic product (GDP) and its components—the usual starting point—are important, other parts of the national accounts system are also useful and achievable.
- Seasonally adjusted data, trend data, and unadjusted data all provide useful perspectives, but the unadjusted data should be the foundation of national accounts compilation.

Within these guidelines, the sources, methods, and scope of each country's QNA system will differ according to circumstances such as user preferences, availability of source data, and economic conditions. Accordingly, our objective is not to give fixed answers but to indicate the range of alternatives and to supply general principles that can be applied to develop a QNA system suitable for each country's circumstances.

We hope that the *Manual* will find its way to a broad readership and will support the introduction, improvement, and wise use of QNA in many countries.

Carol S. Carson
Director
Statistics Department
International Monetary Fund

Acknowledgments

The authors are grateful for comments from IMF colleagues, particularly from Carol S. Carson, Paul Armknecht, Paul Cotterell, Jemma Dridi, Segismundo Fassler, Cor Gorter, John Joisce, Sarmad Khawaja, Manik Shrestha, and Kim Zieschang. The authors are also grateful for comments from the participants in a workshop held in July, 2000 to discuss the draft manual, namely, Mr. Roberto Barcellan (Eurostat), Mr. Raúl García Belgrano (ECLAC), Ms. Marietha Gouws (South Africa), Mr. Peter Harper (Australia), Ms. Barbro Hexeberg (World Bank), Ms. Olga Ivanova (World Bank), Mr. Ronald Janssen (The Netherlands), Mr. Paul McCarthy (OECD), Mr. Dave McDowell (Canada), Ms. Chellam Palanyandy (Malaysia), Mr. Robert Parker (USA), Mr. Eugene Seskin (USA), Mr. Jan van Tongeren (UN), and Mr. Agustín Velázquez (Venezuela). Useful comments were also received through the IMF's website. The authors retain full responsibility for any remaining omissions and errors.

I Introduction

A. Introduction

1.1. Quarterly national accounts (QNA) constitute a system of integrated quarterly time series coordinated through an accounting framework. QNA adopt the same principles, definitions, and structure as the annual national accounts (ANA). In principle, QNA cover the entire sequence of accounts and balance sheets in the *System of National Accounts 1993 (1993 SNA)*; in practice, the constraints of data availability, time, and resources mean that QNA are usually less complete than ANA. The coverage of the QNA system in a country usually evolves. In the initial stage of implementation, only estimates of gross domestic product (GDP) with a split by industry and/or type of expenditure may be derived. Gross national income (GNI), savings, and consolidated accounts for the nation can follow fairly soon. Extensions can be made as the use of the system becomes more established, resources become available, and users become more sophisticated; additional breakdowns of GDP, institutional sector accounts and balance sheets, and supply-use reconciliation may be added.[1]

1.2. This manual is written for both beginning and advanced compilers. In addition, it may be of interest to sophisticated data users. Most of the *Manual* addresses issues, concepts, and techniques that apply to the whole system of national accounts. The discussion of indicators in Chapter III focuses on components of GDP. Although this reflects the interest of first-stage compilers, it should not be taken to mean that QNA should stop there. As shown in Chapter IV,

GNI and savings for the total economy can be readily derived in most cases, and further extensions are also feasible. In particular, the quarterly expenditure and income components of GDP, in conjunction with balance of payments data, provide all items for the full sequence of consolidated accounts for the total economy. Several countries have expanded their QNA systems to cover selected institutional sector accounts. A number of countries are currently aspiring to expand their QNA systems to include a more complete set of institutional sector accounts and balance sheets.

1.3. This manual is intended for readers who have a general knowledge of national accounts methodology. The *Manual* aims at full consistency with the *1993 SNA*, and duplication of material presented in the latter is avoided as much as possible. Thus, for general national accounts issues, readers are referred to the *1993 SNA*.

1.4. This introductory chapter discusses the main purposes of QNA and the position of QNA between ANA and short-term indicators. This chapter also discusses some important aspects of QNA, such as their relation to ANA, their time-series character, the usefulness of seasonally adjusted QNA data, and the importance of transparency.

B. Purposes of Quarterly National Accounts

1.5. The main purpose of QNA is to provide a picture of current economic developments that is more timely than that provided by the ANA and more comprehensive than that provided by individual short-term indicators. To meet this purpose, QNA should be timely, coherent, accurate, comprehensive, and reasonably detailed. If QNA fulfill these criteria, they are able to serve as a framework for assessing, analyzing, and monitoring current economic developments.

---

[1] Another extension could be the development of monthly national accounts. This would be particularly useful in a situation of high inflation. To justify the extra resources needed, such an extension should provide a system of monthly data and not be limited to one single GDP number. A single GDP number offers little added value beyond the underlying indicators. Also, higher volatility in monthly data may make it more difficult to pick up underlying trends. Monthly national accounts compilation raises no new methodological issues compared with QNA.

Furthermore, by providing time series of quarterly data on macroeconomic aggregates in a coherent accounting framework, QNA allow analysis of the dynamic relationships between these aggregates (particularly, leads and lags). Thus, QNA provide the basic data for business cycle analysis and for economic modeling purposes. Also, QNA have a particular role to play for accounting under high inflation and where annual source data are based on varying fiscal years. In addition, as with the annual accounts, QNA provide a coordinating conceptual framework for design and collection of economic source statistics and a framework for identifying major gaps in the range of available short-term statistics.

1.6. QNA can be seen as positioned between ANA and specific short-term indicators in many of these purposes. QNA are commonly compiled by combining ANA data with short-term source statistics and ANA estimates, thus providing a combination that is more timely than that of the ANA and that has increased information content and quality compared with short-term source statistics.

1.7. QNA are usually available within three months after a quarter. ANA, on the other hand, are produced with a considerable time lag. The initial ANA (accounts based on annual data as opposed to first estimates on the basis of the sum of the four quarters) are often only available six months or more after the end of the year. Thus, ANA do not provide timely information about the current economic situation, which hampers monitoring the business cycle and the timing of economic policy aimed at affecting the business cycle. The strength of the ANA is to provide information about economic structure and long-term trends, not to provide data needed for monitoring the business cycle.

1.8. Lack of timeliness is also a major disadvantage for the use of ANA for constructing forecasts, which are best based on up-to-date information on the current economic situation. Furthermore, quarterly data more adequately reflect the dynamic relationships between economic variables, leads and lags in particular, and they provide four times as many observations, which is very helpful when using mathematical techniques such as regression analysis.

1.9. ANA are less suitable than QNA for business cycle analyses because annual data mask short-term economic developments. In-year economic developments are not shown in the ANA. In addition, develop-

ments that started in one year and end in the next may not show up in the ANA (see Example 1.1[2]).

1.10. ANA are also less useful at times of high inflation, when QNA are virtually indispensable, for two reasons. First, in these circumstances one of the basic axioms of the ANA is violated, namely, the assumption of price homogeneity over time. Although this basic axiom never fully applies (unless there are no price changes), in times of low inflation it does not negate the usefulness of the ANA. However, in the situation of high inflation, summing of current price

---

Example 1.1. Monitoring Business Cycles—Quarterly GDP Data (Seasonally Adjusted) versus Annual GDP Data

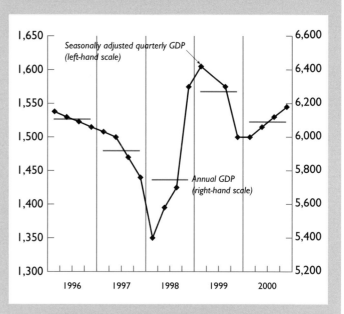

The chart shows quarterly and annual constant price GDP for an imaginary economy and illustrates how annual data may mask the cyclical movements. In this example, the QNA data show that the economy was growing during 1998 and that the upturn from the preceding slump started around the first quarter of 1998. In contrast, the ANA data show that the economy contracted in 1998 compared with 1997. The growth during 1998 first shows up in the ANA when the annual estimates for 1999 become available.

The situation is further aggravated by the usual time lag of the ANA, with the first annual estimates for 1999 not available until 2000. While the QNA will show the upturn in the first quarter of 1998 in 1998, the ANA will not show that upturn until 2000. By that time, the economy in this example has just gone through a second downturn. Thus, an upturn in economic activity would already have changed into a downturn while the ANA would still show positive growth.

---

[2]The use of QNA data exemplified in the example is best made with seasonally adjusted data or trend estimates.

data over a year becomes meaningless because the prices vary so much within the year. QNA are much less affected by this situation (although under extreme circumstances the accounting period should even be shorter). Second, the problem of holding gains is much less severe for QNA than for ANA and can more easily be eliminated because changes in valuation are less in a shorter accounting period.

1.11. QNA are less timely than individual short-term indicators, but they provide a more comprehensive picture of current economic developments organized in an integrated framework for analyzing the data. Short-term indicators, such as price indices, labor market indicators, industrial production indices, and turnover data for retail trade are often available on a monthly basis shortly after the reference period. These short-term indicators provide invaluable information on specific aspects of current economic developments. However, for want of integration into a consistent analytical framework such as the national accounts, these indicators do not provide a coherent, comprehensive, and consistent picture of the different aspects of the current economic situation. This hampers tracing the causes of current problems and identifying potential future developments. For instance, for a country facing decreasing domestic output growth, in addition to identifying affected industries (as a detailed production index would allow), it would be helpful to identify causes, such as decreasing domestic demand or falling exports, and to further trace deeper causes, such as income, saving, and investment patterns affecting demand categories.

1.12. A critique of QNA is that quarterly GDP is not a good business cycle indicator because GDP includes activities such as government and agriculture that do not necessarily respond to changes in the business cycle. For this reason, it is argued that a less comprehensive measure, such as a volume index for manufacturing industries, is preferable as a business cycle indicator. This critique seems pertinent only if the QNA were to be restricted to GDP as a single indicator. However, the QNA should not be regarded as only a vehicle for compiling summary aggregates such as GDP; it also provides an integrated framework for analyzing economic statistics, thus allowing examination and analyses of developments and behavior. Furthermore, breaking down GDP into specific economic activities would allow a view of economic activities that are deemed more relevant for business cycle analyses.

C. Quarterly National Accounts as Time Series

1.13. It is important for QNA to have a time-series character. A time series is defined here as a series of data obtained through measurement of the same concept over time that allows different periods to be compared. Thus, to form a time series, the data have to be comparable over time. Most important, this implies that the data have to be consistent over time with respect to concepts and measurement. Among other things, this requires that the time periods have to be identical (e.g., months, quarters). Cumulative data (that is, data that cover, for instance, January through March, January through June, January through September, and so on), as commonly used in formerly centrally planned economies, do not constitute time series. Series of measures of changes from the same period of the previous year (for instance, the growth between the third quarter of the previous year and of the current year) also do not constitute time series, because they do not allow for the comparison of different time periods. The same applies to period-to-period changes (for instance, the growth between the second and the third quarter of a year), although period-to-period changes can be linked together to form a proper time series (in the format of an index series).

1.14. Having QNA data in a time-series format is essential for business cycle analysis, for identifying turning points, for trend-cycle analyses, for studying the dynamic relationships between economic variables (in particular, leads and lags), and for forecasting. For these purposes it is also important that the time series are sufficiently long. In a situation where QNA have only recently been started, it is recommended to extend the series backward. As a rule of thumb, for purposes of regression analyses and seasonal adjustment, the time series should cover at least five years. A QNA series that is restricted to the quarters of the preceding year and the current year, even if it fulfills the criteria in paragraph 1.13, cannot be considered a time series, because such a presentation would not allow comparisons with previous years. This requirement for a time-series character for the QNA has important implications for the design of QNA compilation techniques, as will be evident in later chapters.

1.15. The importance of presenting monthly and quarterly data as time series for the purposes of analyzing trends and turning points in the data is illustrated in Annex 1.1. The numerical example provided there shows that in measures of change from the same period of the previous year, turning points in the data show up with a systematic delay, which in most circumstances can be substantial. The average delay can be shown to be around half a year in discrete data and around three-quarters of a year in cumulative data. Thus, as shown in the example, rates of change from the same period in the previous year can, for example, indicate that an economy is still in recession when it has actually been recovering for some time.

D. Seasonally Adjusted Data and Trend-Cycle Estimates

1.16. Seasonal adjustment[3] means using analytical techniques to break down a series into its seasonal, trend-cycle, and irregular components. The purpose is to identify these components and to allow, for certain uses, a view of the series where some of these components have been removed. In seasonally adjusted data, the effects of recurrent within-a-year patterns—the seasonal pattern—are removed, and in trend-cycle estimates the impact of irregular events are adjusted for as well. Seasonal patterns may be caused by economic behavior or recurrent exogenous factors such as weather patterns, holidays, religious events, and calendar effects such as variations in the number and type of trading days and paydays. Although it is feasible to focus seasonal adjustment on any of such factors in isolation or in sequence (for instance, calendar effects only or first), all seasonal patterns should be taken into account simultaneously, for reasons that are explained in Chapter VIII.

1.17. Opinions differ among both users and compilers on the appropriateness of statistical offices producing seasonally adjusted and trend-cycle estimates. These differences are caused both by differences in opinion over the usefulness of seasonally adjusted data as such for various uses of the data, and by differences in opinion over whether seasonal adjustment and trend-cycle estimation should be undertaken by users or by compilers of official statistics. Consequently, country practices in this respect differ. Some statistical offices do not publish any seasonally adjusted data or trend-cycle estimates at all, considering it to be outside the responsibility of producers

of official statistics and part of users' analysis of the data. Others focus mainly on seasonally adjusted data/trend-cycle estimates and may not even compile or publish unadjusted QNA estimates, but rather compile seasonally adjusted QNA estimates directly from seasonally adjusted source data. Most publish seasonally adjusted and trend-cycle data at least for the main aggregates, and this practice is strongly encouraged.

1.18. A basic premise of this manual is to compile QNA from unadjusted source data and apply seasonal adjustment/trend-cycle estimation on the resulting estimates. The discussions on sources and methods in this manual, and in particular the discussions concerning benchmarking, are all based on this premise. This premise is derived from the need to serve different users' needs as well as from practical compilation considerations. As illustrated in Box 1.1, unadjusted data, seasonally adjusted data, and trend-cycle estimates are useful for different purposes. The unadjusted data tell what actually happened in each period, while the seasonally adjusted data and the trend-cycle estimates tell what the underlying movements in the series are. Thus, users should have access to all three sets of data. Obviously, while QNA estimates based on unadjusted data allow seasonal adjustment, deriving unadjusted QNA estimates from seasonally adjusted estimates is not possible. Thus, if QNA compilation is based on adjusted data, providing unadjusted QNA estimates necessitates a separate compilation process, using a separate set of (unadjusted) data.

1.19. Seasonally adjusted data and trend-cycle estimates are indispensable for identification of changes in the business cycle and turning points in particular. Identifying turning points in the business cycle is an important purpose of QNA that can be significantly impeded if seasonal patterns and one-time events in the data are not separated out. One alternative to seasonal adjustment is to use growth rates from the corresponding quarter of the previous year rather than from the previous quarter. This is not an adequate solution, as explained in paragraph 1.15 above (see Annex 1.1 for further explanation of this issue). Furthermore, growth rates from the corresponding quarter do not fully exclude seasonal elements (for instance, Easter may fall in the first or in the second quarter, and the number and type of working days in a quarter differ from year to year).

1.20. Unadjusted data and other components of the series are needed for other purposes, including various

---

[3]Well-established techniques are available for seasonal adjustment, such as the Census X11/X12 method; these will be discussed in Chapter VIII.

aspects of monitoring current economic developments. For short-term forecasting of highly seasonal series, all components may be needed, particularly the seasonal component. Economic policy formulation may also require information on all components of the series, while for analysis of the effects of particular events, identification of the irregular component may be most important. Unadjusted data are also required for purposes such as econometric modeling, where the information contained in the seasonal component of the series may play a particular role in determining the dynamic relationship among the variables.[4] A further argument for requiring that unadjusted data always be provided is that for the most recent data in the series, seasonally adjusted and trend-cycle estimates are subject to additional revisions compared with the unadjusted series (the "wagging tail" problem—see Chapter VIII.)

1.21. Some users may prefer the unadjusted data because they regard seasonally adjusted data as artificial and arbitrary, or they may want to seasonally adjust the data themselves by applying their own seasonal adjustment preferences. Seasonally adjusted data represent one answer of several to the hypothetical question "What would the data have been if no seasonal factors affected them?" In that respect, seasonally adjusted data are obviously artificial. However, most economic analysts find the answer to this hypothetical question indispensable for business cycle analysis. Still, various aspects of seasonal adjustment remain controversial,[5] partly reflecting the many subjective and somewhat arbitrary choices involved in seasonal adjustment, including the choice of method (e.g., X11/X12 versus TRAMO-SEATS, BV4, SABLE, STAMP) and model (additive or multiplicative), the treatment of outliers, and the choice of filter lengths. For these and other reasons it has been argued that statistical offices "should produce the raw data and the users can then use their own software for treating seasonal data in the way they want and in which their analysis calls for."[6] However, while sophisticated users can and sometimes may want to seasonally adjust the data themselves, the public at large require that the data be adjusted for them. In addition, the statistical office may have particular information about special events impacting on the series and thus have advantages in carrying out seasonal adjustment.

1.22. Compilation considerations also support the basic premise of statistical offices compiling seasonally adjusted data and trend-cycle estimates based on unadjusted QNA estimates. When compiling QNA estimates, seasonally adjusted versions of the estimates may assist in detecting abnormalities in the data and allow better checks on plausibility of data (in particular, growth rates.) Thus, it may be easier to identify errors or discrepancies and their causes with adjusted data than with unadjusted data. On the other hand, the adjustments may obscure discrepancies and abnormalities in the unadjusted data that do not relate to seasonality. Also, it is more difficult to interpret discrepancies in the adjusted data because it is uncertain to what extent the discrepancies were already implicit in the unadjusted data. Finally, practice has shown that seasonally adjusting the data at the detailed level needed for compiling QNA estimates can leave residual seasonality in the aggregates.

1.23. Although seasonal adjustment removes the identifiable regular repeated influences on the series, it does not and should not remove the impact of irregular events. Consequently, if the impact of irregular events is strong, seasonally adjusted series may not represent a smooth and easily interpretable series. To further highlight the underlying trend-cycle, most standard seasonal adjustment packages also calculate a smoothed trend-cycle series running through the seasonally adjusted data (representing an estimate of the combined long-term trend and the business cycle movements in the series). Several countries include these estimates in their publications, and this practice is strongly encouraged.

E. Conceptual Links between Quarterly and Annual Accounts

1.24. To avoid confusion about interpreting economic developments, it is imperative that the QNA[7] are consistent with the ANA. Differences in growth rates between QNA and ANA would perplex users and cause uncertainty about the actual situation. Concerning the level of the data, this means that the sums of the estimates for the four quarters of the year should be equal to the annual estimates. In a situation where the ANA or ANA components are built up from the QNA, this is more or less self-evident. However, more commonly, the ANA are based on different sources than the quarterly estimates, and if that is the case, differences could

---

[4]See, for instance, Bell and Hillmer (1984), pp. 291-320.
[5]See, for instance, Chapter 5 of Alterman, Diewert, and Feenestra (1999) for a discussion of many of these controversial issues.
[6]Hyllenberg (1998), pp. 167-168.

[7]That is, the non-seasonally adjusted QNA.

Box 1.1.   Seasonal Adjustment: Unadjusted Data, Seasonally Adjusted Data, Trend-Cycle Estimates— What Do Users Want?

Main use of the data	Components that are:	
	Of interest	Not of interest
Business cycle analysis	Trend-cycle and irregular component	Unadjusted data
Turning point detection	Trend-cycle and irregular component	Unadjusted data
Short-term and medium-term forecasts	The original unadjusted series and all its components (trend-cycle, irregular, seasonal factors, preadjustment factors, etc.)	
Short-term forecasts of stable but highly seasonal items such as electricity consumption	The seasonal factors plus the trend-cycle component	
Long-term forecasts	Annual data and possibly the trend-cycle component of monthly and quarterly data	Unadjusted monthly and quarterly data, seasonally adjusted data and the irregular components
Analysis of the effect of particular events, such as a strike	The irregular component and any preadjustment factors	
To determine what actually happened (e.g., how many people were unemployed in November)	The original unadjusted series	Seasonally adjusted data and trend-cycle data
Policy formulations	The original unadjusted series and all components (trend-cycle, irregular, seasonal factors, preadjustment factors, etc.)	
Macroeconomic model building	Could be unadjusted, adjusted, trend-cycle, or all components, depending on the main purpose of the model	
Estimation of behavioral relationships	Could be unadjusted, adjusted, trend-cycle, and all components, depending on the main use of the estimated relationships	
Data editing and reconciliation by statistical compilers	Original unadjusted series, seasonally adjusted data, irregular component, and trend-cycle component	

develop. To avoid this, the QNA data should be aligned with the annual data; the process to achieve this is known as "benchmarking." One advantage of benchmarking is that incorporating the usually more accurate annual information into the quarterly estimates increases the accuracy of the quarterly time series. Benchmarking also ensures an optimal use of the quarterly and annual source data in a time-series context.

1.25. Benchmarking deals with the problem of combining a time series of high-frequency data (e.g., quarterly data) with less frequent but more accurate data (e.g., annual or less frequent data). Benchmarking issues arise both in QNA and ANA compilations. For the ANA, benchmarking arises when the estimates are anchored to more comprehensive and detailed surveys and censuses that are performed only every few years. The same basic principle applies to quarterly and annual benchmarking; however, as apparent from the technical discussion in Chapter VI, quarterly benchmarking is technically more complicated.

1.26. Benchmarking has two main aspects, which in the QNA context are commonly looked upon as two different topics; these are (a) *quarterization*[8] of annual data to construct time series of historical QNA estimates ("back series") and to revise preliminary QNA estimates to align them to new annual data when they become available, and (b) *extrapolation* to update the series by linking in the quarterly source data (the indicators) for the most current period ("forward series").

1.27. The general objective[9] of benchmarking is to preserve as much as possible the short-term movements in the source data under the restrictions

---

[8]Quarterization is defined here as generation of quarterly data for past periods from annual data and quarterly indicators; it encompasses the techniques of interpolation for stock data and temporal distribution for flow data. For more on this, see Chapter VI.
[9]The only exceptions to this general objective concern the rare cases where (a) the relationship between the indicator and the target variable follows a known short-term pattern or (b) knowledge about the underlying error mechanism indicates that the source data for some quarters are weaker than for others and thus should be adjusted more.

provided by the annual data and, at the same time, for forward series, ensure that the sum of the four quarters of the current year is as close as possible to the unknown future annual data. It is important to preserve as much as possible the short-term movements in the source data because the short-term movements in the series are the central interest of QNA , about which the indicator provides the only available explicit information. Optimally preserving the short-term movements in the data is one of the basic premises of this manual. Therefore, the core problem of benchmarking in a quarterly context is how to align a quarterly time series to annual data while maintaining the quarterly pattern and without creating a discontinuity in the growth rate from the last quarter of one year to the first quarter of the next year. This problem is known as the "step problem." To solve the step problem, several mathematical techniques have been developed. Chapter VI presents one technique, the proportional Denton technique with enhancements, that by logical consequence is optimal[10] under the general benchmarking objective stated above. The other techniques proposed in the literature are reviewed in Annex 6.1.

1.28. To be consistent, QNA and ANA should use the same concepts. As mentioned, this manual seeks full consistency with the *1993 SNA* and aims to avoid any unnecessary duplication. Nevertheless, some conceptual issues have a stronger emphasis and more substantial consequences in QNA than in ANA, which necessitates some further discussion. The most important conceptual issue in this respect is time of recording, particularly in two cases, namely, (a) long production cycles, and (b) low-frequency payments. Long production cycles, or production cycles that are longer than one accounting period, mainly concern construction, manufacturing of durable goods, and agriculture and forestry. The problems involved can be very substantial for QNA compilation and are discussed in Chapter X. Low-frequency payments are payments made on an annual basis or in infrequent installments over the year. Examples of such payments are dividends, end-of-year bonuses, vacation bonuses, and taxes on the use of fixed assets and other taxes on production. These issues are discussed in Chapter IV.

F. Transparency in Quarterly National Accounting

1.29. Transparency[11] concerning QNA is a fundamental requirement of users, and is particularly pertinent in dealing with revisions. To achieve transparency, it is important to provide users with documentation regarding the source data used and the way they are adjusted. As well, documentation should be provided on the compilation process. This will enable users to make their own judgments on the accuracy and the reliability of the QNA and will preempt possible criticism of arbitrary data manipulation. In addition, it is important to inform the public at large about release dates so as to prevent accusations of manipulative timing of releases. To avoid misperceptions, it is advisable to take a proactive approach to educate users.

1.30. Revisions are undertaken to provide users with data that are as timely and accurate as possible. Resource constraints and respondent burden, in combination with user needs, cause tension between timeliness of published data, on the one hand, and reliability, accuracy, and comprehensiveness on the other hand. To balance these factors, preliminary data are compiled that later are revised when more and better source data become available. Revisions provide the possibility to incorporate new and more accurate information into the estimates, and thus to improve the accuracy of the estimates, without introducing breaks in the time series.

1.31. Although revisions sometimes may be perceived as reflecting negatively on the trustworthiness of official statistics, delaying the implementation of revisions may cause later revisions to be greater if successive revisions are in the same direction (because they are cumulative). In fact, experience has shown that more sophisticated users understand that letting large revisions through is a sign of integrity. Not incorporating known revisions actually reduces the trustworthiness of data because the data do not reflect the best available information, and the public may know this or find out (for instance, the public may wonder why a revision in the monthly production index is not reflected in the QNA). In a time-series-oriented compilation system, suppression of revised information can also be cumbersome and costly and can cause estimation errors.

---

[10]The enhancements developed in Chapter VI also provide for superior solutions in the case of the two exceptions to this objective presented in footnote 9.

[11]Which can be described with terms such as openness, candor, and so on.

1.32. To minimize the number of revisions needed without suppressing information, it is advisable to coordinate statistical activities. The revision schedule should be largely driven by arrival of source data, and coordinating their arrival would help reduce the number of revisions needed.

1.33. To face any concerns users may have about revisions, it is important to have both an established and transparent publication policy and a revision policy in place. In addition, users need to be educated about the causes of revisions and the policies for dealing with them. Countries have adopted different approaches to revisions in response to their own circumstances. However, some important elements that constitute best practice are (a) candid and easily available documentation of sources and methods, (b) easily available documentation of the size and causes of revisions, and (c) release and revision dates that are well known and published through an advance release calendar. These practices are all required or encouraged by the IMF's Special Data Dissemination Standard (SDDS) and the General Data Dissemination System (GDDS). In addition, electronic release of the complete time series, not only the data for the most recent periods, will make it easier for users to update their databases. These issues will be further discussed in Chapter XI.

1.34. To avoid unwanted perceptions, it is advisable to take a proactive approach to educate users. Educating users, while valuable for most statistical areas, is particularly important for QNA because of their policy relevance and technical complexity. This introductory chapter has emphasized the usefulness of QNA, but also has pointed out inherent weaknesses. Compilers must be candid about these issues with the public and pursue transparency of sources and methods for compiling their QNA. For instance, experience has shown that a proactive approach can help reduce complaints about revisions. Although beginning compilers may well face more difficulties in this respect than well-established ones, the valuable experience gained by the latter should be a stimulus to move to a proactive approach as soon as circumstances permit. Also, compilers are often ahead of users in terms of sophistication of analysis and potential uses of the data. Compilers should educate users about the analytical possibilities and other benefits of the QNA data. Enhanced contact with users may also help compilers detect weaknesses in the estimates or their presentation. In addition, users

sometimes have their own economic information that could be helpful to compilers.

1.35. Users should be informed about the meaning of the data and their limits, and inappropriate uses should be discouraged. Given the likelihood of future revisions, users should be cautioned against overemphasizing the most recent release. To achieve a prudent appraisal of developments, users should be advised to consider the trend in the data over several quarters rather than the latest quarter. As well, if QNA data are presented in an annualized format, either as compounded growth rates or as levels multiplied by four, it is important to explain that this presentation magnifies the irregularity and uncertainty of QNA data (for further explanation, see Chapter VIII). Similarly, using growth rates with more than one digit behind the decimal point gives the impression that the data are significantly more precise than they generally are.

1.36. Several approaches can be taken to educate users. Seminars could be conducted for specific audiences, such as specialized journalists, interested parliamentarians, users within the central bank, or government agencies such as the ministry of finance or the department of commerce. Direct inquiries by users are good occasions for compilers to explain specific issues. For the general public, the occasion of new releases, which often brings the QNA to public attention, can be used to highlight points of interest. In particular, attention should be given to revisions and their causes. Also, in presenting the data, care should be taken to exemplify proper use, as indicated above. The best way to go about this is to provide press releases tailored to the style of the media, ready to print.

G. Flash Estimates

1.37. In some countries, the term "flash estimates" is used for a first release of QNA data fairly shortly after the reference period. The terminology is designed to emphasize that shortcuts have been taken and that, consequently, the data are particularly subject to revision. The shortcuts usually include use of data for only one or two months of the quarter for some or all components, with the missing month(s) estimated by extrapolation using mechanical methods such as those discussed in Chapter VII. Another common shortcut is use of data with less complete response rates than the data used for subsequent QNA estimates. Because the use of shortcut sources and methods is a general feature of QNA compilation, flash estimates only differ from subsequent QNA estimates in that they use a higher proportion of such methods. Consequently, flash estimates do not raise additional conceptual issues, although the practical concerns about informing users of their limitations and assessing the record of revisions for QNA are even more crucial. The flash estimates may be more limited in coverage of the *1993 SNA* variables (for instance, they may cover variables from the production account only) or be published in a more aggregated form. Publication of less detail is a recognition that the statistical noise is greater in disaggregated data and will emphasize the limitations of the estimates to users. Preferably, the level of compilation would be the same as for subsequent estimates, because a different level of compilation requiring use of different methods may cause unnecessary revisions.

1.38. In some cases, flash estimates may be used to describe data derived from aggregated econometric models that use factors such as behavioral relationships, leading indicators, or other indicators that do not have a close measurement relationship to the variable. These techniques are not a substitute for statistical measurement and are outside the scope of QNA compilation. As they require different skills from those used in statistical compilation, they are best undertaken by other agencies.

H. An Outline of the *Manual*

1.39. The outline of this manual can be summarized as follows. The *Manual* discusses strategic and organizational matters (Chapter II), the source data that are the foundation of QNA (Chapters III-V), mathematical techniques that are applied to data (Chapters VI-VIII), and, finally, a number of specific issues (Chapters IX-XI).

1.40. Chapters II-V are intended to be of particular interest to those setting up a new system. In addition, these chapters will be useful to those reviewing existing systems. In Chapter II, strategies for a QNA system and the management of QNA compilation are discussed, with the warning that data are the foundation of QNA and mathematical techniques are not a substitute. The chapter introduces the benchmark-indicator framework used throughout the *Manual* to understand QNA compilation and its relationship to ANA. It emphasizes the nature of QNA data as time series and the necessity of closely linking QNA and ANA using benchmarking techniques.

1.41. The commonly used sources and the issues that arise concerning them are outlined in Chapters III (GDP and its components, according to the production, expenditure, and income approaches) and IV (institutional accounts). The *Manual* recommends that even when GDP can only be estimated from a single approach, other splits of GDP should be produced with one category as a residual. Chapter IV points out that completion of some of the institutional accounts is usually feasible and always desirable.

1.42. Chapter V advises on good practices for handling data through checking and reconciliation.

1.43. Chapters VI-VII deal with benchmarking and projection techniques. The *Manual* warns against methods that introduce a step problem and presents an optimal benchmarking technique to solve the step problem under the general benchmarking objective presented in Section C above. The technique presented should be applied even in a newly established QNA system, and an understanding of the basic aspects of the technique and its compilation implications is fundamental for QNA compilers. However, the detailed discussions of the mathematics behind it, enhancements, and possible alternatives provided toward the end of the chapter and in the annexes are considered optional and are intended for more advanced readers.

1.44. Basic principles of seasonal adjustment are covered in Chapter VIII. The chapter is intended particularly for those starting a new system as well as those with existing systems that do not yet have seasonally adjusted data.

1.45. Chapter IX deals with issues in price and volume measurement. The problem of aggregation over time is relevant to all compilers, while the issues associated with annual chaining pertain to more advanced systems.[12]

---

[12]The term **volume** is used for measures that exclude the effects of changes in prices of the components that make up the item. The exclusion of the effect of price changes means that changes in a time-series of volume measures are driven by quantity and quality changes. Volume can be contrasted with **quantity**, which is limited to data that can be expressed in physical units. Accordingly, quantity measures do not take into account quality change and are not applicable for unquantifiable items or aggregates of different items. Volume can also be contrasted with estimates in **real** terms which refer (in precise national accounts terminology) to measures of the purchasing power of an item, that is, in reference to prices of other items. In common usage, "real" is often used for purchasing power as well as volume measures. While constant price estimates are a common form of volume measure, the term also includes fixed-base and chain-linked volume indices.

1.46. Work in progress is dealt with in Chapter X. The issues are relevant to all national accounts compilers, but the degree of sophistication of methods used will depend on the stage of QNA compilation.

1.47. Chapter XI discusses revision policy and the compilation cycle. Although policies need to differ according to the circumstances of each country, a transparent policy is required in all cases.

Annex 1.1. Identification of Turning Points

1.A1.1. This annex provides a numerical example illustrating the importance of presenting monthly and quarterly economic information as time series and the derived rates of change in the time series on a period-to-period basis, for the purposes of analyzing trends and turning points in the data, as emphasized in Chapters I and VIII. In the absence of seasonally adjusted time series and trend-cycle estimates, it is common practice to present changes from the same period in the previous year, instead of period-to-period changes. As shown in the numerical example, rates of change from the same period of the previous year can be inadequate in identifying the current trend in economic activity—indicating, for example, that an economy is still in recession when it has actually been recovering for some time. If changes from the same period of the previous year are used, turning points in the data show up with some delay, which in some circumstances can be substantial. The average delay can be shown to be around half a year in discrete data and around three-quarters of a year in cumulative data.

1.A1.2. In addition to delaying identification of turning points, changes from the same period of the previous year do not fully exclude all seasonal elements (e.g., Easter may fall in the first or second quarter, or the number of working days of a quarter may differ from year to year.) Moreover, in addition to any irregular events affecting the current period, these year-to-year rates of change will reflect any irregular events affecting the data for the same period of the previous year.

1.A1.3. Consequently, year-to-year rates of change are not suitable for business cycle analysis, and analyzing the economy on the basis of these rates of change can have an adverse impact on the soundness of macroeconomic policy.

1.A1.4. If the changes from the same period in the previous year are based on cumulative data (e.g., data that cover January, January through March, January through June, and so on), which has been the tradition in some countries, the delays in determining the turning points are even longer.

1.A1.5. The numerical example presented in Example 1.A1.1 is based on a time series of hypothetical data, starting in the first quarter of 1996, that can be viewed as representing tons of steel produced in each quarter, or, alternatively, quarterly GDP at constant prices. It contains three turning points. The first turning point occurs in quarter 1 of 1998, the second occurs in quarter 1 of 1999, and the third in quarter 4 of 1999.

1.A1.6. From the discrete quarterly data presented in the first column of Example 1.A1.1, these three turning points are easily seen as the series (a) turns from decreasing to increasing in quarter 1 of 1998, (b) turns from increasing to decreasing in quarter 1 of 1999, and (c) turns from decreasing to increasing in quarter 4 of 1999.

1.A1.7. Similarly, from the quarter-to-quarter rates of change presented in the third column of Example 1.A1.1, the first turning point is indicated by the change in quarterly rates of change from a negative rate in quarter 1 of 1996 to a positive rate in quarter 2 of 1998, the second turning point by the change from a positive to a negative rate of change between quarter 1 and quarter 2 of 1999, and the third turning point by the change from a negative to a positive rate of change between quarter 4 of 1999 and quarter 1 of 2000.

1.A1.8. When using changes from the same period of the previous year (e.g., the change from quarter 1 of 1996 to quarter 1 of 1997) instead of quarter-to-quarter changes, the delays in identifying the turning points can be substantial. In the example, the changes from the same quarter of the previous year are presented in the fourth column and show the third turning point as having taken place in quarter 3 of 1999—that is, three quarters after it actually occurred.

1.A1.9. If the changes from the same quarter in the previous year are based on cumulative data, as shown in the final column, the analysis gives the impression that the turning point took place even one quarter later.

Example 1.A1.1. Identification of Turning Points

Tons of Steel Produced

Bold type indicates turning points.

Quarter	Discrete Data	Cumulative Data	Quarter-to-Quarter	Rates of Change	
				Changes from the Same Quarter of the Previous Year (Discrete Data)	Changes from the Same Quarter of the Previous Year (Cumulative Data)
q1 1996	1,537.9	1,537.9			
q2 1996	1,530.2	3,068.1	−0.5%		
q3 1996	1,522.6	4,590.7	−0.5%		
q4 1996	1,515.0	6,105.8	−0.5%		
q1 1997	1,507.5	1,507.5	−0.5%	−2.0%	−2.0%
q2 1997	1,500.0	3,007.5	−0.5%	−2.0%	−2.0%
q3 1997	1,470.0	4,477.5	−2.0%	−3.5%	−2.5%
q4 1997	1,440.0	5,917.5	−2.0%	−5.0%	−3.1%
q1 1998	**1,350.0**	1,350.0	−6.3%	−10.4%	−10.4%
q2 1998	1,395.0	2,745.0	**3.3%**	−7.0%	−8.7%
q3 1998	1,425.0	4,170.0	2.2%	−3.1%	−6.9%
q4 1998	1,575.0	5,745.0	10.5%	**9.4%**	−2.9%
q1 1999	**1,605.0**	1,605.0	1.9%	18.9%	**18.9%**
q2 1999	1,590.0	3,195.0	**−0.9%**	14.0%	16.4%
q3 1999	1,575.0	4,770.0	−0.9%	10.5%	14.4%
q4 1999	**1,500.0**	6,270.0	−4.8%	**−4.8%**	9.1%
q1 2000	1,500.0	1,500.0	**0.0%**	−6.5%	**−6.5%**
q2 2000	1,515.0	3,015.0	1.0%	−4.7%	−5.6%
q3 2000	1,530.0	4,545.0	1.0%	−2.9%	−4.7%
q4 2000	1,545.0	6,090.0	1.0%	**3.0%**	−2.9%

Example 1.A1.1. *(continued)*

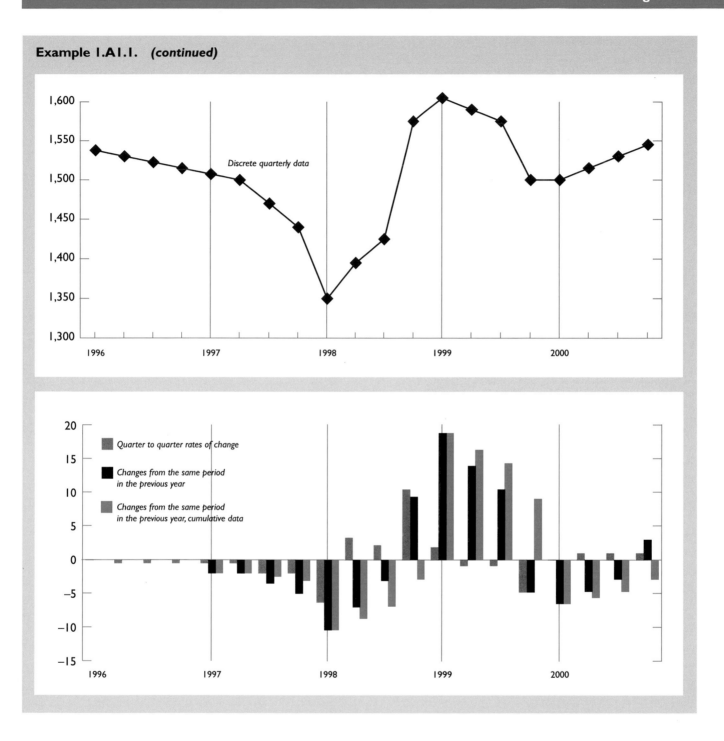

II Strategic Issues in Quarterly National Accounts

A. Introduction

2.1. Strategic statistical and managerial issues have to be dealt with to facilitate a smooth and efficient operation of quarterly national accounts (QNA). These issues arise when QNA are being set up, and it could be useful to revisit them from time to time once the QNA are fully operational. The most important statistical issues to be considered are the relationship of the QNA to the annual national accounts (ANA), coverage of the QNA, assessment of quarterly source data, and statistical compilation processes. Important managerial aspects concern the release cycle, the timing of the compilation process, and organizing the staff involved in the compilation. In this chapter, both statistical and managerial issues are examined from a strategic perspective, without much detail (statistical issues will be discussed in more detail in later chapters).

2.2. When considering these strategic issues, it is essential to have a broad understanding of the overall process. The main steps in establishing and maintaining QNA are summarized in Box 2.1. In this box, two related phases are distinguished, namely, an establishing phase and an operational phase. In the establishing phase, the compilation approach is decided, source data are selected and assessed, compilation processes are developed and assessed, and the whole compilation system is used to establish time series of QNA data on past years ("back series"). An important first step in this phase is to consult with potential users to see what kind of use they could make of QNA data. Obviously, consulting users should not be restricted to the first phase, because user wishes will probably evolve as the QNA develop.

2.3. In the operational phase, the compilation system is used to compile estimates for the current quarters; these estimates are subsequently revised when new quarterly and annual information becomes available. The sources, statistical techniques, and compilation system used for establishing the back series in the establishing phase and for updating the series in the operational phase should be identical. In contrast, managing the work on QNA may differ between the preparatory and the operational phase, and the alternatives countries have developed are discussed in this chapter.

B. Statistical Issues

1. The Link between Quarterly and Annual National Accounts

2.4. It is generally agreed that QNA estimates should be kept consistent with ANA estimates (that is, the non-seasonally adjusted QNA estimates). Reasons for this were discussed in Chapter I and include aspects of quality and transparency. Ideally, the QNA should be based on the same data sources and methods as the ANA and compiled using the same system. However, in practice, this ideal is generally not achievable. To achieve both timeliness and accuracy within resource constraints, it is common to collect detailed and comprehensive source statistics only annually or less frequently, and to compile a more limited set of short-term indicators on a monthly and quarterly basis using smaller sample surveys. For the same reasons, it is common to compile a detailed and more comprehensive system of national accounts only annually, and to compile a simplified and aggregated set of QNA estimates immediately after each quarter based on less comprehensive source data.

2.5. A QNA compilation system may be separate from the ANA compilation system or integrated with it. *Separate systems* are commonly found in countries with a comprehensive and detailed ANA system, including a supply and use (SU) table. Applying an SU framework implies an extensive cross-sectional reconciliation that these countries do not find feasible on a quarterly basis, at least not on the same level of detail. This implies that some of the transformation to

Box 2.1. Main Steps to Establish and Maintain Quarterly National Accounts

To Establish QNA

1. **Consult potential users**
    - Concerning possible uses
    - Concerning required coverage, detail, and so on
2. **Take inventory**
    - Of annual compilation methods
    - Of available quarterly and annual source data
3. **Design compilation methods and procedures**
    - Consider relationship to sources and methods used in the annual accounts
    - Decide coverage of QNA, including which parts of the 1993 SNA are to be implemented
    - Determine compilation level
    - Choose integrated or separate ANA-QNA compilation system
    - Make compilation schedule, including timeliness of first estimates and revision policy
4. **Review the quality of source data and compilation procedures**
    - Study correlation between annual and quarterly source data
    - Study revisions to main aggregates based on historic data (historic simulation of the compilation system)
      ▶ Revisions to the quarterly compilation system
5. **Generate time series of QNA data for past years ("back series")**
    - Benchmark the time series of quarterly source data to the time series of annual data (using methods such as the enhanced proportional Denton method)
      ▶ To be done for a sufficiently long time series
      ▶ To be done at the most detailed compilation level
6. **Perform real-time test runs and update the quarterly time-series with estimates for the quarters of the current year (year y)**
    - Link monthly and quarterly source data for the current quarters with estimates for the back series
      ▶ Extrapolation with indicators—Benchmark the time series of quarterly source data to the time series of annual data (using methods such as the enhanced proportional Denton method)
    - Fill information gaps
7. **First release**

To Maintain QNA

8. **Revise the quarterly estimates for the current year when new quarterly data become available**
    - Link monthly and quarterly source data for the current quarters with estimates for the back series
      ▶ Extrapolation with indicators—Benchmark the time series of quarterly source data to the time
9. **Revise the quarterly estimates when new annual data become available**
    - Revise the quarterly estimates for year y (and preceding years) to incorporate new benchmark data without introducing steps in the series
      ▶ Benchmark the time series of quarterly source data to the new series of annual data
      ▶ To be done at the most detailed compilation level
10. **Update the quarterly time series with estimates for the next current year (year y+1)**
    - Compile quarterly estimates for year y+1 by linking monthly and quarterly source data for the quarters of year y+1 with the revised and benchmarked QNA estimates for year 1 to year y
      ▶ Extrapolation with indicators—Benchmark the time series of quarterly source data to the time series of annual data
      ▶ To be done at the most detailed compilation level.

which the annual source data are subjected cannot be performed quarterly. As a result, the QNA sources have to be benchmarked to ANA estimates derived from the transformation that takes place in the ANA compilation process. *Integrated ANA-QNA systems* are typically found in countries not using an SU framework for their ANA, which makes it easier to use the same system for QNA as for ANA. In an inte-

grated system, the data storage and calculation functions for both ANA and QNA are carried out within the same processing system, although the level of detail may differ. In this situation, QNA sources may be benchmarked to annual source data,[1] rather than to

---

[1]These may have been pre-benchmarked to more comprehensive and detailed surveys and censuses that are performed only every few years.

ANA estimates. A variant is the situation in which a perfect one-to-one correspondence exists between the *annual levels* and *annual movements* in the quarterly data and the corresponding annual data; in such cases, the annual data may even be derived from the QNA data. However, this situation occurs for only a few components.

2.6. The choice between these alternative compilation styles depends on circumstances in each country. One factor is whether the annual data are subject to a detailed reconciliation process that cannot be applied each quarter. Another factor is whether the existing annual system has a time-series dimension or a year-by-year style of calculation, as the time-series focus is a requirement for QNA. A third factor is whether revisions of annual data sources tend to arrive at the same time of year or spread throughout the year, because in a separate ANA-QNA system, revised annual source data cannot be taken into account in the QNA until after the ANA are revised. It is important that QNA system designers think about these issues explicitly and do not choose one style without considering the alternatives.

2.7. Consequently, QNA are commonly compiled by benchmarking the quarterly source data to annual source data or to ANA estimates derived from a separate ANA system. In the benchmarking procedure, the quarterly source data serve only to determine the short-term movements in the series, while the annual data determine the overall level and long-term movements in the series (see Chapter VI for a detailed discussion of benchmarking). Thus, the quarterly source data are used as **indicators** to
- split ANA estimates into quarters for years for which ANA estimates are available; and
- update the QNA series by using the short-term movements in the QNA source data to generate QNA estimates for the most current period that are consistent with the QNA estimates for years for which ANA are available.

As shown in Chapter VI, the level and movements in the final QNA estimates will depend on the following:
- the movements, but not the level, of the short-term indicators;
- the level of the ANA estimates for the current year; and
- the level of the ANA estimates for several preceding and following years.

2. Coverage of QNA

a. General issues

2.8. When establishing QNA, one of the first choices that has to be made is which parts of the *1993 SNA* should be implemented initially. The choice will depend on availability of quarterly source data, the ANA system in place, available capacity, and user requirements. As mentioned in the introduction to this chapter, an important first step is to consult with potential users to see what kind of use they could make of QNA data. This implies assessing what kind of detail, coverage, and so on users would find desirable. Because potential users may not be aware of the possible benefits of QNA, statistical leadership is needed in this phase, and statisticians may have to set the stage by anticipating future needs.

2.9. When establishing QNA, ANA are usually already in place, along with supporting source data. Also, countries considering establishing QNA usually have some monthly or quarterly source data available. The next step in designing QNA is to take an inventory of available source data to decide which parts of the ANA can be implemented on a quarterly basis. The initial design of QNA should be based on the ANA as much as possible, although it is usually simpler and more aggregated.

2.10. In the initial stage of implementation, only estimates of GDP with corresponding components from the production or expenditure side as well as GNI and savings may be derived. Over time, it may be useful to revisit the extent of coverage of the QNA in view of changes in the availability of source data and changes in the coverage of the ANA. As the QNA become more established and as problems and gaps are identified, users needs for additional data may guide future extension. Experience has shown that once QNA are well-established, users become more sophisticated and may promote providing increased resources to extend the QNA to include supply-use reconciliation, institutional sector accounts, and balance sheets.

2.11. Extending the QNA beyond basic compilation of GDP has several advantages. It provides users with a more comprehensive picture of the various aspects of the current economic developments organized in an integrated framework for analyzing the data. Also, the extended accounting framework enables cross-checking of the data.

2.12. Because, as argued above, QNA should be anchored on ANA, the coverage of the QNA should be consistent with the coverage of the ANA, which means that it should either be the same as the ANA or constitute a subset of the ANA. For instance, if the ANA covers only compilation of GDP estimates, with components from the production and the expenditure sides, the initial coverage of the QNA will have to be restricted to compilation of GDP from the same sides or at least one of them.

2.13. Obviously, establishing QNA requires that human resources and equipment should be available. If no extra capacity is forthcoming and it is not possible to realize efficiency gains, reprioritizing will be needed with ANA or other statistical tasks. If the capacity needed for the development of the QNA has to be found from the resources currently used for the ANA, this may imply cutting back on developments; for instance, this may imply that the *1993 SNA* cannot be fully implemented as rapidly as otherwise would have been possible. In a more dire scenario, generating capacity for the development of QNA may necessitate cutting back on the existing ANA program; the alternative of decreasing accuracy should be avoided. Rather, capacity should be generated by discontinuing marginal activities or by discontinuing parts of the ANA that have not been in demand. It is important to consult users on the choices to be made in such a situation.

2.14. The introduction of a QNA system is similar for both developing and developed countries. The need for the type of information provided through QNA may be as urgent in developing as in developed countries, although more efforts may be needed to convince users of the importance of QNA data and inform them about the limitations of QNA data. Countries now starting QNA have the advantage that software supporting the implementation of the required techniques (such as benchmarking) is now widely available.

b. Measurement of GDP and its components

2.15. Measurement of GDP constitutes a core part of almost all national accounts systems, and a breakdown of GDP into its components is usually one of the first QNA results available. Traditionally, a distinction is made among three approaches[2] to GDP measurement, namely, (a) the production approach, (b) the expenditure approach, and the (c) the income

---

[2]A distinction is made between a compilation approach (which leads to a GDP total) and production of splits (in which a GDP total is derived from one approach, but some components of another approach are derived, so the remaining item can be derived as a residual).

approach. This distinction is somewhat artificial because these three approaches often use the same source data. For instance, government output and government consumption estimates are often based on the same source data; the estimates of fixed capital formation for the expenditure approach are partly based on output estimates of construction and production of machinery, which are also used in the production approach; and the wages and salaries estimates used in the income approach are often derived from the same statistics that provide the data on industry output and value added that are used in the production approach. However, the various approaches also use specific source data and allow a distinct perspective on development and level of GDP. Although, as argued, these approaches are not fully independent, applying various approaches facilitates cross-checking of data. Therefore, this manual recommends that countries should aspire to estimate GDP from at least two of the three sides. Because of their relative strength, it would be particularly useful to apply both the production and the expenditure approach.

2.16. Another important reason to apply at least the production and expenditure approaches is that they provide different breakdowns of GDP. To the extent that demand is driving short-term changes in the economy, the expenditure split provides particularly useful data for business cycle and macroeconomic policy analysis and for forecasting. The industry composition of growth provides a useful but less important supplementary perspective.

2.17. The production approach is the most widely used in the QNA for measuring GDP, probably because of a traditional focus in many countries on short-term statistics on manufacturing industries as major indicators. The production approach involves calculating output, intermediate consumption, and value added at current prices as well as in volume terms by industry. However, the available source data are usually restricted to either output or intermediate consumption, and the situation in which both types of source data are available is relatively rare. In most countries, output data are reasonably well covered for manufacturing industries, but the coverage of construction and services is usually less comprehensive. Components missing from output, intermediate consumption, and value added are estimated using ratios that reflect fixed input-output (IO) coefficients. Single-indicator-based estimates will be biased to the extent that the ratios vary with factors such as seasonal effects, capacity utilization, change in composition, technological change, and productivity trends.

2.18. The expenditure approach for measuring GDP is less common than the production approach among QNA-compiling countries. This is because of problems in availability, timing, valuation, and coverage in expenditure source data. The expenditure side usually has two strong pillars of quarterly data, namely, foreign trade and government consumption; the other categories are often less well covered. The major components of external transactions are usually available from the balance of payments and through merchandise trade statistics that often have a strong basis in comprehensive data collection for customs purposes. Data on government consumption can usually be derived from government administrative data. Other expenditure components (namely, household final consumption, parts of fixed capital formation, and changes in inventories) are usually covered less well. Directly observed data on fixed capital formation and changes in inventories may in many cases be lacking.

2.19. If expenditure data are incomplete, it may still be possible to derive a useful split of GDP by type of expenditure. For example, if total GDP is derived by the production approach and the available source data allow some of the key expenditure components to be estimated, the missing items may be derived as a residual. This situation can arise because data on changes in inventories are incomplete or inadequate. Although not an independent check of the GDP estimates, use of incomplete expenditure data in this way provides benefits for analysis in addition to plausibility checks of GDP.

2.20. The expenditure split is, in some ways, the most practical to measure in constant price or volume terms because there is a relatively clear concept of price and valuation for each demand category. In contrast, the price and volume dimensions of value added are more complex because value added cannot be directly observed, and the income approach is not suited for price and volume measures. As mentioned, the expenditure split also provides particularly useful data for business cycle and macroeconomic policy analysis and for forecasting. Also, this split is most useful for policy reasons because, over the short-term, demand can be more easily influenced than supply.

2.21. The income approach is the least commonly used of the three approaches but is potentially useful

as an alternative measure of GDP. The income approach avoids some of the problems the production and expenditure approaches may have, such as the reliance on fixed IO ratios in production data; however, it lacks a constant price dimension. Also, it requires that businesses have quarterly data on profits and some expenses. The income approach may have a sound underpinning in wage statistics or in administrative data on wages (for instance, for social security purposes), but quarterly observations of operating surplus/mixed income are often unavailable, particularly for unincorporated enterprises.

2.22. Even if income data are incomplete, it may still be possible to derive an income split of GDP where one of the categories (usually gross operating surplus) is derived residually. The distribution of income from GDP provides a useful alternative perspective on economic development. For a country interested in issues such as profitability and wage bargaining, this could be an important economic statistic. It also shows the link between business accounting and the national accounts, particularly if a bridge table from profits to operating surplus/mixed income is provided.

2.23. The weaknesses of the various methods for compiling GDP can be mitigated by combining several of them. Production and expenditure data can be combined using the commodity flow method. This method is based on the fundamental national accounting identity shown in the goods and services account and SU tables, namely, that total supply (by product) must equal total use. The commodity flow method can be applied on different levels, for instance, for groups of commodities or for individual commodities. The more detailed the level at which the method is applied, the more accurate the result (detailed information requires fewer assumptions on origin and use). This method is particularly strong if applied in an SU[3] framework, even one of limited dimensions (see next section). Production and income data can be checked if both are classified by industry, which is particularly meaningful if the value added data for industries can be broken down into compensation of employees, operating surplus, and mixed income (for a discussion on reconciliation issues, see Chapter V).

c. Quarterly GDP by the supply and use approach

2.24. Several countries have developed quarterly SU tables as the basis for their quarterly compilation of

---

[3]Input-output tables may also be used. For simplicity, we will refer to this whole area as supply and use (SU).

the GDP-related part of the national accounts. Compilation of SU tables is basically a common-sense method of compiling the GDP-related part of the overall national accounts system. For each individual product—at a more or less detailed level—SU tables show the sources of supply (production and imports) and the uses (intermediate consumption, households and nonprofit institutions serving households final consumption, government final consumption, and gross capital formation and exports). If supply and use for each individual product is balanced, the aggregated goods and services accounts for the total economy will also be balanced.

2.25. Application of an SU framework may seem daunting in a quarterly context, but it has proved feasible.[4] In particular, if SU tables are used as a compilation tool without being published, less rigor may be applied in balancing conflicting data and removing discrepancies. For instance, it may not be necessary to remove minor discrepancies that remain after major imbalances have been solved, as is usually done if SU tables are to be published.

2.26. SU tables provide an instrument to make maximum use of whatever information is available. SU tables are particularly suitable for filling gaps and reconciliation of data. With problems of data gaps caused by unrecorded economic activities and errors in the reported data, it is particularly desirable to use the SU framework to organize and coordinate the compilation work. The SU framework is, therefore, suitable for good data systems as well where the data sources are limited in coverage or are of poor quality.

2.27. The SU framework also allows the generation of more detailed data; for instance, retail sales may be available only for broad product groups, but the reconciliation with detailed production and external trade data can enable the production of detailed data on household consumption. Such detailed data can be useful to some users and can also help improve the quality of deflation. Making calculations at a more detailed level reduces the dependence on the fixed weights used in Laspeyres price indices, resulting in aggregate implicit deflators that are closer approximates to the preferred Paasche deflators. The SU framework also provides the ideal basis for making separate volume measures for output and

intermediate consumption, and thus for value added, using the double indicator method.

2.28. A few advanced countries compile both current and constant price SU tables. SU tables at current prices alone are more common. However, many of the assumptions about relationships are more likely to hold in constant price data. Having both current and constant price tables also makes it possible to separate price and volume aspects and to balance price, volume, and value (current price) data simultaneously.

2.29. The production of components of a quarterly SU system is broadly the same as for the equivalent components in the other approaches, as already discussed. However, there is an extra element of overall balancing and reconciliation. In effect, the use of the other approaches often involves elements of the SU approach. For example, the production approach often involves using fixed ratios on partial data, and commodity balances are often used to derive estimates. Each of these is a typical element of the SU approach. Using them is like using the SU approach for particular industries or products, but without the benefits of using the overall accounting framework for checking the aggregates. For all these reasons, countries that have a developed system of annual SU tables should consider using them systematically as a basis for QNA estimation.

3. Compilation Level

2.30. QNA are almost always compiled at a lesser level of detail than the annual estimates. Of course, it is not easy to draw the line on the level of detail required, but it should maintain separate data for items that are large, of interest to data users, or behave in atypical ways. Less detail does not always mean making the compilation process simpler, faster, and less resource demanding, because sometimes a more detailed level of compilation makes it easier to eliminate differences between indicators. For instance, when balancing supply and use of vehicles, having more details about different types of vehicles (such as trucks and passenger cars) makes balancing of supply and use easier (the use of trucks is mostly for fixed capital formation, while use of passenger cars can be both for fixed capital formation and for household consumption). Also, in automated compilation processes, more detail need not make much of a difference in compilation speed and resource needs. Finally, as mentioned above, making the calculations at a more detailed level reduces the dependence on fixed IO assumptions or

---

[4]For instance, these methods are being used in the QNA context in Denmark, France, the Netherlands, and Norway.

the fixed weights used in Laspeyres price indices, resulting in improved estimates.

4. Assessing Source Data and the Compilation System

2.31. Before commencing publication of QNA estimates, it is important to review the quality of both source data and the proposed compilation procedures. Because of the general demand for long time series, this review should go back as many years as feasible. The main purpose of the review is to identify weaknesses in the quarterly compilation system and possibilities for improvements to minimize future revisions of the main aggregates. It is important to establish whether source statistics properly indicate the direction and overall size of the changes and whether they enable catching turning points. The review also gives an indication of the quality of the estimates and the degree of revisions that can be expected in the future. Because of resource constraints and lack of sufficiently accurate and detailed source statistics, weaknesses will remain and revisions are inevitable; for some series, the revisions may be large. Thus, upon release of the first quarterly estimates, it is vital that the users are well informed of the accuracy and the reliability of the estimates and the degree of revisions that can be expected in the future.

2.32. In the national accounts context, the term "accuracy" is used to mean "closeness to the truth," while "reliability" is used to mean "degree of revisions the series is subject to." Because QNA are anchored to the ANA, the accuracy of the ANA sets a ceiling on the accuracy of the QNA; the reliability of the QNA is also thus determined because the extent of revisions depends on the closeness of the initial QNA estimates to the ANA estimates and the extent of revisions to the ANA estimates (for a more comprehensive discussion of revisions, see Chapter XI).

2.33. It is essential that decisions about sources and methods be well documented. The documentation is useful for compilers when problems arise or when there is staff turnover or absence. It also provides the basis for documentation for users, who often wish to know more about the data.

2.34. Assessing the source data and the compilation system involves conducting the following three tracking exercises:

(a) To assess the ability of the quarterly source data for individual series to track the annual estimates.

(b) To assess preliminary quarterly source data for the individual series to track the final quarterly source data.

(c) To assess the ability of the overall compilation system to track the annual estimates for major aggregates.

The overall tracking exercise will also, on an ex ante basis, provide a measure of the reliability of the QNA in the sense discussed in paragraph 2.31. Assessing the source data and the compilation system should be seen as a continuous process that should also be conducted regularly in the operational phase (in the operational phase this concerns ex post revision studies). The main aspects of assessing the source data and the compilation system are summarized in Box 2.2.

a. Assessing individual source data

2.35. Source data should be assessed for accuracy, reliability, and timeliness. Such an assessment is important for several reasons. First, it will reveal whether a specific series of source data is suitable for QNA purposes; second, where more than one data source is available for a particular variable, it will aid

---

Box 2.2. Review: Assessment of Indicators and Compilation Methods

1. Relationship to the sources and methods used in the annual estimates
   - Are the same sources available quarterly?
   - Are other sources/indicators available quarterly?
   - Are several alternative sources/indicators available for the same item?
2. Compilation level
   - As detailed as possible?
   - At the level of the main aggregates?
3. Coverage
   - What parts of the ANA can be covered?
4. Assessment of sources and methods
   - Accuracy in predicting annual changes
   - Systematic bias or noise
   - Individual and aggregated tracking exercises
   - Definitions of source data
     ► Coverage
     ► Units
     ► Classifications
   - Reliability (revision of indicators)
     ► Systematic bias
     ► Noise
   - Timeliness
     ► Reliability of preliminary estimates
     ► Amount of gap filling and guess estimation
5. Do the annual sources and methods need to be changed?

in choosing among them; third, when source data are conflicting, it will facilitate a choice on where to adjust; fourth, it will help to identify areas for improvement; and fifth, it will facilitate informing users about the quality of the estimates and expected future revisions to the individual series. Of course, in many cases, there will be little or no choice about the source to be used—in particular, in the short term. However, it is still necessary to assess indicators that could possibly be used. These assessments should be discussed with the data providers, who may be able to give additional background information. (In addition, national accountants are sometimes able to identify problems that the data collectors had not discerned.)

2.36. The main criterion for the accuracy of quarterly source data is to what extent they are successful in indicating annual movements. This follows from the need to keep QNA consistent with ANA and the assumed higher quality of the annual source data. The accuracy of the short-term source statistics as indicators for the annual movements depends on definitions and specification of the variables and on issues such as coverage, units, and classifications.

2.37. The ability of the quarterly source data to track the annual estimates should be assessed by *comparing the growth rates* in the annual sum of the quarterly source data with growth rates in the corresponding ANA estimates (this is the first of the three tracking exercises listed in paragraph 2.34). Large differences in the rates of change indicate inconsistencies between the quarterly and annual source data for that series and potential weaknesses in the quality of either the quarterly or the annual source data. Large differences in the annual rates of change in the quarterly and annual source data for the back series also indicate that large revisions can be expected in the future as additional source data become available. Mathematical techniques can be used to more formally study the correlation between annual and quarterly data and to identify and remove any systematic errors (that is, bias) in the quarterly source data's long-term movements. Use of mathematical techniques to identify and adjust for biases is discussed in Chapter VI.

2.38. Specific problems may arise if annual reporting is on a fiscal year basis rather than a calendar year basis. In this respect, the main problem is that in annual statistics, respondents with a nonstandard reporting year (that is, a reporting year that differs from the rest of the industry) are usually included in the statistics for the year that has the largest overlap,

which will then create a mismatch with the sum of the quarters. A solution to this problem with the annual data could be found if the annual source statistics would use the information from the quarterly source statistics to allocate the data of an individual respondent to the standard accounting period using the benchmarking technique presented in Chapter VI.

2.39. The reliability of the quarterly source data has important implications for how early sufficiently reliable initial QNA estimates can be prepared. Often the first estimates will have to be based on published or unpublished preliminary versions of source data that are still open to revisions. One important reason for such revisions to the source data is that early response rates are lower, and estimates may change as response increases. These changes may follow a consistent pattern, which implies a "bias," or the changes may be irregular, which implies "noise." A bias in early estimates of an indicator may be caused by selectivity in the response. The reliability of the quarterly source data can be assessed by comparing period-to-period rates of change in the preliminary versions with the corresponding rates of change in the final versions of the series. Obviously, this can only be done if the preliminary versions of the data have been retained in the databases rather then being continually overwritten.

2.40. The timeliness of the quarterly source data also has important implications for how early sufficiently reliable initial QNA estimates can be prepared. Often the first estimates will have to be based on an incomplete set of source data. For some series, data for only two months of the last quarter may be available, while data for other series may be missing altogether. To fill these source data gaps, provisional estimates will have to be made based on simple trend extrapolation or on alternative indicators that are more timely but less accurate. For each individual variable, the impact of these provisional estimates on the reliability of the first estimates can be assessed by constructing provisional estimates for the past years *as if one were in the past* and comparing the period-to-period rate change in those estimates with corresponding rates of change in the final quarterly source data for that variable. This and the assessment of the reliability of the quarterly source data described in paragraph 2.39 represent the second of the three tracking exercises listed in paragraph 2.34.

2.41. The assessment of possible source data will determine what source data are suitable for QNA purposes and, from there, which parts of the 1993 SNA can be implemented. Sometimes the assessment will lead to the conclusion that biases and noise are too substantial for a particular set of data to be used to compile QNA data. This can imply that the QNA compilers have no other choice than to not use these data, but it would be important to discuss with the compilers of the source data whether improvements can be made (see below). While the decision not to use a certain data set might mean that the system cannot be fully implemented, this is likely to be preferable to the use of data that can result in misleading results.

2.42. Sometimes, a choice has to be made among various sources for the same variable. Although in most cases QNA compilers face a lack of source data rather than an abundance, the situation may occur in which several indicators are available for one particular variable. If alternative indicators are available for the same variable, it is important to have some knowledge of their accuracy and reliability to choose between them. Note that the lesser quality data may still be useful as a check on the preferred series.

2.43. Often, QNA compilers need to adjust the source data in the QNA compilation process. If data on supply and use are confronted through SU tables or in a commodity flow equation, it is likely that inconsistencies will emerge. In such cases, knowledge about the accuracy and reliability of the data will provide guidance on how much leeway there is for adjusting the data.

2.44. Assessment of the source data may also help identify areas that need improvement, both for the QNA and the ANA. Necessary improvements may concern coverage, definitions, units, and so on. Obviously, it will be easier for QNA compilers to request improvement of statistics collected by the same agency, but even data from other agencies may be improved. Agencies collecting data for their own use that do not fit well into the QNA compilation might prefer adapting their questionnaires to allow use in the QNA context rather than having their respondents exposed to a new survey.

2.45. In setting priorities for improvements, the relative importance of an indicator should be one of the considerations. For many components, the basic data are so poor that refinement of methods would be of doubtful benefit. There are also likely to be components of little economic significance that have poor data. National accountants need to be careful about expending too much effort on numerous, trivial items at the expense of large, important items. Of course, the fact that an item is small cannot be an excuse for deliberately choosing a poor method when a better one is available, and the methods adopted for even the smallest components need to be defensible to inquisitive users. Also, it should be noted that small items may have a substantial effect on growth estimates (changes in inventories are an example of this).

2.46. In some cases, the development of QNA methods also leads to improvements in the ANA. The process of review often brings to light outdated or unrealistic assumptions in annual estimation, as well as faulty annual compilation practices. In a few cases, the quarterly data may be superior and so may be used to replace the annual data. One instance is annual deflators that are best built up from quarterly data as the ratio between the annual sum of quarterly current and constant price data (see Chapter IX, Section B), instead of constructed as a simple annual average of monthly price data for the year. Similarly, data on inventories and work-in-progress are best built up from short-term data. QNA can also contribute to an improved allocation of fiscal year data to calendar years in cases where the two do not coincide.

b. Assessing the overall compilation system

2.47. Before QNA estimates are published, an aggregate tracking exercise should be undertaken to assess the overall consistency of the quarterly and annual source data and compilation systems with respect to annual rates of change for major aggregates (this is the third of the three tracking exercises listed in paragraph 2.34). Errors in the individual series may go in opposite directions and, thus, may not give a good indication of the degree of future revisions of the main aggregates that can be expected. To undertake an aggregate tracking exercise, the entire compilation process needs to be simulated on historic data to produce time series of unbenchmarked estimates for the major aggregates. That is, the proposed QNA compilation system should be used to produce estimates of QNA aggregates for the past years *as if one were in the past* and were producing the first preliminary sum of four quarter estimates for those years without later annual benchmarks. If feasible, it is preferable to perform the aggregate tracking exercise based on the incomplete set of source data that would actually have been available when the first sum of four quarter estimates would have been produced.

2.48. Later, in the operational phase, the aggregate tracking exercise should be repeated by comparing the various releases of annual data from the QNA system with the eventual ANA data. As emphasized in Chapter XI, best practice also involves periodically conducting and publishing studies of long-term trends in the revision patterns. Summaries of these studies may accompany the regular quarterly release of data to remind users that data are subject to revisions.

2.49. It is advisable to also perform test runs in real time before going public with the QNA. Only experience from such test runs can sufficiently ensure the robustness of a QNA system and its ability to cope with unexpected problems. Although user demands and other compelling reasons may provide a push for going public as soon as possible, in the establishment phase, QNA compilers should endeavor to schedule sufficient time to run one or two real-time test runs.

2.50. The tracking exercise on the aggregate level can be used to remove weaknesses in the system overall. For instance, the exercise may indicate that estimates from the production approach are more robust than the estimates from the expenditure approach, which would provide guidance to adjustments in the course of the compilation process.

5. Statistical Processing

2.51. Statistical processing encompasses the assembly of data, benchmarking, deflation, seasonal adjustment, aggregation, and other calculations. In designing a processing system, it is useful to anticipate the differences and links between the preparatory and operational phases of QNA compilation so that different needs can be satisfied using the same processing system. In general, the processes for compiling data in the preparatory and operational phases will be the same. However, the operational phase has some extra complexities that may not be evident in the preparatory phase.

2.52. In the QNA preparatory phase, the objective is to compile data on past years (back series). Compilation of QNA data for a single quarter or year is of little value. The back series of historical data provide greater perspective on economic developments, and for that reason should go as far back as feasible. Long back series also allow compilers setting up a new system to check the data, gain experience in the behavior of the series, and support seasonal adjustment.

2.53. In the operational phase, the objective is to update the time series with data for the current quarters as well as revising the data for past years. The operational phase differs from the preparatory phase in several respects. These differences arise because, in the preparatory phase, compilation was done after the fact with existing ANA totals as benchmarks, which would not be available for the most recent quarters. Other differences are that in the operational phase, the data will be less complete for the most recent quarters, data source revisions will be an issue, and the timing of data supply in a proper sequence becomes much more important. Only running the quarterly compilation system in real time will reveal all the implications. A trial run of a quarter or two before the official release (as recommended above) will allow these problems to be identified and resolved without delays the public may notice.

2.54. For the operational phase, the forward or extrapolation part of the series presents its own difficulties because there will be no annual benchmarks for that part of the series. The challenge is to extend the series beyond the end of the last benchmark, tracking the likely future ANA estimates so that future revisions are minimized while preserving the short-term movements in the quarterly source data (to the extent possible).

2.55. Finally, during the operational phase, there are continuing cycles of revisions to quarterly indicators, revisions to annual benchmarks, and the receipt of annual benchmarks for the most recent years. This new information needs to be incorporated in the QNA estimates as it becomes available.

2.56. The calculations applied to the data are diverse and depend on the characteristics of the series. Some data will be received in a form ready to use without adjustment, but more commonly there will be the straightforward manipulations familiar in annual compilation—addition, subtraction, multiplication (whether called scaling, grossing up, or quantity revaluation), and division (e.g., deflation). However, the mathematical techniques used to produce QNA estimates by combining a quarterly indicator and an annual benchmark series are more complex. Inevitably, the movements in any two nonidentical quarterly and annual series will differ. The challenge is to align the QNA estimate to the ANA estimate while preserving the time-series properties of the data. This process—

called benchmarking—is not an easy matter because simple methods such as pro rata distribution of the annual total introduce a discontinuity in the series between years—the "step problem." Benchmarking improves the quarterly data by taking into account the superior annual information.

2.57. The proportional Denton benchmarking technique with enhancements as presented in this manual, is recommended as an integrated way of dealing with these tasks for both the back and forward parts of the series. It gives results superior to those methods that treat the back data in the preparatory phase, the extrapolation phase, and the arrival of new benchmarks separately. In practice, the Denton technique can be readily automated so that it is not time-consuming. It is worthwhile to set up the system correctly because using alternative methods with step problems can undermine the time-series properties that are the key focus of QNA. The importance of good benchmarking methods increases as quarterly indicators show more divergence in movements from annual data. The Denton method with enhancements is presented in Chapter VI, along with some discussion of its implications and the alternatives.

2.58. It should be emphasized that in the case of incorporation of revised or new benchmarks, the calculations should be based on the original quarterly indicator, not on the preliminary QNA estimates that have already been adjusted. Otherwise, the compilation process risks deteriorating into an unorganized data hashing, in which the compilers lose track of the original data, the effects of benchmarking, and the effects of other adjustments.

2.59. To avoid introducing distortions in the series, incorporation of new annual data for one year will generally require previously published quarterly data for the past several years to be revised. This is a basic feature of all acceptable benchmarking methods. As explained in paragraph 6.30 and as illustrated in Example 6.3, in addition to the QNA estimates for the year for which new annual data are to be incorporated, the quarterly data for one or several preceding and following years may have to be revised. In principle, previously published QNA estimates for all preceding and following years may have to be adjusted to maximally preserve the short-term movements in the indicator if the errors in the indicator are large. However, in practice, with most benchmarking

methods, the impact of new annual data will gradually diminish until it no longer has any impact on sufficiently distant past years. With the recommended proportional Denton benchmarking technique, the impact on data for proceeding years will normally become insignificant after three to four years. One of the advantages of the Denton technique is that it allows for revisions to as many preceding years as desired.

6. Relationship between QNA and Source Data Statistics

2.60. As a consequence of benchmarking and calculations in the QNA compilation process, the QNA data may differ from the source statistics. Subjecting data to a balancing process in a commodity flow or SU framework will also generate differences with the source data. Users may find these differences puzzling and awkward, and efforts should be made to work the differences back into the source data. Certain limitations may apply; for instance, the implicit deflator of household consumption in the QNA may differ from the consumer price index (CPI), owing to differences in coverage and differences caused by the use of different index formulas. However, if the variables in the QNA are basically identical to those in the source statistics, consistency should be pursued. Owing to consistency requirements, this consistency should be sought through adjustments in the source statistics. For instance, output and value added data from a production index should tally with the corresponding data from the QNA. At the very minimum, causes for differences should be explored, and they should be documented in a way that facilitates access by users.

2.61. Initially, working the differences resulting from the QNA compilation process back into the source statistics may not be popular with the compilers of these statistics, if only because this would entail a revision process that they may not be accustomed to. However, compilers of source statistics may come to accept that adjusting their statistics to the QNA is beneficial to the consistency of the statistical system and to the quality of their own statistics. One important effect of adjustment may be an increased awareness among the compilers of source statistics of the need to ensure consistency between data from high-frequency statistics (monthly and quarterly data) and annual data; these compilers may also be encouraged to apply benchmarking procedures. Discussions with the compilers of source statistics about the differences will most likely increase their involvement in the way their data are used in the QNA compilation process. For instance, they may develop an interest in participating in the deliberations during the balancing process, for which they could provide valuable input. Obviously, the adjustment process of the QNA source statistics will be easier to establish if a similar process is in place for the ANA. If this is not the case, starting a QNA system is a good opportunity to initiate an adjustment process for the ANA source statistics as well.

C. Dissemination

2.62. Dissemination of QNA has much in common with dissemination of other statistics, and general guidance can be found in the IMF's SDDS and GDDS. These standards center on integrity, and important themes include avoiding nonstatistical interference with the data, simultaneous release to all users, general accessibility of the data, and transparency. These issues are mentioned in Chapter I and elaborated on in Chapter XI.

2.63. This section focuses on some QNA-specific dissemination issues, especially concerning release and presentation. With regard to release, owing to the nature of QNA and their importance for decision making, the predominant condition is that the release should be fast. Rather than spending time on preparing and printing a glossy and comprehensive publication, the emphasis should be on releasing the QNA data as soon as they are available or, if a release calendar is in place, on the scheduled release date.

2.64. Thus, the first release may be a rather limited one, focusing on the most important data. For instance, the focus could be on GDP growth in current and constant prices—both seasonally adjusted and nonadjusted—as well as on trend estimates. As a further extension, it could include breakdowns of expenditure categories and industries. Also, it is important to mention the most important revisions concerning earlier releases (see Chapter XI for more on this subject).

2.65. The quickest ways to release these data are through a press release and the Internet. The press release text should be short (as a rule, not longer than one typed page) and ready for use without

rewriting. These conditions promote acceptance by the media and also prevent misrepresentation by hasty or less knowledgeable media staff. Media often mention the source of press releases, which may generate the perception that the published article reflects the view of the statistical agency. Thus, it is important to prepare press releases in a way that prevents tinkering with the text by the media. Try to have a catchy heading; if the press release does not have one, the media will make one up that might be more creative than statisticians would like. Also, because the media shorten articles by simply removing text at the end, the most important news should be first. Furthermore, it is advisable to support the press release with a small table containing the most important data. For easy recognition by the general public, it makes sense to standardize such a table and to consult with media staff about its content. Consulting with the media about press releases is good advice in general. Publication through the Internet should be simultaneous with the press release, and to promote speed it could simply have the same text. Preparation of the releases should start as early as possible and need not wait until all the publishable data are ready; usually an impression of the important news can be developed on the basis of the data that become available in the last phases of the compilation process.

2.66. Many countries also publish a more comprehensive quarterly statistical publication dedicated to the QNA. These publications provide a more thorough analysis of the data, supported by charts depicting the economic developments in various ways. Pie charts depicting contributions to GDP growth from demand categories or from industries are often used; such charts are usually based on seasonally adjusted constant price data. Column diagrams showing the composition of GDP and the changes in this composition are also often published.

2.67. The extent to which statisticians comment on the data differs among countries. In some countries, statistical offices basically provide only the data with technical explanation as needed; in other countries, statistical organizations see it as their task to interpret economic developments. Either way, keep close to the facts to avoid giving the impression that the statistical agency wishes to influence public opinion by taking a position on economic and political issues.

D. Managerial Issues

I. General

2.68. Management of QNA differs from that of ANA because of the greater intensity of work and tightness of deadlines. Also, compilation of QNA is more creative because more assumptions need to be used and more use is made of indirect indicators, with less "bean counting." This implies a need for staff with a solid economic background. As well, because of the more intensive use of mathematical techniques, some staff with a background in mathematical statistics are needed.

2.69. As mentioned before, QNA can only start when sufficient quarterly source data are available. These source data are more efficiently managed in the compilation of QNA when they are available in electronic databases.

2.70. There is no single best way of organizing QNA compilation. Each country develops its system according to its own experience and circumstances. The objective of this chapter is to raise some issues for consideration rather than to give recommendations or answers.

2.71. The pattern of workload peaks is quite different for QNA than for ANA. A statistical office that produces only annual estimates is accustomed to a production cycle spread over a year. The annual estimation may often have some clustering of tasks toward the end of the cycle, and there may be tight deadlines to be met. In a quarterly compilation system, the workload is typically relatively low at the beginning of each quarter because data on the previous quarter are not yet available and compilation of the preceding quarter should be finalized.

2.72. For both ANA and QNA compilation, data from a wide range of sources are brought together. Data are sometimes collected by national accountants themselves; more typically, data come from other parts of the same organization or from other organizations. The sequencing and timing of QNA compilation are complex because it needs to be built around the arrival of the results from numerous collections and suppliers.

2.73. An important organizational issue to be dealt with at an early stage concerns the release cycle—the timing of the first release of the data on a quarter and of subsequent revisions. In a QNA system that is linked closely to the ANA, as promulgated in this manual, the release cycle will also depend on the release cycle of the ANA. As mentioned in Chapter I, it is best practice to publish first results within the next quarter. After the first release, revisions are usually needed, depending on, among other things, the arrival of new or revised source material and, eventually, the arrival of annual data. The release cycle derives directly from the revision policy, which is discussed in Chapter XI.

2. Timing of the Compilation Process

a. Structuring the compilation process

2.74. Sequential and "big bang" processing are alternative ways to structure the compilation process. The sequential approach involves processing in stages (data entry, basic checks, aggregation at lower levels, deflation, seasonal adjustment, overall aggregation). In contrast, with the big bang approach, the data are entered and the whole system is run simultaneously; the results are then viewed in detail in the context of the aggregate trends. This may be done iteratively several times as new data arrive and adjustments are made. In practice, there may be some blending of these two approaches. Some of the considerations to be taken into account in designing the processing system are whether the source data arrive within a short period of time or over several weeks, how much checking of source data is necessary, and the nature of the computer system being used. The big bang approach lends itself to SU methods because it emphasizes interrelationships between different data.

b. Planning workloads

2.75. Because the point of QNA is timeliness, deadlines are necessarily short and tight. This means that QNA compilers are subject to pressure. QNA compilation is also particularly vulnerable to problems like delays in major data inputs or bugs in computing systems.

2.76. To deal with timing problems, a quarterly work schedule should be drawn up. The schedule should take into account the agreed-upon release schedule, the expected time of arrival of each of the required data sources, the period required to carry out each process, and the flow of data from one stage to the next. In this way, it is possible to predict when the results will be ready for publication. It will also help in identifying the sequence of tasks and calculating the effects of delays. The work schedule should identify the following:

- the data inputs and when they are expected to arrive;
- the tasks of the national accounts compilers, including how long each task is expected to take and the order in which they are carried out; and
- the delineation of responsibility for each task.

2.77. The work schedule should account for unforeseen delays. As discussed in Chapter XI and as required by the SDDS, release dates should be preannounced. However, unforeseen problems occur and failure to release the estimates as announced may create suspicion of manipulation for political reasons. When compilers first start compiling QNA, there is a greater potential for unforeseen problems. Therefore, countries might initially provide for a longer compilation period and greater margin for delay and gradually increase timeliness as they gain QNA compilation experience.

c. Methods of speeding compilation

2.78. Because source data are often released only after the end of the quarter and QNA are produced quickly, compilation is necessarily concentrated in a short period. This situation makes accelerating jobs particularly important. Compilation can be speeded up in a number of ways.

2.79. First, it is important to reduce peaks in processing workloads. One way to reduce the burden during the peak processing period is to do as much work as possible in advance. For example, monthly data for the first one or two months of the quarter can be processed early. Similarly, it may be possible to implement revisions made to data for earlier quarters before compilation for the new quarter begins. Some problems in data can be foreseen and dealt with in advance. For example, if a series will be rebased or its coverage changed, it may be possible to set up a program that splices together the old and new series before the data become available.

2.80. Second, QNA often achieve earlier release by improving the arrangements for the supply of source data. Data suppliers may be able to provide preliminary data. Data may be supplied by faster methods, such as by e-mail, on a shared database, on diskettes, or on printouts rather than in a more polished publication that takes longer to produce. Also, data should be supplied in the most efficient format, with the data in the required order and excluding irrelevant data.

2.81. Third, printing of statistical publications can be slow. Timeliness is more important for QNA, so it may be necessary to develop dissemination procedures as discussed in Section C of this chapter.

2.82. The practice runs recommended above will also help to identify general problems that would cause delays and undermine punctuality.

3. Organizing Staff

2.83. The topic of organizing staff needs to be considered according to circumstances in each country. Concerns include the agency involved in compiling QNA, the unit compiling QNA, the number of staff involved, the organization of this staff, and the place of the QNA unit (if there is one) in the compiling agency. The most common situation is for all national accounts data, including QNA, to be compiled in the national statistical office, often by the same part of that institution. In some countries, compilation of quarterly accounts is done in the central bank. In some cases, QNA estimates are done by yet another organization, such as a research institute. Unless there are particular problems with staff and other resources, it is generally undesirable to have different organizations involved because of the potential problems of inconsistent data and methods as well as the loss of synergies between the annual and quarterly systems.

2.84. All too often, the national accounts compilers will have little say in the total number of staff, although they may be able to determine the allocation of staff between quarterly and other activities. Obviously, a small staff means a much more basic quality of estimation and a lower level of detail and timeliness.

2.85. The organization of national accounting divisions varies. In a small organization, there may be no division. In a larger organization, units can be divided in one or more of the following ways:
- detailed sources/integrating data and working on aggregates;
- quarterly data/annual data;
- industries/expenditure components/income components;
- current price data/constant price data;
- orientation on process/orientation on product; and
- development and analyses/operational work.

2.86. Some of the considerations regarding allocation of staff are balancing peaks and troughs in workloads, linking common subject matters and techniques, and having teams that are easy to manage (too large makes communication harder, too small means fewer skills and more vulnerability to absences and departures). When related issues are dealt with by different teams, there is a risk of duplication or conflicting opinions about methods.

2.87. An important organizational choice to be made is whether there should be a unit focused specifically on QNA or whether QNA or annual national accounts should be compiled within the same unit by the same staff. The pattern of workload peaks is quite different, so peaks in the annual compilation may not crowd out activities in QNA (and vice versa). An advantage of combining both functions is that harmonization between QNA and ANA is more likely if the same staff are working on both.

2.88. When setting up a new QNA system, it is often desirable to identify a separate QNA team. Otherwise, the developmental work may be hampered if staff are continually being called to other, more urgent, tasks. The development of a new system requires a high level of conceptual ability, so the staff should have a good knowledge of the *1993 SNA* and the annual compilation system. Some staff with good background knowledge on monthly and quarterly surveys may complement the knowledge of ANA compilers.

4. Organizing Data Supply

2.89. National accounts are unique in their use of many data sources from different agencies. Because the timing of QNA is typically more crucial than the timing of ANA, coordination with data suppliers is one of the important tasks of the QNA compiler. This issue is discussed in Section D.2.c. of this chapter in the context of speeding compilation.

2.90. National accountants need to be in close contact with their suppliers so that both sides understand the other's needs and problems. The timing, content, and formats of data supply can be arranged. Data sources can have changes in base year, coverage, definitions, procedures, and classifications that need to be identified in advance so that there is no unpleasant surprise during data compilation. Data suppliers can also be good sources of information on what is happening in the economy, shortcomings of the data, and how to deal with problems such as breaks in the series.

2.91. Data suppliers are not always aware of how their data are used. It is the responsibility of national accountants to provide them with this information through meetings or discussions. In some countries, national accountants run seminars or courses for data suppliers.

5. Managing Data Compilation Systems

2.92. For QNA data, the time-series dimension is the dominant feature of the data. Thus, any computer system for compiling QNA estimates must be time-series oriented. Box 2.3 sets out the main elements of a compilation system built on time-series-oriented database software. Most elements are also relevant for spreadsheet-based systems.

2.93. National accounts data processing systems are developed to meet the situations of each country. As noted in paragraph 2.5, some countries have separate QNA and ANA systems while others use the same system. Some countries base their national accounts processing system on spreadsheets such as *Lotus* or *Excel*. For large-scale systems, a processing system based on a general database package is preferable. The structure of a database package is built on data series and algorithms to manipulate them. In contrast, the structure of a spreadsheet is based on individual cells linked by formulas. The large volumes of data involved in national accounts compilation favor the use of databases. Databases are more efficient in handling large volumes of data and are also more suitable for handling data transfer to and from seasonal adjustment and benchmarking packages. In spreadsheets containing massive amounts of numbers, making errors is easy and tracing them difficult. Transfer of data between spreadsheets is clumsy, and it is hard to keep track of different versions of data. Spreadsheets also make it difficult to change compilation methods and to ensure that changes are correctly put through.

2.94. Accordingly, as a general guideline, spreadsheets are useful in small-scale tasks like development work, pre-editing, and summary measures. As the system moves from development to operations, it is desirable to shift to a compilation system built on database software and use it for the large-scale tasks of data storage, calculations, seasonal adjustment, and benchmarking. A database system should allow for receiving and downloading data in spreadsheet format, which will facilitate transition from a spreadsheet-based QNA system and assist in data exchange with suppliers and users. With good interfaces, it is also possible to have mixed systems that use spreadsheets for some functions, such as data supply or editing charts, while using a database for others, such as large-scale storage and calculation.

2.95. The core of a national accounting processing system built on database software is generally a general-purpose, commercially available database package. A custom-made interface to the database may be needed to ease data exchange between the database and other software packages; smaller tailor-made compilation modules may also be needed. *Access*, *Oracle*, *Sysbase*, and *dBase* are relational database packages specialized for cross-sectional operations. In contrast *Fame*, *Dbank*, and *Aremos* are specialized for time-series operations. None of the database packages currently available is optimal for both types of operations. Time-series databases treat all data objects (data arrays or data vectors) as time series and are particularly suitable when the time dimension is the dominant feature of the data, such as for QNA. Relational databases are more suitable when the time dimension is not the most important feature of the data. Compilation of SU tables and editing and aggregation of microdata are examples of operations best undertaken with relational databases.

2.96. A well-thought-out naming structure for the series is essential for the functionality of a compilation system built on time-series-oriented database software. The naming structure determines how the data are organized and thus how to navigate within the database. The structure should be easy to understand, follow the classification system, show the type of data (frequency, value/price index), and show the stage of processing. Other aspects of a well-designed system include well-documented programs and easy operation of the system. The programs should be documented by descriptive files and by comments and notes within the programs themselves. Finally, the system should be able to be run by national accounts compilers, rather than by computer specialists without any national accounts expertise.

2.97. In a spreadsheet-based system, or in spreadsheet components of a system otherwise built on database software, some good practices to be followed include these:

- Separate sheets should be used for data entry and subsequent stages of processing. Each figure should be entered only once and subsequently always referenced by links so that all consequential changes are made in the event of revisions.
- Documentation of sources, processes, assumptions, and adjustments to assist later compilers

---

Box 2.3. Elements of a QNA Processing System Built on Database Software

The core of a well-designed computer system for compiling QNA estimates should contain the following main elements:

- Databases for data input
  - ▶ A set of databases for storage of monthly quarterly and annual source data
  - ▶ A database for storage of ANA estimates
  - ▶ A set of databases for storage of annual source data
- Compilation routines
  - ▶ Benchmarking of time series of indicators to time series of annual data—quarterization and extrapolation
  - ▶ Deflation/reflation
  - ▶ Source data assessment procedures—tracking on a detailed level, editing
  - ▶ Compilation system assessment procedures—simulations on historical data/tracking on an aggregated level
  - ▶ Reconciliation/comparison of GDP estimates from the production, expenditure, and income sides
  - ▶ Seasonal adjustment (link to X-11-Arima and/or X-12-Arima)
- Databases for storage of compiled QNA data
  - ▶ Database(s) for official published data
  - ▶ Archived copies of previous quarters—published data, to facilitate studies of revisions
  - ▶ Working databases for unpublished estimates
  - ▶ Storage of alternative versions of data (i.e., both before and after adjustments/revisions) to facilitate verifiability and checking
- Routines for tabulation of the data to construct publication tables and for transferring data to diskettes and external databases

---

should be included in spreadsheets as text or notes. Data should have headings that describe the series and its units.

- Standardized formats should be used for all parts of the system (e.g., basic sheets for input, deflation, checking, aggregation; time series as either rows or columns, not both; several years of data should be visible on the screen; choose millions or billions, not both). The formats should be designed for compatibility with input formats required by seasonal adjustment and benchmark tasks that need to be done outside the spreadsheet.
- Multiple layers of worksheets should be used to show stages separately while allowing links to related stages.
- Color and font options should be used to separate inputs, outputs, data that have a different reference base (to facilitate later changing of the base), and edit checks.
- Spreadsheets should be dated (e.g., printed copies can be dated by using the Excel function "=today()"). Backups of previous versions should be stored. One option would be to store

all the spreadsheets from a quarter in a single folder to separate them from other quarters without having to rename each file. As well, the practice of automatic overwriting of previous versions means that a mistake may be hard to undo. Within each quarterly run, it may be safer to rename files each time they are changed (e.g., "Manufacturing Aug22-B" for the second time it was saved on August 22; after completion, the last version could be archived and the others deleted).

- Files and worksheets should have meaningful names (e.g., not "Sheet1" and "Sheet 2" but "CPI Data Entry" and "CPI Rereferencing").
- Formulas should be double-checked to see that they do what was intended and have not been unintentionally affected by other changes.
- The chart facility of the spreadsheet package should be used frequently.
- Row and column headings should always be visible (in Excel, applying the "split" command followed by the "freeze panes" option achieves this result).

III Sources for GDP and its Components

A. General Issues

1. Introduction

3.1. This chapter deals with the process of identification and assessment of quarterly data sources. Because circumstances differ, it is not possible to create a standard set of sources that can be applied in all countries. Rather, the approach taken in this chapter is to describe the alternatives that are used in quarterly national accounts (QNA) compilation in various countries and some of the considerations that need to be taken into account in choosing among them.

3.2. In general, the same principles for designing sources and methods apply to both annual national accounts (ANA) and QNA. Accordingly, this chapter does not seek to provide a general introduction to national accounts sources and methods. Rather, it deals with issues that are specific to or are of heightened importance in a QNA context.

3.3. This section deals with general issues that apply to more than one component of GDP compilation. The remaining sections of this chapter cover the components of each of the production, expenditure, and income splits of GDP. Even if expenditure or income data are incomplete, it may still be possible to derive a useful split of GDP by type of expenditure or income, as noted in Chapter II. For the production approach, the presentation in this chapter is by type of indicator, because there are common issues in data sources that cut across a wide range of industries. In contrast, a presentation arranged by output, intermediate consumption, and value added would not show the links between the compilation of these items, and a presentation by industry would be repetitive because some issues apply across many industries. The other approaches are discussed by component— expenditure by household consumption, government consumption, and so on; income by compensation of employees, operating surplus, and so on. Some indicators are used in more than one approach; for example, the same construction indicators are used for the construction industry in the production approach and for capital formation in the expenditure approach. In these cases, specific issues for such indicators are discussed under the heading of expenditure.

2. Data Sources

3.4. The basic principle in selecting and developing QNA sources is to obtain indicators that best reflect the items being measured. In some cases, source data are available in a form ready for use in the ANA or QNA with little or no adjustment. In other cases, the source data will differ from the ideal in some way, so that the source data will need to be adjusted. These adjustments may typically be established for one or a few *main benchmark years* for which additional sources such as the results of more comprehensive and detailed surveys or censuses may be available. In these cases, the annual and quarterly time series are anchored to these main benchmark years and the regular source data are *used as indicators* to update the benchmark estimates (extrapolation or, equivalently, forward carrying of the benchmark adjustments). As the ANA provide the benchmarks for QNA they should be the starting point in selecting and developing QNA sources. In some cases, the same sources that are used annually or for the main benchmark years may also be available on a quarterly basis, most commonly foreign trade, central government, and financial sector data. More commonly, QNA data sources are more limited in detail and coverage than those available for the ANA because of issues of data availability, collection cost, and timeliness. For each component, the available source that best captures the movements in the target variable both in the past and in the future constitutes the best indicator.

3.5. The use of an indicator implies an assumption that it is representative of the target variable. The best strategy is to make such assumptions explicit and review them regularly. When assumptions are not made explicit, there is a greater risk that they are not being carefully evaluated. As well, the economic conditions that underlie an assumption may be initially realistic, but later change, so the assumptions need to be reviewed from time to time.

3.6. The suitability of an indicator can be assessed qualitatively by looking at the differences from the target variable in coverage, definitions, and so on. There are a range of possibilities for the closeness of the indicator and the target variable. After the ANA data sources themselves, the most desirable indicators differ only slightly from those used in the ANA, for example, by being based on a sound sample but with less detailed data. Less satisfactory are indicators that cover only a part of the total, such as the major products or largest establishments in an industry. Even less satisfactory as indicators are those that measure something related to the process or population of the target variable, but less directly, such as labor inputs as an indicator of service industry outputs. Least acceptable are indicators that apply past trends or measure something that is connected to the target variable only by a behavioral relationship or statistical correlation. Such indicators should be avoided because the underlying relationships can be expected to be less stable than is the case for an indicator with a direct intrinsic relationship to the target variable.

3.7. The indicator and the assumptions behind its use can also be assessed quantitatively by *comparing the growth rates* in the annual sum of the quarterly indicator with growth rates in the corresponding ANA estimate. Equivalently, the ratio of the ANA estimate to the sum of the quarterly indicator shows the relationship between the two series as a single figure, which in this manual is called the benchmark-indicator ratio. (The process of indicator assessment is described in depth in Chapter II.)

3.8. A stable benchmark-indicator ratio shows that the indicator represents the movements in the target variable well. Changes in the ratio may point to problems and help identify ways to improve the indicator in the future. The benchmark-indicator ratio does not have to equal one, as differences between the levels of the annual estimate and the quarterly indicator can easily be solved by multiplication. For example, a quarterly indicator in the form of an index can readily be converted to a money value. This lack of concern about levels is an important difference in focus

between QNA and ANA compilation: while establishing correct **levels** is essential in ANA compilation, levels in QNA can be derived from the ANA. The essential task in QNA is to obtain the data sources that provide the best indication of quarterly **movements.**

3.9. Even with careful selection of the most suitable indicators and improvements to data sources, benchmark-indicator ratios will vary over time, because indicators are not fully representative of the target variable. Chapter VI deals with the mathematical processes used to make a QNA estimate that follows the movements of the indicator as closely as possible while being fully consistent with the levels and growth rates of the annual estimates. Use of fixed ratio adjustments is another way of using an indicator in conjunction with a benchmark. However, the adjustment of indicators to the levels of the annual data should be done through the benchmarking process, not using fixed ratios, because benchmarking takes into account changes in the ratios as smooth changes and so avoids step problems. (This issue is discussed in more detail in Section D.1 of Chapter VI.)

3.10. Two or more indicators may be available for the same item. In some cases, the indicators may represent different parts of the item. For example, clothing may have separate indicators for men's, women's, and children's clothing. In these cases, the best solution is to split the annual data into each component and benchmark each indicator and component separately. If that is not possible, the components should be added or weighted together to form a single indicator before benchmarking. Alternatively, if the various indicators do not represent different parts of an item but rather are alternative indicators, the one that is most representative in terms of concept and past annual movements should be adopted. If they are equally suitable, the indicators could be added or weighted together to produce a single indicator.

3. Issues with Surveys

3.11. A common problem for surveys is the delay in the inclusion of new businesses and deletion of non-operating businesses in survey frames and estimation procedures. This problem is more serious for QNA than for ANA because of the more limited collection time for the quarterly source data and because the information needed to update the survey frames may be more limited on a quarterly basis. The continuing process of births and deaths of establishments and enterprises occurs in all industries but particularly in those with a large number of small-scale, short-lived establishments, such as retailing and consumer services. Births and deaths of establishments and enterprises are an important factor in changes in the overall trends. In fact, growth often occurs largely through increases in the number of businesses rather than through growth in the output of existing businesses. Moreover, new businesses are particularly likely to have higher rates of growth and high levels of capital formation (particularly in the start-up quarter), as well as being more likely to be established during economic upturns. Closed businesses are included in the scope of surveys but may be misclassified as nonresponse. Because of these factors, quarterly business surveys should be designed to reflect changes in the population of businesses or they will tend to understate growth for a booming economy and understate declines for an economy in recession.

3.12. For the survey results to reflect changes in the population of businesses, the following considerations need to be taken into account when designing business surveys:
- The business register that provides the population frame[1] for the survey needs to be updated on a continuous basis to ensure complete coverage of the entire population of businesses in the frame.
- New businesses should be incorporated in the survey as soon as they start, either by drawing supplementary samples of new businesses or redrawing the sample for the whole population.
- Deceased businesses need to be separated from nonresponding businesses in the original sample. The contribution of deceased businesses to their industry should be recorded as nil; for nonresponding businesses, values should be estimated.
- For each industry, the original sample and the supplementary samples should be stratified by size, location, age, and other dimensions of businesses that may explain major variations in the level and growth rates of the target variable for each business for which corresponding population-wide information is available in the frame. Different stratification principles may have to be used for new and continuing businesses in cases where the available population-wide information differs for the two subgroups.

[1]The sources of information available to update the business register depend on the legal and economic conditions in each country. Sources include business licenses, taxation registers, business bank accounts, and telephone directories.

- The estimation procedure should be level oriented, not index oriented, because the introduction of new businesses and products is more difficult in an index framework. In contrast to an index formulation, a level formulation of the estimation procedure allows different grossing-up factors to be used for different parts of the sample. Levels can be easily converted to indices for presentation purposes.

3.13. If new businesses cannot be incorporated in the survey as soon as they start or there is a large informal economy, household labor force surveys may provide information that can be used to adjust incomplete coverage of business surveys. To be useful for this purpose, household surveys should include questions about the kind of work done and the number of hours worked by each resident of the household, as well as information that allows the place of employment to be identified from the business register, if possible. The survey should include each position held by those with more than one job. Business surveys would need corresponding questions about the number of employees and the number of hours worked. The comparison of labor force and business survey results would give adjustment factors for undercoverage in business surveys. The adjustments, or grossing-up procedures, should be conducted at a detailed industry level with stratification by dimensions that explain variations in the ratio between the target variable and the grossing-up factor. If used to derive measures of business survey undercoverage in this way, monthly or quarterly labor force surveys can be an important data source for QNA.

3.14. Infrequent changes in survey frames or other changes in survey methodology can lead to distortions in the time-series qualities of the QNA. Movements in the indicator will be misleading if caused by changes in survey methods or coverage, rather than actual changes. In these cases, it is essential to separate the causes of movements in the data. If an overlapping period is available for both the old and new survey bases, it would be possible to separate the effect of frame and method changes from the quarterly change. In the case of changes in the frame, the adjustment should be allocated over all the periods since the frame was last updated. For other changes in methods, the old and new series would be linked by a factor to take into account the effect of the change. If it were not possible to have an overlapping period, adjustments could be based on indicators not affected by the change, sometimes including the household labor surveys mentioned in the previous paragraph, or derived from any other available information comparing the old and new survey bases.

4. Issues with Administrative Byproduct Data

3.15. Administrative byproduct data tend to be used more in QNA than in ANA. These data are derived from information gathered in the process of government taxation or regulation, rather than from a survey designed for statistical purposes. For example, taxation and control of foreign trade, taxation of payrolls and collection of social security contributions, and regulation of particular activities such as transport or land transfer all generate information that can be useful for QNA purposes. As these systems were designed with other objectives than obtaining statistics, there may be limitations from a national accounts perspective in matters such as coverage, units, data definitions, period covered, and level of detail. For these reasons, direct statistical collections may be preferred for annual data. On the other hand, if the administrative information has already been collected, the costs and response burden associated with a survey can be avoided. As well, governments often ensure high or even universal compliance on a timely basis. However, timing problems from differences in periods covered can become be a problem with administrative data and can be more severe in QNA, as any timing difference is relatively larger in a quarterly context. For example, a biweekly system could have six two-week periods in some quarters and seven two-week periods in others.

3.16. An important type of administrative data for QNA is from value added tax (VAT) systems (also called "goods and services tax" in some countries). VAT systems collect monthly or quarterly data on sales and purchases as part of the tax collection process. The data may also be suitable for statistical purposes and are being used in an increasing number of countries. VAT systems have the benefit of offering comprehensive or, at least, very wide coverage. Since the VAT system would collect information in any case, the extra cost and burdens of statistical collections can be avoided. However, VAT systems are not always designed with statistical objectives in mind, so there may be problems with regard to national accounts requirements on issues such as timeliness, timing, tax exemptions, industry classifications, units, the effects of rebates or backdated assessments, and limited product detail.[2] Because VAT is usually collected from legal entities

rather than establishments, VAT data from multi-industry enterprises lacks industry detail. VAT data for the single industry enterprises could be supplemented by a survey of multi-industry enterprises. If such a survey is not possible, data by industry of enterprise could be used as an indicator of data by industry of establishment. There may also need to be extensive communication with the tax collection authorities to understand the data, to produce tabulations in a form suitable for national accounts compilation, and to make adjustments to tax forms and procedures to better meet statistical objectives. Other product tax systems may also provide data on the underlying flows of taxable products, such as alcohol and petroleum.

5. Sources in the Absence of Surveys or Administrative Data

3.17. If no statistical collections or administrative data are available, industry associations, industry experts, or leading enterprises in a particular industry may be able to assist with finding or making quarterly indicators.

3.18. If no quarterly indicator is available, there is still a need to fill gaps to ensure a comprehensive total. Ideally, these gaps will be few in number, represent a small proportion of the total, and be closed later as other data sources become available. Among the alternatives for such items are use of:
- a somewhat related item as an indicator;
- totals of a wide range of other items as an indicator;
- the overall economy as an indicator; or
- mathematical methods based on distribution of annual data and extrapolation of past annual trends.

3.19. In choosing among alternatives, past patterns in the annual data for that variable can be used as a guide. If a series is volatile and related to the economic cycle, growth rates of the rest of the economy could be a suitable indicator. If the annual series does not relate to fluctuations in the rest of the economy, a growth rate based on past trends may be suitable. Extrapolation on the basis of past trends is generally not desirable, as it tends to hide the actual data on current trends. If there really is no suitable indicator, a simple method that is transparent may be more appropriate than something that is time-consuming and complicated but not necessarily any better. Mathematical techniques for generating synthetic data in the absence of indicators are discussed in Chapter VII.

---

[2]Some product details may be available if different tax rates are applied.

B. GDP by Industry

I. General Issues

3.20. The production approach is the most common approach to measuring quarterly GDP. To some extent, this may reflect the availability of data before the introduction of QNA. In addition, the production approach shows the industry composition of growth, which provides a useful perspective on economic performance. The production approach is also particularly suitable for deriving productivity measures because industries for which output volumes are poorly measured can be excluded for this type of analytical use.

3.21. The general principles of deflation and choice of double and single indicator methods are the same for QNA and ANA. The production approach involves calculating output, intermediate consumption, and value added at current prices as well as in volume terms by industry. Because of definitional relationships, if two out of output, intermediate consumption, and value added are available, the third can be derived residually. Similarly, if two out of values, prices, and volumes are available, the third can be derived. (See Box 3.1.)

3.22. Observed data on both output and intermediate consumption at current prices may be available quarterly in some cases; in these cases, the double indicator method for value added can be used. For example, in some countries, government-owned enterprises in industries such as oil, transport, or telecommunications may be economically significant and able to supply data directly. Commodity flow methods may be used to generate information on some specialized inputs, for example, pesticides and fertilizers for agriculture. In a system of quarterly supply and use tables, the required data can be generated on the basis of available data, past tables, and national accounting identities.

3.23. However, the data required for the production approach are commonly incomplete on a quarterly basis. Because compiling the production accounts at current prices and in volume terms requires detailed accounting information on both output and current expenses, the required data may not be available quar-

terly or may not be collected with the speed needed for timely QNA compilation. Then the missing data must be estimated by using another series as an indicator. Most commonly, output data are available, while data on intermediate consumption are not. In other cases, data on total intermediate consumption, component(s) of intermediate consumption, labor inputs, or capital inputs may be available as indicators. The quality of the estimate depends on the assumption of a stable relationship between the indicator and the target variable.

3.24. Relationships between inputs and outputs (input-output or IO coefficients) may change as a result of technological changes, differences in the seasonal patterns of outputs and inputs, or variations in capacity utilization caused by changes in the business cycle. The impact of technological changes may not be significant in the short term and can be handled through the benchmarking process if they happen gradually over a longer period. As discussed in Section D of Chapter VI, it is preferable to use benchmarking rather than fixed ratios. The reliance on fixed coefficients is particularly unsatisfactory for calculations at current prices because of the additional factor of changes in relative prices.

3.25. It is recommended that output, intermediate consumption, and value added—at current prices, in volume terms, and the corresponding deflators—always be derived and published in a complete presentation. In some countries, value added is derived directly, without explicitly calculating output and intermediate consumption. This practice is undesirable for several reasons. It is not consistent with the *1993 SNA* presentation of the production account or with supply and use tables. It reduces the analytical usefulness of the data. Also, because value added is not able to be directly observed or deflated, it encourages the use of inappropriate calculation or deflation methods when better options are available. It does not facilitate comparison of quarterly estimates with subsequent annual output data or help in pinpointing weaknesses. As an example, compiling the full production account by industry makes explicit the assumptions about IO ratios that might otherwise be implicit or ignored. An assumption of fixed IO ratios at both current and constant prices might be highlighted in

Box 3.1. Data for the Production Approach

	Current price values	Prices/price index	Volumes/constant price values
Output	✔	✔	✔
Intermediate consumption	✔	✔	✔
Value added	(usually derived indirectly)	(usually derived indirectly)	(usually derived indirectly)

implausible implicit price deflator movements, or deflating value added by an output price index[3] might result in unacceptable changes in IO ratios.

3.26. If data on intermediate consumption are not available, the preferred method is first to obtain an estimate of intermediate consumption at constant prices using constant price output as an indicator. This method uses an assumption of a stable IO ratio modified by annual trends in the ratio that are incorporated through the benchmarking process. Intermediate consumption at current prices can then be derived by reflating the constant price estimate by price indices that reflect the product composition of intermediate inputs. In the likely event that there is not a specific producer price index (PPI) for inputs, industry-specific intermediate consumption price deflators can be constructed by weighting together relevant price index components from, for example, the consumer price index (CPI), PPI, and foreign trade price indices according to the composition of inputs. A use table[4] for a recent year would provide weights to derive industry-specific intermediate consumption deflators (or reflators). A more detailed level of reflation is preferable as it allows the effect of changes in the composition of output to be captured in the estimates.

3.27. Output and value added should be estimated at basic prices according to the *1993 SNA*, although producers' prices are an acceptable alternative. A number of countries that follow the *1953 SNA* or *1968 SNA* use factor cost valuation.[5] Measurement of value added at basic prices is preferred in the *1993 SNA* and

is increasingly common in practice. To derive GDP from value added at basic prices, customs duties, VAT, and other taxes on products are added and subsidies on products are subtracted. This measure is consistent with the expenditure-based estimate of GDP, while separating the processes of production and taxation of products in the generation of GDP.[6]

2. Sources for Industries

3.28. Commonly used types of source data for the production approach on a quarterly basis include current price data from accounting and administrative systems, quantity indicators, labor and other input measures, and price indices. Most commonly, deflation will be used to derive a volume measure, that is, a current price value is divided by a corresponding price index. Due to problems that are discussed below, deflation is usually preferable to direct measures of volumes. In other cases, there may be volume and price indicators only or current price value and volume indicators only. Box 3.2 provides an overview of the value and volume indicators most commonly used for the production approach.[7]

a. Current price data on outputs and/or inputs

3.29. Current price data can be obtained from accounting systems through surveys or as administrative byproducts. Accounting data are particularly suited for the collection of aggregates. Compared with volume measures, these data have the advantages of being comprehensive and cutting the costs associated with collecting detailed data, which reduces respondent burden. In contrast, quantities of different products need to be collected separately for each product, and there are potential serious problems if new products are omitted.

3.30. The sources of accounting aggregates may be direct surveys, published accounts, or administrative systems for regulation or taxation.

3.31. For goods-producing industries, the values of sales together with opening and closing values of inventories of finished goods and work-in-progress[8] are required to derive an output indicator. The simplest indicators cover only total sales of goods manufactured by the enterprise. A more sophisticated system may collect separate data by product group and/or

---

[3]Unlike the other single indicator methods, deflation of value added by output price indices assumes that prices of inputs, outputs, and value added are all moving in the same proportions. Relative prices can often be quite volatile because of factors such as changes in exchange rates, wage rates, profitability, and commodity prices. It is almost always possible and better to
- deflate output at current prices by the output deflator; then
- estimate intermediate consumption at constant prices by using output as an indicator (assumes a stable input-output ratio, although this will be modified by annual trends by the benchmarking process); then
- derive value added as the difference between the estimates of output and intermediate consumption, all at constant prices.
This method requires no additional data; rather, it uses more realistic assumptions.
[4]A use table shows use by industry of each product. When a use table is not available, an industry-by-industry input-output table may be considered as a less satisfactory substitute. An industry-by-industry input-output table shows the use by industry of the output of each industry, and it is less useful in this context because it is more difficult to relate the price data (as they typically refer to products) and because product prices tend to be more homogeneous than industry prices.
[5]The factor price concept has virtually been dropped in the *1993 SNA* because factor cost does not correspond to observable prices in contrast to basic, producers', and purchasers' prices and is actually a measure of income, not production.

---

[6]Note that the effects of nonproduct taxes and subsidies on production are reflected in basic prices along with other production costs.
[7]The Organisation for Economic Co-Operation and Development (1996) provides information about sources in its member countries.
[8]Output = sales + changes in inventories of finished goods and work-in-progress (excluding any revaluation effects).

Box 3.2. Overview of Value and Volume Indicators Commonly Used for Quarterly GDP by Industry

	Current price data on outputs and/or inputs	Data on quantities of outputs and/or inputs	Labor input measures	Other indicators
Agriculture, forestry, fishing, hunting	X	X		Population (subsistence)
Mining	X	X	X	Industrial Production Index (may be derived from range including output, quantities, and input)
Manufacturing, utilities	X	X	X	Industrial Production Index (may be derived from range including output, quantities, and input)
Construction	X	X		Supply of building materials
Wholesale and retail trade	X			Supply of goods handled
Restaurants and hotels	X	X	X	
Transport, storage, and communications	X	X		Volume of goods transported
Financial intermediation	X	X		Value of loans/ deposits
Real estate, business services	X		X	
Ownership of dwellings		X		Stock of dwellings (capital input)
Public administration and defense	X	X	X	
Education, health, other services	X	X	X	
Net taxes on products (including import duties, VAT)	X			Constant price value of relevant products (equivalent to applying base year tax rates)

establishment. (In establishment-level data for multi-establishment enterprises, shipments of goods and provision of services to other establishments in the enterprise need to be recorded.) Other revenue, such as sales of goods not produced by the factory, repairs, or rental services, might also be collected in total or separately. Data on inventories used in calculations should have the effects of valuation changes excluded.

3.32. Value data for construction projects are collected in some countries. If only the total value of a project is available, it is necessary to allocate it over the life of the project and exclude holding gains (see Chapter X). Otherwise, data are collected on value of work done during the quarter. Collecting this kind of data avoids the difficulties of making assumptions about the allocation of a total value for a whole project to particular quarters. However, the feasibility is limited by the availability of data, as construction enterprises are often small scale and work done may be hard to separate into quarters. Progress payments

for work done may be an acceptable approximation if interviews suggest that they approximate the value of work put in place. (Construction indicators are discussed further in Section C.2 of this chapter.)

3.33. Sales data are commonly used as quarterly indicators for the output of wholesale and retail trade. Sales data could be obtained from a business survey or as an administrative byproduct of a tax on sales. Output at current prices is defined as the trader's margin, that is, sales less the replacement cost of goods sold.

3.34. Output at current prices of other business and consumer services can be measured by turnover or sales. In some countries, there are surveys of sales of services such as restaurants, hotels, clubs, hairdressers, theaters, and repairers.

3.35. Government agencies are an important source of quarterly accounting data for activities that they operate, regulate, or tax. Publicly owned corporations are important in some activities, for example, transport, post, and telecommunications. General government dominates the service industries of public administration, defense, and community services. Government regulation of activities such as banking, insurance, and health may give rise to quarterly value data. Sales information concerning products subject to a specific tax—gambling, for example—may be obtained from governments. In some of these cases, it may be possible to use the same methods used for the annual estimates; in others, a less detailed version may be acceptable.

3.36. VAT systems can supply helpful data that can be used for the production approach. In addition to the general issues discussed in Section A of this chapter, VAT systems have the problem that they do not take changes in inventories into account because the data cover sales (not output) and purchases (not intermediate consumption). Also, purchases of goods and services that are deductible for VAT usually include both capital formation and intermediate consumption. For national accounts indicators, it is highly desirable to separate these two components. Otherwise, the purchases data would not be usable as an indicator of intermediate consumption because fixed capital formation is usually large, lumpy, or both.

b. Data on quantities of output and/or inputs

3.37. Data on quantities of output are available for many products. Quantities are easy to define for the goods-producing industries, for example, metric tons of wheat and coal, kiloliters of beer, and numbers of cars. Less tangible quantities can be measured for other industries, for example, kilowatts of electricity, floor area of construction, and ton-kilometers of freight.

3.38. The concepts of quantity measures and volume measures should be distinguished. Quantity data are expressed in terms of physical units. Volume data are expressed in terms of constant price values or volume indices; these data differ from the quantity data because quality changes are accounted for and because the measures can be meaningfully aggregated. Quantity data can be converted to constant price values by multiplying them by base year prices and making adjustments (if any) for quality change.

3.39. In some cases, businesses can supply quantity data more readily than they can supply financial information on a quarterly basis. The businesses may not compile quarterly accounts, or they may take longer to complete than simply collecting numbers that do not require processing or valuation. Quantity indicators can be multiplied by price indices or average prices for the quarter to obtain current price indicators. Such estimates avoid the inventory valuation issues that arise for current price values that have been derived from data that include inventories measured at historic cost.

3.40. The limitations of quantity data are significant, and quantity data should be avoided if products are heterogeneous or subject to quality change. The range of products in an economy is enormous, so the list of products is limited to the major ones and is usually far from comprehensive. Products are not the same as industries, so secondary production should be included with the industry of actual production, not with the industry to which they are primary. The usefulness of quantity data is limited by the homogeneity of the products. For basic commodities, such as wheat and base metals, there is often relatively little variation in quality over time, particularly if data are broken down by grades of quality, so quantity indicators may be suitable. However, many products vary considerably in quality—that is, they are heterogeneous. For such goods, deflated current price data should be used. This situation applies to a large number of manufactured goods and to some agricultural and mining products. The more narrowly such products are defined, the more the estimates will be able to reflect the actual volume of output. For example, if cars are treated as a single product, changes in the mix of output toward larger cars or cars with more accessories or better quality will not affect the number of cars but should be treated as an increase in the volume of output. There are many products for which quantities are poor indicators or for which output is not readily quantifiable, such as clothing, medicines, and specialized equipment. One way of dealing with the problems of heterogeneity of products is to collect extra detail, although it may not be practical owing to greater collection costs, respondent burden, and delay in tabulation.

3.41. Quantity indicators are usually developed on a case-by-case approach for each industry, rather than as a unified system. The following are some examples of quantity indicators:
- Agriculture: quantities are usually closely monitored, heavily regulated, or subsidized by Ministries of Agriculture. Quantity data for agricultural products may be obtained from some point along the distribution chain if the number of farms is large and the distributors few. However, differences between quantity of products at the farm and quantity of products at the distribution site can be caused by

wastage, timing differences, double counting, grower-consumed products, informal sales, and other factors. Conceptual issues associated with the timing of agricultural production are dealt with in Chapter X.

- Construction: floor area built, preferably divided by type of building. (Indicators for construction are discussed further under gross fixed capital formation on construction in the expenditure approach in Section C of this chapter.)
- Hotels and restaurants: numbers of bed-nights; numbers of meals. Numbers of foreign tourists may be an acceptable indicator in countries where expenditures by foreign tourists are a high proportion of the total.
- Transport: numbers of passengers or passenger-kilometers; metric tons of freight or ton-kilometers; numbers of licensed taxis and hire cars. To the extent that prices, and therefore the volume of service, reflect distance, data with a kilometer dimension are better indicators. For example, metric ton-kilometers would be a better indicator of the volume of freight than a measure of metric tons that did not take into account differences in distances carried. (Ideally, if there were both fixed and distance-related elements to the price, the two would be weighted together.)
- Services to transport: numbers of ships handled in ports; numbers of aircraft and passengers handled at an airport; numbers of days for which cars are hired; weight or volume of goods stored or refrigerated; numbers of cars parked in pay parking; numbers of journeys on toll roads.
- Communications: numbers of letters, parcels, or local telephone calls; minutes of long-distance or international telephone calls; numbers of telephone lines. In view of technological change in the area of communications, it is important to include new products, such as electronic data lines, internet connections, and mobile phones.
- Ownership of dwellings: numbers of dwellings, preferably broken down by location, size, and type of dwelling and with adjustments for new dwellings and alterations and quality change. (Sources and methods are covered later in more detail in the discussion of indicators for household consumption of rent.)
- Other business services: numbers of wills, court cases, and divorces for lawyers; numbers of registered land transfers for real estate agents; numbers of deaths for undertakers; stock market turnover for stock market dealers.
- Public administration services: numbers of pen-

sions processed, licenses issued, and court cases processed. Because these indicators are partial and do not reflect quality well, they are used to only a limited extent.
- Other services: numbers of tickets sold by theaters and other forms of entertainment; numbers of vehicle repairs.

3.42. The potential range of sources is very wide. Unlike industrial production indices, these indicators are not usually part of a comprehensive system of indicators. As a result, there are typically many gaps, and data often need to be obtained from different agencies. Some potential indicators may be unpublished but could be obtained by making a request to the relevant agency.

c. Labor input measures

3.43. Labor input measures are sometimes used as indicators of the volume of output of service industries. The assumption behind the use of this method is that employment is directly related to output and value added in volume terms. Labor is a major input to the service industries, and compensation of employees plus mixed income typically constitute very high proportions of value added. As well, comprehensive monthly or quarterly data on employment by industry are available in many countries, from specific surveys or as a byproduct of a payroll or social security tax system.

3.44. Number of hours worked is preferable to number of employees as an indicator of labor input. Output is affected by changes in standard weekly working hours, the proportions of part-time employees, and hours of overtime. Hours worked takes into account these effects, but numbers employed does not. However, hours worked is still an imperfect measure of labor input. Ideally, labor input measures would take into account different types of labor (e.g., disaggregating by occupation or skill level) weighted by their different rates of remuneration. The total value of wages and salaries divided by a fixed specifications wage and salary index would give an indicator that also takes into account such compositional effects, but it would need to be supplemented by a measure for self-employed labor. It is preferable that actual hours worked be covered, rather than paid hours which include sick leave, vacations, and public holidays but exclude unpaid work. The labor input measure should include working proprietors and the self-employed as well as employees.

3.45. Labor input would seldom be preferred as a volume measure because the relationship of labor to output is variable. Because of the delays and costs associated with hiring and firing, labor tends to be less responsive to output than some other inputs. The relationship between labor input and output also changes as a result of changes in capital intensity and total factor productivity.

3.46. In the case of the nonmarket activities of general government and nonprofit institutions serving households, current price output is measured on the basis of the cost of inputs. It is preferable that the output volume measure take into account the services provided by the government or nonprofit institution, if measurable. It is common, however, to use input indicators if suitable volume measures are not available.

3.47. As with other sources, calculations at a greater level of detail will usually improve the estimates. For example, cleaning and litigating may both be in the business services industry category, but the output per hour worked of a cleaning business is much less than that of a law firm. Accordingly, an indicator that separates the two activities will better reflect changes in output.

d. Indirect indicators

3.48. Where direct measures are not available, a diverse range of indirect indicators may be considered. It is sometimes possible to identify a downstream or upstream activity that can be used as a basis to generate indicators. For example, the supply of building materials can be used as an indicator of construction activity. Construction is often difficult to measure because of the large number of small-scale and ephemeral contractors, own-account work, and work done without permits. The supply of building materials, on the other hand, can often be obtained from a relatively small number of manufacturers and quarries (with adjustments for exports and imports, if applicable). To the extent that there is a stable relationship between building material inputs and output, this is a suitable indicator that can be obtained with relatively little cost or compilation time. The quality of the assumption deteriorates if there are changes in any of the mix of types of building, techniques of building, productivity, and inventories of building materials. If changes in these factors are known to be occurring, it may be desirable to explore more complex methods (e.g., a calculation that takes into account the different products used by different types of construction or collection of data on inventories).

3.49. An indicator for the wholesale and/or retail industries could be obtained from the supply of goods that are distributed by these industries. Although it would be conceptually preferable to obtain data on sales and purchases directly from the enterprises, data on the supply of goods handled are often better or easier to collect[9] because many wholesalers and retailers are small scale. (Data on sales of goods to consumers are discussed later in this chapter in the context of GDP by expenditure category.) Similarly, if the types of commodities handled by wholesalers are known, the value of supply of those commodities can be used as an indicator for wholesale output. The wholesaling activity of specialist importers can be measured by the volume of imports. As the estimation procedures rely on an assumption of fixed markups (i.e., the margin as a percentage of the price), the method will give better results if calculated at a greater level of product detail to take into account the combined effect of changes in the product mix with varying markups of different products.

3.50. If data on road freight transport activities are inadequate, it may be possible to derive an indicator based on the supply of goods that are usually transported, or at least the major components. Indicators for other supporting industries may also be derived from the output of the industries served, such as services to agriculture, mining, and transport.

3.51. Population is sometimes used as an indicator in areas where nothing more specific is available, such as subsistence agriculture, housing, and some consumer services. The indicators should be adjusted for long-term trends; for example, population could be used to represent dwelling services, but adjustments should be used to account for trends in quality of dwellings and persons per household. Adjustments for divergence in long-term trends between the population indicator and the annual estimates can be incorporated through the benchmarking process.

3.52. All of the methods discussed in this section assume ratios based on the benchmark data. Such

---

[9]The supply of goods is derived from output less exports plus imports (plus any other adjustments for any other known use in intermediate consumption, inventories, or capital formation, or tax or distribution margins).

ratios are more likely to be stable in constant price terms, so it is generally better to make the assumption in constant price terms and then reflate to current prices. Also, in all of these cases, if the benchmark data are more detailed, the quarterly estimates will tend to be better if the calculations are done at a detailed level.

e. Price indicators

3.53. If a current price value is available for an item, a volume measure can be obtained by deflating with a price index. Alternatively, if a volume measure is available, a current price measure can be obtained by reflating (or inflating) with a price index. Often appropriate deflators will already be available in the form of published price indices, but sometimes deflators will need to be derived by the national accounts compiler by recombining components of other indices or obtaining supplementary price information.

3.54. For manufacturing output, relevant detailed components of the producer price index (PPI) are usually available. PPI measures prices at the factory gate (usually at basic values, sometimes at producer's prices) and is, therefore, most suitable for deflating data at basic values, such as output. In an increasing number of countries, PPIs are extended to cover a wider range of industries beyond manufacturing, possibly including agriculture, mining, construction, and services. For consumer services, particular components of the consumer price index (CPI) could be used. A wholesale price index (WPI) measures prices including transport and distribution margins (and sometimes product taxes) and also covers imports. As a result, WPIs are less suitable for deflating output measures than is PPI, but WPI may be more suitable for deflating intermediate consumption that has passed through the distribution system and includes inputs.

3.55. In some cases, national accountants may be able to develop specific-purpose price indices to fill in gaps. For example, if there are a small number of airports or rail operators, it may be possible to obtain a selection of their charges directly (e.g., from their rate sheets if these show actual transaction prices). When a product is largely exported, average unit values may be used. Professional associations, such as those of lawyers or architects, may have information on fees. Ministries of agriculture and other government bodies that regulate or monitor agricultural activities are often sources of price data for agricultural products. The data are usu-

ally expressed in terms of average prices. It is necessary to exclude transport and distribution costs to derive "farm gate" prices.

3.56. Where no direct data are available, prices of one or more similar or closely related products or industries that have a tendency to move in the same way may be suitable. Suitable comparable products or industries should have somewhat related cost structures or demand. For example, CPIs for domestically produced components are more likely to be representative for unmeasured domestic products than the total CPI, which includes imports and so is more affected by exchange rate movements. Similarly, CPI service items are more likely to be representative of unmeasured services than the total CPI to the extent that services tend to have similar, labor-dominated cost structures.

3.57. It may be necessary to produce output deflators or reflators based on input costs, for example, weighting together wage indices or information on wage rates with the prices of major intermediate inputs. Because this technique does not account for operating surplus, it is unsatisfactory to the extent that profitability varies. However, to the extent that profitability and productivity are taken into account in annual data, the benchmarking process will incorporate the annual variations.

3.58. Wholesaling and retailing present special difficulties in identifying the price dimension. The difficulty arises because they are industries that predominantly produce margins; the service components are combined with the prices of the goods, and the quality aspects are difficult to measure. The preferred solution is to avoid deflating the margin directly by deriving independent volume and value measures. A volume indicator of the margin service can be made from the volume of goods bought or sold using an assumption of a stable volume of the distribution service per unit of goods, that is, no quality change in the service. The suitability of the assumption is improved by compiling at a greater level of detail, as markups differ among products and between outlet types. The price indices of the goods should not be used as a proxy deflator or reflator of margins because margins have different cost structures and can vary differently than goods prices.

3.59. Like output of wholesaling and retailing, the output of financial intermediation services indirectly measured (FISIM) is a margin and so is not readily observable. The recommended approach for QNA estimation is to use the deflated values of loans and deposits as volume indicators for the service provided in conjunction with the annual benchmarks. The value of loans and deposits should be deflated by a price index measuring the general price level (e.g., the CPI). The method would ideally be applied at a disaggregated level, with a detailed breakdown of types of assets and types of liabilities, because the interest margin varies among different types of assets and liabilities, reflecting the fact that the value of service provided varies for different categories. Note that interest margins for financial services can be quite volatile. Interest margin changes are price effects and do not affect the volume of loans, so they will be correctly shown as a price effect with this method. A less satisfactory alternative would be direct deflation of the value of FISIM by a general price index or by financial service input prices. However, these deflators do not measure the price of FISIM and ignore interest margin changes. As a result, changes in financial institutions' profitability would be wrongly shown as a volume change.

3.60. In cases where independent current price and volume measures for output are obtained, the corresponding implicit price deflator should be checked for plausibility.

3.61. Intermediate consumption usually has no specific aggregated deflators, so it is necessary to build them from components of other price indices for the relevant products. Note that even when a fixed coefficient method has been used to derive volume measures for an industry, it is desirable to reflate intermediate consumption and output separately and undesirable to use the fixed coefficient method at current prices.

f. Industrial production indices

3.62. An industrial production index (IPI) is typically already available in countries that compile QNA. It is usually at least quarterly and sometimes monthly. IPIs can use any of the methods used for industry volume indicators, namely deflated values, quantity measures, or selected inputs. In some cases, the IPI may use a mix of methods, such as quantities for homogeneous goods and deflation for others.

3.63. It is preferable to compile QNA estimates from the IPI source data or from IPI components at a disaggregated level, rather than from the total IPI. The more detailed compilation allows differences in cov-

erage and concepts between the IPI and QNA to be resolved. Benchmarking, structural assumptions, and reflation tend to be better when carried out at a greater level of detail. The national accounts measure of output requires weights to reflect output at basic prices or producers' prices, while the IPI may use other weights or valuations. The IPI may have gaps in coverage that may need supplementary sources, for example, particular industries, goods that are not easily quantified, repair service revenue, newspaper advertising revenue, hiring revenue, and secondary output. The base years may also differ. Published IPIs are sometimes adjusted for variations in the number of working days, rendering them unsuitable as QNA indicators. For compilation of non-seasonally adjusted QNA, the data should reflect the actual activity in each quarter, without adjustments for working days or other calendar and seasonal effects.

3.64. If different methods are used in the IPI and QNA, it will prevent confusion if the QNA sources and methods documentation clearly states the differences. These differences should be explained (e.g., weights, coverage, valuation) and quantified, if possible.

3. Adjustment Items

3.65. To derive GDP at market prices, total value added of industries at basic prices needs to have net taxes on products added and unallocated FISIM deducted.

3.66. Net taxes on products consists of import duties, value added taxes, and other taxes less subsidies on products. Data on net taxes on products at current prices are normally available from government finance statistics and present few problems. In a few countries, some components, such as state and local product taxes, may need to be estimated. Such estimates can be based on data on the supply of the taxed products.

3.67. Net taxes or subsidies in volume terms can be defined as the base year rate of tax (or subsidy) applied to the current volume of the good or service. Technically, this is equivalent to the base year value of taxes (or subsidies) extrapolated by the volume of the taxed (or subsidized) goods and services. To the extent that tax (or subsidy) rates differ, it is desirable to do the calculations at a more detailed level to take into account the differing rates.

3.68. The QNA treatment of FISIM should follow the ANA treatment. Under the preferred *1993 SNA* treatment, FISIM should be allocated to users (viz., intermediate consumption by industries, final consumption expenditure, exports) and so would not be an adjustment item to total GDP. In the *1968 SNA,* FISIM was treated as the intermediate consumption of a nominal industry rather than allocated across users. With the *1968 SNA* treatment, it is necessary to deduct unallocated FISIM in aggregate from value added by industry in order to derive GDP. The same indicators that are used to derive and deflate output of financial services should be used for the adjustment. The *1993 SNA* also permits the use of the *1968 SNA* treatment.

C. GDP by Type of Expenditure

1. General Issues

3.69. GDP by type of expenditure shows the final demand for goods and services and so is particularly useful for economic analysis. One benefit for compilation of the expenditure approach is that prices are readily observable; also, this approach does not rely as much on fixed ratios as the quarterly production estimates. Nevertheless, the expenditure approach is less common than the production approach among QNA compiling countries because of problems of availability, timing, valuation, and coverage of expenditure source data, as detailed in the following:
- Government and international trade are typically well covered by quarterly data, but the timing of recording of data is often inconsistent with the national accounts requirements. Government data are usually recorded on a cash basis, although accrual adjustments are sometimes made for particular, identifiable items and accrual accounting is becoming more common in government accounts. Merchandise trade data are recorded when the merchandise passes through the customs frontier, although adjustments may already have been made for some timing problems in balance of payments statistics. Inconsistencies in the timing of transactions may lead to discrepancies and errors. Timing differences are a much more important issue in quarterly data than in annual data: with the same timing differences affecting the annual and quarterly series, the relative impact of an error is four times more significant.
- Expenditure estimates are more strongly influenced by coverage problems in the business register. This influence arises because of the high proportion of retailing and consumer services output that goes to household consumption and the high proportion of building output that goes to capital formation. These

activities often have high proportions of smaller, shorter-lived, less formal businesses. The same activities are included in GDP by industry, but only to the extent of their value added.
- Changes in inventories have serious valuation problems. These problems also occur in production and income approach estimates, although they may be partly avoided by use of quantities of output in the production estimates.

3.70. If the available expenditure data have serious gaps, the expenditure approach cannot be used. However, it may still be possible to derive a useful split of GDP by type of expenditure. The sum of the available expenditure components can be derived so that the total of the missing components can then be derived as the residual from total GDP from the production approach. For example, many countries derive changes in inventories in this way. Although not an independent check on the production estimates, use of incomplete expenditure data in this way is helpful to data analysts.

2. Sources

a. Household final consumption expenditure

(i) Value indicators

3.71. Household final consumption is usually the largest component of GDP by expenditure. The main sources of data on household consumption are surveys of retailers and service providers, value added tax (VAT) systems, and household surveys. Also, data on the production and foreign trade in consumer products can be used to derive estimates by commodity flow methods.

3.72. Business surveys of retailers and providers of other consumer services are a common data source for household consumption at current prices. Many types of retailers and almost all services are fairly specialized, but supermarkets and department stores sell a wide range of goods, so that collecting product breakdowns for these stores is desirable. A detailed breakdown by product improves the quality of the deflation and provides extra information to users. If product mixes are stable, satisfactory quarterly data by product can be estimated by using total sales of a retail industry as an indicator for the benchmark values of sales by product.

3.73. A VAT or sales tax system may be able to provide data on sales by type of enterprise. Such a tax system may also divide sales into different product categories if different tax rates are applied. It is necessary to identify which sales are indicators of household consumption, for example, sales by retailers and consumer services. The systems used to collect other taxes, such as taxes on alcohol or tobacco, may also be a potential source of information.

3.74. Some countries conduct continuous household expenditure surveys. If the results are processed on a timely basis by quarter, they could be useful indicators for QNA. Data collected from households have different benefits and shortcomings compared with business data. Reporting quality and omissions of small or sensitive items may be a problem in household surveys, depending on the behavior of respondents. For example, expenditure on socially sensitive items such as alcohol and tobacco is often understated, requiring adjustments to be made on the basis of other information.[10] As well, there are often problems with purchases of consumer durables as a result of recall and infrequency of purchases. On the other hand, household surveys ensure good coverage of purchases from informal, small-scale retailers and service providers. These are difficult to cover in business surveys, but the purchaser has no reason to understate this expenditure, which is no more difficult to report than any other expenditure. Household surveys may be favored in developing and transition economies because they cover purchases from the informal activities. In countries with small informal sectors, business surveys may be preferred because of issues such as collection cost, delay, and reporting quality of quarterly household expenditure data. For QNA estimation, a level bias in household surveys is not a problem as long as the bias is stable so that it gives a correct indication of movement. In general, a combination and reconciliation of data from several sources will give the best results.

3.75. In addition to broad sources such as retail sales, VAT systems, and household surveys, there are a range of specific indicators for components of household consumption. The sources of specific indicators include specialized statistical surveys, major supplying enterprises, and regulators. Where there are a small number of large suppliers of a particular item but no currently published data, the information can sometimes be collected specifically for QNA. Examples could include sales to residences of electricity and gas, as well as some components of transport, communication, and gambling.

3.76. Household consumption expenditure estimates that are based on indicators from the retailers and service providers will need adjustments for expenditure by residents when abroad and expenditure by nonresidents while in the country. Both of these can be obtained from balance of payments statistics, if available on a quarterly basis (and, if not, by using the methods discussed in the IMF's *Balance of Payments Compilation Guide*).

3.77. Commodity flow methods can be used in cases where there are good data on the supply of products. Total supply to the domestic market at purchasers' prices for a product can be derived as
• domestic output at basic prices,
• plus changes in inventories,
• less exports,
• plus imports,
• plus taxes on products,
• less subsidies on products, and
• plus trade and transport margins.

3.78. To obtain household consumption as a residual, other uses (i.e., intermediate consumption, government consumption, fixed capital formation, and changes in inventories) should be deducted from total domestic supply. This method often relies on ratios to fill in gaps, for example, taxes and margins may be calculated as a proportion of the underlying flows. As explained in Chapter VI, variation in the annual ratios is taken into account through the benchmarking process. In some cases, particular components are nil. The commodity flow method can be particularly useful for goods because goods are often supplied by a relatively small number of producers and importers, and data on the supply of the goods are easier to collect than data on sales at the retail level. Where a significant part of retailing is informal, surveys of retailers are likely to have incomplete coverage, so the commodity flow method could provide more suitable indicators than a survey of retailers.

(ii) Volume indicators

3.79. Data on consumption of dwelling services can be estimated by extrapolation on the basis of the number of dwellings. If construction data do not allow estimates of the net increase in the number of dwellings, population could be used as a proxy (preferably adjusted for any trends in the average number of persons per dwelling). Because of differences in the average rent per dwelling, the quality of the estimation would be improved by doing separate calculations by location and for different dwelling

---

[10]For example, from tax data if smuggling and tax evasion are not major problems.

types (e.g., house/apartment; number of bedrooms). It would also be desirable to put in an adjustment factor to account for any shortcomings in this method (e.g., for long-term changes in the size and quality of dwellings). These factors should be accounted for annually so that their effects can be incorporated in the QNA by the benchmarking process. Because the stock of dwellings is large and changes slowly, acceptable estimates can be derived for dwelling services, even in the absence of quarterly volume indicators. The methods used should be consistent with those used in the production estimates.

3.80. Indicators for some services, such as insurance, education, and health, may be obtained as a byproduct of government regulation. In addition, motor vehicle regulation may provide indicators for the volume of vehicle purchases. The components to be included are household purchases of cars and other light vehicles, both new and secondhand, from businesses and governments.

3.81. Administrative byproduct data may help fill other gaps. For example, taxis, financial intermediation, insurance, health, and gambling are often regulated. As a result, indicators may be published or potentially available on request to the regulatory authorities. Other administrative data can be used as indirect indicators. For example, numbers of divorces and wills in probate are a potential indicator for legal services; numbers of deaths for funeral services; total numbers of vehicles and numbers of road accidents for vehicle repairs. In each case, a direct survey would usually be better but may not be justifiable on a quarterly basis because of the data collection cost and the relative unimportance of the activity. (Value may also sometimes be available from these sources.)

3.82. Consumption from subsistence production of food can be quite important in expenditure estimates for developing countries. The methods should be consistent with those used in the production estimates. In some cases, estimates of agricultural output include subsistence agriculture, so that the consumption can be identified separately or derived by the commodity flow method. In the absence of quarterly surveys of subsistence production, population trends may be an acceptable indicator.

(iii) Price indicators
3.83. CPI components usually provide appropriate deflators for household consumption expenditure.

The coverage of household consumption expenditure is typically fairly close to that of the CPI.

3.84. Deflation should be carried out at a detailed level to ensure that each component is deflated by the price index that most closely matches its actual composition and to minimize the impact of using deflators constructed using the Laspeyres formula and not the preferred Paasche formula. For example, it would be better to deflate each type of food separately to account for different price movements. It is seldom justifiable to use the total CPI in deflation. National accountants should work closely with price statisticians to have consistent classifications and coverage of all required components.

3.85. There may be gaps where a component of expenditure is not covered by a matching CPI item. An example is insurance, which is measured as a margin in the national accounts and which CPI compilers may exclude or measure as total premiums. A possible alternative as a deflator is a price indicator based on input costs (e.g., a weighted index of wages, taxes, and intermediate consumption components such as office-related items, together with an adjustment for profitability, if available). In other cases, it may be necessary to take the most closely related CPI item or group of items.

3.86. For expenditure by residents abroad, the CPIs of the main destination countries adjusted for exchange rate movements could be used as deflators. If available, it would be preferable to obtain specific indices for the most relevant components, for example, hotels, transport, meals, or any particularly important categories of goods, rather than the total CPI. Expenditure of nonresidents could be deflated by the domestic CPI items that relate to the major components of tourist expenditures, that is, hotels, transport, meals, and so on.

b. Government final consumption expenditure
(i) Value indicators
3.87. Government accounting data are often available on a monthly or quarterly basis. These could be prepared on the basis of the various international handbooks or country-specific accounting systems. The most important need for QNA is to have expenditures classified by economic type, in particular, consumption of goods and services, capital formation of goods and services, other expenditures, and

data on offsetting sales. Even if not published, the data may be available on request. Government accounts usually have the advantage of being reported on the same basis as the annual data so that the quarterly data are consistent.

3.88. Data for the central government are generally readily available. In some cases, lack of data or delays may require estimation for state, provincial, or local government. In the absence of comprehensive data, consideration can be given to alternative indicators that relate to the actual level of activity in the quarter, such as the following:
- a sample collection for local governments;
- wages paid by the governments concerned (preferably excluding those involved in own-account capital formation such as road building);
- expenditure data not classified by economic type;
- central government payments where these are the major source of funds; or,
- where actual data are not yet available, government budget estimates. Before forecasts are used, the track record should be checked to see whether they are reliable.

3.89. Government accounts are traditionally prepared on a cash basis. Government cash payments can be large and lumpy, and their timing can be determined by political or administrative concerns. Differences between the cash basis used and the accrual basis required by the *1993 SNA* could cause errors and discrepancies in the estimates. These timing errors are the same in both QNA and ANA, but the impact in QNA is relatively larger since they have a magnitude only about 25 percent of the corresponding ANA estimates. A particular instance of a distortion caused by cash recording is where government employees are paid every two weeks. While some quarters will have six paydays, others will have seven, causing fluctuations in the quarterly data that would not be a serious issue in annual data. To the extent that such timing problems can be identified, adjustments that are supported by evidence can be used to get closer to an accrual basis. Information may be available for some large individual transactions, such as the payday effect or large purchases of weapons.[11] Accrual accounting has already been introduced by some governments, and the 2001 IMF *Manual on Government Finance Statistics* recommends accrual accounting.

---

[11]These issues also occur for government gross fixed capital formation derived from cash-based sources.

3.90. The links to the production estimates for general government should be noted. If inconsistent methods or data are used, errors in the residual item or discrepancies will occur. The scope of government consumption and general government output differ in that government consumption is equal to:
(a) general government nonmarket output;
(b) less own-account capital formation included in output;
(c) less any sales and fees recovered, i.e., government output paid for by others;
(d) plus purchases that government provides free to households without processing.

Although the same indicators can often be used for both production and expenditure, the factors causing differences between them need to be taken into account, especially if they are changing proportions of the total.

(ii) Volume indicators

3.91. In a few cases, it may be possible to obtain quantity measures for output of government services. For example, numbers of students at government schools, numbers of operations or bed-nights for patients in public hospitals, and numbers of benefit recipients served by a government social assistance office may be available. However, these indicators fail to take into account important quality aspects. Further, there are many other activities of government where output is difficult to quantify, such as research and policymaking.

3.92. In the absence of suitable output volume indicators, an indicator based on labor inputs may be used, such as number of employees or hours worked. Because government consumption is a labor-intensive service, this is a more acceptable assumption than it would be for other expenditure components. In addition to the limitations of labor input measures for measuring production, measuring consumption is more difficult because of work contracted out to the private sector, capital work on own account, and the offsetting effect of charges for some services. Structural changes in the proportions of staff engaged in capital work, the proportions of output recovered through charges, or the proportion of work outsourced could be significant on a quarterly basis.

(iii) Price indicators

3.93. Although current price measures for government are clearly defined as being based on costs, the price and volume dimensions are less clearly defined and have several alternatives. Prices are usually not directly observable. One option is to derive independent value and volume measures so that the price dimension is obtained indirectly. Alternatively, a deflator could be obtained as a weighted average of input costs. The usual input costs are wage indices or pay scales of civil servants and military staff, combined with relevant components of price indices reflecting typical input costs such as rents, electricity, stationery, and repairs.

3.94. Methods based on input costs have the shortcoming that they do not account for productivity changes. Of course, these measurement problems are the same for annual and quarterly estimates. For the quarterly national accounts compiler, the simplest solution is usually to adopt the annual method and allow the benchmarking techniques to incorporate any adjustment factors.

c. Final consumption expenditure by nonprofit institutions serving households

(i) Value indicators

3.95. Much of the discussion on measurement of government consumption also applies to nonprofit institutions serving households (NPISHs). Like general government, their output and consumption of nonmarket services at current prices is measured at cost. However, quarterly accounting data are less available than for general government. However, data for some larger institutions may be published or available on request. Governments may be a good source of statistical indicators if they monitor, regulate, or provide transfers to charities, private schools, and similar institutions. Otherwise, since they are mainly involved in services, wages and salaries paid may be an acceptable substitute. Balance of payments data on transfers to nongovernment institutions may be an important indicator in countries where foreign aid is a major source of funding for NPISHs.

(ii) Volume indicators

3.96. Labor input measures may be suitable indicators. If data are unavailable and the NPISH sector has been shown to be economically stable in annual data, past trends may be an acceptable volume indicator. The method for the expenditure estimates should be consistent with that for the equivalent production estimates.

(iii) Price indicators

3.97. The methods are analogous to those used for general government consumption, where output at current prices is also defined as the sum of costs. A weighted average of input costs may be used for consumption by nonprofit institutions serving households so that the deflator corresponds with the composition of the current price value measured from input costs. Items could include wages, rents, repairs, stationery, and electricity.

d. Gross fixed capital formation

(i) General value indicators

3.98. Annual and quarterly surveys of capital expenditure by businesses are the conceptually preferred sources of capital formation data. However, capital formation surveys are particularly expensive and difficult to conduct on a quarterly basis for the following reasons. First, such surveys are very sensitive to coverage problems in the business register because new enterprises, which may not yet even be in operation, are particularly likely to have higher rates of capital formation than established businesses. Second, the potential population is almost every enterprise in the economy, and there will be a large number of enterprises having little or no capital formation in any particular quarter. As a consequence, the sample frame needs frequent updating and the samples have to be relatively large. Product splits are also more difficult to obtain than from the supply side. Another problem is that the *1993 SNA* includes work done on contract as capital formation of the final purchaser at the time it is done, while only progress payments will be known to the purchaser. If possible, it would be desirable to compare data from the alternative indicators for construction and equipment noted in this section.

3.99. Where a VAT system requires capital and intermediate purchases to be split, a useful indicator of capital formation can be obtained. However, VAT lacks a product split and excludes capital work on own account. VAT returns in some countries do not separate capital and intermediate purchases. (The lumpiness of capital purchases may assist in identifying enterprises undertaking capital formation during the period and provide the basis for generating a split at the level of individual enterprise.)

3.100. The largest components of gross fixed capital formation are construction and equipment. In addition, capital formation includes cultivated assets (such as livestock and orchards) and intangible assets (such as mineral exploration; computer software; and entertainment, literary, and artistic originals; but not research and development). Costs associated with the purchase of fixed and other assets are also included, such as transfer costs (including real estate agents' commissions, legal costs, and taxes on real estate purchases), architects' fees, and installation costs. In addition to purchases, own-account production of capital can be important in some cases, including construction, computer software, and legal work, and can be hard to include other than directly in surveys.

(ii) Specific value, volume, and price indicators

Construction

Value indicators

3.101. Gross fixed capital formation on construction assets includes the nonmaintenance parts of the output of the construction industry, own-account construction of other industries, and associated expenses such as architectural services and real estate agents' commissions.

3.102. Estimates of capital formation on construction raises a number of special measurement issues and problems, such as the following:

• Large numbers of small businesses. Construction is typically carried out by numerous enterprises that are often small and informal. Data collection and obtaining sufficient coverage from construction businesses can, therefore, be particularly difficult.

• Long projects. The length of construction projects gives rise to issues of holding gains and allocation of the output to quarters (as will be discussed in Chapter X).

• Subcontracting. Work is often arranged by a prime contractor with a number of specialized subcontractors which means that several enterprises may be involved in the same project, giving rise to the possibility of double counting or omissions.

• Speculative construction. Where the work is undertaken by a developer with no final buyer, the price is not known at the time after the work is done. In addition, land costs are included in the price, and holding gains and operating surplus are mixed together.

3.103. These problems apply to the corresponding estimates for construction industry by the production approach as well. They also apply to annual data, but quarterly data are more sensitive to the slowness or high cost of data collection and more subject to difficulty allocating the value of long-term projects to quarters.

3.104. Gross fixed capital formation of construction can be measured in various ways, corresponding to different stages in the building process, include the following:
• supply of building materials,
• issue of government permits for particular projects,
• data reported by construction businesses,
• data reported by construction-purchasing businesses, and
• data reported by households engaged in own-account construction.

3.105. In many countries, construction requires permits from local or regional governments, and the permit system can be used as a source for estimates of construction in the national accounts. The permit system may cover only larger projects or urban areas, while in other cases it may cover all except minor construction work. Permits usually show the type of construction, value, size, proposed starting and ending dates, and the name and address of the owner and/or builder. If the data are in volume terms only (e.g., numbers of dwellings, number of square meters) or the value data are of poor quality, then an average price per unit is also necessary to derive current price values for national accounts purposes. Data in this form need to be allocated to periods (see Example 10.2 in Chapter X), usually with information from builders, approval authorities, or engineers in order to obtain average construction times for each building type. It is also necessary to make adjustments, to the extent practical, for realization ratios (i.e., to account for projects that do not go ahead), biases in builders' estimation of their costs, the effect of holding gains included in prices, and the proportion of projects that are carried out without a permit. Government decisions and newspapers may be used to identify large-scale work that otherwise may be missed.

3.106. In some countries, the approval process is used to identify construction projects, and this process then provides the frame for a separate survey. Direct information about the project, such as the value of work done each quarter and changes from the original proposal in the cost or size or starting/ending dates, can be collected in such a survey. Using survey information prevents the need for making the kind of assumptions that have to be made when permit data are used directly. The survey method is conceptually much closer to statistical requirements, but it is more expensive and time-consuming to perform. The usefulness of the survey is also limited by the degree of sophistication of builders' accounting records about the value of work done in the period. In practice, the value of work done may have to be represented by progress payments.

3.107. Architectural and approval costs are a part of capital formation on construction and need to be added to the values that represent construction output. These items are related to construction activity, so construction indicators could be used as indirect indicators if more direct data are not available. However, as some of these expenses precede construction work, their timing is different. As a consequence, the timing pattern built into construction estimates may have to be adjusted.

3.108. Real estate transfer costs consist of items such as lawyers' fees, real estate agents' commissions, land title transfer taxes, loan application fees and other set-up costs for finance, and inspection fees. These costs relate both to new construction and to purchases of land and existing dwellings. If these land dealings are registered with a government agency, it may be possible to obtain a quarterly indicator from this source. Data on financing of land and building purchases is a poorer indicator; an even worse indicator is the value of new construction. For real estate transfer expenses, numbers of transfers may be used as a volume indicator. To take into account compositional changes, it would be better to classify by type of property (e.g., houses, apartments, shops, complexes) and other variables that may affect the cost (e.g., by state or province if charges are different). In some cases, it may be necessary to derive a current price measure from the volume measure, which would require information about transfer tax rates, real estate commission rates, lawyers' fees, and so on.

3.109. Speculative construction raises special issues regarding valuation and timing. With speculative construction, the work is undertaken by the builder before a purchaser is identified. Under the *1993 SNA*, speculative construction is regarded as inventories of work-in-progress. (In contrast, the *1968 SNA* treated it as capital formation at the time the work was done.) Whatever the conceptual considerations, the availability of data tends to determine the treatment of speculative construction. For example, data based on supply of building materials only suit the *1968 SNA* treatment because they would not allow speculative construction to be identified separately. Surveys of builders or building permits could be designed to

meet either treatment, although extra information would need to be collected to separate speculative construction. Surveys of construction purchasers are more suited to the *1993 SNA* treatment. Note that the net effect on GDP of the different treatments should be nil, since they cause offsetting differences in gross fixed capital formation and changes in inventories. If, contrary to the *1993 SNA* recommendations, it is decided to include unsold speculative construction work in gross fixed capital formation, there is a valuation issue in that the estimated price may differ from the realized price. If unsold speculative construction work is shown as changes in inventories, there needs to be a valuation adjustment to make the withdrawal from inventories consistent with the gross fixed capital formation. This topic is discussed further in Chapter X.

3.110. Construction in rural areas in developing countries is often carried out by households on their own account and made with their own labor, outside the scope of official permits. A household survey may provide information on the numbers of households involved and the cost of materials. These results would need to be adjusted to an estimated market price by taking the equivalent market prices (if such a market exists) or a shadow price based on costs (including labor). Usually, these indicators would only be available for a benchmark period and not on a quarterly basis. The building material approach captures some of this activity to the extent that a significant proportion of materials is produced by factories, although some materials may be made by the household. In the absence of other data, the size of the rural population could be used as a quarterly indicator for this type of construction.

3.111. It is desirable to obtain data on gross fixed capital formation of construction by type of asset, both for economic analysis and for improving deflation. Data by the industry and institutional sector of the purchaser are also useful for analysts. The estimates based on building materials give little or no breakdown, while other estimation methods can give more. In some cases, the general government sector data could be obtained from the government finance statistics, allowing the nongovernment component to be derived as a residual. Because residuals magnify the effects of errors, implausible values of the residuals may point to data problems.

3.112. Gross fixed capital formation of construction and construction industry output will often be estimated from the same data sources. The estimates, however, will differ because of different treatment of the following:

• repair work (part of output, but not fixed capital formation);
• secondary activity (secondary capital construction by establishments outside the construction industry is part of capital formation, while construction establishments may have secondary activity in nonconstruction goods and services);
• speculative construction work (output of the industry when the work is put in place; in the 1993 SNA, it is included in inventories when produced and in fixed capital formation when sold); and
• associated expenses, such as nonconstruction goods included in a structure; architectural, legal, and approval fees (which are not part of construction output, but are fixed capital formation); or the effect of any product taxes and subsidies.

Volume indicators

3.113. Building permit systems may provide volume indicators such as floor area. To the extent that the composition of the variable is stable, quality changes per unit will not distort the estimates, so calculation in more detail is beneficial.

3.114. The supply of building materials is often the most readily available construction volume indicator. While builders are often small and dispersed, building materials are often produced by a relatively small number of large factories and quarries. Data on exports and imports of building materials are also generally available and may be important for some kinds of building materials in some countries. Therefore, measures of the total supply of building materials or selected major building materials to the domestic market can be obtained as output plus imports less exports. Preferably, trade, tax, and transport markups would be taken into account, to the extent that they have changed or that differential markups affected the weights of different components. A lag factor may be included to take into account the time it takes for materials to get from the factory (local production) and customs frontier (imports) until they are incorporated in construction work.

3.115. The advantages of the building materials method are the ready availability of data and the data's inclusion of informal and unapproved work. (Use of materials is one of the few ways that informal construction leaves a statistical trace.) The limitation

of this indicator is that it assumes a stable relationship between building materials and output. The assumptions may not be stable because different kinds of construction work use different materials and have different materials-to-output ratios. Preferably, this method would only be used quarterly, so the benchmarking process would capture changes in these relationships as shown in the annual data. There may also be variations in the lags between production and use. As well, the building materials method does not provide details that may be of interest, for instance, by type of building, industry of purchase or use, or institutional sector.

Price indicators

3.116. Because each construction project differs, compiling a price of construction presents special difficulties. Three alternative methods that are used to derive construction price indices are
• model specifications,
• hedonic techniques, and
• input costs.

3.117. One method of obtaining output prices is to collect or derive hypothetical prices for construction output. House builders may have standard models of houses that are offered. Although options and individual circumstances mean that the model is not implemented in every case, it can still form the basis of the builder's pricing, and it would be relatively easy to obtain quotations from the builder for the standard model on a consistent basis. However, standard models are usually only found for dwellings, where a mass market exists, but not for other types of construction. Another approach to model specification is to divide construction into a number of particular tasks, for example, painting a certain area of wall, laying a certain height and type of brick, cost per hour of electrical work, and so on. A weighted total of each of these components could be used to represent overall prices for a particular type of construction. A possible shortcoming is that the most difficult jobs might be omitted, such as the prime contractor's organizational work and unique, large-scale engineering tasks. Construction is usually highly cyclical, with margins cut or increased in line with conditions. Because the prices are hypothetical, the statistician needs to be careful if list prices are being reduced by discounts or bargaining during a recession or if more is charged during a busy period to cover overtime costs.

3.118. In recent years, some countries have explored the use of hedonic techniques to measure prices of one-off goods. In addition to collecting the prices of a range of buildings, these countries also collect data on characteristics of the building that affect the price (such as floor area, height, fittings, materials, and location). A regression model is then developed to identify the effect of each characteristic on the price. This allows the prices of the different kinds of buildings to be converted to a standard basis and, hence, allows a price index to be derived. This method requires a great deal of work in data collection and analysis of data. A limitation is that characteristics may be too numerous or abstract to be quantified, so the model would only explain a limited part of the price variation. Also, the coefficients of the model may not be stable over time.

3.119. Input cost measures are based on the prices of construction materials and labor. These should include building materials (from a producer or wholesale price index[12]) and wages (preferably specifically for occupations employed in construction). An adjustment could also be made for changes in markups to account for builders' operating surplus and mixed income, if indicators were available, because these represent a major part of the price and could be quite variable. Data on intermediate consumption by product supplied to the construction industry would be required for a benchmark period. Use tables could present these data or they could be obtained directly from surveys of construction enterprises. Otherwise, it would be necessary to seek expert advice or a sample of bills of quantities for building projects. Data on employment in construction by type of employee (occupation groups) would also be useful for weighting the labor cost part of the index. Because of different input structures, it would be desirable to compile separate indices for different types of building and construction (i.e., houses, apartments, offices, shops, etc.)

3.120. Generally, it is desirable to avoid using input costs to represent output prices, because input costs ignore changes in productivity and profitability. However, the input cost method avoids the difficulties of obtaining an output price index for heterogeneous products. Many types of construction are one-off, and even where the same model is used in different places,

---

[12]Wholesale price indexes (WPIs) would generally be more suitable than producer price indexes (PPIs), because they include taxes, imports, and distribution costs. If a WPI is not available to deflate items that include margins, taxes, and imports, a PPI could be used as a substitute, preferably with adjustments for changes in import prices, tax rates, and other markups (if available).

differences in soil type, slope, or options mean that it is not possible to find exactly comparable observations. Finding actual buildings that are representative and consistently priced is close to impossible.

3.121. In practice, countries may often use a mix of different pricing measures for the different types of construction.

3.122. In situations where independent volume and value indicators are available, it is beneficial to derive an implicit price per unit to check that the result is plausible. Erratic results may mean that one of the indicators is unsuitable (e.g., the implicit deflator may fluctuate because of quality changes that were not taken into account in floor area data used as a volume indicator).

Equipment

Value indicators

3.123. The four sources for measuring equipment, reflecting the stages along the distribution process, are the following:
- survey data on supply of capital goods,
- survey data reported by the purchasing businesses,
- VAT data on purchases of capital goods (if identified separately from intermediate goods), and
- registration data from governments.

3.124. Derivation of the supply of capital goods is an application of the commodity flow method. The supply of capital goods is measured, most simply, as the value of domestically produced capital goods plus imported capital goods, less exported capital goods. Changes in tax rates and margins should be taken into account, if possible, because they are subject to change. Deductions should also be made for capital goods that were used for intermediate consumption (e.g., parts for repairs), final consumption (e.g., computers, cars, and furniture that are used for nonbusiness purposes), or inventories, and for net sales of capital goods (e.g., company cars sold secondhand to households).

3.125. Data from the supply side provide totals and splits by asset type, but not estimates by industry or institutional sector of use, which are of analytical interest. Like construction, government finance data could be used to obtain government capital formation of equipment, and then a private total could be calculated as a residual.

3.126. Transactions in secondhand goods present some additional issues. Some sources may only provide data on new products. Data on some second-hand components—such as government asset sales, goods sold or purchased internationally, or vehicles—may be available. Data in some cases may not need to be collected if the transactions are small, stable, or occur within a single component.

Volume indicators

3.127. Capital goods tend to be heterogeneous, so quantities are unavailable or meaningless. A possible exception is transport equipment, where government registration systems sometimes provide numbers. These systems usually cover motor vehicles, aircraft, and seacraft. From these systems, it is often possible to obtain indicators of capital formation in these assets. Ideally, the registration authorities would be able to supply information on numbers and values and distinguish among types of owner (corporations, government, nonprofit institutions serving households—all capital; household purchases are more complicated in that they can be capital, consumption, or a mix), and between new and secondhand acquisitions.

Price indicators

3.128. Data derived from a survey of equipment purchases are at purchasers' prices. The most appropriate price indicators are the capital goods components of a WPI, because wholesale prices would take into account trade, transport, and tax margins and would generally include both imported and locally produced goods. If data on wholesale prices are not available, components of the PPI and import price index could be weighted and used as a proxy. However, PPIs are designed to deflate output rather than capital formation and, thus, exclude the margins. It would be desirable to make adjustments if trade, transport, and tax margins were known to be unstable. The most likely instance is taxes, where information on tax rates to adjust producer prices for taxes would generally be available. Similarly, import price indices are typically measured at the point of arrival in the country rather than the point of final purchase and, thus, exclude domestic trade, transport, and tax margins.

3.129. If the equipment data had been derived from the supply side, the current values for domestically-produced goods would have been reported at basic or producers' prices. If so, the best method would be to develop volume indicators by deflating the supply values of domestically-produced equipment by the relevant PPI component. As the value and price measures would be consistent, it would be expected to be a superior volume indicator to one derived from value and price measures that were based at inconsistent pricing points.

3.130. Imports are a major component of capital formation in many countries. Import unit values would be expected to be poor indicators of prices. If no import price index is available for some or all types of equipment, a solution may be to take advantage of the producer price or export price indices of the main equipment-supplying countries. These should be obtained at a detailed level so that the components can be weighted to reflect the composition of imported equipment in the importing country. The data should also be adjusted for exchange rate movements and lagged to account for shipping times, if the lag is substantial. It would also be desirable to take into account changes in shipping costs if an indicator were available. It is possible in practice that the effect of exchange rate changes is lagged or smoothed by forward exchange cover and by squeezing or expansion of margins. Because of changes in exchange rates and international specialization in types of equipment, prices of imported and domestically produced equipment may move in quite different ways.

Other fixed capital formation and acquisitions less disposals of valuables

3.131. Computer software was included separately in fixed capital formation for the first time in the *1993 SNA*. As with other capital items, the estimates could be made on the supply side (manufacture plus software developers plus imports less exports) or the demand side. Supply data may be easier to collect because of the relatively smaller number of businesses involved; demand data are complicated by the fact that almost all businesses are potentially involved in using software. However, the data on the supply side have the limitation—as do the data for motor vehicles—that a substantial proportion of computer software is for household consumption. Another issue is that some software can be developed in-house. If important, data on own-account software expenditure should be collected in surveys. A further issue is that some software is sold in conjunction with hardware, possibly raising questions of double counting. Price indices are also problematic; possible alternatives are cost-based measures, hedonic techniques, or the relevant indices of software-exporting countries.

3.132. Indicators for other components of gross fixed capital formation—such as mineral exploration, forests, orchards, livestock, and intangible assets—are less commonly available. If significant, a survey could be considered. For example, in countries where mining or forestry is important, a specific survey on the topic would be justified. In some cases, administrative requirements for copyright registration or mining exploration permits may give rise to information that could be used as an indicator. Even in those cases, the timing of registration or permission could differ substantially from the time of economic activity.

3.133. In the *1993 SNA*, an additional category of capital formation is created for "valuables" such as paintings and jewelry. These were previously largely included in household consumption. They could be recorded from the point of production (e.g., factories) or import (customs data), from the point of sale (usually retailers), or from purchasers (household expenditure survey).

e. Changes in inventories

(i) Introduction

3.134. Inventories are defined as goods and some services that were produced or imported but have not yet been used for consumption, fixed capital formation, or export. This delay between supply and use brings about valuation issues. Inventories appear explicitly only in the expenditure estimates. They must, however, be taken into account in both the production estimates (both output and intermediate consumption) and income estimates (operating surplus and mixed income). The valuation issues also arise in the other approaches, except where output or input measures are expressed in quantity terms for production estimates.

3.135. Inventories consist of finished goods, work-in-progress, goods for resale, raw materials, and auxiliary materials.[13] These components of inventories differ according to their stage and role in the production process. Finished goods are part of output and are of the same form as their consumed equivalents. Work-in-progress is also part of output, but is harder to quantify than finished goods because the product is incomplete. Inventories of goods for resale, that is, goods held for the purpose of wholesaling and retailing are neither part of output nor future intermediate consumption of the holder. Net increases in inventories of goods for resale need to

---

[13]Called "stocks" in the *1968 SNA*. In the *1993 SNA*, the term "stocks" refers to balance sheet items in general and is used as a contrast to the term "flows."

be deducted from purchases of goods for resale to derive cost of goods sold and, hence, wholesale and retail margins, which are defined as the value of goods sold less the cost of goods sold. Raw materials are goods intended for intermediate consumption by the holder. Auxiliary materials are also to be used for intermediate consumption but are not physically part of the final goods—office stationery, for example. Because auxiliary materials are typically minor, they are usually included as part of intermediate consumption at the time of purchase. The separation of different components is important because they include different products, and, therefore, the price indices to be used in deflation will also differ. In practice, attention can be confined to those components of inventories that are important; for instance, quarterly surveys could be limited to miners, manufacturers, wholesalers, and retailers.

3.136. Although changes in inventories are a small component of GDP, they can swing substantially from strongly positive to strongly negative. Consequently, this small component can be a major factor in GDP movements. In the quarterly data, the average absolute quarterly contribution to growth can be large, often being one of the major quarterly growth factors. Over the long term, the contribution of changes in inventories to GDP growth tends to be small because some of the quarterly volatility will cancel itself out over the year. The importance of inventories follows from its nature as a swing variable in the economy. It represents the difference between total demand (the sum of the other components of GDP expenditure) and total supply. An increase in inventories would represent supply that was not used during the period, while a reduction would show the amount of demand that was met from previous supply. Without these data, the expenditure estimates would show demand, not production. Data on changes in inventories are also important for analysis because the gap between demand and supply can be an indication of future trends. For example, a decrease in inventories suggests that demand exceeds supply, and output or imports will need to increase just to keep pace with the existing level of demand.

3.137. Changes in inventories present particular difficulties in terms of valuation. Businesses use several different varieties of historic cost, none of which match national accounting valuation concepts. Measurement practice also varies, from complete physical stock-takes to samples and estimates. The valuation problems are sometimes ignored but are significant, as can be illustrated with some simple but conservative assumptions: if inventories are stable, the total holdings of inventories of inputs and outputs are equivalent to three months of output, and if value added is half of output, then 1 percent of price change in inventories will amount to a valuation effect of 2 percent of quarterly value added. Thus, even quite low rates of inflation can cause a significant overstatement of the level of value added, and this effect will be concentrated in the major inventory-holding industries. Similarly, a small increase in the rate of inflation will overstate the growth of GDP.

(ii) Value indicators

3.138. The *1993 SNA*[14] sets out the perpetual inventory method to produce estimates of changes in inventories. The method requires that data be reported transaction by transaction, with continuously updated replacement prices. While ensuring that valuation is consistent throughout the system, this method requires so much respondent and compilation time that it is not implemented in practice, and simplified methods have to be used. With advances in accounting software and sophisticated computing-based inventory monitoring, however, there is potential for improvements in the future through compiling perpetual inventory model data at the establishment level.

3.139. A number of issues arise concerning data on inventories. Some businesses may have computerized inventory controls; others have full physical stock-takes at less frequent intervals with sampling or indicator methods for more frequent measures; and some small enterprises may not measure inventories on a quarterly basis at all. The values of inventories may also be a particularly sensitive commercial issue. Valuation effects can generally be better calculated with higher frequency data. This is because higher frequency data reduce the possibility of uneven price and volume movements within the period. As a consequence, the annual sum of the quarterly valuation adjustments may be superior to annually calculated ones, unless there is some other compelling difference, such as differences in coverage or detail. Similarly, if monthly data are available, the calculation should generally be done on a monthly basis for use in quarterly estimates. These factors all need to be assessed in light of each country's conditions.

[14]See 1993 SNA, Chapter XII Annex.

3.140. Annex 3.1 shows how values of changes in inventories on a national accounts basis can be derived from business accounting data. The method involves conversion from historic cost prices to constant prices, then reflation to current prices. Because valuation changes can occur within the period and interact with changes in volume, better estimates can be obtained by making calculations for shorter periods. (Indeed, the perpetual inventory method involves the same calculations effectively made for every instant.) As a result, a quarterly estimate from the sum of monthly data will differ from and be better than one calculated from quarterly data. Similarly, the annual estimate would be better if made as a sum of the quarters than if made from annual data.

3.141. Some countries derive changes in inventories in GDP by expenditure as a residual. The residual method could be used quarterly even if the annual measures were obtained directly. This method is only possible if there is a complete measure of GDP from the production approach and estimates are available for all other expenditure categories. However, because inventories should also be included in estimates of output and intermediate consumption, the measurement problems still need to be dealt with, even though quantity data that sidestep these valuation issues can sometimes be used. Derived as a residual, changes in inventories would also include the net effect of errors and omissions. In that light, compilers should review it carefully for signs of any errors that could be dealt with directly. As well, users should be advised to use caution in interpreting the estimate of changes of inventories, which should be labeled as being "changes in inventories plus net errors and omissions" to emphasize the limitations.

3.142. One method that should not be used is to accept changes in inventories at book values as reported by enterprises without adjustment. Business accounting practices typically use historic costs, which result in the inclusion of holding gains in the value of changes in inventories.

(iii) Volume indicators

3.143. Inventory data may be available in quantity terms for some products held by some enterprises. Because inventories include almost every type of goods (as well as a few kinds of services) and firms typically use a range of products (especially their inputs), this solution cannot be implemented comprehensively. However, it may be available for some of the major components of inventories, such as principal agricultural commodities, oil, or some minerals. (These goods have the most volatile prices, and inventory holdings are often large.) With quantity data, valuation problems can be side-stepped by directly revaluing the change in the quantity over the period by the base year average prices (constant price measures) and average prices of the period (current price measures).[15]

(iv) Price indicators

3.144. Price indicators can be chosen according to the composition of the inventories, making use of CPIs, PPIs, trade prices, and average prices for specific commodities. The opening and closing levels of inventories (never the change in inventories) should always be deflated. If inventories are usually valued at historic cost, prices of several preceding periods may be relevant.

f. Exports and imports of goods and services

(i) Value indicators

3.145. Countries that compile QNA data typically have a well-developed system of trade and balance of payments statistics that produce quarterly data on trade in merchandise and services. Merchandise data are derived from customs records, surveys of trading enterprises, or both. Services data are typically derived from specific surveys, administrative systems, and international transaction reporting (exchange record) systems.

(ii) Volume indicators

3.146. Quantity data on merchandise are usually obtained in a customs system. For homogeneous products, they may be used to derive volume estimates.

3.147. Quarterly balance of payments data on services may have been derived using volume indicators, for example, international arrivals and departures for travel and air and ship movements for passenger, freight, port, and airport services. Although the focus of balance of payments is toward value data, the derivation of volume measures for national accounts purposes may be of special interest to balance of payments analysts because they provide a perspective on whether price or volume forces are

driving changes in values. Specific volume indicators may also be available. For example, for freight and passenger services it may be possible to obtain volume indicators, such as ton-kilometers or passenger-kilometers, from the carriers.

(iii) Price indicators

Merchandise

3.148. Customs and other trade data systems usually collect quantity information (e.g., metric tons, liters, numbers). These data are often processed to provide volume and unit value indices directly from the information already included on customs declarations. The unit values and volumes at the most detailed level of classification are combined to derive aggregate indices using weights from the value data.

3.149. Some countries have import and/or export price indices. These are collected from businesses in the same way as wholesale and producer price indices. Components of these indices can also be used to deflate the current price value data at the most detailed level to derive volume measures. If available, this will be the preferred method. The price indicators should be consistent with any adjustments for transfer pricing in the value data.

3.150. A price index is a better way of dealing with heterogeneous products than is a unit value index. The price index approach of identifying products with fixed specifications and transaction conditions for each product allows price effects to be isolated. However, a trade price index system has the disadvantages of high cost and respondent burden. Also, the actual transaction prices that make up trade may be affected by factors such as the mix of prices from contracts made at different times and the effects of foreign exchange hedging. These effects may not be easy to capture in a price index.

3.151. Unit values are derived by dividing the value of trade in a product by its quantity. Unit values have the advantage of being able to be derived from information collected by the customs system. However, the unit values, like the corresponding volume measures, often cover quite diverse products, even at the most detailed level of classification. For example, as discussed under capital formation, large-scale equipment, such as ships or heavy machinery, is often one-off in nature. Even for other products, changes in composition within the product group can be important, for example, a particular class of clothing can vary substantially in quality

---

[15]The result will be an estimate of the value of the physical change in inventories. At current prices, this is only an approximation of the *1993 SNA* concept, which also includes adjustments for all valuation changes that occur between the time of production and the time of final expenditure. The two concepts will be the same if price changes and transactions are spread evenly over the quarter.

of material, workmanship, and fashionableness. It is usually possible to identify the products affected by serious compositional changes by examining the variances in the average unit values of the product.

3.152. There are several ways of dealing with heterogeneous products in unit value indices. One possibility is to supplement the customs data with specific price surveys. Another possibility is to narrow the specifications by also taking into account the partner country. A further option is to use unit values and volumes only for those products with unit values not subject to high variance. In cases where unit values are too variable, the unit values of the most closely related homogeneous products could be used. The use of this price indicator assumes that prices for related products move in similar ways, which is often realistic—certainly more realistic than assuming that volumes of related products move in similar ways. This method works best for the "not elsewhere classified" products within a group, as there are usually readily identifiable related products with similar price behavior in the same group.

3.153. In some cases, both unit value and price indices may be unavailable or unsuitable. In these cases, a solution may be to use price indices from other countries. In the case of imports, the export price indices of the main supplying countries can be used. If export prices are not available for some supplying countries, a producer price index may be an acceptable substitute, although factory gate prices are less relevant than export prices. Preferably, the indices would be obtained at a fairly detailed level so that different imported products could be deflated separately to reflect the actual composition of trade, rather than the fixed composition used in the indices of the supplying country or countries. It would also be desirable to obtain price index data from several of the main supplying countries, to take into account different composition and price pressures. The price indices should be adjusted for exchange rate movements between the currencies of the supplying countries and the importing country. If the source of the trade is remote, it may be desirable to allow a lag to account for shipping times (e.g., if shipping takes two months, the January export price represents the March import price).

3.154. Similarly, for exports, the import price indices of the customer countries could be used. Alternatively, for major agricultural commodities, the world prices shown

in the IMF's *International Financial Statistics* and other publications could be used.

3.155. Imports are deducted from total expenditure to derive GDP. In other words, the imported component of each type of final expenditure and intermediate consumption is excluded from total expenditure to derive the expenditure on domestic output. It is therefore highly desirable that the deflation of imports and the imported components in the corresponding other expenditure categories be as consistent as possible, so as not to create inconsistencies that lead to errors in total GDP. For example, different deflation methods for imported capital equipment in capital formation and imports could generate differences in data that would affect GDP.

Services

3.156. Overall price indices for international trade in services are not usually available. However, price or volume indicators are often available for many components of traded services. If the current price data have been derived by balance of payments compilers, it is essential to find out the methods they have used, because the data may sometimes have been compiled from volume and price indicators. In other cases, other price indices may be relevant. Hotels and transport components of the consumer price index may be relevant to travel service exports, while hotels and transport in the main destination countries may be relevant to travel service imports (adjusted for exchange rate movements). Price indices and implicit price deflators from particular industries in GDP by the production approach (exports) or from the supplying country (imports) may be useful. In the case of FISIM, the deflated value of loans and deposits may be used, as discussed under the production approach.

D. GDP by Income Category

I. General Issues

3.157. The income approach is built up from components of compensation of employees, operating surplus, mixed income, and taxes less subsidies on products, production, and imports. It is the least commonly used of the three approaches. Income estimates are particularly suitable for data by institutional sector, while industry data are more difficult to obtain. Income data provide a useful perspective on the distribution of income from GDP, for example, looking at compensation of employees and operating surplus as a proportion of value added for the nonfinancial corporations sector. The income approach requires that businesses have quarterly data on, at least, profits, depreciation, and net interest paid, so the availability of data on business incomes determines whether independent quarterly income estimates are developed. The data could be particularly important in analyzing issues such as rates of return and profitability. The income approach is potentially useful as an alternative measure of GDP if the other approaches have serious data problems; for example, if IO ratios in production data are known to be changing rapidly with the business cycle.

3.158. The drawbacks of the income approach should also be noted. It does not support constant price and volume estimation because not all of the income components of GDP have a price dimension. In addition, the ability to produce data by industry of establishment on a quarterly basis is limited because some income components are only obtainable at the enterprise level.

3.159. Benchmark data for the income approach can be compiled in two ways. The income estimates can be compiled in the same way as value added in the production approach—that is, from goods and services produced less goods and services used—with the additional step of using expense data to split value added among compensation of employees, net taxes on production, and the residual, namely, operating surplus/mixed income. As for the production approach, getting this information is not usually feasible in a quarterly context. Alternatively, income estimates can be built up from the primary income components. This method is viable in some countries on a quarterly basis using profits, interest, and depreciation as indicators.

3.160. In the absence of an independent estimate of GDP from the income side, an income split can usually be derived with one category as a residual. Such data are as analytically useful as the full approach. Operating surplus/mixed income is always the residual in countries that use this method, because it is the most difficult component to measure.

2. Value Indicators

a. Compensation of employees

3.161. Data on compensation of employees are readily available in many countries. The major indicators are

- administrative byproducts from the collection of social security or payroll taxes,
- business surveys of employment and wages and salaries, and
- business or household surveys of numbers of employees in conjunction with business surveys of average wages.

Where government regulates employment, clear definitions of employment and data are usually readily available. The data may refer to total compensation of employees paid or received, but an industry or institutional sector split may also be available.

3.162. Often only wages and salaries are available quarterly. Pension fund contributions and other social contributions paid by employers are also included in the definition of compensation of employees. Data may be available for programs run or highly regulated by government, but data are less likely to be available for private programs, where they would need to be collected by survey or derived using wages and salaries as an indicator. There is also a wide variety of supplements and fringe benefits that vary from country to country, such as annual bonuses, thirteenth month of salary, profit sharing, stock plans, concessional loans, discounts on purchases, commissions, redundancy payments, and remuneration in kind. Ideally, quarterly source data would also cover these items. If some items are not available, and especially if these items are small and/or stable, use of the available items to indicate the unavailable ones will be quite acceptable (i.e., an implicit ratio adjustment through benchmarking the quarterly data to annual data that include these items). However, the larger or more volatile they are, the stronger the case for collecting additional data to record them separately.

3.163. In quarterly estimates, there are potentially important questions of allocation over time that are more significant than in annual data. The usual national accounting concept requires that compensation of employees be recorded on an accruals basis. For payments that are paid once a year but earned during the year, it would be desirable that they be allocated over the time they accrued, not just the quarter in which they are paid.

b. Operating surplus/mixed income

3.164. An indicator that approximates gross operating surplus or mixed income can be derived by adding operating profits, net interest paid, and depreciation. These kinds of business accounting data can potentially be collected directly from businesses by surveys.

3.165. Profits data should be collected with definitions as close as practical to national accounts concepts. "Operating profit" is closer to the national accounts concept than some bottom-line profit measures, to the extent that it excludes one-off items such as capital gains, foreign exchange gains and losses, and insurance claims. It also excludes income from the operation of other enterprises, that is, profits received as dividends from subsidiaries and other share holdings. The *1993 SNA* definitions of production and, therefore, operating surplus also exclude the effect of provisions for bad debts, so these should be added back. In a quarterly context, some adjustments may need to be made implicitly through benchmarking an incomplete quarterly indicator to the more comprehensive annual data. Business accounting measures of profits include the effect of price changes from inventories, which should be excluded in national accounts measures. (The adjustment would be the same as the corresponding adjustments made to the production and expenditure estimates, that is, the inventory valuation adjustment discussed in Annex 3.1.)

3.166. Net interest paid and depreciation also need to be added back to profits to get closer to gross operating surplus and mixed income. It would, therefore, be worth collecting data on these items at the same time as profits, because the relationship of operating surplus to profits is likely to be much less stable than the relationship of operating surplus to profits plus net interest and depreciation. Expense data from detailed annual or benchmark surveys would allow the identification of other expenses that are not intermediate consumption, compensation of employees, or taxes on production. Similarly, detailed income data would allow the exclusion of any items that were not from production. If these factors are small and stable, an implicit ratio adjustment through the benchmarking process may be suitable. Otherwise, consideration may need to be given to collecting the data quarterly.

3.167. Large enterprises often calculate their incomes on a quarterly or even monthly basis, and publicly listed companies are often required to release quarterly or half-yearly information. Similarly, data may be available for government enterprises and market producers within general government. Privately held corporations and unin-

corporated enterprises are typically less inclined to have sophisticated monthly or quarterly accounting systems. This is changing, however, with computerization of business accounts. Standard accounting software packages can make quarterly and even monthly data available to even the smallest of businesses. Once the basic transactions are recorded, these packages can generate data for any required period or level of detail at little extra cost. Many small enterprises do not have quarterly accounts, particularly in developing countries. In these cases, their operating surplus cannot be collected, but it may be derived by estimating their output, intermediate consumption, and compensation of employees. The same indicators used for estimating value added under the production approach could be used and estimates of their wages and net taxes on production deducted. In the case of ownership of dwellings, the sources for estimating output and value added can be used with the addition of data on property taxes paid and compensation of employees. To the extent that the same indicators are used in the income and production approaches, they become less independent and more integrated.

c. Taxes and subsidies on products, production, and imports

3.168. Data on total taxes on imports, value added taxes, other taxes and subsidies on products, and other taxes and subsidies on production are usually available from a government finance statistics (GFS) system. Although GFS systems are generally among the most accurate and timely data sources, the data can suffer from problems of time of recording and may not provide any industry/institutional sector split.[16] Typically, GFS data have been compiled on a cash basis, not on an accrual basis as required in the national accounts. However, an accrual basis is becoming more common and will be recommended in the forthcoming *Manual on Government Finance Statistics.* Knowledge of the tax payment regulations may provide a basis for adjusting cash-based data to an approximately accrual basis. In some cases, state, provincial, or local government data may not be available for the most recent quarters. If this is the case, it would be necessary to make estimates. For large components, the estimate should be based on actual data on trends in the tax base and changes in tax rates, while simpler methods could be used on small items.

---

[16]An industry and/or sector split may sometimes be possible from the underlying administrative data.

3. Volume and Price Indicators

3.169. The income approach is oriented to current price data only because prices of some income components are not observable. It is possible to measure labor inputs in volume terms and make estimates of net taxes on products at base year rates, but there is no meaningful price or volume dimension to operating surplus/mixed income and other taxes on production.

3.170. A few countries derive GDP by the income approach at constant prices by deflating by the implicit price deflator for GDP from the production or expenditure-based estimates. Only if the income-based GDP figure differs from the other approach will this give a different GDP, and it will differ from the other approach by the same percentage as at current prices. This treatment is valid only for total GDP and is not valid for splits by type of income. Deflating income components by a generalized price index, such as the CPI, is a measure of purchasing power (called "real" income in the *1993 SNA*) that should not be confused with volume measures of product.

Annex 3.1. Estimation of Changes in Inventories

3.A1.1. This annex discusses the calculation of changes in inventories from business accounting data and gives a simple example. In most countries, accounting practice is to value withdrawals from inventories at historic cost, that is, the prices at the time of acquisition or some notional approximation, rather than the prices at the time of withdrawal as required by the *1993 SNA* and economic concepts. In a few countries, most of which have had high inflation, accounting principles use a current replacement price concept approximating the one used by the *1993 SNA*. If prices are changing, the change in the book value of inventories between the beginning and end of the period will be affected by valuation changes. Changes due to price movements do not contribute to GDP and should be excluded from production, income, and expenditure data. The valuation effects are usually removed by an inventory valuation adjustment (IVA). The IVA should be deducted/added to the book value of changes in inventories, operating surplus, and value added.[17]

3.A1.2. The inventory valuation practices of businesses need to be understood before making calculations. In historic cost measures, inventories as of the end of each quarter are valued at a mix of prices paid over several earlier periods. If data are at historic cost, the periods that prices relate to need to be known in order to adjust from those prices to current prices. Historic cost has several variations, of which the most common are FIFO (first in, first out), LIFO (last in, first out), WAC (weighted average cost), and "specific cost." Note that, other than specific cost, the valuation methods do not necessarily reflect actual ages of products in the inventory—they are simply valuation conventions.

3.A1.3. FIFO means that withdrawals are valued at the earliest prices, and hence the stock of inventories is valued at relatively recent prices. In contrast, under LIFO, the withdrawals are at recent prices, but the stock of inventories is valued at old prices. Thus,

FIFO usually results in lower values of withdrawals and higher values of inventories, and it usually requires larger valuation adjustments to withdrawals than does LIFO. However, under FIFO, the valuation of stocks of inventories is more stable and recent, so inventory valuation calculations are more straightforward. The specific cost valuation is the least abstract and is now feasible as a result of computer-based inventory recording. Rather than using a hypothetical valuation rule, with specific cost valuation, each item is valued individually at its actual price at the time of its purchase or production. In many businesses, this will approximate FIFO to the extent that inventory management practice is to turn goods over quickly.

3.A1.4. Sometimes, the historic cost principle is modified to allow for declines in value (COMWIL valuation, i.e., "cost or market, whichever is less"). If price declines are major, this may need to be taken into account.

3.A1.5. The *data required* to derive value of physical change in inventories are the following:
- Values of opening (beginning of period) and closing (end of period) stocks of inventories. Preferably, these would be classified by product groups and/or industries and/or stages of processing (raw materials/work-in-progress and finished goods/goods for resale). If available, product data would be preferable to industry data because the price behavior would be more homogeneous.
- Price indices for relevant products.
- Information on the product composition of inventories.
- Information on the valuation methods used by enterprises.
- Information on the age structure of inventories.

3.A.1.6. The steps involved in the calculation are the following:
- Create an inventory-specific book value deflator. The deflator should reflect both the product composition and the valuations used for the items included in the book values.

---

[17]Note that "holding gains" in the 1993 SNA sense arise from changes in prices during the period. If the source data are at historic cost, the inventory valuation adjustment (IVA) will cover holding gains from changes in prices between the time of initial valuation and the current period.

- Deflate the opening and closing book values to obtain constant price values.
- Obtain changes in inventories at constant prices as the difference.
- Create reflators to convert from constant price to current price values.
- Reflate constant price values of levels and changes in inventories to obtain current price values.

3.A1.7. The price indices would also need to reflect the products included in inventories. These would not necessarily be in the same proportions as in sales, production, or intermediate consumption. Data on inventories should be collected in detail, if possible. For a quarterly collection, this may not be viable, so more aggregated data may have to be collected.

3.A1.8. The appropriate price index for raw materials would be input prices; for work-in-progress and finished goods, it would be output prices. Goods for resale are the typical holdings of retailers and wholesalers, but manufacturers and others may also act as wholesalers. The appropriate price index would reflect these goods and could be different from the equivalent finished goods indices because goods for resale could include imports and different types of goods. More detailed information on the product composition of inventories could be obtained in annual or less frequent business surveys or in a survey or interview program for a subsample of firms. In a quarterly system, a range of producer, wholesale, import, and consumer prices may be combined in fixed proportions. It would be desirable to assess the stability of the composition of inventories to see whether the fixed proportions need to be changed.

3.A1.9. Note that two price indices usually need to be derived for each period and component: first, a price index to deflate historic cost data to constant prices, and second, a price index to reflate constant price data to current prices. The two indices are different because the historic cost prices of goods in inventories differ from current replacement prices. For the first price index—the historic cost deflator—a mix of historic prices is obtained. For instance, if the producer price index relates to average prices of the month and if investigations have shown that the inventory is valued by FIFO principles at prices of the previous three months—each month with an equal quantity and none from earlier months—the deflator for the book value on December 31 would be an equally weighted average of the October, November, and December price indices. (This treatment assumes that the prices and transactions were spread evenly over the period.) The most sophisticated inventory valuation adjustment calculations have proportions for weighting previous months' prices that take into account fluctuations in the level of inventories (e.g., when inventory levels fall, the proportions of newer inventories rise).

3.A1.10. The second price index is for converting from base period prices to current replacement prices. For example, for flow data for the fourth quarter, the index would be an average of October, November, and December prices. The required current price measure should reflect the average prices of the whole quarter. Note that prices used for the end of the period would not be comparable to prices used for other transactions during the quarter.

3.A1.11. Even when balance sheets are not calculated, it is necessary to obtain both the opening and closing values in order to make valuation adjustments to inventory data in value terms. Direct data on the changes in inventories are almost useless because valuation effects occur on the whole value and so cannot be calculated without data on the inventory levels.

3.A1.12. The quality of all these calculations would usually be improved by working at a more detailed level of product or industry dissection. This is because price movements are more likely to be homogeneous at a more detailed level. To the extent that price movements are similar across different types of goods, the results will not be affected so much by aggregation or choice of index. Primary commodity prices that are particularly volatile and differ from product to product are a higher priority for disaggregation.

Example 3.A.1. Calculation of Changes in Inventories

Information

The book values of inventories of coal for use as a raw material are as follows:

December 31, 2000	1,000.0
March 31, 2001	1,500.0

Both are valued at historic cost on a first-in, first-out valuation basis.

The inventory holdings at both points represent three months of purchases. The coal was acquired evenly over the previous three months.

Price indices and constant price data use a reference base of 2000.

The price index for coal is as follows:

	2000	2001
January	94.5	106.5
February	95.5	107.5
March	96.5	108.5
April	97.5	109.5
May	98.5	110.5
June	99.5	111.5
July	100.5	112.5
August	101.5	113.5
September	102.5	114.5
October	103.5	115.5
November	104.5	116.5
December	105.5	117.5
Average	100.0	112.0

The price indices are based on average prices for the month.

Calculations

(1) Derive an inventory-specific price index to deflate the book value of inventories.

	Weight	Dec. 31, 2000	Mar. 31, 2001
2-3 months	0.3333333	103.5	106.5
1-2 months	0.3333333	104.5	107.5
< 1 month	0.3333333	105.5	108.5
Total index	1.0000	104.5	107.5

The resulting index reflects the book valuation of the inventories, based on equal proportions of coal from each of the three previous months.

A more complex example would involve several price indices and differing proportions being assigned to each month (typically showing a tapering off for earlier months). If the weights for each month are based on quantities or volumes, the indices can be combined in this way; but if the weights are based on values, the total value should be split into component months of purchase according to the proportions and each month deflated by its price index.

(2) Deflate the opening and closing book values of inventories to obtain constant price values.

	Dec. 31, 2000	Mar. 31, 2001
Book value of inventories	1,000.0	1,500.0
Deflators	104.5	107.5
Value of inventories at average 2000 prices	956.9	1,395.3
(Derived by dividing the book value by the book value deflator.)		

(3) Derive the change in inventories at constant prices.

The change in inventories from January through March 2001 at average prices of the year 2000 is 438.4 (=1,395.3 − 956.9)

(continued on next page)

Example 3.A.1. *(continued)*

(4) Derive price indices to reflate from constant price to current price values.

Index for flows, q1 2001	107.5	(average January 2001 through March 2001)
Index for stocks, Dec. 31, 2000	106.0	(average December 2000 through January 2001)
Index for stocks, Mar. 31, 2001	109.0	(average March 2001 through April 2001)

As the original price index data relate to the average for the month, an end-of-month value (required for balance sheet items) can be approximated, in the absence of better information, as the (geometric) mean of the two surrounding months.

(5) Reflate constant price values to obtain current price values.

Estimated change in inventories at average prices of January through March 2001 $\quad 471.3 \ = \quad 438.4 / 1.075$

Inventory valuation adjustment $\quad 28.7 \ = \quad 500.0 - 471.3$
(book value of inventory changes less estimated change in inventories at average prices of January through March 2001 where book value of inventory changes are equal to $500.0 = 1500.0 - 1000.0$)

Stock data at current prices

Inventory value at current prices on December 31, 2000	$1014.4 \ =$	$956.9 \cdot 1.060$
Inventory value at current prices on March 31, 2001	$1,520.9 \ =$	$1,395.3 \cdot 1.090$
Total change in inventory current price values January through March 2001	$506.6 \ =$	$1,520.9 - 1,014.4$
"Holding gains" in the 1993 SNA sense	$35.3 \ =$	$506.6 - 471.3$

IV Sources For Other Components of the *1993 SNA*

A. General Issues

4.1. The *1993 SNA* presents a comprehensive set of related accounts that are of considerable analytical interest and were designed with a wide range of economic analyses in mind. The accounts can also help compilers identify inconsistencies and errors in the data. Just as compilers are urged to extend their annual data to a wider range of accounts, a quarterly national accounts (QNA) system should seek to cover more than GDP and its components.

4.2. For the convenience of countries at the first stage of development of QNA, the previous chapter presented sources organized around the three approaches to GDP measurement. The splits of GDP by expenditure and income components discussed in Chapter III, however, also provide the foundation for the wider sequence of accounts. The expenditure approach to GDP provides components of the goods and services, income, and capital accounts. The income approach to GDP provides data used in the income accounts.

4.3. The general issues associated with the identification and evaluation of sources discussed in the introduction to Chapter III also apply to the other accounts. As with data used in estimating GDP components, quarterly indicators for other national account variables often have shortcomings and need to be benchmarked.

4.4. QNA potentially can include the whole sequence of accounts, but coverage invariably is more limited. There are no recommendations on which accounts should be given priority to be produced quarterly; rather, the choice will depend on user priorities, the availability of indicators, and the stage of development of QNA in the country. The choice will also be influenced by the range of accounts published annually. Data for items beyond GDP and its components may not be included in the initial stage of QNA development and may have lower priority and accuracy than the quarterly GDP measures, but they should not be ignored, especially in the plans for future improvements. Several countries produce some of the accounts in the *1993 SNA* sequence quarterly. Although the coverage differs, the most common are the transaction accounts for the total economy, general government, and financial corporations.

4.5. The sequence of accounts can be presented in gross or net terms, that is, with or without deducting consumption of fixed capital. For simplicity, the following discussion will refer to gross measures, but quarterly consumption of fixed capital can be obtained. Annual estimates of capital consumption that follow *1993 SNA* concepts are usually derived by the perpetual inventory method (PIM); in the same way, quarterly estimates could be derived by enhancing the PIM calculations with a quarterly dimension. Alternatively, capital consumption is typically a relatively stable item because the stock of capital is large in relation to additions and retirements, so quarterly distribution and extrapolation of annual data would usually give acceptable estimates.[1]

B. Main Aggregates for the Total Economy

4.6. The main aggregates for the total economy include important balancing items such as national and disposable income, saving, and net lending/net borrowing. They can usually be compiled at an early stage in the development of QNA because the data requirements are quarterly splits of current price GDP by type of expenditure and quarterly balance of payments. Splits of GDP by expenditure can be derived either directly or, if necessary, by treating one component as a residual. In the usual pattern of statistical evolution,

---

[1]See Chapter VII for methods of distribution without use of indicators that avoid step problems.

Box 4.1. Main Aggregates for the Total Economy

Goods and Services Account in the *1993 SNA*   (consolidated)

GDP	**1,854**	
= Government consumption expenditures	368	
+ Households consumption expenditures	1,015	
+ NPISHs* consumption expenditures	16	
+ Acquisitions less disposals of nonfinancial assets	414	
+ Exports	540	
− Imports	499	

Current and Capital Accounts in the 1993 SNA   (consolidated)

GDP		**1,854**	Source
+ Net primary income received from abroad		29	BOP**
= ***National income, gross***		**1,883**	
+ Net current transfers received from abroad		−28	BOP
= ***Disposable income, gross***		**1,855**	
− Final consumption expenditures		1,399	
Government	368		
Households	1,015		
NPISHs	16		
= ***Saving, gross***		**455**	
+ Net capital transfers received from abroad		−3	BOP
− Gross capital formation (fixed, inventories, valuables)		414	
= ***Net lending (+)/Net borrowing (−)***		**38**	BOP

Financial Account in *1993 SNA*

Net acquisition of financial assets less net acquisition of liabilities	38	BOP
Errors and omissions	0	BOP
= ***Net lending (+)/Net borrowing (−)***	**38**	BOP

*NPISHs = nonprofit institutions serving households

**BOP = balance of payments

More detail of the financial account, including gross flows by type, may be available from the BOP.

Numbers are from the example in the *1993 SNA*. Figures in italics are derived.

quarterly balance of payments data are already available in a country setting up a new QNA system. National accounting systems usually work "down" the *1993 SNA* sequence of accounts—starting with GDP and subsequently deriving balancing items for income and capital accounts. It is also possible in a country where financial data are better than production data to start with the balance on the financial accounts and subsequently derive saving, income, and GDP by working "up" the sequence of accounts. An example of consolidated and simplified accounts is shown in Box 4.1.[2]

C. Accounts for the Total Economy

4.7. A further step in the development of a QNA would be the development of the unconsolidated accounts for the economy as they appear in Annex V

---

[2]The presentation in Box 4.1 is derived from the *1993 SNA* sequence of accounts by consolidation, that is, removing flows between residents that appear on both sides of the same account.

to the *1993 SNA*. The data required for this presentation differ from the presentation of main aggregates because income and transfer flows among residents are also shown. This presentation makes the links to the *1993 SNA* formats and institutional sector accounts more obvious and facilitates observation of some relationships. The unconsolidated accounts require more data than the consolidated presentation, however, and thus tend to occur at a later stage in the development of QNA. Because many of the data sources for transactions among residents have an institutional sector perspective, compilation of unconsolidated accounts for the total economy also contributes to some institutional sector data.

1. Production Account

4.8. The production account in gross terms shows output at basic prices plus net taxes on products as resources, and intermediate consumption as a use. GDP is the balancing item. The estimation of GDP at current prices by the production approach provides these items by industry. In addition to the presentation of the whole production account and a fuller presentation of the production process, the explicit calculation of output and intermediate consumption is recommended as good compilation practice for reconciling data with other sources and manifesting the implications of assumptions.

2. Income Accounts

4.9. The four income accounts shown in the *1993 SNA* are each discussed separately in this subsection. In addition to the specific issues for each account, there are some timing issues that are particularly serious in QNA and that apply to more than one of the income accounts.

4.10. Timing issues become particularly significant for some quarterly income account items. Incomes may be paid in lumps, rather than evenly through the year. Examples of paying in lumps include dividends, interest, taxes, and employee bonuses. The basic principle on the timing of recording in the *1993 SNA* is the use of the time of accrual. In the case of distributive transactions, the time of accrual is when the claim arose rather than when it was paid. This issue of timing of recording also plays a role in the annual national accounts (ANA), to the extent that some payments may partly relate to another year, but the effect is more pronounced in the QNA.

4.11. In order to deal with timing issues, it is useful to identify two categories of payments based on their relationship to previous periods:
(a) Payments that have a purely ad hoc character should be recorded in the period in which they are actually made. Dividends, for example, are usually determined only after the books are closed on a fiscal year and may not even relate to the company's profits over that year.
(b) Payments that have a fixed relation to a particular period (e.g., accrued in a previous period or accrued over a number of accounting periods) should be allocated to the periods in which they accrued. Examples are taxes on incomes and products that may be collected in a subsequent period and vacation bonuses that build up over the period of a year and on which employees have a claim if they leave the employment before payment is due. To obtain accrual-based data, the options may include surveys if businesses use accrual principles, allocating data on payments back to the relevant periods, or estimating the accrual of income from data on the underlying flow (e.g., income

taxes from wages and profits, possibly subject to a lag). Once these issues are considered on a quarterly basis, it may also be realized that the annual data need to be adjusted to meet accrual principles.

4.12. The application of accrual principles to quarterly data in such cases may present such serious practical and conceptual problems that it becomes an obstacle to completion of the data. In these cases, it may be better to publish data on a cash basis while clearly stating the problems than to publish nothing or publish something that has been subject to adjustments without a firm foundation.

a. Generation of income account

4.13. The generation of income account shows the derivation of operating surplus/mixed income as GDP less the sum of compensation of employees and taxes less subsidies on production and on imports. This account shows the identity that underlies the calculation of GDP by the income approach. Accordingly, the required data have already been compiled if the income approach has been used or an income split has been compiled with operating surplus/mixed income as a residual.

b. Allocation of primary income account

4.14. The allocation of primary income account shows the derivation of national income. Primary incomes include compensation of employees and property income (interest, dividends, etc.). The distributive income transactions paid between residents cancel out for the whole economy. As a result, gross national income (GNI) can be derived simply as GDP plus primary income receivable from the rest of the world less primary income payable to the rest of the world. The external primary income items can be obtained from the balance of payments and are usually derived from surveys or banking records.

4.15. The allocation of primary income account in unconsolidated form, as recommended in the *1993 SNA,* requires estimates of property income paid by residents to other residents. The interest and insurance components may be available as byproducts of the system of financial regulation or financial sector surveys. Alternatively, the flows may have to be estimated from the levels of the assets and liabilities and raised by a rate of return. Dividends could be estimated from a survey of businesses, from published statements of companies listed on the stock exchange, or from (lagged) estimates of operating surplus. Dividend behavior depends on national circumstances such as company law, business practices, and tax law. The predictability of this behavior can be assessed from past annual patterns. Seasonal patterns within the year may be unknown without extra information but present fewer serious problems for analysis (see Chapter VIII).

c. Secondary distribution of income account

4.16. The secondary distribution of income account shows the derivation of disposable income from national income by taking into account redistribution of income through taxes, social security contributions and benefits, and other transfers. Transfers paid by governments are usually available from government finance statistics. Other items include non-life insurance premiums and claims, which may be available from regulators or may be estimated based on distributed annual values if they are accrued evenly throughout the year. Note that these transactions within the country cancel out in total and so can be ignored in a consolidated presentation. International aid, social contributions and benefits to governments of other countries, and other current transfers to and from the rest of the world can be obtained from the balance of payments.

d. Use of disposable income account

4.17. The use of disposable income account shows disposable income as a resource. It shows household, nonprofit institutions serving households (NPISHs), and government consumption as uses, and saving as the balancing item. Disposable income is obtained from the secondary distribution of income account, while consumption is derived as part of the expenditure approach to measuring GDP.

3. Capital Account

4.18. The capital account shows how saving and capital transfers are available to fund capital formation and capital consumption with net lending or borrowing as the balancing item. Saving is obtained from the use of disposable income account, while capital formation is obtained as was shown under the expenditure approach to GDP. Capital transfers payable or receivable by government, if needed for an unconsolidated presentation, can be obtained from a system of government finance statistics. Capital transfers between residents and nonresidents can be obtained from the balance of payments. Following the harmonization of statistical concepts between the *1993 SNA* and the fifth edition of the *Balance of Payments Manual,* net lending/borrowing is equivalent to the sum of the current and capital account balances in the balance of payments. The elaboration of saving and lending is important in understanding the forces behind current account imbalances.

4. Financial Accounts

4.19. The financial accounts show changes caused by transactions in financial assets and liabilities classified by type of instrument. Data on stocks of financial assets or liabilities by counterpart sectors are often readily available from the financial corporations as a byproduct of regulation or monitoring of the financial sector. Data on transactions, however, are less readily available, so there may be problems in splitting changes in stocks into transactions and other changes in volumes and values. Financial corporations tend to be relatively large and have sophisticated records, however, making collection of data on transactions and other flows practical and feasible. In contrast, the counterparts to the financial corporations in these transactions are widespread and often small, making data collection less feasible.

4.20. Other sources may be available to check or complement data from the financial corporations. Data on government financial transactions can often be obtained directly. The financial account of the balance of payments records transactions with nonresidents. It is important that consistent classifications and valuations be used in all these sources. If all are consistently defined, the government and external transactions with the financial sector can be reconciled. Also, the transactions not involving the financial sector can be obtained to complete the totals. The data will also support the simultaneous development of the accounts by institutional sector.

4.21. If transactions data are not available, the differences between opening and closing balance sheets may have to be used as a proxy. In addition to changes caused by transactions, however, the difference between opening and closing values includes revaluation and other changes in volumes of assets.

4.22. Information on financing through shares and other equities can be more difficult to obtain. This financing occurs outside the financial sector, and thus data are frequently less complete. For listed companies, data may be available from stock-exchange registers. In other cases, company registration requirements include issue of equity. In still other cases, surveys would be necessary.

4.23. The balancing item on the financial account is net lending or borrowing. Net lending or borrowing is conceptually the same as in the capital account. In practice, if the measure is derived independently, it could differ significantly because of net errors and omissions. In a country with well-developed financial statistics, the net errors and omissions may help point to problems in other accounts. Alternatively, net lending or borrowing derived from the financial account can be used to obtain a missing item in the capital account as a residual (or vice versa).

4.24. In consolidated form, the financial account of the *1993 SNA* presents the same information as the financial account of the balance of payments. The total economy and balance of payments are the same because all the internal transactions net out.

5. Balance Sheets

4.25. The balance sheets show the opening and closing values of assets and liabilities. The financial assets and liabilities part of the balance sheets use similar sources as, and should be compatible with, the transactions data shown in the financial accounts. The international investment position is the balance of payments equivalent of the national accounts balance sheets for the financial assets and liabilities, and the net values for each type of instrument are the same.

4.26. Estimates for nonfinancial assets are derived by methods similar to those used annually. For inventories, the same source as for changes in inventories can provide either inventory levels or an estimate of the change in the levels since the previous estimate of the level. For land, the basic volume is fixed or changes only slowly. For fixed capital, these estimates tend to be based on calculations with the perpetual inventory method. The same issues arise as for estimates of consumption of fixed capital. The calculations could be made quarterly, or, alternatively, they could be made as interpolations from the annual values. The stability of capital is typically strongest in volume terms, while asset prices can be volatile. As a result, current price measures should preferably be derived from the volume measures for each component if there are price indices available for each of the major asset types (e.g., land, buildings, various categories of equipment).

4.27. The collection of balance sheet data is more subject to problems in valuation than transaction data. Because some stock data in business accounts are valued at historic costs rather than current values, adjustments may be needed. It is a good practice to obtain information on valuation methods at the same time the value data are collected.

4.28. Balance sheet data are useful in measuring productivity (using capital input) and analyzing spending and saving decisions (through wealth effects). As a result, interest in these items on a quarterly basis has been increasing among economists.

4.29. The difference between the opening and closing values in the balance sheets is explained by transactions, revaluations, and other changes. The transactions are shown in the capital account for nonfinancial assets and financial accounts for financial assets. The revaluations could be obtained separately or residually.

D. Institutional Sector Accounts

4.30. In addition to the sequence of accounts for the total economy, a more advanced QNA system may consider the compilation of the *1993 SNA* sequence of accounts by institutional sector. The institutional sector accounts could be introduced simultaneously or, more commonly, be gradually developed in several stages. For example, central or total general government accounts may be introduced first because of availability of data and the desirability of having the data in a national accounting framework to allow them to be linked to the rest of the economy. Households and other sectors could initially be combined and calculated as a residual. For some institutional sectors, income accounts may be developed before capital accounts because of lack of data on transactions in second-hand assets. Financial accounts may be easier to implement than the nonfinancial accounts because data on transactions and stocks of financial assets or liabilities by counterpart sectors often are available readily from the financial corporations as a byproduct of regulation or monitoring of the financial sector. Data compilers often find the usefulness of institutional accounts is not appreciated until after the data become available, so statistical compilers should anticipate future uses.

4.31. In order to assist in understanding the following discussion of the institutional sector accounts, Box 4.2 shows the sequence (excluding balance sheets) in matrix form, similar to Table 2.8 in the *1993 SNA*. The tabulation here emphasizes the interrelationships between sectors. It is intended for presentational purposes and should not be taken as a recommended main presentation of the data for a QNA publication; first, because it would be expected in practice that some accounts and sectors would be missing; and second, because the QNA usually emphasize time series, the main presentation should be time-series oriented.

4.32. A basic principle of compiling institutional sector accounts is making use of counterpart information; that is, in any transaction involving two parties, information can be collected from the party from which it can be most efficiently collected. For instance, interest paid by government to households can be obtained from one or a small number of government agencies, rather than a large number of households. Counterpart information is the equivalent of using commodity balances in the goods and services and production accounts to fill gaps. Counterpart information becomes particularly important in a quarterly context when there are more likely to be gaps. One issue to be taken into account is that data providers may not always be able to provide data on the institutional classification of the counterparts if they do not have sufficient information or motivation to do so.

4.33. If the production accounts are based on surveys of businesses and other units, the derivation of production by institutional sector is practical. All that is required is that the institutional sector of the unit be identified in the relevant survey. Some of the less direct methods, however, may not provide any institutional sector splits.

4.34. The income approach to GDP is a foundation for the income accounts by institutional sector. The availability of GDP by income component and institutional sector provides the primary income accounts to be completed by institutional sector. As a result, countries that use the income approach in the QNA system typically have better-developed quarterly institutional sector accounts.

4.35. Estimates of capital formation by institutional sector are practical if the data are collected from the purchaser rather than the supplier of the capital. These estimates are an important component of the capital accounts. The institutional sector capital accounts are more difficult to prepare than the accounts for the total economy. For institutional sec-

tor data, it is necessary to cover the secondhand assets (including land), while for the total economy, transactions in existing assets largely cancel out (except for transactions with nonresidents, which can be obtained from trade and balance of payments statistics, and sales of used vehicles from businesses and governments to households). The same considerations apply to the stocks of nonfinancial assets for balance sheets. Similar to the stocks for the whole economy, they are likely to be stable in aggregate, although transactions in secondhand assets may be a more significant issue. From the value of net lending or borrowing obtained in the financial accounts, it may be possible to derive a net estimate of acquisition of secondhand assets as a residual (although large errors and omissions may make this unacceptable, as they would all accumulate in this small item).

4.36. The financial accounts and the financial components of the balance sheets are usually among the more complete institutional sector data. Balance sheet or transaction data are often already collected from financial corporations. If the counterparts in each transaction, asset, or liability are classified by institutional sectors, there is a strong basis for compiling the data for all the sectors, not only the financial corporations themselves. In addition, balance of payments and international investment position data would show transactions, assets, and liabilities between nonresidents and residents that are not financial corporations. One should also pay attention to financial transactions and stocks of assets and liabilities not included in financial sector and balance of payments data, such as household equity in corporations and direct financial relationships between nonfinancial corporations.

4.37. Net lending/borrowing is the balancing item for both the capital and financial accounts. If the accounts are derived independently, they will act as checks on each other. Alternatively, if only one account is available, the balancing item can be used as a starting point for compiling the other. Of course, although the relationship between the balancing items on the two accounts is a conceptual identity, the balancing item is a small residual of a number of large items and could turn out to be of poor quality if there are problems in any of the component series.

1. General Government

4.38. Quarterly data are often readily available for general government or at least central government. The *1993 SNA* presentation may involve some reformatting or supply of more detailed data from the

Box 4.2. The Sequence of Institutional Sector Transactions Accounts

Uses						Transaction	Resources					
Rest of the World	Total economy	Non-financial corporations	Financial corporations	General government	Households + NPISHs*		Non-financial corporations	Financial corporations	General government	Households + NPISHs*	Total economy	Rest of the World
						I. Production Account/External Account of Goods and Services						
						Output, basic prices	1,753	102	440	1,309	3,604	
	1,883	899	29	252	703	Intermediate consumption						
	1,721	*854*	*73*	*188*	*606*	*Gross value added*						
						Taxes less subsidies on products					133	
	1,854					*GDP*						
						Imports of goods and services						499
540						Exports of goods and services						
-41						*External balance of goods and services*						
						II.1.1 Generation of Income Account						
						Value added/ GDP	854	73	188	606	1,854	
	762	545	15	140	62	Compensation of employees						
	133					Taxes less subsidies on products						
	58	51	3	2	2	Other taxes less subsidies on production						
	901	*258*	*55*	*46*	*542*	*Gross operating surplus/mixed income*						
						II.1.2 Allocation of Primary Income Account						
						Operating surplus/mixed income	258	55	46	542	901	-41
6						Compensation of employees				766	766	2
						Taxes less subsidies on productions			191		191	
63	391	135	167	42	47	Property income (interests, dividends, rents, withdrawals)	86	141	32	157	416	38
	1,883	*209*	*29*	*227*	*1,418*	*Balance of primary income/national income*						

II.2/3 Secondary Distribution of Income Account

Resources

Item	(1)	(2)	(3)	(4)	Total economy
Balance of primary income/national income	209	29	227	1,418	1,883
Current taxes on income and wealth			213		213
Social contributions		54	268		322
Social benefits				332	332
Other current transfers	10	49	108	73	240

Uses

Item	(1)	(2)	(3)	(4)	Total economy
Current taxes on income and wealth	34			178	212
Social contributions				322	322
Social benefits		43	289		332
Other current transfers		57	139	73	269
Disposable income, net	185	32	388	1,250	1,855

II.4 Use of Income Account

Resources

Item	(1)	(2)	(3)	(4)	Total economy
Disposable income, net	185	32	388	1,250	1,855
Adjustment for the change in net equity of households on pension funds				11	11

Uses

Item	(1)	(2)	(3)	(4)	Total economy
Final consumption expenditures			368	1,031	1,399
Adjustment for the change in net equity of households on pension funds		11			11
Saving, Gross	185	21	20	230	456
Current external balance					−42

III.1 Capital Account

Changes in assets

Item	(1)	(2)	(3)	(4)	Total	Rest of world
Gross fixed capital formation	250	9	37	80	376	
Changes in inventories	26			2	28	
Acquisitions less disposals of valuables	2		3	5	10	
Acquisitions less disposals of nonproduced/nonfinancial assets	−7		2	5	0	
Net lending(+)/Net borrowing(−)	−69	5	−50	153	39	−39

Changes in liabilities and net worth

Item	(1)	(2)	(3)	(4)	Total	Rest of world
Saving, Gross	185	21	20	230	456	
Current external balance						−42
Capital transfers, receivable	33	6	23	62		4
Capital transfers, payable	−16	−7	−34	−8	−65	−1

III.2 Financial Account

Changes in assets

Item	(1)	(2)	(3)	(4)	Total	Rest of world
Net lending(+)/Net borrowing(−)	−69	5	−50	153	39	−39
Net acquisition of financial assets	71	237	120	214	642	49

Changes in liabilities and net worth

Item	(1)	(2)	(3)	(4)	Total	Rest of world
Net incurrence of liabilities	140	232	170	61	603	88

*NPISHs = nonprofit institutions serving households

accounting system; however, government accounting systems have traditionally not emphasized balance sheets, so that data may be limited to the transaction accounts. In addition, issues of timing may be a problem in countries where the government accounts are on a cash basis because timing issues are more significant in quarterly data. The *Government Finance Statistics Manual* is used as a basis for presentation of government data in many countries and provides data that can be converted to *1993 SNA* formats. With the revision of the *Government Finance Statistics Manual,* most conceptual differences with the *1993 SNA* will be resolved, although the presentation will differ.

4.39. Quarterly government accounting data that do not follow national accounts principles may already be available in some countries. Analysts may already use these data to meet many needs. It is worthwhile, however, to also produce the national accounts presentation of government, as it adds value by facilitating analysis of links between government and other parts of the economy and requires relatively little extra compilation cost.

4.40. In most countries, central government data can be obtained relatively easily. As with government data for measuring GDP discussed in Chapter 3, state/provincial and local data may be available only later or in less detail. Even if all data are available at the same time, it may be desirable for analytical purposes to show the accounts for each level of government separately.

2. Financial Corporations

4.41. There is often a wide range of data obtained as a byproduct of regulation of the financial corporations sector. As mentioned in the context of financial assets and liabilities, this sector is usually relatively good in terms of the availability of administrative byproduct data and ability to provide survey data. As for general government data, the *1993 SNA* provides a presentation for quarterly financial data in an internationally standard manner that is designed to support general economic analysis.

3. Households

4.42. A few countries have continuous household surveys that collect revenue and expenditure that would provide a basis for some of the accounts. As mentioned in Chapter III in the discussion of sources for household consumption, household surveys may suffer from level biases; for QNA purposes, however, the data are suitable indicators of movement if the bias is consistent.

4.43. Alternatively, the specialized nature of many components of household income and expenditure means that many of the items of the accounts can be completed from income, expenditure, and counterpart accounts. Households receive almost all compensation of employees, mixed income, and social benefits, with the only adjustments for payments to and from nonresidents that can be obtained from the balance of payments. Households typically receive most of the operating surplus of dwellings. Pensions and annuities are also specific to households, and data are often available from pension providers or are likely to be relatively stable from quarter to quarter. Interest receivable and payable by households could be available separately from financial corporations, or it could be estimated from data on household deposits and loans if those assets and liabilities are identified separately by the financial corporations. The remaining major income component is dividends. The timing and data issues for dividends were discussed in the context of accounts for the total economy. Dividends received by households may be able to be estimated from lagged operating surplus of corporations and (in some cases) property income data from the balance of payments, if they show a stable relationship with the corresponding household income items in annual data.

4.44. For the uses of income, a range of indicators is usually already available. Household final consumption is derived as part of the expenditure approach to GDP and relates entirely to the household sector. Social contributions are obtainable from government accounts and are also specialized to households. Taxes have varying degrees of specificity to households. Interest and insurance premiums payable by households can be obtained or estimated in similar ways to the corresponding income items discussed in the previous paragraph. A capital formation survey covering businesses may be designed to produce gross capital formation by institutional sector by identifying the institutional sector of each business in the survey. If all the above items were obtained, it would be possible to derive income and capital accounts for households, and, hence, the analytically important household saving and net lending balancing items.

4. Nonfinancial Corporations

4.45. A direct survey of corporations would provide the necessary data, but such surveys are seldom conducted on a quarterly basis. Data may be available for nonfinancial corporations as a result of the lodgment of information under company legislation. Alternatively, companies listed on the stock exchange or foreign corporations may be required to disseminate quarterly or half-yearly data, and these companies may constitute a significant or representative proportion of the nonfinancial corporations sector. It would be necessary to investigate from annual data whether the other nonfinancial corporations behaved in the same way as the unobserved ones.

4.46. If such direct sources are unavailable, data for nonfinancial corporations may be obtained from counterpart transactions with the other sectors or as a residual. Dividends play a large part in the income accounts for nonfinancial corporations. Taxes and dividends are often not determined on a quarterly basis; for example, dividends may be payable twice a year, and profits tax four times a year on the basis of the previous year's earnings.

5. Nonprofit Institutions Serving Households

4.47. NPISHs often receive little attention in ANA and are not always economically volatile enough to justify high priority in quarterly data. NPISHs may be quite significant in some countries, however. The NPISH sector is defined more narrowly in the *1993 SNA* than the normal use of the term nonprofit may suggest, as it is confined to institutions that do not charge economically significant prices and may differ from some sources of information about nonprofit institutions. For example, private schools, private

hospitals, and trade unions that charge fees that cover a substantial proportion of costs are not included in the NPISHs sector.

4.48. Government transfers or transfers from the rest of the world may be major contributions to disposable incomes of NPISHs. When that is the case, such indicators would be available from counterparts through government accounts or the balance of payments, respectively. A household expenditure survey could provide data on donations and other revenue from households. If the NPISHs sector is economically significant, as it is in some countries, surveys of the institutions themselves would be necessary. Although undesirable for analytical purposes, the NPISHs sector is sometimes combined with the household sector in quarterly data.

6. Rest of the World

4.49. Balance of payments statistics provide all the data required for the rest of the world accounts. As a result of the harmonization of balance of payments and national accounts concepts, there is simply a need for rearrangement of items to a different presentation. Because the rest of the world accounts are from the perspective of the nonresidents, the signs are reversed compared to the balance of payments, which are presented from the point of view of the country itself. A terminological difference is that the balance sheets in the balance of payments are called "international investment position."

V Editing and Reconciliation

A. Introduction

5.1. Editing and reconciliation are essential stages of statistical production and are among the tasks in national accounts compilation that require the greatest skill. While other chapters deal with the sources of data and techniques, this chapter emphasizes reviewing and understanding the data. The process of reviewing and understanding data can be called "editing," "checking," or "data validation." It should occur at all stages—before, during, and after—of the calculation of the estimates. "Reconciliation" or "confrontation" is a special kind of editing done after initial compilation, in which alternative data are checked in the context of national accounting relationships. Editing and reconciliation may involve fixing errors or adopting alternative sources and methods; these tasks should, however, never be an excuse for manipulating data without evidence or adjusting data to fit forecasts or for political reasons.

5.2. National accounts compilation is a complicated process, bringing together a wide range and large volume of data. The data cover different periods; come from varying sources; are of varying quality; and may have different units, concepts, and timing. Large volumes of data mean that mistakes are easy to make and hard to find. In addition, when a method or program has worked well in the past, the production process has gone smoothly, or the calculations are complicated, there is a natural tendency for busy compilers to accept the data without close scrutiny, resulting in a risk of errors.

5.3. Data suppliers are an integral part of national accounts compilation, so editing should be supplemented by continuing contact with suppliers to gain knowledge from them about problems they have identified or suspect. In addition, the national accounts compilation process itself may shed new light through volume measures, seasonally adjusted and trend-cycle data, analysis of revision patterns, and reconciliation with related data sources. Thus, communication needs to be in both directions.

5.4. Many of the reconciliation and editing issues in quarterly national accounts (QNA) are the same as in annual national accounts (ANA). However, these issues are particularly important in the compilation of QNA. Deadlines for QNA are usually much tighter than for ANA, work is more rushed, and a higher proportion of source data may be preliminary or unpublished. As a result, errors are more likely to occur. There is typically less detailed information in QNA. The tight deadlines applying to quarterly compilation impose a severe limit on the amount of investigation done for the latest quarter. In the time available, it may be necessary to limit checks to known problem areas, the most recent periods, and some major ratios. In the time between the end of one quarterly compilation cycle and the beginning of the next, however, there may be opportunities to undertake further investigation.

5.5. The highest priority in editing is usually to *identify and remove errors* before publication; however, there are other benefits. Editing helps national accountants *understand the data and the economy better.* It also helps national accountants *anticipate queries from users,* because unusual movements will already have been identified; explanations for the expected queries can thus be given immediately. Successful editing enhances both the quality of the data and the confidence of users in the compilation procedures.

5.6. Editing procedures usually rely on *relationships within data* to identify problems and questions. Only rarely will looking at a single number help point to anomalies. The foundation of editing is to compare observations of the same variable in different periods or to compare one variable with other variables that are expected to have some linkage.

5.7. Editing and reconciliation may result in changes in the estimates. It is important that such changes are justified and documented. For example, sometimes mistakes are identified and the correct figure can be used instead. In other instances, a method may have become unsuitable because the assumptions behind it have become obsolete, or the source data may have problems in reporting or coverage. A distinction needs to be made, however, between editing and unacceptable manipulation of data. An unexpected change in a series should lead to checking that there is no error or problem with the data source. Editing may suggest that an alternative source or method is justified; however, data should not be changed just because they are unexpected, as this may lead to charges of manipulation and may undermine the reputation of compilers if it becomes known. Further, in reality, many unexpected developments occur, and the purpose of QNA is to show actual developments in the economy, particularly when they are unexpected. In line with principles of integrity and transparency, QNA estimates should be able to be explained by reference to source data, publicly available compilation methods, and adjustments documented with the supporting evidence.

B. Causes of Data Problems

5.8. There is a range of causes for failure of data to fit expected relationships. When there is a data problem, it is first necessary to confirm that the input data are consistent with those supplied by the data collectors. If the QNA are compiled by computer, as is the usual case, it is necessary to confirm that the computer program is doing what was intended. This check will show whether any anomalies were due to mistakes made in the national accounts compilation system itself. In the interest of good relationships with data suppliers, the possibility of an error in the compilation system should be excluded before pursuing other avenues of inquiry. Causes of data failing to fit expected relationships include the following:

(a) *Errors in data entry by national accounts compilers.* These include mistyping of numbers, putting numbers in the wrong place, and using old data that should have been updated.

(b) *Errors in national accounts compilation systems.* At a basic level, these include wrong formulas, which are particularly likely when changes are made to programs, especially in spreadsheets. In addition, the assumptions and indicators may become inappropriate as conditions change; for example, use of a generalized deflator or direct deflation of value added may give acceptable results when there is little relative price change but may become quite misleading under different economic circumstances. Adjustments are required when data sources do not fully meet national accounts requirements and are particularly prone to becoming outdated by economic changes. Examples are adjustments for timing, valuation, and geographic/size/product coverage.

(c) *Errors in data recording by respondents.* Reporting quality is often a problem, but it can be improved by good questionnaire design, helpful completion instructions, and availability of assistance in completing forms. Timing problems can be particularly important in QNA. Timing problems occur when transactions are not recorded at the time required by the *1993 SNA.* The 1993 SNA standard is based on accrual principles and change of ownership; however, many data sources do not meet these requirements. Government data are often recorded on a cash basis. International trade data are typically recorded at the time the goods cross the customs frontier or when the customs authorities process the form. Administrative byproduct data (e.g., value added or payroll tax data) may cover periods that do not coincide with a quarter because the agency is more interested in tax collection than statistical objectives. Businesses may also use different accounting periods that do not exactly match the three-month period used in the QNA, such as weeks, four-week periods, or nonstandard quarters. These problems are also found in annual data but are more significant in QNA because a timing error of the same size is relatively larger in quarterly data.

(d) *Errors and problems in source collection systems.* Problems can occur in classification, data entry, estimation of missing items or returns, sample design, tabulation, treatment of late response, incomplete business registers, and omitted components. Estimation of nonreporting units is a particularly important issue for QNA because of the higher proportion of missing data owing to earlier deadlines. Early estimates are often based on incomplete response, complemented by estimation processes for the missing respondents. Treatments of outliers may also differ. A systematic difference between early and late estimates suggests that the estimation for the missing components is biased. Large but nonsystematic errors suggest that it would be desirable to put more effort into early follow-up. National accounts compilers need to be sympathetic to the constraints of resources and respondent cooperation faced by their data collection colleagues.

(e) *Changes in the structure of economy.* In many instances, it is possible to confirm that there has been a surprising but valid change in the series owing to a known cause, such as a large individual transaction or a business closure. This information helps the national accountant understand the data and deal with queries from users. Some changes in the structure of the economy have the effect of making assumptions used in the national accounts compilation obsolete and so may require changes in methods. For example, the representativeness of an indicator that does not fully match the required coverage may deteriorate.

(f) *Inexplicable reasons.* There is also likely to be a residue of cases where the movement is surprising, and neither an error nor an actual cause can be found. It is still better to know about such cases, so that a query from a user is not a surprise and in case an explanation subsequently comes to light.

5.9. The causes of some data problems are obvious, while in other cases investigation is needed to identify the cause. Some can be easily resolved, while others involving data collection will take longer to implement; examples of the latter may include problems that require changes in survey coverage or questionnaire design, design of new imputation methods for nonresponse, or revised procedures for incorporation of new businesses in surveys. Even where it is not possible to fix or explain data immediately, it is important that the issues be identified for later investigation and resolution.

C. How To Identify Data Problems

5.10. In this chapter, various ways of identifying data problems are presented. The terminology and classification were developed for this chapter because there is little or no literature about its subject and no standard terminology.

1. Eyeball Testing

5.11. "Eyeball testing"—that is, just looking at the numbers as they will be published, without any additional calculations, tabulations, or charts—is the most basic kind of editing. Even with this limited presentation of data, a number of potential problems will be apparent to the careful eye:
- Different orders of magnitude, different numbers of digits.
- Numbers that change too much—excessive growth or decline.

- Numbers that do not change at all—no change at all may suggest that numbers have been copied into the wrong period.
- Numbers that change too little—a much slower growth than other items may point to a problem.

5.12. Eyeball testing does not use a computer or other tools to pinpoint problems, so it depends solely on the editor's ability. As a result, many data problems will not be apparent and may be missed. Despite these limitations, such a basic examination can be implemented quickly and is much better than no editing at all. Someone who was not involved in the original calculations is more likely to notice potential problems.

5.13. A slightly more sophisticated check is to present the numbers as charts. Charts of data can be generated readily with spreadsheet and other packages. Unusual movements and inconsistencies stand out in charts to a much greater extent than they do in tables.

2. Analytical Testing

5.14. A more advanced form of editing uses additional calculations or charts to assist in checking data. It is a more sophisticated and time-consuming form of editing but will usually reveal more problems than eyeball testing alone.

a. Logical

5.15. Logical edits are those in which exact relationships must hold, based on mathematical identities or definitions, such as in the following examples:
- Total is equal to the sum of components (e.g., GDP = Household final consumption + Government final consumption + Gross fixed capital formation + Changes in inventories + Acquisitions less disposal of valuables [if applicable] + Exports of goods and services – Imports of goods and services; Manufacturing = Food + Textiles + Clothing, etc.).
- Commodity balances, which are checks of the relationship between supply and use when they have been derived independently. They can best be done as a part of a comprehensive supply and use framework in which balancing and interrelationships between components are dealt with simultaneously. Even without a comprehensive supply and use framework, however, balancing supply and uses of particular products is a useful way to find errors or inconsistencies between data from different data sources. (If the supply and use data are complete, this is a logical edit.)
- Year is equal to the sum of the quarters (in original data; not necessarily true in seasonally adjusted or trend-cycle data).

- Definitions of specific terms (e.g., Implicit price deflator = Current price value/Constant price value; Value added = Output – Intermediate consumption).

5.16. Rounding errors may sometimes disturb these relationships slightly, but they should be relatively minor and not used as an all-purpose excuse for acceptance of inconsistency.

b. Plausibility

5.17. Edits of plausibility rely on expectations of how series should move in relation to past values of the same series and to other series. In contrast to logical edits, there is not an exact requirement that the data must satisfy; rather, data can be seen as being in a spectrum that goes from expected values, to less expected but still believable values, to unusual values, and on to unbelievable values. This assessment requires an understanding of what is a realistic change; that is, the national accountant must have a good grasp of economic developments as well as an understanding of the statistical processes.

5.18. It is important to assess QNA indicators for their ability to track movements in the corresponding annual series. As explained in Chapters II and VI, the annual benchmark-indicator (BI) ratio shows the relationship between the two series. A stable annual BI ratio shows that the indicator is representative. Alternatively, a trend increase or decrease in the BI ratio points to bias in the movements of the indicator series. Volatile changes in the annual BI ratio point to problems that are less easily diagnosed and solved.

5.19. The following are some other editing calculations that can be made to assess the plausibility of data:
- Percentage changes (e.g., for quarterly estimates, compared with one quarter or four quarters earlier) can be calculated. These can help identify cases where rates of growth or decline are excessive, or where one component is moving in a different way from a related series. It may be feasible to develop thresholds to identify unusual changes on the basis of past behavior. As well as being useful in editing, percentage change tables are a useful supplementary way of presenting data.
- Contributions to growth,[1] which show the factors behind growth in aggregates (rather than just

growth of series in their own right), can be calculated.
- Commodity balances can be made. (These are already discussed under logical edits. If the supply and use data are incomplete, this is more a test of plausibility.)
- Ratios of various kinds can be calculated (particularly where series have independent sources):
  - ▸ Implicit price deflators—that is, the ratio of current price values to constant price values, are a kind of price index.
    - ↳ At a detailed level, if the value and volume measures have been obtained independently, a peculiar implicit price deflator movement will indicate incompatible trends.
    - ↳ At an aggregated level, it is useful to calculate the corresponding Laspeyres price indices. Comparison between the Laspeyres price indices and implicit price deflators points to the effect of compositional changes on the implicit price deflators. No extra data are required to calculate the Laspeyres price indices, and they are of analytical interest in their own right.
  - ▸ Productivity measures show the relationship between inputs and output/value added and, hence, may point to problems in input or output data. The most common and simple measure is labor productivity, that is, output or value added at constant prices per employee or hour worked. For example, the output, value added, and employment series may not look unreasonable individually, but they could be moving in incompatible ways. In this case, the productivity measure will highlight the inconsistency in the trends by the implausible movement. Some countries publish labor or total factor productivity estimates; again, these are of analytical interest.
  - ▸ Ratios between other closely related series (e.g., construction in gross fixed capital formation and construction output in production estimates; value added and output for the same industry; components to total ratios, such as manufacturing/total; inventories/sales).
  - ▸ Other ratios between series. Less stable ratios will occur for series that are linked by behavioral relationships, for example, consumption and saving to income, current account deficit to saving. However, changes in these ratios can point to data problems and also help national accounts compilers advise data users.
- Implicitly derived series should be examined closely, as they may highlight data problems, for example, intermediate consumption when value added has been derived with an output indicator.

---

[1]Calculated as $(x_t - x_{t-1})/A_{t-1}$ where x is the component series and A is an aggregate. For example, if household consumption has increased by 5 since the previous period, and GDP was 1000 in the previous period, the change in household consumption makes a contribution to GDP growth of 0.5 percentage point.

• Revisions (since the previous publication or several publications earlier) should be examined. Newly introduced mistakes will show up as revisions. Consistent patterns of revisions (i.e., consistently upward or downward) suggest a biased indicator. Large, erratic revisions may indicate a problem with early data that can be investigated. The incorporation of annual benchmarks into quarterly estimates will cause revisions and could reflect problems in the sources or methods for either annual or quarterly data. To calculate and track down the causes of revisions, it is necessary to archive data from previous releases, by keeping printouts and copies of computer files or by saving earlier data in the computing system under separate identifiers.

5.20. It is not a coincidence that many of these tools for plausibility editing are also of interest to users of the statistics. Both editors and analysts are performing similar tasks of looking at how the data are moving and why.

5.21. Analytical editing can be done with charts or tables. Usually, the interest in this case is in big changes rather than precise relationships. Charts are particularly suitable in this task because they can be read by glancing, especially to identify outliers. Line charts and bar charts are alternative presentations that give different emphases. Charts may sometimes take more time to set up than tables but are worth it because of their usefulness. Tables allow errors to be traced more easily because an exact number is known, so they might be used to investigate a problem detected by a chart. Choices between charts and tables are often influenced by the capacities of the computer processing system being used. Different formats each have their own uses, so it is desirable to have a range of presentations.

5.22. In general, editing and reconciliation are best done at both detailed and aggregate levels. In aggregate form, problems can be hidden by large values of data or by errors in offsetting directions canceling each other out. With more specific identification of the affected components, it is possible to focus on the cause of the problem. Some problems are only apparent at a detailed level, because they get swamped at a higher level of aggregation. In other cases, the level of "noise" or irregular movements in the series is high at a micro level, so problems may become more obvious at a higher level, as the noise in the series becomes relatively smaller.

5.23. Problems are sometimes more apparent in constant-price or seasonally adjusted data. These presentations remove some sources of volatility and hence isolate remaining fluctuations. For example, an unadjusted series may have a strong seasonal pattern, with quarter-to-quarter changes so large that trends and irregularities are hidden.

5.24. Discrepancies and residual items should receive particular attention because they are not derived directly, and problems in certain components are often highlighted by the balancing item.

D. Reconciliation

5.25. When there are two or more independent measures of an item, inconsistencies inevitably will arise. The inconsistencies could be between two measures of GDP estimated by different approaches or, in a detailed system, between the supply and use of a particular product. Reconciliation is the process of dealing with these inconsistencies. This section discusses different options for reconciliation and the considerations that need to be taken into account in choosing among them. Reconciliation issues arise in both annual and quarterly estimates. The approach to ANA reconciliation will typically be the starting point for QNA, although some different approaches may emerge because of the quarterly emphasis on speed and time-series maintenance. In addition, the QNA data will be strongly influenced by the reconciliation carried out in the annual data because the annual balances (or imbalances) will be passed to QNA through the benchmarking process. The options available are reconciliation by detailed investigation, reconciliation by mathematical methods, or publication of discrepancies in varying ways.

5.26. One important type of reconciliation is the process of balancing data at a detailed level within a full *supply and use (or input-output)* table framework or through commodity balances for key products. Supply and use tables provide a coherent framework to identify inconsistencies at the detailed product level. Supply and use balancing is at its most useful when investigations are used to identify the cause of discrepancies. Even if supply and use data are not available in a comprehensive framework, a partial version in the form of commodity balances for particular products can provide some of the benefits of supply and use tables for reconciliation. A few countries use a supply and use framework on a quarterly basis, typically at a less detailed level than annually and as a compilation tool that is not intended for publication.

5.27. Another type of reconciliation occurs when there are *independent estimates of GDP* by two or more approaches but without the details of a supply and use framework.[2] In such cases, discrepancies become apparent only when the data are aggregated, making well-based reconciliation difficult or impossible because the aggregate discrepancies provide no indications of which components are causing the discrepancies. Investigations may still prove useful, however, as patterns in the discrepancies may point to specific problems (e.g., reversed fluctuations point to timing problems, persistent differences of a similar size point to a bias in a major source, and procyclical differences may point to problems in measuring new businesses).

5.28. Some countries have a mix of methods in which supply and use balancing occurs on an annual or less frequent basis, while independent estimates are made quarterly. In these cases, the quarterly discrepancies will cancel out within the quarters of balanced years and generally tend to be smaller because of the benchmarking process.

5.29. A number of countries do not have an apparent problem of reconciliation because they do not have supply and use tables; they have only one approach to measuring GDP; or they have two or more approaches, but only one is derived independently, with one component in the other(s) derived as a residual. Besides the analytical interest of having different approaches, however, discrepancies can be useful pointers to data problems that would otherwise be undiagnosed.

5.30. For both supply-use and independent measures of GDP, investigation and resolution of the problems is the ideal method of reconciliation. The processes of confrontation and reconciliation at a detailed level can identify many issues and are highly regarded by national accounts compilers. The extent of adjustment that can be made should depend on the expertise of the statistical compilers. Adjustment should not be made lightly but should be based on evidence and be well documented. There is potential for concern if uninformed guesses are made or adjustments are made with a view to meeting some political objective (or that accusations could be made that politically-motivated manipulation has occurred). Adjustments should be monitored to see if they later need to be reversed.

5.31. For cases in which there is insufficient time, expertise, or information for investigation to achieve

complete reconciliation, there are a number of alternatives for treating the discrepancies. There is no international consensus, however, and treatments must account for national circumstances.

5.32. One technique to remove discrepancies is the allocation of discrepancies to a single category by convention. The discrepancy is, then, no longer apparent. Usually the chosen category is large (such as household consumption) or poorly measured (such as changes in inventories). In effect, the estimates are no longer independent, and one source is forced to equal the other. As a consequence, the information content of the chosen component is reduced or even lost. And although the discrepancy is hidden in this way, it is not solved. At least, the component should be properly labeled, for example as "changes in inventories plus net errors and omissions."

5.33. A related option for removing the remaining discrepancies is to allocate them by mathematical or mechanical techniques across a number of categories. The chosen categories could be a selected group or all categories. Methods may involve simple or iterative prorating; for example, the RAS method is an iterative prorating method used for supply and use tables and other multidimensional reconciliation situations. The selection of which categories to adjust by prorating and which categories to leave unchanged should be based on explicit assessments of which estimates were better. Like allocation to a single category, the problem with allocation across several categories is that the process removes some of the information content of the original data. As a result, balance may be achieved at the expense of damaging the time-series quality of the individual components. If an error that belongs in one component is distributed across a number of components, all the components will be less accurate. If the discrepancies are trivial, this may not be of concern. But if they are significant, these techniques merely hide the problem rather than solving it. It is a disservice to users to leave them unaware of the actual extent of uncertainty. Minimizing problems in data sources can also undermine the attempts of national accountants to highlight those problems and reduce the chance of bringing about improvements. Because of the greater significance of timing problems in source data and the reduced time for investigation of the causes of inconsistencies, the limitations of reconciliation are more serious in QNA than in ANA. As a result, some countries that have balanced ANA allow imbalances in QNA.

---

[2]These issues are dealt with in Bloem et. al. (1997).

5.34. The alternative to reconciliation by investigation, allocation to a single component, or mathematical removal is to present the remaining discrepancies openly. Within that alternative, one presentation is to publish more than one measure of GDP or supply and use of a product. Alternatively, a single measure can be identified as preferred on the basis of a qualitative assessment of data sources or mathematical testing of the properties of the alternative measures (or a mixture of them). Explicit statistical discrepancy items would then be needed (in aggregate for independent measures of GDP; at the product level for supply and use), so that the sum of the items equals the preferred total.

5.35. The main concerns about showing explicit discrepancies are that they may cause confusion among users and criticism or embarrassment to the compilers. To the extent that the discrepancies represent problems that have identifiable causes and can be solved, the criticism is justified and investigations should have been carried out to make appropriate adjustments. To the extent that the discrepancies are trivial, mechanical techniques would be justified to remove them. In the remaining cases where the differences are significant and the causes unknown, however, it is better to admit the limitations of the data because the uncertainty is genuine. The ultimate objective must be to solve the problem, and being transparent to users about shortcomings is more likely to help bring about the required changes in data collection or compilation resources. While it is understandable that some compilers might be inclined to "sweep problems under the carpet," in the longer term, being open will avoid even more serious—and valid—criticism about secretiveness and covering up important problems.

5.36. The objective of soundly based reconciliation is the same in both ANA and QNA. Similarly, the options and considerations to be taken into account in choosing between them apply in both situations. There are, however, some procedural and practical differences. Procedurally, QNA reconciliation problems are likely to be most severe for the most recent quarters, because for earlier quarters the same issues would already have been identified in the ANA. Benchmarking brings the benefits of annual reconciliation to QNA, so that additional quarterly reconciliation may be a lower priority. There are also practical considerations, because there is less opportunity to investigate discrepancies during quarterly compilation.

5.37. Benchmarking means that QNA will benefit indirectly from the reconciliation carried out on the annual data, so that discrepancies may be smaller and reconciliation less urgent. If the ANA are already balanced and the QNA are benchmarked, the need for separate reconciliation is reduced. For the balanced years, discrepancies within quarters will cancel out over the whole year and tend to be small. For quarters outside the annually reconciled period, the discrepancies will tend to be smaller close to the benchmark years. For the most recent quarters that have no annual benchmark, if the indicators correctly track their benchmarks, previously identified causes of inconsistencies will already have resulted in adjustments that are carried forward. Accordingly, the QNA discrepancies will tend to be limited to those caused by noise, divergence between benchmarks and indicators, or data problems that have emerged since the last benchmark. Of course, if the annual data contain unreconciled inconsistencies, they will also be carried forward to the QNA, which will be at least as imbalanced as their ANA equivalents. The implications of benchmarking for reconciliation are discussed further in Chapter VI.

5.38. QNA are typically compiled with less time, information, and detail than ANA. The reduced time and information tend to restrict the capacity to investigate problems that have emerged in the most recent quarters. Timing errors and statistical noise may be difficult to resolve by investigation. These issues are more significant in QNA because they tend to cancel out over a whole year. In terms of user interests, analysis of QNA tends to strongly emphasize the time-series aspects of QNA data rather than structural relationships. Also, in a quarterly supply and use system, the tables are compilation tools and are not generally published in their own right, so that time-series consistency is given more weight then structural balance. Therefore, there is likely to be less investigation and more acceptance of unresolved discrepancies in a QNA system than an ANA system.

E. Editing as Part of the Compilation Process

5.39. Editing can occur at all stages of data processing:
(a) before receipt by the national accounts compilers,
(b) during data input (i.e., the data as supplied to the national accounts compilers),
(c) during data output (i.e., the data as planned to be published), and
(d) during intermediate stages:

(i)   before and after benchmarking,

(ii) before and after deflation,

(iii) before and after reconciliation, and

(iv) before and after seasonal adjustment.

5.40. Good editing practices should be applied by all compilers of statistical data. Those who collect the data need to monitor the results and anticipate queries for their own purposes. In some countries, the national accounts compilers have contributed toward educating the data collection staff through the perspective that comes from seeing macroeconomic links, from undertaking deflation and seasonal adjustment, and from maintaining consistent time series. In addition, national accounts compilers may have meetings or standardized data supply forms to allow the data collectors to notify them of major movements in the data, known economic developments, response rates, standard errors, changes to questionnaires, and other changes in methods. Good procedures or structures for interaction between data collection staff and national accounts compilers help maintain effective cooperation and avoid conflicts.

5.41. Editing at each stage through the compilation process is desirable. Each stage of processing and adjustment can introduce new errors or hide earlier ones. Earlier identification of problems and errors is generally preferable.

5.42. Original estimates, adjustments, and reasons should be documented along with supporting evidence. As a good practice, when national accounts data are changed during the editing process, the source data, original estimates, and adjusted estimates should be stored. Although only the adjusted data will be published, it is important to be able to document how the source data were amended and the cause of the problem. Documentation is necessary so that the reasons may be understood and verified later. While it is tempting to put off documentation work, memories are not a good substitute, because people move on to other jobs, forget, are on leave at a crucial time, or have conflicting recollections. Documentation is a defense against accusations of manipulation. As later data become available, patterns may be more apparent from a consistent series of original data, or alternative adjustments may be developed. Later information may lead to the conclusion that some adjustments were ill-advised and should be revised. Documentation could be on paper files or, better still, on the computer system if it allows different versions of a series to be saved and associated metadata to be linked to a series.

5.43. The ability of the national accounts compiler to make adjustments is limited if consistency with some or all published source data is a constraint. In some countries, particular data are regarded as binding for QNA compilation because of their relatively high quality or need for consistency. While some sources may not be published, making overt inconsistency not an issue, the basic criterion for adjustments should be their justifiableness. In some countries, data that are known to be particularly poor are identified as being subject to adjustments (e.g., consistency between the production and expenditure estimates being achieved by adjustments to changes in inventories because that component is known to be of poor quality).

5.44. Deciding how much editing work to do depends on staffing, deadlines, and knowledge of the kinds of problems that typically arise. In the abstract, more editing is always better. In practice, the extra work and time required to establish editing systems and then check the data mean that edits must be limited to the types that are most likely to be useful.

5.45. Computers have greatly increased the capacity for editing. At the first stage of computerizing the national accounts, the tasks from clerical systems are often transferred directly to computers without changes. However, this does not fully use the capacity of computers to do additional tasks. The next stage in the evolution of processing is to use the strengths of the computer to implement new tasks, especially editing. Calculations for editing (such as percentage changes and ratios) that would be time consuming in a clerical system involve very little cost in a computerized system and so are much more feasible. At the same time, computerized systems may need more checking because the data processing itself involves less human observation.

5.46. The compilation schedule needs to allow time for editing and subsequent investigation and revision of data. If time is only allocated to carry out basic data entry and calculation tasks, it will not be possible to make any changes before the publication deadline.

5.47. More complicated estimation methods for particular components are at more risk of mistakes. Similarly, the need for editing is stronger when data or methods are weak because the risk of inappropriate results is greater. Because numbers in a computer are all treated as numbers regardless of their origin, it is important for the compiler to bear in mind the link between the quality of data input and the quality of data output: "garbage in, garbage out."

VI Benchmarking

A. Introduction

6.1. Benchmarking deals with the problem of combining a series of high-frequency data (e.g., quarterly data) with a series of less frequent data (e.g., annual data) for a certain variable into a consistent time series. The problem arises when the two series show inconsistent movements and the less frequent data are considered the more reliable of the two. The purpose of benchmarking is to combine the relative strengths of the low- and high-frequency data. While benchmarking issues also arise in annual data (e.g., when a survey is only conducted every few years), this chapter deals with benchmarking to derive quarterly national accounts (QNA) estimates that are consistent with annual national accounts (ANA) estimates, where the annual data[1] provide the benchmarks.[2] Quarterly data sources often differ from those used in the corresponding annual estimates, and the typical result is that annual and quarterly data sources show inconsistent annual movements. In a few cases, the quarterly data may be superior and so may be used to replace the annual data.[3] More typically, the annual data provide the most reliable information on the overall level and long-term movements in the series, while the quarterly source data provide the only available explicit[4] information about the short-term movements in the series, so that there is a need to combine the information content of both the annual and quarterly sources.

6.2. Benchmarking has two main aspects, which in the QNA context are commonly looked upon as two different topics; these are (a) *quarterization*[5] of annual data to construct time series of historical QNA estimates ("back series") and revise preliminary QNA estimates to align them to new annual data when they become available, and (b) *extrapolation* to update the series from movements in the indicator for the most current period ("forward series"). In this chapter, these two aspects of benchmarking are integrated into one common **benchmark-to-indicator (BI) ratio framework** for converting individual indicator series into estimates of individual QNA variables.

6.3. To understand the relationship between the corresponding annual and quarterly data, it is useful to observe the ratio of the annual benchmark to the sum of the four quarters of the indicator (the annual BI ratio). Movements in the observed annual BI ratio show inconsistencies between the long-term movements in the indicator and in the annual data.[6] As a result, movements in the annual BI ratio can help identify the need for improvements in the annual and quarterly data sources. The technical discussion in this chapter treats the annual benchmarks as binding and, correspondingly, the inconsistencies as caused by errors[7] in the indicator and not by errors in the annual data. Benchmarking techniques that treat the benchmarks as nonbinding are briefly described in Annex 6.1.

---

[1] That is, the annual source data, or ANA estimates based on a separate ANA compilation system.

[2] A trivial case of benchmarking occurs in the rare case in which annual data are available for only one year. In this case, consistency can be achieved simply by multiplying the indicator series by a single adjustment factor.

[3] One instance is annual deflators that are best built up from quarterly data as the ratio between the annual sums of the quarterly current and constant price data, as discussed in Chapter IX Section B. Another case is that of nonstandard accounting years having a significant effect on the annual data.

[4] The annual data contain implicit information on aspects of the short-term movements in the series.

[5] Quarterization refers to generation of quarterly data for the back series from annual data and quarterly indicators, and encompasses two special cases, namely:
(a) Interpolation—that is, drawing a line between two points—which in the QNA mainly applies to stock data (except in the rare case of periodic quarterly benchmarks).
(b) Temporal distribution, that is, distributing annual flow data over quarters.

[6] See Section B.4 of Chapter II for a further discussion of this issue.

[7] The errors can be systematic ("bias") or irregular ("noise").

6.4. The general objective of benchmarking is
- to preserve as much as possible the short-term movements in the source data under the restrictions provided by the annual data and, at the same time,
- to ensure, for forward series, that the sum of the four quarters of the current year is as close as possible to the unknown future annual data.

It is important to preserve as much as possible the short-term movements in the source data because the short-term movements in the series are the central interest of QNA, about which the indicator provides the only available explicit information.

6.5. In two exceptional cases, the objective should not be to maximally preserve the short-term movements in the source data: (a) if the BI ratio is known to follow a short-term pattern, for example, is subject to seasonal variations; and (b) if a priori knowledge about the underlying error mechanism indicates that the source data for some quarters are weaker than others and thus should be adjusted more than others.

6.6. As a warning of potential pitfalls, this chapter starts off in Section B by explaining the unacceptable discontinuities between years—the "step problem"—caused by distributing annual totals in proportion to the quarterly distribution (pro rata distribution) of the indicator. The same problem arises if preliminary quarterly estimates are aligned to the annual accounts by distributing the differences between the annual sums of the quarterly estimates and independent annual estimates for the same variable evenly, or pro rata, among the four quarters of each year. Techniques that introduce breaks in the time series seriously hamper the usefulness of QNA by distorting the view of developments and possible turning points. They also thwart forecasting and constitute a serious impediment for seasonal adjustment and trend analysis. In addition to explaining the step problem, section B introduces the BI ratio framework that integrates quarterization and extrapolation into one framework.

6.7. Subsequently, the chapter presents a BI ratio-based benchmarking technique that avoids the step problem (the "proportional Denton" technique with extensions).[8] The proportional Denton technique generates a series of quarterly estimates as proportional to the indicator. as possible subject to the

restrictions provided by the annual data. The chapter goes on to propose an enhancement to the Denton technique to better deal with the most recent periods. Other enhancements to the Denton are also mentioned and some other practical issues are considered.

6.8. Given the general objective stated above it follows that, for the back series, the proportional Denton is by logical consequence[9] **optimal**, if
- maximal preservation of the short-term movements in the indicator is specified as keeping the quarterly estimates as proportional to the indicator as possible; and
- the benchmarks are binding.
Under the same conditions, it also follows that for the forward series, the enhanced version provides the best way of adjusting for systematic bias and still maximally preserving the short-term movements in the source data. In addition, compared with the alternatives discussed in Annex 6.1, the enhanced proportional Denton technique is relatively simple, robust, and well suited for large-scale applications.

6.9. The technical discussion in this chapter also applies to estimates based on periodically "fixed" ratios in the absence of direct indicators for some variables that also result in a step problem. As mentioned in Chapter III, these cases include cases in which (a) estimates for output are derived from data for intermediate consumption, or, estimates for intermediate consumption are derived from data for output; (b) estimates for output are derived from other related indicators such as inputs of labor or particular raw materials; and (c) ratios are used to gross up for units not covered by a sample survey (e.g., establishments below a certain threshold). In all these cases, the compilation procedure can be expressed in a benchmark-to-(*related*) indicator form, and annual, or less frequent, variations in the ratios result in step problems. The proportional Denton technique can also be used to avoid this step problem and, for the reasons stated above, would generally provide optimal results, except in the case of potential seasonal and cyclical variations in the ratios. This issue is discussed in more detail in Section D.1, which also provides a further enhancement to the proportional Denton that allows for incorporation of a priori known seasonal variations in the BI ratio.[10]

---

[8]Some of the alternative techniques that have been proposed are discussed in Annex 6.1, which explains the advantages of the proportional Denton technique over these alternatives.

[9]Because the proportional Denton is a mathematical formulation of the stated objective.

[10]Further enhancements, which allow for incorporating a priori knowledge that the source data for some quarters are weaker than others, and thus should be adjusted more than others, are also feasible.

6.10. In the BI ratio benchmarking framework, only the short-term movements—not the format and overall level[11]—of the indicator are important, as long as they constitute continuous time series.[12] The quarterly indicator may be in the form of index numbers (value, volume, or price) with a reference period that may differ from the base period[13] in the QNA; be expressed in physical units; be expressed in monetary terms; or be derived as the product of a price index and a volume indicator expressed in physical units. In the BI framework, the indicator only serves to determine the short-term movements in the estimates, while the annual data determine the overall level and long-term movements. As will be shown, the level and movements in the final QNA estimates will depend on the following:

- The movements, but not the level, in the short-term indicator.
- The level of the annual data—the annual BI ratio—for the current year.
- The level of the annual data—the annual BI ratios—for several preceding and following years.

Thus, it is not of any concern that the BI ratio is not equal to one,[14] and the examples in this chapter are designed to highlight this basic point.

6.11. While the Denton technique and its enhancements are technically complicated, it is important to emphasize that shortcuts generally will not be satisfactory unless the indicator shows almost the same trend as the benchmark. The weaker the indicator is, the more important it is to use proper benchmarking techniques. While there are some difficult conceptual issues that need to be understood before setting up a new system, the practical operation of benchmarking is typically automated[15] and is not problematic or time-consuming. Benchmarking should be an integral part of the compilation process and conducted at the most detailed compilation level. It represents the QNA compilation technique for converting individual indicators into estimates of individual QNA variables.

---

[11]The overall level of the indicators is crucial for some of the alternative methods discussed in Annex 6.1.
[12]See definition in paragraph 1.13.
[13]For traditional fixed-base constant price data, see Chapter IX.
[14]In the simple case of a constant annual BI ratio, any level difference between the annual sum of the indicator and the annual data can be removed by simply multiplying the indicator series by the BI ratio.
[15]Software for benchmarking using the Denton technique is used in several countries. Countries introducing QNA or improving their benchmarking techniques, may find it worthwhile to obtain existing software for direct use or adaptation to their own processing systems. For example, at the time of writing, Eurostat and Statistics Canada have software that implement the basic version of the Denton technique; however, availability may change.

B. A Basic Technique for Distribution and Extrapolation with an Indicator

6.12. The aim of this section is to illustrate the step problem created by pro rata distribution and relate pro rata distribution to the basic extrapolation with an indicator technique. Viewing the *ratio of the derived benchmarked QNA estimates to the indicator* (the quarterly BI ratio) implied by the pro rata distribution method shows that this method introduces unacceptable discontinuities into the time series. Also, viewing the quarterly BI ratios implied by the pro rata distribution method together with the quarterly BI ratios implied by the basic extrapolation with an indicator technique shows how distribution and extrapolation with indicators can be put into the same BI framework. Because of the step problem, the pro rata distribution technique *is not acceptable*.

1. Pro Rata Distribution and the Step Problem

6.13. In the context of this chapter, distribution refers to the allocation of an annual total of a flow series to its four quarters. A pro rata distribution splits the annual total according to the proportions indicated by the four quarterly observations. A numerical example is shown in Example 6.1 and Chart 6.1.

6.14. In mathematical terms, pro rata distribution can be formalized as follows:

$$X_{q,\beta} = A_\beta \cdot \left(\frac{I_{q,\beta}}{\sum_q I_{q,\beta}} \right) \quad \text{Distribution presentation} \quad (6.1.a)$$

or

$$X_{q,\beta} = I_{q,\beta} \cdot \left(\frac{A_\beta}{\sum_q I_{q,\beta}} \right) \quad \begin{array}{l} \text{Benchmark-to-indicator} \\ \text{ratio presentation} \end{array} \quad (6.1.b)$$

where

$X_{q,\beta}$ is the level of the QNA estimate for quarter q of year β;

$I_{q,\beta}$ is the level of the indicator in quarter q of year β; and

A_β is the level of the annual data for year β.

6.15. The two equations are algebraically equivalent, but the presentation differs in that equation (6.1.a) emphasizes the distribution of the annual benchmark (A_β) in proportion to each quarter's proportion of the

Example 6.1. Pro Rata Distribution and Basic Extrapolation

	Indicator				Derived QNA Estimates				
	The Indicator (1)	Period-to-Period Rate of Change	Annual Data (2)	Annual BI ratio (3)	Distributed Data				Period-to-Period Rate of Change
					(1)	·	(3)	=	(4)	
q1 1998	98.2				98.2	·	9.950	=	977.1	
q2 1998	100.8	2.6%			100.8	·	9.950	=	1,003.0	2.6%
q3 1998	102.2	1.4%			102.2	·	9.950	=	1,016.9	1.4%
q4 1998	100.8	−1.4%			100.8	·	9.950	=	1,003.0	−1.4%
Sum	**402.0**		**4000.0**	**9.950**					**4,000.0**	
q1 1999	99.0	−1.8%			99.0	·	10.280	=	1,017.7	1.5%
q2 1999	101.6	2.6%			101.6	·	10.280	=	1,044.5	2.6%
q3 1999	102.7	1.1%			102.7	·	10.280	=	1,055.8	1.1%
q4 1999	101.5	−1.2%			101.5	·	10.280	=	1,043.4	−1.2%
Sum	**404.8**	**0.7%**	**4161.4**	**10.280**					**4,161.4**	**4.0%**
q1 2000	100.5	−1.0%			100.5	·	10.280	=	1,033.2	−1.0%
q2 2000	103.0	2.5%			103.0	·	10.280	=	1,058.9	2.5%
q3 2000	103.5	0.5%			103.5	·	10.280	=	1,064.0	0.5%
q4 2000	101.5	−1.9%			101.5	·	10.280	=	1,043.4	−1.9%
Sum	**408.5**	**0.9%**	**?**	**?**					**4,199.4**	**0.9%**

Pro Rata Distribution
The annual BI ratio for 1998 of 9.950 is calculated by dividing the annual output value (4000) by the annual sum of the indicator (402.0). This ratio is then used to derive the QNA estimates for the individual quarters of 1998. For example, the QNA estimate for q1 1998 is 977.1, that is, 98.2 times 9.950.

The Step Problem
Observe that quarterly movements are unchanged for all quarters except for q1 1999, where a decline of 1.8% has been replaced by an increase of 1.5%. (In this series, the first quarter is always relatively low because of seasonal factors.) This discontinuity is caused by suddenly changing from one BI ratio to another, that is, creating a step problem. The break is highlighted in the charts, with the indicator and adjusted series going in different directions.

Extrapolation
The 2000 indicator data are linked to the benchmarked data for 1999 by carrying forward the BI ratio for the last quarter of 1999. In this case, where the BI ratio was kept constant through 1999, this is the same as carrying forward the annual BI ratio of 10.280. For instance, the preliminary QNA estimate for the second quarter of 2000 (1058.9) is derived as 103.0 times 10.280. Observe that quarterly movements are unchanged for all quarters.

(These results are illustrated in Chart 6.1.)

annual total of the indicator[16] $(I_{q,\beta}/\sum_q I_{4,\beta})$, while equation (6.1.b) emphasizes the raising of each quarterly value of the indicator $(I_{q,\beta})$ by the annual BI ratio $(A_\beta/\sum_q I_{q,\beta})$.

6.16. The **step problem** arises because of discontinuities between years. If an indicator is not growing as fast as the annual data that constitute the benchmark, as in Example 6.1, then the growth rate in the QNA estimates needs to be higher than in the indicator. With pro rata distribution, the entire increase in the quarterly growth rates is put into a single quarter, while other quarterly growth rates are left unchanged. The significance of the step problem depends on the size of variations in the annual BI ratio.

2. Basic Extrapolation with an Indicator

6.17. Extrapolation with an indicator refers to using the movements in the indicator to update the QNA time series

---

[16]The formula, as well as all subsequent formulas, applies also to flow series where the indicator is expressed as index numbers.

with estimates for quarters for which no annual data are yet available (the forward series). A numerical example is shown in Example 6.1 and Chart 6.1 (for 1999).

6.18. In mathematical terms, extrapolation with an indicator can be formalized as follows, when moving from the last quarter of the last benchmark year:

$$X_{4,\beta+1} = X_{4,\beta} \cdot \left(\frac{I_{4,\beta+1}}{I_{4,\beta}} \right) \qquad \text{Moving presentation} \quad (6.2.a)$$

or

$$X_{4,\beta+1} = I_{4,\beta+1} \cdot \left(\frac{X_{4,\beta}}{I_{4,\beta}} \right) \qquad \text{BI ratio presentation} \quad (6.2.b)$$

6.19. Again, note that equations (6.2.a) and (6.2.b) are algebraically equivalent, but the presentation differs in that equation (6.2.a) emphasizes that the last quarter of the last benchmark year $(X_{4,\beta})$ is extrapolated by the movements in the indicator from that period to the current quarters $(I_{q,\beta+1}/I_{4,\beta})$, while equation (6.2.b) shows that this is the same as

Chart 6.1. Pro Rata Distribution and the Step Problem
The Indicator and the Derived Benchmarked QNA Estimates

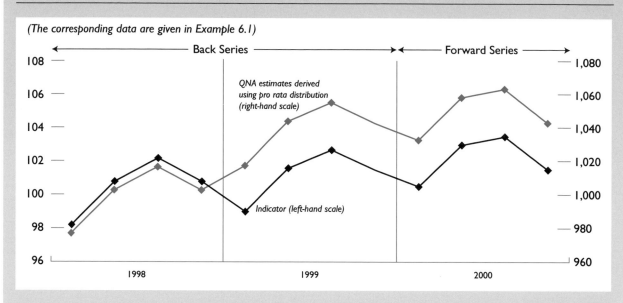

(The corresponding data are given in Example 6.1)

In this example, the **step problem** shows up as an increase in the derived series from q4 1998 to q1 1999 that is not matched by the movements in the source data. The quarterized data erroneously show a quarter-to-quarter rate of change for the first quarter of 1999 of **1.5%** while the corresponding rate of change in source data is **–1.8%** (in this series, the first quarter is always relatively low because of seasonal factors).

Benchmark-to-Indicator Ratio

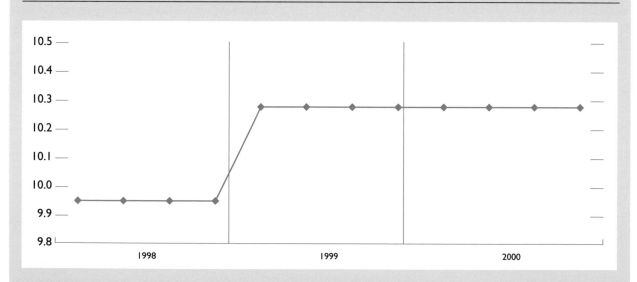

It is easier to recognize the step problem from charts of the BI ratio, where it shows up as abrupt upward or downward steps in the BI ratios between q4 of one year and q1 of the next year. In this example, the step problem shows up as a large upward jump in the BI ratio from q4 1998 to q1 1999.

scaling up or down the indicator $(I_{q,\beta+1})$ by the BI ratio for the last quarter of the last benchmark year $(X_{4,\beta}/I_{4,\beta})$.

6.20. Also, note that if the quarterly estimates for the last benchmark year $X_{4,\beta}$ were derived using the pro rata technique in equation (6.1), for all quarters, the implied quarterly BI ratios are identical and equal to the annual BI ratio. That is, it follows from equation (6.1) that

$$(X_{4,\beta}/I_{4,\beta}) = (X_{q,\beta}/I_{q,\beta}) = (A_\beta/\sum_q I_{q,\beta}).^{17}$$

6.21. Thus, as shown in equations (6.1) and (6.2), distribution refers to constructing the back series by using the BI ratio for the current year as adjustment factors to scale up or down the QNA source data, while extrapolation refers to constructing the forward series by carrying that BI ratio forward.

C. The Proportional Denton Method

1. Introduction

6.22. The basic distribution technique shown in the previous section introduced a step in the series, and thus distorted quarterly patterns, by making all adjustments to quarterly growth rates to the first quarter. This step was caused by suddenly changing from one BI ratio to another. To avoid this distortion, the (implicit) quarterly BI ratios should change smoothly from one quarter to the next, while averaging to the annual BI ratios.[18] Consequently, all quarterly growth rates will be adjusted by gradually changing, but relatively similar, amounts.

2. The Basic Version of the Proportional Denton Method

6.23. The basic version of the proportional Denton benchmarking technique keeps the benchmarked series as proportional to the indicator as possible by minimizing (in a least-squares sense) the difference in relative adjustment to neighboring quarters subject to the constraints provided by the annual benchmarks. A numerical illustration of its operation is shown in Example 6.2 and Chart 6.2.

6.24. Mathematically, the basic version of the proportional Denton technique can be expressed as[19]

$$\min_{(X_1,...,X_{4\beta},......X_T)} \sum_{t=2}^{T}\left[\frac{X_t}{I_t} - \frac{X_{t-1}}{I_{t-1}}\right]^2 \qquad (6.3)$$

$$t \in \{1,...(4\beta),...T\}$$

under the restriction that, for flow series,[20]

$$\sum_{t=2}^{T} X_t = A_y, \quad y \in \{1.....\beta\}.$$

That is, the sum[21] of the quarters should be equal to the annual data for each benchmark year,[22]

where

t is time (e.g., $t = 4y - 3$ is the first quarter of year y, and $t = 4y$ is the fourth quarter of year y);

X_t is the derived QNA estimate for quarter t;

I_t is the level of the indicator for quarter t;

A_y is the annual data for year y;

β is the last year for which an annual benchmark is available; and

T is the last quarter for which quarterly source data are available.

---

[17]Thus, in this case, it does not matter which period is being moved. Moving from (a) the fourth quarter of the last benchmark year, (b) the average of the last benchmark year, or (c) the same quarter of the last benchmark year in proportion to the movements in the indicator from the corresponding periods gives the same results. Formally, it follows from equation (6.1) that

$$X_{q,\beta+1} = X_{4,\beta} \cdot \left(\frac{I_{q,\beta+1}}{I_{4,\beta}}\right)$$

$$= X_{q,\beta} \cdot \left(\frac{I_{q,\beta+1}}{I_{q,\beta}}\right)$$

$$= A_\beta \cdot \left(\frac{I_{q,\beta+1}}{\sum_q I_{q,\beta}}\right)$$

[18]In the standard case of binding annual benchmarks.

[19]This presentation deviates from Denton's original proposal by omitting the requirement that the value for the first period be predetermined. As pointed out by Cholette (1984), requiring that the values for the first period be predetermined implies minimizing the first correction and can in some circumstances cause distortions to the benchmarked series. Also, Denton's original proposal dealt only with estimating the back series.

[20]For the less common case of stock series, the equivalent constraint is that the value of the stock at the end of the final quarter of the year is equal to the stock at the end of the year. For index number series, the constraint can be formulated as requiring the annual average of the quarters to be equal to the annual index or the sum of the quarters to be equal to four times the annual index. The two expressions are equivalent.

[21]Applies also to flow series in which the indicator is expressed as index numbers; the annual total of the indicator should still be expressed as the sum of the quarterly data.

[22]The annual benchmarks may be omitted for some years to allow for cases in which independent annual source data are not available for all years.

Example 6.2. The Proportional Denton Method
Same data as in Example 6.1.

	The Indicator	Indicator Period-to-Period Rate of Change	Annual Data	Annual BI Ratios	Derived QNA Estimates	Estimated Quarterly BI ratios	Period-to-Period Rate of Change
q1 1998	98.2				969.8	9.876	
q2 1998	100.8	2.6%			998.4	9.905	3.0%
q3 1998	102.2	1.4%			1,018.3	9.964	2.0%
q4 1998	100.8	−1.4%			1,013.4	10.054	−0.5%
Sum	402.0		4000.0	9.950	4,000.0		
q1 1999	99.0	−1.8%			1,007.2	10.174	−0.6%
q2 1999	101.6	2.6%			1,042.9	10.264	3.5%
q3 1999	102.7	1.1%			1,060.3	10.325	1.7%
q4 1999	101.5	−1.2%			1,051.0	10.355	−0.9%
Sum	404.8	0.7%	4161.4	10.280	4,161.4		4.0%
q1 2000	100.5	−1.0%			1,040.6	10.355	−1.0%
q2 2000	103.0	2.5%			1,066.5	10.355	2.5%
q3 2000	103.5	0.5%			1,071.7	10.355	0.5%
q4 2000	101.5	−1.9%			1,051.0	10.355	−1.9%
Sum	408.5	0.9%	?	?	4,229.8		1.6%

BI Ratios
- For the back series (1998–1999):
  In contrast to the pro rata distribution method in which the estimated quarterly BI ratio jumped abruptly from 9.950 to 10.280, the proportional Denton method produces a smooth series of quarterly BI ratios in which:
  ▸ The quarterly estimates sum to 4000, that is, the weighted average BI ratio for 1998 is 9.950.
  ▸ The quarterly estimates sum to 4161.4, that is, the weighted average for 1999 is equal to 1.0280.
  ▸ The estimated quarterly BI ratio is increasing through 1998 and 1999 to match the increase in the observed annual BI ratio. The increase is smallest at the beginning of 1998 and at the end of 1999.
- For the forward series (2000), the estimates are obtained by carrying forward the quarterly BI ratio (10.355) for the last quarter of 1999 (the last benchmark year).

Rates of Change
- For the back series, the quarterly percentage changes in 1998 and 1999 are adjusted upwards for all quarters to match the higher rate of change in the annual data.
- For the forward series, the quarterly percentage changes in 1999 are identical to those of the indicator; but note that the rate of change from 1999 to 2000 in the derived QNA series (1.6%) is higher than the annual rate of change in the indicator (0.9%). The next section provides an extension of the method that can be use to ensure that annual rate of change in the derived QNA series equals the annual rate of change in the indicator, if that is desired.

(These results are illustrated in Chart 6.2.)

6.25. The proportional Denton technique *implicitly constructs* from the annual observed BI ratios a time series of *quarterly benchmarked QNA estimates-to-indicator* (quarterly BI) ratios that is as smooth as possible and, in the case of flow series:
- For the back series, $(y \in \{1,...\beta\})$ averages[23] to the annual BI ratios for each year y.
- For the forward series, $(y \in \{\beta + 1.....\})$ are kept constant and equal to the ratio for the last quarter of the last benchmark year.

We will use this interpretation of the proportional Denton method to develop an enhanced version in the next section.

---

[23]annual weighted average
$$\left(\sum_{q=1}^{4} \frac{X_{q,y}}{I_{q,y}} \cdot w_{q,y} = A_y \middle/ \sum_{q=1}^{4} I_{q,y} \right)$$

where the weights are
$$w_{q,y} = I_{q,y} \middle/ \sum_{q=1}^{4} I_{q,y}$$

6.26. The proportional Denton technique, as presented in equation (6.3), requires that the indicator contain positive values only. For series that contain zeroes but not negative values, this problem can be circumvented by simply replacing the zeroes with values infinitesimally close to zero. For series that can take both negative and positive values, and are derived as differences between two non-negative series, such as changes in inventories, the problem can be avoided by applying the proportional Denton method to the opening and closing inventory levels rather than to the change. Alternatively, the problem can be circumvented by temporarily turning the indicator into a series containing only positive values by adding a sufficiently large constant to all periods, benchmarking the resulting indicator using equation (6.3), and subsequently deducting the constant from the resulting estimates.

6.27. For the back series, the proportional Denton method results in QNA quarter-to-quarter growth rates that differ from those in the indicator (e.g., see

Chart 6.2. Solution to the Step Problem: The Proportional Denton Method
The Indicator and the Derived Benchmarked QNA Estimates

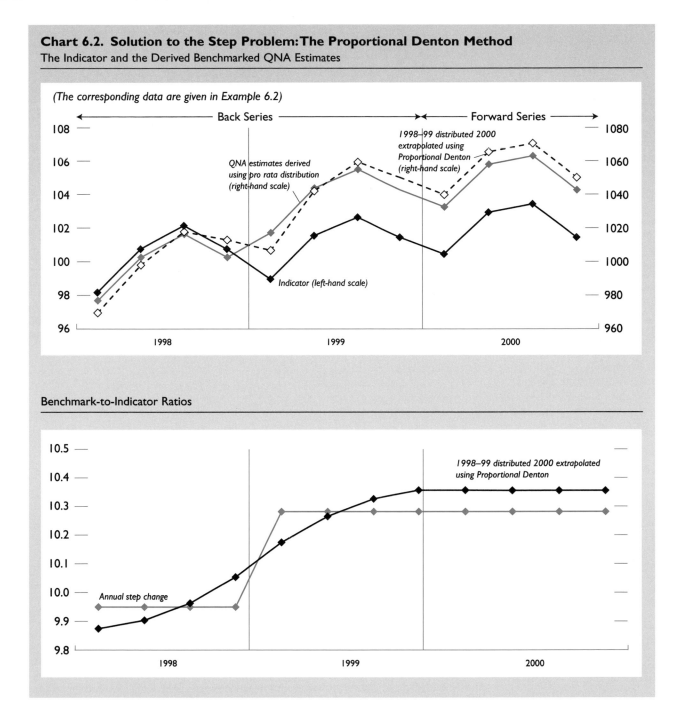

(The corresponding data are given in Example 6.2)

Benchmark-to-Indicator Ratios

Example 6.2). In extreme cases, the method may even introduce new turning points in the derived series or change the timing of turning points; however, these changes are a necessary and desirable result of incorporating the information contained in the annual data.

6.28. For the forward series, the proportional Denton method results in quarter-to-quarter growth rates that are identical to those in the indicator but also in an annual growth rate for the first year of the forward series that differs from the corresponding growth rate of the source data (see Example 6.2). This difference in the annual growth rate is caused by the way the indicator is linked in. By carrying forward the quarterly BI ratio for the last quarter of the last benchmark year, the proportional Denton method implicitly "forecasts" the next annual BI ratio as different from the last observed annual BI ratio, and equal to the quarterly BI ratio for the last quarter of the last benchmark year. As explained in Annex 6.2, the proportional Denton method will result in the following:

- It will partly adjust for any systematic bias in the indicator's annual rate of change if the bias is sufficiently large relative to any amount of noise, and thus, on average, lead to smaller revisions in the QNA estimates.
- It will create a wagging tail effect with, on average, larger revisions if the amount of noise is sufficiently large relative to any systematic bias in the annual growth rate of the indicator.

The next section presents an enhancement to the basic proportional Denton that better incorporates information on bias versus noise in the indicator's movements.

6.29. For the forward series, the basic proportional Denton method implies moving from the fourth quarter of the last benchmark year (see equation (6.2.a)). As shown in Annex 6.2, other possible starting points may cause a forward step problem, if used together with benchmarking methods for the back series that avoid the step problem associated with pro rata distribution:

- Using growth rates from four quarters earlier. Effectively, the estimated quarterly BI ratio is forecast as the same as four quarters earlier. This method maintains the percentage change in the indicator over the previous four quarters but it does not maintain the quarterly growth rates, disregards the information in past trends in the annual BI ratio, and introduces potential sever steps between the back series and the forward series.
- Using growth rates from the last annual average. Effectively, the estimated quarterly BI ratio is forecast as the same as the last annual BI ratio. This method results in annual growth rates that equal those in the indicator; however, it also disregards the information in past trends in the annual BI ratio and introduces an unintended step between the back series and the forward series.

6.30. When the annual data later become available, the extrapolated QNA data would need to be re-estimated. As a result of the benchmarking process, new data for one year will also lead to changes in the quarterly movements for the preceding year(s). This effect occurs because the adjustment for the errors in the indicator is distributed smoothly over several quarters, not just within the same year. For example, as illustrated in Example 6.3 and Chart 6.3, if the

1999 annual data subsequently showed that the downward error in the indicator for 1998 for Example 6.2 was reversed, then

- the 1999 QNA estimates would be revised down;
- the estimates in the second half of 1998 would be revised down (to smoothly adjust to the 1999 values); and
- the estimates in the first half of 1998 would need to be revised up (to make sure that the sum of the four quarters was still consistent with the 1998 annual total).

While these effects may be complex, it should be emphasized that they are an inevitable and desired implication of incorporating the information provided by the annual data concerning the errors in the long-term movements of the quarterly indicator.

3. Enhancements to the Proportional Denton Method for Extrapolation

6.31. It is possible to improve the estimates for the most recent quarters (the forward series) and reduce the size of later revisions by incorporating information on past systematic movements in the annual BI ratio. It is important to improve the estimates for these quarters, because they are typically of the keenest interest to users. Carrying forward the quarterly BI ratio from the last quarter of the last year is an implicit forecast of the annual BI ratio, but a better forecast can usually be made. Accordingly, the basic Denton technique can be enhanced by adding a forecast of the next annual BI ratio, as follows:

- If the annual growth rate of the indicator is systematically biased compared to the annual data,[24] then, on average, the best forecast of the next year's BI ratio is the previous year's value multiplied by the average relative change in the BI ratio.
- If the annual growth rate of the indicator is unbiased compared to the annual data (i.e., the annual BI follows a random walk process), then, on average, the best forecast of the next year's BI ratio is the previous annual value.

---

[24]The indicator's annual growth rate is systematically biased if the ratio between (a) the ratio of annual of change in the indicator and (b) the ratio of annual change in the annual data on average is significantly different from one or, equivalently, that the ratio of annual change in the annual BI ratio on average is significantly different from one, as seen from the following expression:

$$\frac{A_y/A_{y-1}}{\sum\limits_{q=1}^{4} I_{q,y} \Big/ \sum\limits_{q=1}^{4} I_{q,y-1}} <=> \frac{A_y \Big/ \sum\limits_{q=1}^{4} I_{q,y}}{A_{y-1} \Big/ \sum\limits_{q=1}^{4} I_{q,y-1}} = \frac{BI_y}{BI_{y-1}}$$

Example 6.3. Revisions to the Benchmarked QNA Estimates Resulting from Annual Benchmarks for a New Year

This example is an extension of Example 6.2 and illustrates the impact on the back series of incorporating annual data for a new year, and subsequent revisions to the annual data for that year.

Assume that preliminary annual data for 2000 become available and the estimate is equal to 4,100.0 (annual data A). Later on, the preliminary estimate for 2000 is revised upwards to 4,210.0 (annual data B). Using the equation presented in (6.3) to distribute the annual data over the quarters in proportion to the indicator will give the following sequence of revised QNA estimates:

Date	The Indicator	Indicator Period-to Period rate of Change	Annual Data 2000A	Annual BI Ratio 2000A	Annual Data 2000B	Annual BI Ratio 2000B	Revised QNA Estimates Derived in Example 6.2	With 2000A	With 2000B	Quarterized BI Ratios Derived in Example 6.2	With 2000A	With 2000B
q1 1998	98.2						969.8	968.1	969.5	9.876	9.858	9.873
q2 1998	100.3	2.6%					998.4	997.4	998.3	9.905	9.895	9.903
q3 1998	102.2	1.4%					1,018.3	1,018.7	1,018.4	9.964	9.967	9.965
q4 1998	100.8	−1.4%					1,013.4	1,015.9	1,013.8	10.054	10.078	10.058
Sum	**402.0**		**4,000.0**	**9.950**	**4,000.0**	**9.950**						
q1 1999	99.0	−1.8%					1,007.2	1,012.3	1,008.0	10.174	10.225	10.182
q2 1999	101.6	2.6%					1,042.9	1,047.2	1,043.5	10.264	10.307	10.271
q3 1999	102.7	1.1%					1,060.3	1,059.9	1,060.3	10.325	10.321	10.324
q4 1999	101.5	−1.2%					1,051.0	1,042.0	1,049.6	10.355	10.266	10.341
Sum	**404.8**	**0.7%**	**4,161.4**	**10.280**	**4,161.4**	**10.280**						
q1 2000	100.5	−1.0%					1,040.6	1,019.5	1,037.4	10.355	10.144	10.323
q2 2000	103.0	2.5%					1,066.5	1,035.4	1,061.8	10.355	10.052	10.308
q3 2000	103.5	0.5%					1,071.7	1,034.1	1,065.9	10.355	9.991	10.299
q4 2000	101.5	−1.9%					1,051.0	1,011.0	1,044.9	10.355	9.961	10.294
Sum	**408.5**	**0.9%**	**4,100.0**	**10.037**	**4,210.0**	**10.306**	**4,229.8**	**4,100.0**	**4,210.0**			

As can be seen, incorporating the annual data for 2000 results in (a) revisions to both the 1999 and the 1998 QNA estimates, and (b) the estimates for one year depend on the difference in the annual movements of the indicator and the annual data for the previous years, the current year, and the following years.

In **case A**, with an annual estimate for 2000 of 4100.0, the following can be observed:
- The annual BI ratio increases from 9.950 in 1998 to 10.280 in 1999 and then drops to 10.037 in 2000. Correspondingly, the derived quarterly BI ratio increases gradually from q1 1998 through q3 1999 and then decreases through 2000.
- Compared with the estimates obtained in Example 6.2, incorporating the 2000 annual estimate resulted in the following *revisions to the path of the quarterly BI ratio through 1998 and 1999:*
  ‣ To smooth the transition to the decreasing BI ratios through 2000, which are caused by the drop in the annual BI ratio from 1999 to 2000, the BI ratios for q3 and q4 of 1999 have been revised downwards.
  ‣ The revisions downward of the BI ratios for q3 and q4 of 1999 is matched by an upward revision to the BI ratios for q1 and q2 of 1999 to ensure that the weighted average of the quarterly BI ratios for 1999 is equal to the annual BI ratio for 1999.
  ‣ To smooth the transition to the new BI ratios for 1999, the BI ratios for q3 and q4 of 1998 have been revised upward; consequently, the BI ratios for q1 and q2 of 1998 have been revised downwards.
- As a consequence a turning point in the new time series of quarterly BI ratios has been introduced between the third and the fourth quarter of 1999, in contrast to the old BI ratio time series, which increased during the whole of 1999.

In **case B**, with an annual estimate for 2000 of 4210.0, the following can be observed:
- The annual BI ratio for 1999 of 10.306 is slightly higher than the 1999 ratio of 10.280, but:
  ‣ The ratio is lower than the initial q4 1999 BI ratio of 10.325 that was carried forward in Example 6.2 to obtain the initial quarterly estimates for 2000.
  ‣ Correspondingly, the initial annual estimate for 2000 obtained in Example 6.2 was higher than the new annual estimate for 2000.
- Consequently, compared with the initial estimates from Example 6.2, the BI ratios have been revised downwards from q3 1999 onwards.
- In spite of the fact that the annual BI ratio is increasing, the quarterized BI ratio is decreasing during 2000. This is caused by the steep increase in the quarterly BI ratio during 1999 that was caused by the steep increase in the annual BI ratio from 1998 to 2000.

(These results are illustrated in Chart 6.3.)

- If the annual BI is fluctuating symmetrically around its mean, on average, the best forecast of the next year's BI ratio is the long-term average BI value.
- If the movements in the annual BI ratio are following a stable, predictable time-series model (i.e., an ARIMA[25] or ARMA[26] model) then, on average, the best forecast of the next year's BI ratio may be obtained from that model.
- If the fluctuations in the annual BI ratio are correlated with the business cycle[27] (e.g., as manifested in the indicator), then, on average, the best forecast of the next year's BI ratio may be obtained by modeling that correlation.

---

[25]Autoregressive integrated moving average time-series models.
[26]Autoregressive moving average time-series models.

[27]Lags in incorporating deaths and births of businesses in quarterly sample frames may typically generate such correlations.

Chart 6.3. Revisions to the Benchmarked QNA Estimates Resulting from Annual Benchmarks for a New Year

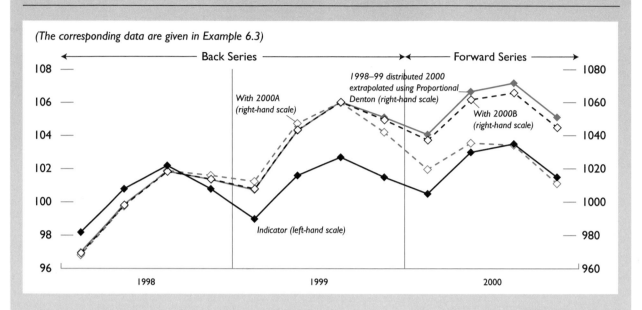

(The corresponding data are given in Example 6.3)

Benchmark-to-Indicator Ratios

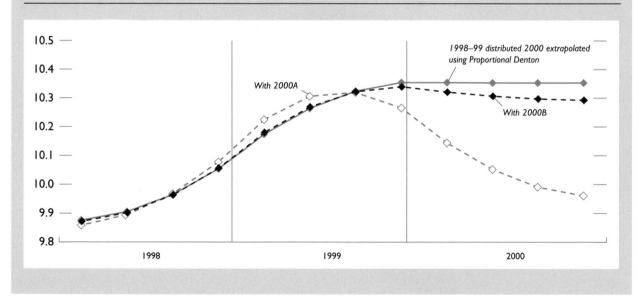

Note that only the annual BI ratio and not the annual benchmark value has to be forecast, and the BI ratio is typically easier to forecast than the annual benchmark value itself.

6.32. To produce a series of estimated quarterly BI ratios taking into account the forecast, the same principles of least-square minimization used in the Denton formula can also be used with a series of annual BI ratios that include the forecast. Since the benchmark values are not available, the annual constraint is that the weighted average of estimated quarterly BI ratios is the same as the corresponding observed or forecast annual BI ratios and that period-to-period change in the time series of quarterly BI ratios is minimized.

6.33. In mathematical terms:

$$\min_{(QBI_1,....,QBI_{4\beta},.......QBI_T)} \sum_{t=2}^{T}\left[QBI_t - QBI_{t-1}\right]^2 \quad (6.4.a)$$

$$t \in \left\{1,...(4\beta),....T\right\}$$

under the restriction that

(a) $$\sum_{t=4y-3}^{4y} QBI_t \cdot w_t = ABI_y$$

for $t \in \left\{1,...(4\beta)\right\}, y \in \left\{1,...\beta\right\}.$

and

(b) $$\sum_{t=4y-3}^{4y} QBI_t \cdot w_{t-4} = \hat{ABI}_{y+1}$$

for $t \in \left\{(4\beta)......T\right\}, y \in \left\{\beta+1,....\right\}.$

Where $w_t = I_t \Big/ \sum_{t=4y-3}^{4y} I_t$ for $t \in \left\{1,...(4\beta)\right\},$

and where

QBI_t is the estimated quarterly BI ratio (X_t/I_t) for period t;

ABI_y is the observed annual BI ratio $(A_t/\sum_q I_{q,y})$ for year $y \in \{1,...\beta\}$; and

$\hat{ABI}_y$ is the forecast annual BI ratio for year $y \in \{\beta+1.....\}.$

6.34. Once a series of quarterly BI ratios is derived, the QNA estimate can be obtained by multiplying the indicator by the estimated BI ratio.

$$X_t = QBI_t \cdot I_t \quad (6.4.b)$$

6.35. The following shortcut version of the enhanced Denton extrapolation method gives similar results for less volatile series. In a computerized system, the shortcut is unnecessary, but it is easier to follow in an example (see Example 6.4 and Chart 6.4). This method can be expressed mathematically as

(a) $\hat{QBI}_{2,\beta}$ $= QBI_{2,\beta} + 1/4 \cdot \eta$ (6.5)

       $\hat{QBI}_{3,\beta}$ $= QBI_{3,\beta} + 1/4 \cdot \eta$

       $\hat{QBI}_{4,\beta}$ $= QBI_{4,\beta} - 1/2 \cdot \eta$

(b) $\hat{QBI}_{1,\beta+1}$ $= \hat{QBI}_{4,\beta} - \eta$

       $\hat{QBI}_{q,\beta+1}$ $= \hat{QBI}_{q-1,\beta+1} - \eta$

where

$\eta = 1/3(QBI_{4,\beta} - \hat{ABI}_{\beta+1})$ (a fixed parameter for adjustments that ensures that the estimated quarterly BI ratios average to the correct annual BI ratios);

$QBI_{q,\beta}$ is the original BI ratio estimated for quarter q of the last benchmark year;

$\hat{QBI}_{q,\beta}$ is the adjusted BI ratio estimated for quarter q of the last benchmark year;

$\hat{QBI}_{q,\beta+1}$ is the forecast BI ratio for quarter q of the following year; and

$\hat{ABI}_{\beta+1}$ is the forecast average annual BI ratio for the following year.

6.36. While national accountants are usually reluctant to make forecasts, all possible methods are based on either explicit or implicit forecasts, and implicit forecasts are more likely to be wrong because they are not scrutinized. Of course, it is often the case that the evidence is inconclusive, so the best forecast is simply to repeat the last observed annual BI ratio.

D. Particular Issues

I. Fixed Coefficient Assumptions

6.37. In national accounts compilation, potential step problems may arise in cases that may not always be thought of as a benchmark-indicator relationship. One important example is the frequent use of assumptions of fixed coefficients relating inputs (total or part of intermediate consumption or inputs of labor and/or capital) to output ("IO ratios"). Fixed IO ratios can be seen as a kind of a benchmark-indicator relationship, where the available series is the indicator for the missing one and the IO ratio (or its inverse) is the BI ratio. If IO ratios are changing from year to year but are kept constant within each year, a step problem is created. Accordingly, the Denton technique can be used to generate smooth time series of quarterly IO ratios based on annual (or less frequent) IO coefficients. Furthermore, systematic trends can be identified to forecast IO ratios for the most recent quarters.

2. Within-Year Cyclical Variations in Coefficients

6.38. Another issue associated with fixed coefficients is that coefficients that are assumed to be fixed may in fact be subject to cyclical variations within the year. IO ratios may vary cyclically owing to inputs that do not

Example 6.4. Extrapolation Using Forecast BI Ratios

Same data as Examples 6.1 and 6.3

Date	Indicator	Annual data	Annual BI ratios	Original estimates from Example 6.2		Extrapolation using forecast BI ratios		Quarter to quarter rates of change		
				BI ratios	QNA estimates for 1997–1998	Forecast BI ratio	Estimate	Original indicator	Original Estimates from Example 6.2	Based on forecast BI ratios
q1 1998	98.2			9.876	969.8					
q2 1998	100.8			9.905	998.4			2.60%	3.00%	3.00%
q3 1998	102.2			9.964	1,018.3			1.40%	2.00%	2.00%
q4 1998	100.8			10.054	1,013.4			−1.40%	−0.50%	−0.50%
Sum	**402.0**	**4,000.0**	**9.950**		**4,000.0**					
q1 1999	99.0			10.174	1,007.2			−1.80%	−0.60%	−0.60%
q2 1999	101.6			10.264	1,042.9	10.253	1,041.7	2.60%	3.50%	3.40%
q3 1999	102.7			10.325	1,060.3	10.314	1,059.2	1.10%	1.70%	1.70%
q4 1999	101.5			10.355	1,051	10.376	1,053.2	−1.20%	−0.90%	−0.20%
Sum	**404.8**	**4,161.4**	**10.280**		**4,161.4**	**10.280**	**4,161.4**	**0.70%**	**4.00%**	**4.00%**
q1 2000	100.5			10.355	1,040.6	10.42	1,047.2	−1.00%	−1.00%	−0.60%
q2 2000	103			10.355	1,066.5	10.464	1,077.8	2.50%	2.50%	2.90%
q3 2000	103.5			10.355	1,071.7	10.508	1,087.5	0.50%	0.50%	0.90%
q4 2000	101.5			10.355	1,051	10.551	1,071	−1.90%	−1.90%	−1.50%
Sum	**408.5**			**10.355**	**4,229.8**	**10.486**	**4,283.5**	**0.90%**	**1.60%**	**2.90%**

This example assumes that, based on a study of movements in the annual BI ratios for a number of years, it is established that the indicator on average understates the annual rate of growth by 2.0%.

The forecast annual and adjusted quarterly BI ratios are derived as follows:

The annual BI ratio for 2000 is forecast to rise to 10.486, (i.e., 10.280 · 1.02).

The adjustment factor (η) is derived as −0.044, (i.e., 1/3 · (10.355 − 10.486).

q2 1999: 10.253 = 10.264 + 1/4 · (−0.044)
q3 1999: 10.314 = 10.325 + 1/4 · (−0.044)
q4 1999: 10.376 = 10.355 − 1/2 · (−0.044)

q1 2000: 10.420 = 10.376 − (−0.044)
q2 2000: 10.464 = 10.420 − (−0.044)
q3 2000: 10.508 = 10.464 − (−0.044)
q4 2000: 10.551 = 10.508 − (−0.044)

Note that for the sum of the quarters, the annual BI ratios are as measured (1999) or forecast (2000), and the estimated quarterly BI ratios move in a smooth way to achieve those annual results, minimizing the proportional changes to the quarterly indicators.

(These results are illustrated in Chart 6.4.)

vary proportionately with output, typically fixed costs such as labor, capital, or overhead such as heating and cooling. Similarly, the ratio between income flows (e.g., dividends) and their related indicators (e.g., profits) may vary cyclically. In some cases, these variations may be according to a seasonal pattern and be known.[28] It should be noted that omitted seasonal variations are only a problem in the original non-seasonally adjusted data, as the variations are removed in seasonal adjustment and do not restrict the ability to pick trends and turning points in the economy. However, misguided attempts to correct the problem in the original data could distort the underlying trends.

---

[28]Cyclical variations in assumed fixed coefficients may also occur because of variations in the business cycle. These variations cause serious errors because they may distort trends and turning points in the economy. They can only be solved by direct measurement of the target variables.

6.39. To incorporate a seasonal pattern on the target QNA variable, without introducing steps in the series, one of the following two procedures can be used:

(a) **BI ratio-based procedure**

Augment the benchmarking procedure as outlined in equation (6.4) by incorporating the a priori assumed seasonal variations in the estimated quarterly BI ratios as follows:

$$\min_{\left(QBI_1,\dots QBI_{4\beta},\dots QBI_T\right)} \sum_{t=2}^{T}\left[\frac{QBI_t}{SF_t} - \frac{QBI_{t-1}}{SF_{t-1}}\right]^2 \quad (6.6)$$

$$t \in \left\{1,\dots(4\beta),\dots T\right\}$$

under the same restrictions as in equation (6.4), where SF_t is a time series with a priori assumed seasonal factors.

Chart 6.4. Extrapolation Using Forecast BI Ratios

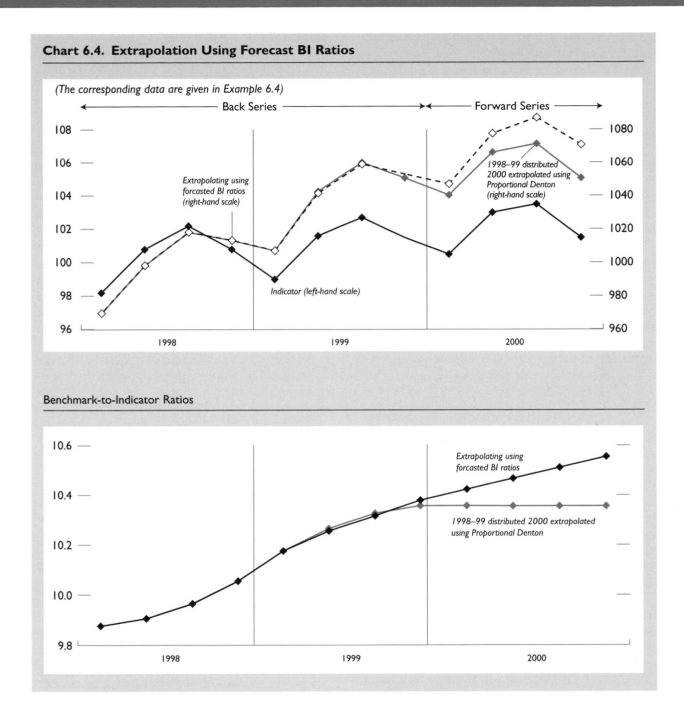

(The corresponding data are given in Example 6.4)

←————————— Back Series —————————→←—— Forward Series ——→

Extrapolating using forcasted BI ratios (right-hand scale)

1998–99 distributed 2000 extrapolated using Proportional Denton (right-hand scale)

Indicator (left-hand scale)

Benchmark-to-Indicator Ratios

Extrapolating using forcasted BI ratios

1998–99 distributed 2000 extrapolated using Proportional Denton

(b) **Seasonal adjustment-based procedure**

(i) Use a standard seasonal adjustment package to seasonally adjust the indirect indicator.

(ii) Multiply the seasonally adjusted indicator by the known seasonal coefficients.

(iii) Benchmark the resulting series to the corresponding annual data.

6.40. The following inappropriate procedure is sometimes used to incorporate a seasonal pattern

when the indicator and the target variable have different and known seasonal patterns:

(a) distribute the annual data for one year in proportion to the assumed seasonal pattern of the series, and

(b) use the movements from the same period in the previous year in the indicator to update the series.

6.41. This procedure preserves the superimposed seasonal patterns when used for one year only. When the QNA estimates are benchmarked, however, this procedure will introduce breaks in the series that can remove or distort trends in the series and introduce more severe errors than those that it aims to prevent (see Annex 6.2 for an illustration).

3. Benchmarking and Compilation Procedures

6.42. Benchmarking should be an integral part of the compilation process and should be conducted at the most detailed compilation level. In practice, this may imply benchmarking different series in stages, where data for some series, which have already been benchmarked, are used to estimate other series, followed by a second or third round of benchmarking. The actual arrangements will vary depending on the particularities of each case.

6.43. As an illustration, annual data may be available for all products, but quarterly data are available only for the main products. If it is decided to use the sum of the quarterly data as an indicator for the other products, the ideal procedure would be first to benchmark each of the products for which quarterly data are available to the annual data for that product, and then to benchmark the quarterly sum of the benchmarked estimates for the main products to the total. Of course, if all products were moving in similar ways, this would give similar results to directly benchmarking the quarterly total to the annual total.

6.44. In other cases, a second or third round of benchmarking may be avoided and compilation procedure simplified. For instance, a current price indicator can be constructed as the product of a quantity indicator and a price indicator without first benchmarking the quantity and price indicators to any corresponding annual benchmarks. Similarly, a constant price indicator can be constructed as a current price indicator divided by a price indicator without first benchmarking the current price indicator. Also, if output at constant prices is used as an indicator for intermediate consumption, the (unbenchmarked) constant price output indicator can be benchmarked to the annual intermediate consumption data directly. It can be shown that the result is identical to first benchmarking the output indicator to annual output data, and then benchmarking the resulting benchmarked output estimates to the annual intermediate consumption data.

6.45. To derive quarterly constant price data by deflating current price data, the correct procedure would be first to benchmark the quarterly current price indicator and then to deflate the benchmarked quarterly current price data. If the same price indices are used in the annual and quarterly accounts, the sum of the four quarters of constant price data should be taken as the annual estimate, and a second round of benchmarking is unnecessary. As explained in Chapter IX Section B, annual deflators constructed as unweighted averages of monthly or quarterly price data can introduce an aggregation over time error in the annual deflators and subsequently in the annual constant price data that can be significant if there is quarterly volatility. Moreover, if, in those cases, quarterly constant price data are derived by benchmarking a quarterly constant price indicator derived by deflating the current price indicator to the annual constant price data, the aggregation over time error will be passed on to the implicit quarterly deflator, which will differ from the original price indices. Thus, in those cases, annual constant price data should in principle be derived as the sum of quarterly or even monthly deflated data if possible. If quarterly volatility is insignificant, however, annual constant price estimates can be derived by deflating directly and then benchmarking the quarterly constant price estimates to the annual constant price estimates.

4. Balancing Items and Accounting Identities

6.46. The benchmarking methods discussed in this chapter treat each time series as an independent variable and thus do not take into account any accounting relationship between related time series. Consequently, the benchmarked quarterly time series will not automatically form a consistent set of accounts. For example, quarterly GDP from the production side may differ from quarterly GDP from the expenditure side, even though the annual data are consistent. The annual sum of these discrepancies, however, will cancel out for years where the annual benchmark data are balanced.[29] While multivariate benchmarking methods exist that take the relationship between the time series as an additional constraint, they are too complex and demanding to be used in QNA.

6.47. In practice, the discrepancies in the accounts can be minimized by benchmarking the different parts of the accounts at the most detailed level and building aggregates from the benchmarked components. If the remaining discrepancies between, for

---

[29]The within-year discrepancies will in most cases be relatively insignificant for the back series.

instance, GDP from the production and expenditure side are sufficiently small,[30] it may be defensible to distribute them proportionally over the corresponding components on one or both sides. In other cases, it may be best to leave them as explicit statistical discrepancies, unless the series causing these discrepancies can be identified. Large remaining discrepancies indicate that there are large inconsistencies between the short-term movements for some of the series.

5. More Benchmarking Options

6.48. The basic version of the proportional Denton technique presented in equation (6.3) can be expanded by allowing for alternative benchmark options, as in the following examples:
- The annual benchmarks may be omitted for some years to allow for cases where independent annual source data are not available for all years.
- Sub-annual benchmarks may be specified by requiring that
  - ▸ the values of the derived series are equal to some predetermined values in certain benchmark quarters; or
  - ▸ the half-yearly sums of the derived quarterly estimates are equal to half-yearly benchmark data for some periods.
- Benchmarks may be treated as nonbinding.
- Quarters that are known to be systematically more error prone than others may be adjusted relatively more than others.

The formulas for the two latter extensions are provided in Section B.2 of Annex 6.1.

6. Benchmarking and Revisions

6.49. To avoid introducing distortions in the series, incorporation of new annual data for one year will generally require revision of previously published quarterly data for several years. This is a basic feature of all acceptable benchmarking methods. As explained in paragraph 6.30, and as illustrated in Example 6.3, in addition to the QNA estimates for the year for which new annual data are to be incorporated, the quarterly data for one or several preceding and following years, may have to be revised. In principle, previously published QNA estimates for all preceding and following years may have to be adjusted to maximally preserve the short-term movements in the indicator, if the errors in the indicator are large. In practice, however, with most benchmarking methods, the impact of new annual data will gradually be diminishing and zero for sufficiently distant periods.

6.50. One of the advantages of the Denton method compared with several of the alternative methods discussed in Annex 6.1, is that it allows for revisions to as many preceding years as desired. If desired, revisions to some previously published QNA estimates can be avoided by specifying those estimates as "quarterly benchmark restrictions." This option freezes the values for those periods, and thus can be used to reduce the number of years that have to be revised each time new annual data become available. To avoid introducing significant distortions to the benchmarked series, however, at least two to three years preceding (and following) years should be allowed to be revised each time new annual data become available. In general, the impact on more distant years will be negligible.

7. Other Comments

6.51. Sophisticated benchmarking techniques use advanced concepts. In practice, however, they require little time or concern in routine quarterly compilation. In the initial establishment phase, the issues need to be understood and the processes automated as an integral part of the QNA production system. Thereafter, the techniques will improve the data and reduce future revisions without demanding time and attention of the QNA compiler. It is good practice to check the new benchmarks as they arrive each year in order to replace the previous BI ratio forecasts and make new annual BI forecasts. A useful tool for doing so is a table of observed annual BI ratios over the past several years. It will be usual for the BI ratio forecasts to have been wrong to varying degrees, but the important question is whether the error reveals a pattern that would allow better forecasts to be made in the future. In addition, changes in the annual BI ratio point to issues concerning the indicator that will be of relevance to the data suppliers.

---

[30]That is, so that the impact on the growth rates are negligible.

Annex 6.1. Alternative Benchmarking Methods

A. Introduction

6.A1.1. There are two main approaches to benchmarking of time series: a purely numerical approach and a statistical modeling approach. The numerical differs from the statistical modeling approach by not specifying a statistical time-series model that the series is assumed to follow. The numerical approach encompasses the family of least-squares minimization methods proposed by Denton (1971) and others,[1] the Bassie method,[2] and the method proposed by Ginsburgh (1973). The modeling approach encompasses ARIMA[3] model-based methods proposed by Hillmer and Trabelsi (1987), State Space models proposed by Durbin and Quenneville (1997), and a set of regression models proposed by various Statistics Canada staff.[4] In addition, Chow and Lin (1971) have proposed a multivariable general least-squares regression approach for interpolation, distribution, and extrapolation of time series. While not a benchmarking method in a strict sense, the Chow-Lin method is related to the statistical approach, particularly to Statistics Canada's regression models.

6.A1.2. The aim of this annex is to provide a brief review, in the context of compiling quarterly national accounts (QNA), of the most familiar of these methods and to compare them with the preferred proportional Denton technique with enhancements. The annex is not intended to provide an extensive survey of all alternative benchmarking methods proposed.

6.A1.3. The enhanced proportional Denton technique provides many advantages over the alternatives. It is, as explained in paragraph 6.7, by logical consequence optimal if the general benchmarking objective of maximal preservation of the short-term

movements in the indicator is specified as keeping the quarterly estimates as proportional to the indicator as possible and the benchmarks are binding. In addition, compared with the alternatives, the enhanced proportional Denton technique is relatively simple, robust, and well suited for large-scale applications. Moreover, the implied benchmark-indicator (BI) ratio framework provides a general and integrated framework for converting indicator series into QNA estimates through interpolation, distribution, and extrapolation with an indicator that, in contrast to additive methods, is not sensitive to the overall level of the indicators and does not tend to smooth away some of the quarter-to-quarter rates of change in the data. The BI framework also encompasses the basic extrapolation with an indicator technique used in most countries.

6.A1.4. In contrast, the potential advantage of the various statistical modeling methods over the enhanced proportional Denton technique is that they explicitly take into account any supplementary information about the underlying error mechanism and other aspects of the stochastic properties of the series. Usually, however, this supplementary information is not available in the QNA context. Moreover, some of the statistical modeling methods render the danger of over-adjusting the series by interpreting true irregular movements that do not fit the regular patterns of the statistical model as errors, and thus removing them. In addition, the enhancement to the proportional Denton provided in Section D of Chapter VI allows for taking into account supplementary information about seasonal and other short-term variations in the BI ratio. Further enhancements that allow for incorporating any supplementary information that the source data for some quarters are weaker than others, and thus should be adjusted more than others, are provided in Section B.2 of this annex, together with a nonbinding version of the proportional Denton.

6.A1.5. Also, for the forward series, the enhancements to the proportional Denton method developed

---

[1]Helfand, Monsour, and Trager (1977), and Skjæveland (1985).
[2]Bassie (1958).
[3]Autoregressive integrated moving average.
[4]Laniel, and Fyfe (1990), and Cholette and Dagum (1994).

in Section C.3 of Chapter VI provide more and better options for incorporating various forms of information on past systematic bias in the indicator's movements. The various statistical modeling methods typically are expressed as additive relationships between the levels of the series, not the movements, that substantially limit the possibilities for alternative formulation of the existence of any bias in the indicator. The enhancements to the proportional Denton method developed in Chapter VI express systematic bias in terms of systematic behavior of the relative difference in the annual growth rate of the indicator and the annual series or, equivalently, in the annual BI ratio. This provides for a more flexible framework for adjusting for bias in the indicator.

B. The Denton Family of Benchmarking Methods

I. Standard Versions of the Denton Family

6.A1.6. The Denton family of least-squares-based benchmarking methods is based on the principle of movement preservation. Several least-squares-based methods can be distinguished, depending on how the principle of movement preservation is made operationally. The principle of movement preservation can be expressed as requiring that (1) the quarter-to-quarter growth in the adjusted quarterly series and the original quarterly series should be as similar as possible or (2) the adjustment to neighboring quarters should be as similar as possible. Within each of these two broad groups, further alternatives can be specified. The quarter-to-quarter growth can be specified as absolute growth or as rate of growth, and the absolute or the relative difference of these two expressions of quarter-to-quarter growth can be minimized. Similarly, the difference in absolute or relative adjustment of neighboring quarters can be minimized.

6.A1.7. The proportional Denton method (formula D4 below) is preferred over the other versions of the Denton method for the following three main reasons:

- It is substantially easier to implement.
- It results in most practical circumstances in approximately the same estimates for the back series as formula D2, D3, and D5 below.
- Through the BI ratio formulation used in Chapter VI, it provides a simple and elegant framework for extrapolation using the enhanced proportional Denton method, which fully takes into

account the existence of any systematic bias or lack thereof in the year-to-year rate of change in the indicator.

- Through the BI ratio formulation used in Chapter VI, it provides a simple and elegant framework for extrapolation, which supports the understanding of the enhanced proportional Denton method; the Denton method fully takes into account the existence of any systematic bias or lack thereof in the year-to-year rate of change in the indicator.

6.A1.8. In mathematical terms, the following are the main versions[5] of the proposed least-squares benchmarking methods:[6]

$$\text{MinD1:} \quad \min_{(x_1,\dots,x_{4\beta},\dots,x_T)} \sum_{t=2}^{T} \left[\left(X_t - X_{t-1} \right) - \left(I_t - I_{t-1} \right) \right]^2 \quad (6.A1.1)$$

$$\Leftrightarrow \quad \min_{(x_1,\dots,x_{4\beta},\dots,x_T)} \sum_{t=2}^{T} \left[\left(X_t - I_t \right) - \left(X_{t-1} - I_{t-1} \right) \right]^2$$

$$\text{Min D2:} \quad \min_{(x_1,\dots,x_{4\beta},\dots,x_T)} \sum_{t=2}^{T} \left[\ln\left(\frac{X_t / X_{t-1}}{I_t / I_{t-1}} \right) \right]^2 \quad (6.A1.2)$$

$$\Leftrightarrow \quad \min_{(x_1,\dots,x_{4\beta},\dots,x_T)} \sum_{t=2}^{T} \left[\ln\left(\frac{X_t / I_t}{X_{t-1} / I_{t-1}} \right) \right]^2$$

$$\Leftrightarrow \quad \min_{(x_1,\dots,x_{4\beta},\dots,x_T)} \sum_{t=2}^{T} \left[\ln\left(X_t / X_{t-1} \right) - \ln\left(I_t / I_{t-1} \right) \right]^2$$

$$\text{Min D3:} \quad \min_{(x_1,\dots,x_{4\beta},\dots,x_T)} \sum_{t=2}^{T} \left[\frac{X_t}{X_{t-1}} - \frac{I_t}{I_{t-1}} \right]^2 \quad (6.A1.3)$$

$$\text{Min D4:}[7] \quad \min_{(x_1,\dots,x_{4\beta},\dots,x_T)} \sum_{t=2}^{T} \left[\frac{X_t}{I_t} - \frac{X_{t-1}}{I_{t-1}} \right]^2 \quad (6.A1.4)$$

---

[5]The abbreviations D1, D2, D3, and D4, were introduced by Sjöberg (1982), as part of a classification of the alternative least-squares-based methods proposed by, or inspired by, Denton (1971). D1 and D4 were proposed by Denton; D2 and D3 by Helfand, Monsour, and Trager (1977); and D5 by Skjæveland (1985).

[6]This presentation deviates from the original presentation by the various authors by omitting their additional requirement that the value for the first period is predetermined. Also, Denton's original proposal only dealt with the back series.

[7]This is the basic version of the proportional Denton.

Min D5:
$$\min_{(x_1,\ldots,x_{4\beta},\ldots,x_T)} \sum_{t=2}^{T}\left[\frac{X_t/X_{t-1}}{I_t/I_{t-1}}-1\right]^2 \quad (6.A1.5)$$

$$\Leftrightarrow \min_{(x_1,\ldots,x_{4\beta},\ldots,x_T)} \sum_{t=2}^{T}\left[\frac{X_t/I_t}{X_{t-1}/I_{t-1}}-1\right]^2$$

$$t \in \{1,\ldots(4\beta),\ldots T\}$$

All versions are minimized under the same restrictions, that for flow series,

$$\sum_{t=4y-3}^{4y} X_1 = A_y, \quad y \in \{1,\ldots\beta\}.$$

That is, the sum of the quarters should be equal to the annual data for each benchmark year.

6.A1.9. The various versions of the Denton family of least-squares-based benchmarking methods have the following characteristics:
- The D1 formula minimizes the differences in the absolute growth between the benchmarked series X_t and the indicator series I_t. It can also be seen as minimizing the absolute difference of the absolute adjustments of two neighboring quarters.
- The D2 formula minimizes the logarithm of the relative differences in the growth rates of the two series. Formula D2 can also be looked upon as minimizing the logarithm of the relative differences of the relative adjustments of two neighboring quarters and as the logarithm of the absolute differences in the period-to-period growth rates between the two series.
- The D3 formula minimizes the absolute differences in the period-to-period growth rates between the two series.
- The D4 formula minimizes the absolute differences in the relative adjustments of two neighboring quarters.
- The D5 formula minimizes the relative differences in the growth rates of the two series. Formula D5 can also be looked upon as minimizing the relative differences of the relative adjustments of two neighboring quarters.

6.A1.10. While all five formulas can be used for benchmarking, only the D1 formula and the D4 formula have linear first-order conditions for a minimum and thus are the easiest to implement in practice. In practice, the D1 and D4 formulas are the only ones currently in use.

6.A.1.11. The D4 formula—the proportional Denton method—is generally preferred over the D1 formula

because it preserves seasonal and other short-term fluctuations in the series better when these fluctuations are multiplicatively distributed around the trend of the series. Multiplicatively distributed short-term fluctuations seem to be characteristic of most seasonal macroeconomic series. By the same token, it seems most reasonable to assume that the errors are generally multiplicatively, and not additively, distributed, unless anything to the contrary is explicitly known. The D1 formula results in a smooth additive distribution of the errors in the indicator, in contrast to the smooth multiplicative distribution produced by the D4 formula. Consequently, as with all additive adjustment formulations, the D1 formula tends to smooth away some of the quarter-to-quarter rates of change in the indicator series. As a consequence, the D1 formula can seriously disturb that aspect of the short-term movements for series that show strong short-term variations. This can occur particularly if there is a substantial difference between the level of the indicator and the target variable. In addition, the D1 formula may in a few instances result in negative benchmarked values for some quarters (even if all original quarterly and annual data are positive) if large negative adjustments are required for data with strong seasonal variations.

6.A1.12. The D2, D3, and D5 formulas are very similar. They are all formulated as an explicit preservation of the period-to-period rate of change in the indicator series, which is the ideal objective formulation, according to several authors (e.g., Helfand, Monsour, and Trager 1977). Although the three formulas in most practical circumstances will give approximately the same estimates for the back series, the D2 formula seems slightly preferable over the other two. In contrast to D2, the D3 formula will adjust small rates of change relatively more than large rates of change, which is not an appealing property. Compared to D5, the D2 formula treats large and small rates of change symmetrically and thus will result in a smoother series of relative adjustments to the growth rates.

2. Further Expansions of the Proportional Denton Method

6.A1.13. The basic version of the proportional Denton technique (D4) presented in the chapter can be further expanded by allowing for alternative or additional benchmark restrictions, such as the following:
- Adjusting relatively more quarters that are known to be systematically more error prone than others.
- Treating benchmarks as nonbinding.

6.A1.14. The following augmented version of the basic formula allows for specifying which quarters should be adjusted more than the others:

$$\min_{\left(X_1,\dots,X_{4\beta},\dots\dots X_T\right)} \sum_{t=2}^{T} w_{q_t} \cdot \left[\frac{X_t}{I_t} - \frac{X_{t-1}}{I_{t-1}}\right]^2 \qquad (6.A1.6)$$

$$t \in \left\{1,\dots(4\beta),\dots T\right\}$$

under the standard restriction that

$$\sum_{t=4y-1}^{4y} X_t = A_y, \quad y \in \left\{1,\dots\beta\right\}.$$

That is, the sum of the quarters should be equal to the annual data for each benchmark year.

Where

w_{q_t} is a set of user-specified quarterly weights that specifies which quarters should be adjusted more than the others.

6.A1.15. In equation (6.A1.6), only the relative value of the user-specified weights (w_{q_t}) matters. The absolute differences in the relative adjustments of a pair of neighboring quarters given a weight that is high relative to the weights for the others will be smaller than for pairs given a low weight.

6.A1.16. Further augmenting the basic formula as follows, allows for treating the benchmarks as non-binding:

$$(6.A1.7)$$

$$\min_{\left(x_1,\dots,x_{4\beta},\dots\dots x_T\right)} \sum_{t=2}^{T} w_{q_t} \cdot \left[\frac{X_t}{I_t} - \frac{X_{t-1}}{I_{t-1}}\right]^2 - \sum_{y=1}^{\beta} w_{a_y} \cdot \left[\sum_{t=4y-3}^{4y} \frac{X_t}{A_y} - 1\right]^2.$$

Where

w_{a_y} is a set of user-specified annual weights that specifies how binding the annual benchmarks should be treated.

Again, only the relative value of the user-specified weights matters. Relatively high values of the annual weights specify that the benchmarks should be treated as relatively binding.

C. The Bassie Method

6.A1.17. Bassie (1958) was the first to devise a method for constructing monthly and quarterly series whose short-term movements would closely reflect those of a related series while maintaining consistency with annual totals. The Bassie method was the only method described in detail in *Quarterly National Accounts* (OECD, 1979). However, using the Bassie method as presented in OECD (1979) can result in a step problem if data for several years are adjusted simultaneously.

6.A1.18. The Bassie method is significantly less suited for QNA compilation than the proportional Denton technique with enhancements for the following main reasons:
- The proportional Denton method better preserves the short-term movements in the indicator.
- The additive version of the Bassie method, as with most additive adjustment methods, tends to smooth the series and thus can seriously disturb the quarter-to-quarter rates of change in series that show strong short-term variations.
- The multiplicative version of the Bassie method does not yield an exact correction, requiring a small amount of prorating at the end.
- The proportional Denton method allows for the full time series to be adjusted simultaneously, in contrast to the Bassie method, which operates on only two consecutive years.
- The **Bassie method can result in a step problem** if data for several years are adjusted simultaneously and not stepwise.[8]
- The proportional Denton method with enhancements provides a general and integrated framework for converting indicator series into QNA estimates through interpolation, distribution, and extrapolation with an indicator. In contrast, the **Bassie method does not support extrapolation**; it only addresses distribution of annual data.
- The Bassie method results in a more cumbersome compilation process.

6.A1.19. The following is the standard presentation of the Bassie method, as found, among others, in OECD (1979). Two consecutive years are considered. No discrepancies between the quarterly and annual data for the first year are assumed, and the (absolute or relative) difference for the second year is equal to K_2.

6.A1.20. The Bassie method assumes that the correction for any quarter is a function of time, $K_q = f(t)$ and that $f(t) = a + bt + ct^2 + dt^3$. The method then stipulates the following four conditions:
(i) The average correction in year 1 should be equal to zero:

Example 6.A1.1. The Bassie Method and the Step Problem

Date	Original Estimates	Annual Estimates	Rate of Error	Adjustment Coefficients Adjustment of Year 2	Adjustment Coefficients Adjustment of Year 3	Adjusted Estimates	Growth Rates	Implied Adjustment Ratio
Year 1								
q1	1,000.0			-0.0981445		990.2		0.990
q2	1,000.0			-0.1440297		985.6	-0.5%	0.986
q3	1,000.0			-0.0083008		999.2	1.4%	0.999
q4	1,000.0			0.25048828		1,025.1	2.6%	1.025
Total year 1	4,000.0	4,000.0	0.00	0.0		4,000.0		
Year 2								
q1	1,000.0			0.57373047	-0.0981445	1,057.4	3.2%	1.057
q2	1,000.0			0.90283203	-0.1440297	1,090.3	3.1%	1.090
q3	1,000.0			1.17911122	-0.0083008	1,117.9	2.5%	1.118
q4	1,000.0			1.34423822	0.25048828	1,134.4	1.5%	1.134
Total year 2	4,000.0	4,400.0	0.10	4.0	0.0	4,400.0		
Year 3								
q1	1,000.0				0.57373047	1,000.0	-11.9%	1.000
q2	1,000.0				0.90283203	1,000.0	0.0%	1.000
q3	1,000.0				1.17911122	1,000.0	0.0%	1.000
q4	1,000.0				1.34423822	1,000.0	0.0%	1.000
Total year 3	4,000.0	4,000.0	0.00		4.0			

In the example, revised annual estimates for years 2 and 3 were made available at the same time. As seen, the first–round adjustment of the quarterly series to align the quarterly estimates to the annual estimate for year 2 results in an upward adjustment in the growth through year 1 and year 2 but no adjustments to year 3, leading to a break in the series between q4 of year 2 and q1 of year 3.

The break introduced by the first round of adjustments is not removed in the second round of adjustments to align the series to the annual estimate for year 3. In the example, the error in year 3 is zero, and the Bassie method, applied as described above, results in no further adjustments of the data.

$$\int_{0}^{1} f(t)dt = 0.$$

(ii) The average correction in year 2 should be equal to the annual error in year 2 (K_2):

$$\int_{1}^{2} f(t)dt = K_2.$$

(iii) At the start of year 1, the correction should be zero, so as not to disturb the relationship between the first quarter of year 1 and the fourth quarter of year 0: $f(0) = 0$.

(iv) At the end of year 2, the correction should be neither increasing nor decreasing:

$$\frac{df(2)}{dt} = 0.$$

6.A1.21. These four conditions allow computing the following fixed coefficients to distribute the

annual error in year 2 (K_2) over the four quarters of year 2 and to adjust the quarterly pattern within year 1:

To be used for year 1		To be used for year 2	
b_1	-0.098145	c_1	0.573730
b_2	-0.144030	c_2	0.902832
b_3	-0.008301	c_3	1.179111
b_4	0.250488	c_4	1.344238
Sum 0.0		4.0	

6.A1.22. The difference between the annual sum of the quarterly estimates and the direct annual estimate in year 2 (K_2) can be expressed either in an additive form or in a multiplicative form. The additive form is as follows:

$$K_2 = A_2 - \sum_{q=1}^{4} X_{q,2} \tag{6.A1.8}$$

leading to the following additive version of the Bassie adjustment method:

$$Z_{q,1} = X_{q,1} + 0.25 \cdot b_q \cdot K_2 \tag{6.A1.9}$$
$$Z_{q,2} = X_{q,2} + 0.25 \cdot c_q \cdot K_2$$

---

[8] This step problem can be reduced, but not removed entirely, by a reformulation of the standard presentation of the method; however, use of the Bassie method is still not advisable.

where

q is used as a generic symbol for quarters;

$Z_{q,y}$ is the level of the adjusted quarterly estimate for quarter q in year 1 ($y = 1$) and 2 ($y = 2$);

$X_{q,y}$ is the level of the preliminary quarterly estimate for quarter q in year y; and

A_2 is the level of the direct annual estimate for year 2.

6.A1.23. The multiplicative form is as follows:

$$K_2 = \left(A_2 \middle/ \sum_{q=1}^{4} X_{q,2} \right) - 1 \qquad (6.A1.10)$$

leading to the following multiplicative version of the Bassie adjustment method:

$$Z_{q,1} = X_{q,1} \cdot (1 + b_q \cdot K_2) \qquad (6.A1.11)$$

$$Z_{q,2} = X_{q,2} \cdot (1 + c_q \cdot K_2)$$

The multiplicative version of the Bassie method does not yield an exact correction, and a small amount of prorating is necessary at the end of the computation.

6.A1.24. The Bassie method only works as long as not more than one year is adjusted each time and the quarterly estimates represent a continuous time series. In particular, it should be noted that (contrary to what is stated in *Quarterly National Accounts* (OECD 1979, page 30), when several years are to be adjusted, the process cannot be directly "continued for years 2 and 3, years 3 and 4, etc., applying the correction factors for the 'first year' to year 2 (which has already been corrected once) and the correction factors for 'the second year' for year 3, and 4, etc." That is, the following generalized version of the multiplicative Bassie method *does not work*:

$$Z_{q,y} = X_{q,y} \cdot (1 + c_q \cdot K_y) \cdot (1 + b_q \cdot K_{y+1}) \qquad (6.A1.12)$$

6.A1.25. Example 6.A1.1, using the multiplicative version of the Bassie method, illustrates the working of the Bassie method as described in OECD (1979) and the step problem inherent in this version of the method when used for adjusting several years simultaneously.

6.A1.26. The break introduced by the use of the Bassie method, as applied above, is caused by the fact that the quarterly time series used in aligning the series to year 3 is not continuous. The time series used consists of the original data for year 3 and the data for year 2 aligned or benchmarked to the annual data for year 2. This discontinuity is carried over into the revised series.

D. The Ginsburgh-Nasse Method

6.A1.27. Ginsburgh proposed a three-step method for distribution of annual data using a related quarterly series. He did not address the problem of extrapolation, or estimation of the forward series. By slightly reformulating the original presentation of the method along the lines suggested by Ginsburgh himself, however, the basic version of the QNA "regression-based" compilation system,[9] as originally formulated by Nasse (1973), for estimating both the back and the forward series emerges. In this section the following is shown:

- The Ginsburgh-Nasse method is in essence identical to the additive Denton (D1) method with a prior adjustment of the indicator for any significant average difference between the level of the indicator and the target variable.
- For both the back and forward series, the Ginsburgh-Nasse method and the D1 method with prior level adjustment result in identical estimates.
- The regression component of the Ginsburgh-Nasse method constitutes an unnecessarily complicated and cumbersome way of prior adjusting the indicator for any significant average difference between the level of the indicator and the target variable.
- The same prior level adjustment can be obtained simply by using the ratio between the annual benchmark and the annual sum of the indicator for one year as an adjustment factor.

6.A1.28. Ginsburgh's proposal was to generate the benchmarked quarterly data by using the following three-step procedure:

(a) Estimate the "quarterly trend" of the annual data A_y and the annual sum of the indicator

$$I_y = \sum_q I_{q,y}$$

using a the following least-squares distribution formula:

$$\min_{(z_1,\dots,z_{4\beta})} \sum_{t=2}^{4\beta} \left[Z_t - Z_{t-1} \right]^2$$

under the restriction that

$$\sum_{t=4y-3}^{4\beta} Z_t = A_y \quad t \in \{1,\dots(4\beta)\}, \; y \in \{1,\dots\beta\},$$

---

[9] As presented in for instance Dureau (1995).

where $Z_t = \hat{A}_t$ and $\hat{I}_t$, respectively. Denote the resulting quarterized series $\hat{A}_{q,y}$ and $\hat{I}_{q,y}$.

(b) Use the standard ordinary-least-squares (OLS) technique to estimate the parameters of the following annual linear regression equation:

$$A_y = f(I_y) = a + b \cdot I_y + \varepsilon_y, \qquad (6.A1.13)$$
$$E(\varepsilon_y) = 0, \quad y \in \{1,....\beta\}$$

where

ε_y stands for the error term assumed to be random with an expected value equal to zero; and
a and b are fixed parameters to be estimated.

(c) Finally, derive the benchmarked data for the back series as follows:

$$X_{q,y} = \hat{A}_{q,y} + \hat{b} \cdot (I_{q,y} - \hat{I}_{q,y}) \qquad (6.A1.14)$$
$$q \in \{1,...4\}, y \in \{1,...\beta\}$$

where $\hat{b}$ is the estimated value of the fixed parameter b in equation (6.A1.13).

6.A1.29. As shown by Ginsburgh, the derived benchmarked series in equation (6.A1.14) can equivalently be derived by solving the following least-squares minimization problem:

$$\min_{(X_1...,X_{4\beta})} \sum_{t=2}^{4\beta} \left[(X_t - X_{t-1}) - \hat{b} \cdot (I_t - I_{t-1}) \right]^2 \qquad (6.A1.15)$$

This equation reduces to the additive Denton (D1) formula in equation (6.A1.1) if $\hat{b}$ is close to 1.

6.A1.30. In equation (6.A1.15), the parameter $\hat{b}$ serves to adjust for the average difference between the level of indicator and the target variable and thus helps mitigate one of the major weaknesses of the standard additive Denton formula. The parameter a, in the linear regression equation (6.A1.13), serves to adjust for any systematic difference (bias) in the average movements of the indicator and target variable. The parameter a does not appear in equations (6.A1.14) or (6.A1.15), however, and thus in the end serves no role in deriving the estimates for the back series.

6.A1.31. The basic set-up of the QNA "regression-based" compilation system proposed by Nasse is the following:

(a) Use an estimated econometric relationship such as in step (b) of the Ginsburgh method above to derive preliminary (nonbenchmarked) QNA time series $(X_{q,y}^p)$ as

$$X_{q,y}^p = \hat{a}/4 + \hat{b} \cdot I_{q,y}, \quad y \in \{1,....\beta\} \qquad (6.A1.16)$$

where $\hat{a}$ is the estimated value of the fixed parameter a in equation (6.A1.13).

(b) Compute the difference between the annual sums of the quarterly estimates derived by using equation (6.A1.16) and the corresponding independent annual data as follows:

$$\hat{\varepsilon}_y = A_y - \sum_q X_{q,y}^p \neq 0 \qquad (6.A1.17)$$

The OLS estimation technique will ensure that the error term sums to zero over the estimation period ($\sum_y \sum_q \varepsilon_{q,y} = 0$) but will not ensure that the annual sum of the error term is equal to zero.

(c) Generate a smooth continuous time series of error terms for year 1 to β using the following least-squares minimization expression:

$$\min_{(\varepsilon_1...,\varepsilon_{4\beta})} \sum_{t=2}^{4\beta} \left[\varepsilon_t - \varepsilon_{t-1} \right]^2, \qquad (6.A1.18)$$

$$y \in \{1,....\beta\}$$

under the restriction that $\sum_{t=4y-3}^{4y} \varepsilon_t = \varepsilon_y$

(d) Finally, derive the benchmarked data for both the back and the forward series as follows:

For the back series,
$$X_{q,y} = \hat{a}/4 + \hat{b} \cdot I_{q,y} + \hat{\varepsilon}_{q,y} \qquad (6.A1.19)$$
$$y \in \{1,....\beta\}$$

For the forward series,
$$X_{q,y} = \hat{a}/4 + \hat{b} \cdot I_{q,y} + \hat{\varepsilon}_{4,\beta} \qquad (6.A1.20)$$
$$y \in \{\beta + 1,.....\}$$

6.A1.32. By combining equations (6.A1.17), (6.A1.18), (6.A1.19), and (6.A1.20), it can be shown that steps (b) to (d) above reduce to

$$\min_{(X_1...,X_{4\beta},......X_{4y})} \sum_{t=2}^{4y} \left[(X_t - X_{t-1}) - \hat{b} \cdot (I_t - I_{t-1}) \right]^2 \qquad (6.A1.21)$$

and thus become identical to the Ginsburgh method in equation (6.A1.15), expanded slightly to also encompass the forward series. Again, observe that the parameter $\hat{a}$ does not appear in equation (6.A1.21) and thus in the end serves no role in deriving the estimates, even for the forward series.

6.A1.33. Equations (6.A1.15) and (6.A1.21) show that the Ginsburgh-Nasse method does not represent any real difference from the additive Denton (D1) method for the following two reasons. First, and most importantly, the regression approach does not provide any additional adjustment for the existence of any bias in the indicator's movements compared with the basic additive Denton method, neither for the back series nor for the forward series. Second, regression analysis represents an unnecessarily complicated way of adjusting for any significant average difference between the level of the indicator and the target variable. This average-level-difference adjustment can be obtained much more easily by a simple rescaling of the original indicator, using the ratio between the annual benchmark and the annual sum of the indicator for one year as the adjustment factor. Thus, as shown, the Ginsburgh-Nasse method in the end constitutes an *unnecessarily complicated and cumbersome*[10] *way of obtaining for both the back and the forward series the same estimates that can be obtained much easier by using the D1 method.*

6.A1.34. As with most additive adjustment formulations, the Ginsburgh-Nasse and D1 methods tend to smooth away some of the quarter-to-quarter rates of change in the indicator series. As a consequence, they can seriously disturb that aspect of the short-term movements for series that show strong short-term variations.[11] This can particularly occur if there is a substantial difference between the level of the indicator and the target variable.

6.A1.35. The procedure set out in (a) to (d) above has also been criticized (Bournay and Laroque 1979) as being inconsistent in terms of statistical models. OLS regression assumes that the errors are not autocorrelated. This is inconsistent with the smooth distribution of the annual errors in equation (6.A1.18), which implies an assumption that the errors are perfectly autocorrelated with a unit autocorrelation coefficient. This inconsistency may not have any significant impact on the back series but may imply that it is possible to obtain a better estimate for the forward series by incorporating any known information on the errors' autocorrelation structure.

6.A1.36. The procedure can also be criticized for being sensitive to spurious covariance between the series. Formulating the econometric relationship as a relationship between *the level of non-stationary time series* renders the danger of primarily measuring apparent correlations caused by the strong trend usually shown by economic time series.

6.A1.37. Compared with the enhanced version of the proportional Denton method, the Ginsburgh-Nasse and D1 methods have two additional distinct disadvantages, namely:[12]
(a) They will only partly adjust for any systematic bias in the indicator's annual movements if the bias is substantial relative to any amount of noise.
(b) They will, on average, lead to relatively larger revisions (a wagging tail effect) if the amount of noise is substantial relative to any bias in the indicator's annual movements.

6.A1.38. The potential wagging tail effect that the Ginsburgh-Nasse and D1 methods suffer from is associated with the inconsistent use of statistical models mentioned above (paragraph 6.A1.35). In particular, estimating the forward series by carrying forward the estimated error term for the fourth quarter of the last benchmark year $\hat{\varepsilon}_{q,\beta}$ is inconsistent with the assumptions underlying the use of OLS to estimate the parameters of equation (6.A1.13). To see this, assume for the sake of the argument that the statistical model in equation (6.A1.13) is correctly specified and thus that the annual error term ε_y is not autocorrelated and has a zero mean. Then the best forecast for the next annual discrepancy $\hat{\varepsilon}_{\beta+1}$ would be zero and not $4 \cdot \hat{\varepsilon}_{\beta+1}$ as implied by equation (6.A1.20).

---

[10]In contrast to the D1 method, the regression approach also requires very long time series for all indicators.
[11]Some of the countries using these additive methods partly circumvent the problem by applying them only on seasonally adjusted source data. However, other short-term variations in the data will still be partly smoothed away, and, as explained in Chapter I, loss of the original non-seasonally adjusted estimates is a significant problem in itself.

[12]The basic version of the proportional Denton also suffers from these weaknesses. A detailed discussion of these issues with respect to the D4 formula is provided in Annex 6.2. The discussion in Annex 6.2 is also applicable to the D1 formula, with the only difference being how the annual movements are expressed: as additive changes in the case of the D1 formula and as relative changes (growth rates) in the case of the D4 formula.

E. Arima-Model-Based Methods

6.A1.39. The ARIMA-model-based method proposed by Hillmer and Trabelsi (1987) provides one method for taking into account any known information about the stochastic properties of the series being benchmarked. As for most of the statistical modeling methods, the method was proposed in the context of improving survey estimates, where the survey design may provide identifiable information about parts of the stochastic properties of the series (the sampling part of the underlying error-generating mechanism). Clearly, incorporating any such information, if available, in the estimation procedure may potentially improve the estimates. In the QNA context, however, this information about the stochastic properties of the series is usually non-existent. Furthermore, non-sampling errors in the surveys may often be more important than sampling errors, and incorporating only partial information about the underlying error-generating mechanism may introduce systematic errors.

6.A1.40. The main advantages of the enhanced proportional Denton method over the ARIMA-model-based methods in the QNA compilation context are the following:
- The enhanced proportional Denton method is much simpler, more robust, and better suited for large-scale applications.
- The enhanced proportional Denton method avoids the danger associated with the ARIMA-model-based method of over-adjusting the series by interpreting as errors, and thus removing, true irregular movements that do not fit the regular patterns of the statistical model.
- The enhanced proportional Denton method avoids the danger of substantially disturbed estimates resulting from misspecification of the autocovariance structure of the quarterly and annual error terms in the ARIMA-model-based method.
- The enhanced proportional Denton method allows for extrapolation taking into account fully the existence of any systematic bias or lack thereof in the year-to-year rate of change in the indicator. In contrast, the proposed ARIMA-model-based method does not accommodate any bias in the indicator's movements.

6.A1.41. The core idea behind the Hillmer-Trabelsi ARIMA-model-based method is to assume the following:

(a) That the quarterly time series is observed with an additive error, $I_{q,y} = \theta_{q,y} + \varepsilon_{q,y}$ where $\theta_{q,y}$ represents the true but unknown quarterly values of the series and is assumed to follow an ARIMA model. The error term $\varepsilon_{q,y}$ is assumed to have zero mean and to follow a known ARMA[13] model. Assuming that the error term has zero mean implies that the observed series is assumed to be an unbiased estimate of the true series.

(b) That the annual benchmarks also are observed with an additive error with zero mean and known autocovariance structure. That is, the annual benchmarks follow the model: $A_y = \sum_q \theta_{q,y} + \xi_y$ where ξ_y represents the annual error term, and is assumed independent of $\varepsilon_{q,y}$ and $\eta_{q,y}$.

Based on the assumed time-series models and assumed known autocovariance structures, Hillmer and Trabelsi obtain the quarterly benchmarked series using what the time-series literature refers to as "signal extraction."

F. General Least-Squares Regression Models

6.A1.42. An alternative, and potentially better, method to take into account any known information about the stochastic properties of the underlying error-generating process is represented by the alternative general-least-squares (GLS) regression models proposed by various Statistics Canada staff.

6.A1.43. The advantages of the enhanced proportional Denton method over the GLS regression model methods, in the QNA compilation context, are basically the same as the advantages over the ARIMA-model-based method listed in paragraph 6.A1.40 above.

6.A1.44. The following three models constitute the core of Statistics Canada's benchmarking program "Program Bench":
- The additive model (Cholette and Dagum 1994)

$$I_t = a + \theta_t + \varepsilon_t, \qquad (6.A1.22a)$$
$$E(\varepsilon_t) = 0, \quad E(\varepsilon_t \varepsilon_{t-k}) \neq 0$$
$$t \ \& \ k \in \{1,...(4\beta),....T\}, \quad y \in \{1,...\beta\}$$

$$A_y = \sum_{t=4y-3}^{4y} \theta_t + w_y, \qquad (6.A1.22b)$$

$$E(w_y) = 0, \quad E(w_y w_{t-k}) \neq 0$$

---

[13]Autoregressive moving average.

where

a is an unknown constant bias parameter to be estimated;

θ_t is the true but unknown quarterly values to be estimated;

ε_t is the quarterly error term associated with the observed indicator and is assumed to have zero mean and a known autocovariance structure; and

w_y is the annual error term associated with the observed benchmarks and is assumed to have zero mean and a known autocovariance structure. The benchmarks will be binding if the variance of the annual error term is zero and non-binding if the variance is different from zero.

- The multiplicative model (Cholette 1994)

$$I_t = a \cdot \theta_t \cdot \varepsilon_t, \qquad (6.A1.23a)$$
$$E(\varepsilon_t) = 0, \quad E(\varepsilon_t\,\varepsilon_{t-k}) \neq 0$$

$$A_y = \sum_{t=4y-3}^{4y} \theta_t + w_y, \qquad (6.A1.23b)$$

$$E\big(w_y\big) = 0, \quad E\big(w_y w_{t-k}\big) \neq 0$$

- The mixed model (Laniel and Fyfe 1990)

$$I_t = a \cdot \theta_t + \varepsilon_t, \qquad (6.A1.24a)$$
$$E(\varepsilon_t) = 0, \quad E(\varepsilon_t\,\varepsilon_{t-k}) \neq 0$$

$$A_y = \sum_{t=4y-3}^{4y} \theta_t + w_y, \qquad (6.A1.24b)$$

$$E\big(w_y\big) = 0, \quad E\big(w_y w_{t-k}\big) \neq 0$$

6.A1.45. Cholette and Dagum (1994) provide the GLS solution to equation (6.A1.22) when the autocovariance structure of the annual and quarterly error terms is known. Similarly, Mian and Laniel (1993) provides the Maximum Likelihood solution to equation (6.A1.24) when the autocovariance structure of the annual and quarterly error terms is known.[14]

6.A1.46. The three GLS models are implemented in Statistics Canada's benchmarking program, assuming that the errors follow the following autocovariance structures:

$$E(\varepsilon_t) = 0, \qquad (6.A1.25a)$$
$$E(\varepsilon_t\,\varepsilon_{t-k}) \neq \sigma_{\varepsilon_t}\,\sigma_{\varepsilon_{t-1}}\,\rho_k$$

$$A_y = \sum_{t=4y-3}^{4y} \theta_t + w_y, \qquad (6.A1.25b)$$

$$E\big(w_y\big) = 0, \quad E\big(w_y^2\big) = \sigma_{w_y}^2$$

where

σ_{ε_t} is the standard deviation of the quarterly errors, which may vary with time t, meaning that the errors may be heteroscedastic;

ρ_k is a parameter indicating the degree of autocorrelation in the errors; and

$\sigma_{w_y}^2$ is the variance of the annual errors, which may vary with time y, meaning that the errors may be heteroscedastic.

and where the autocorrelations ρ_k corresponds to those of a stationary and invertible ARMA process whose parameter values are supplied by the users of the program. This is equivalent to assuming that the quarterly errors follow a time-series process given by $\varepsilon_t = \in_t \cdot \sigma_{\varepsilon_t}$ where $\in_t$ follows the selected ARMA process.

6.A1.47. The regression models in equation (6.A1.22) to (6.A1.25) can be used to approximate the D1, D3, and D4 versions of the Denton method above by specifying the autocovariance structure appropriately. The additive regression model in equation (6.A1.22) approximates D1 if

(a) the bias parameter is omitted;

(b) the benchmarks are binding (zero variances);

(c) the variances of the quarterly errors are constant; and

(d) the ARMA model specified approximates a random walk process (that is $\varepsilon_t = \sigma_{\varepsilon_t} \cdot (\varepsilon_{t-1} + v_t)$ where v_t represents "white noise").

Similarly, the additive regression model in equation (6.A1.22) approximates D4 if

(a) the bias parameter is omitted;

(b) the benchmarks are binding;

(c) the coefficients of variation (CVs, $\sigma_{\varepsilon_t}/\overline{\varepsilon}$ (where $\overline{\varepsilon}$ is the average error) of the quarterly errors are constant; and

(d) the ARMA model specified approximates a random walk process (that is $\varepsilon_t = \sigma_{\varepsilon_t} \cdot (\varepsilon_{t-1} + v_t)$ where σ_{ε_t} is given by the constant CVs).

Finally, the multiplicative regression model in equation (6.A1.24) approximates D3 if

(a) the benchmarks are binding;

(b) the coefficients of variation (CVs) of the quarterly errors are constant; and

(c) the ARMA model specified approximates a random walk process (that is, $\varepsilon_t = \sigma_{\varepsilon_t} \cdot (\varepsilon_{t-1} + v_t)$).

---

[14]The solutions are the "best linear unbiased estimates" (BLUE) under the given assumptions.

G. The Chow-Lin Method

6.A1.48. The Chow-Lin method for distribution and extrapolation of time series is basically a multiple-regression version of the additive GLS model in equation (6.A1.22) above with binding benchmarks. By relating several loosely related indicator series to one annual benchmark series, it does not represent a benchmarking method in a strict sense.

6.A1.49. The main advantages of the enhanced proportional Denton method over the Chow-Lin method are the same as listed above with respect to the GLS regression and ARIMA-model methods. In addition, the Chow-Lin method differs from the above GLS regression methods in the following two fundamental aspects that make it unsuitable for QNA purposes in most circumstances:[15]

- Multiple regression is conceptually fundamentally different from benchmarking. The Chow-Lin method gives the dangerous impression that quarterly estimates of GDP and other national accounts variables can be derived simply by estimating the annual correlation between the national accounts variables and a limited set of some loosely related quarterly source data. In contrast, benchmarking is about combining quarterly and annual source data for the same phenomena. At best, estimating the correlation between, for example, GDP and a set of available quarterly time series is a modeling approach to obtain forecasts or nowcasts of GDP, but it has nothing to do with compiling quarterly national accounts. Furthermore, as a modeling approach for forecasting it is overly simplified and may result in sub-optimal forecasts.

- The multiple-regression approach implicitly assumes that the (net) seasonal pattern of the related series is the same as that of the target aggregate, which is not very likely.

---

[15]The Chow-Lin multiple-regression method may have an application in filling minor gaps with synthetic data where no direct observations are available.

Annex 6.2. Extrapolation Base and the Forward Step Problem

A. Introduction

6.A2.1. The basic version of the proportional Denton method presented in Chapter VI uses the last quarter of the last benchmark year as the extrapolation base.[16] Arguments have been made for using alternative extrapolation bases. It is sometimes argued that using the last quarter of the last benchmark year as the extrapolation base may make the estimates vulnerable to errors in the source data for that quarter, and thus, it may be better to use the last annual average as the extrapolation base. Similarly, it is sometimes argued that to preserve the seasonal pattern of the series, the same quarter in the previous year should be used as the extrapolation base or, alternatively, that a strong seasonal pattern in the series may cause distortions to the estimates if they are not based on moving from the same quarter of the previous year.

6.A2.2. In this annex we will show that these arguments for using alternative extrapolation bases are not correct and that the alternative extrapolation bases generally should not be used. In particular, we will show that use of different extrapolation bases will result in different estimates only if the implied quarterly benchmark-indicator (BI) ratios for the back series differ from quarter to quarter and from the annual (BI) ratio; which they must do to avoid the back series step problem. In those circumstances:

- *The alternative extrapolation bases introduce a step between the back and forward series* that can seriously distort the seasonal pattern of the series.
- Using the last quarter of the last benchmark year as the extrapolation base will result in the following:[17]
  - ▸ It will partly adjust for any systematic bias in the indicator's annual rate of change if the bias is sufficiently large relative to any amount of noise, and

thus, on average, lead to smaller revisions in the quarterly national accounts (QNA) estimates.
  - ▸ It will create a wagging tail effect with, on average, larger revisions if the amount of noise is sufficiently large relative to any systematic bias in the annual growth rate of the indicator.

The annex also demonstrates that using the last quarter of the last benchmark year as the extrapolation base does not make the estimates more vulnerable to errors in the source data for that quarter. Numerical illustrations of these results are given in Examples 6.A2.1 and 6.A2.2, and Chart 6.A2.1.

B. Alternative Extrapolation Bases

6.A2.3. In mathematical terms the use of the alternative extrapolation bases can be formalized as follows:

(a) Fourth quarter of the last benchmark year as the extrapolation base:

$$X_{q,y} = X_{4,\beta} \cdot \left(\frac{I_{q,y}}{I_{4,\beta}} \right) = I_{q,y} \cdot \left(\frac{X_{4,\beta}}{I_{4,\beta}} \right) \qquad (6.A2.1)$$

$$q \in \{1,...4\}, \quad y \in \{\beta+1,...\}$$

(b) Quarterly average of the last benchmark year as the extrapolation base:

$$X_{q,y} = \frac{1}{4} \cdot A_\beta \cdot \left(\frac{I_{q,y}}{\frac{1}{4} \cdot \sum_q I_{q,\beta}} \right) \qquad (6.A2.2)$$

$$= I_{q,y} \cdot \left(\frac{A_\beta}{\sum_q I_{q,\beta}} \right)$$

$$q \in \{1,...4\}, \quad y \in \{\beta+1,...\}.$$

(c) Same quarter of the last benchmark year as the extrapolation base:

$$X_{q,y} = X_{q,\beta} \cdot \left(\frac{I_{q,y}}{I_{q,\beta}} \right) \qquad (6.A2.3)$$

$$= I_{q,y} \cdot \left(\frac{X_{q,\beta}}{I_{q,\beta}} \right)$$

$$q \in \{1,...4\}, \quad y \in \{\beta+1,...\}.$$

---

[16] In contrast, the recommended enhanced version of the proportional Denton presented in section C of Chapter VI does not use any specific extrapolation base.

[2] The enhanced version of the proportional Denton presented in section C of Chapter VI provides means for avoiding the potential wagging tail effect, and for fully adjusting for any systematic bias.

Example 6.A2.1. Extrapolation Bases and the Forward Step Problem

	Indicator	Annual Data	Annual BI Ratios	Quarterized BI Ratios	Estimates for 1998–1999 from 6.2.	Estimates for 2000 (a) Extrapolation of q4 1999 Estimates	BI Ratio Carried Forward
q1 1998	98.2			9.876	969.8		
q2 1998	100.8			9.905	998.4		
q3 1998	102.2			9.964	1,018.3		
q4 1998	100.8			10.054	1,013.4		
Sum	**402.0**	**4,000.0**	**9.950**	**9.950**	**4,000.0**		
q1 1999	99.0			10.174	1,007.2		
q2 1999	101.6			10.264	1,042.9		
q3 1999	102.7			10.325	1,060.3		
q4 1999	101.5			*10.355*	1,051.0		
Sum	**404.8**	**4,161.4**	**10.280**		**4,161.4**		
q1 2000	100.5					1,040.6	10.355
q2 2000	103.0					1,066.5	10.355
q3 2000	103.5					1,071.7	10.355
q4 2000	101.5					1,051.0	10.355
Sum	**408.5**					**4,229.9**	**10.355**

In this example, the following is worth observing:

First, during 1999 the quarterized BI ratio is increasing gradually (10.174, 10.264, 10.325, and 10.355), and consequently the quarter-to-quarter rate of change in the indicator differs from the quarter-to-quarter rates of change in the derived QNA estimates for 1999.

Second, the three different QNA estimates for 2000 can be derived by carrying forward the 1998 BI ratios as follows:
(a) Extrapolating the fourth quarter of 1999:
   q1,00=1040.6 = 100.5 · 10.355   q2,00=1066.5 = 103.0 · 10.355   q4,00=1051.0 = 101.5 · 10.355;
(b) Extrapolating the quarterly average for 1999:
   q1,00=1033.2 = 100.5 · 10.280   q2,00=1058.9 = 103.0 · 10.280   q4,00=1043.4 = 101.5 · 10.280; and
(c) Extrapolating the same quarter in 1999:
   q1,00=1022.5 = 100.5 · 10.174   q2,00=1057.2 = 103.0 · 10.264   q4,00=1051.0 = 101.5 · 10.355.

Third,
(a) Extrapolating the fourth quarter of 1999:
   preserves the quarter-to-quarter rate of changes in the indicator series;
(b) Extrapolating the quarterly average for 1999:
   results in **a break** between the fourth quarter of 1999 and the first quarter of 2000 (period-to-period rate of change of −1.7 and not −1.0% as shown in the indicator); and
(c) Extrapolating the same quarter in 1999:
   results in an **even more severe break** between the fourth quarter of 1999 and the first quarter of 2000 (period-to-period rate of change of −2.7% and not −1.0% as shown in the indicator).
In addition, the breaks between the fourth quarter of 1999 and the first quarter of 2000 introduced by using extrapolation bases (b) and (c) are introduced by a discontinuity in the time series of quarterized BI ratios. That is, when using extrapolation base (b) the BI ratio changes abruptly from 10.355 in the fourth quarter of 1999 to 10.28 in the first quarter of 2000, and when using extrapolation base (c) the BI ratio changes abruptly from 10.355 in the fourth quarter of 1999 to 10.174 in the first quarter of 2000.

Fourth,
(a) Extrapolating the fourth quarter of 1999:
   results in an estimated **annual rate of change** in the QNA series from 1999 to 2000 of 1.6%, which differs from the rate of change from 1999 to 2000 of 0.9% shown in the indicator series;
(b) Extrapolating the quarterly average for 1999:
   results in an estimated rate of change from 1999 to 2000, which is identical to the rate of change shown in the indicator series (0.9%); and
(c) Extrapolating the same quarter in 1999:
   results in an estimated annual rate of change from 1999 to 2000, which is identical to the rate of change shown in the indicator series (0.9%).

Fifth, if the difference of 3.0 percentage points between the rate of change from 1999 to 2000 in the ANA estimate and in the indicator is due to an average downward bias in the annual movements of the indicator of 3.0 percentage points, then the annual data for 2000 can be expected to show an annual rate of change from 1999 to 1999 of 4.0 percent. Thus, the estimate derived by using extrapolation base (a) will still be downward biased.

(These results are illustrated in Chart 6.A2.1.)

| | Estimates for 2000 | | | | Quarter-to-Quarter Rates of Change | | | |
| | (b) Extrapolation of the Average Quarter for 1999 | | (c) Extrapolation of the Same Quarter in the Previous Year | | | | | (c) Extrapolation of the Same Quarter in the Previous Year |
Estimates	BI Ratio Carried Forward	Estimates	BI ratios Carried Forward	Based on the Indicator	(a) Based q4 1999	(b) Based on average 1999	
				2.6%	3.0%		
				1.4%	2.0%		
				−1.4%	−0.5%		
	Identical for All Methods						
				−1.8%	−0.6%		
				2.6%	3.5%		
				1.1%	1.7%		
				−1.2%	−0.9%		
				0.7%	4.0%		
1,033.2	10.280	1,022.5	10.174	−1.0%	−1.0%	−1.7%	−2.7%
1,058.9	10.280	1,057.2	10.264	2.5%	2.5%	2.5%	3.4%
1,064.0	10.280	1,068.6	10.325	0.5%	0.5%	0.5%	1.1%
1,043.4	10.280	1,051.0	10.355	−1.9%	−1.9%	−1.9%	−1.6%
4,199.4	**10.280**	**4,199.3**	**10.280**	**0.9%**	**1.6%**	**0.9%**	**0.9%**

Chart 6.A2.1. Alternative Extrapolation Bases and the Forward Step Problem

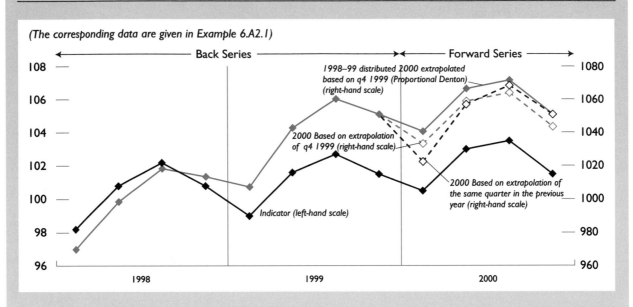

(The corresponding data are given in Example 6.A2.1)

In this example, the **step problem** shows up as a decrease in the derived series from q4 1999 to q1 2000 that is not matched by the movements in the source data. The quarter-to-quarter rate of change for the first quarter of 1999 of **−1.0%** in source data is **−1.0%**. In contrast, the corresponding rate of change in the estimates derived by extrapolating the average of 1999 is **−1.7%**, and the corresponding rate of change in the estimates derived by extrapolating the same quarter of 1999 is **−2.7%**.

Benchmark-to-Indicator Ratio

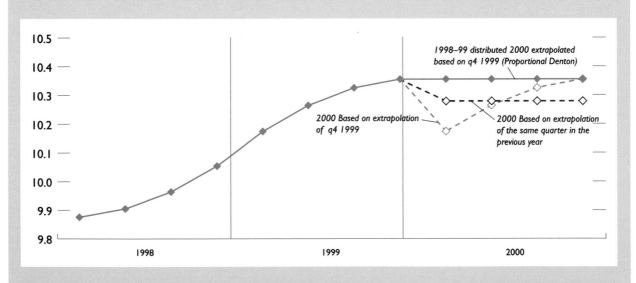

It is easier to recognize the step problem from charts of the BI ratio, where it shows up as abrupt upward or downward steps in the BI ratios between q4 of one year and q1 of the next year. In this example, the step problem shows up as a large upward jump in the BI ratio between q4 1999 and q1 2000.

6.A2.4. The use of different extrapolation bases will result in different estimates only if the implied quarterly BI ratios for the back series differ from quarter to quarter and from the annual BI ratio. That is, if

$$\left(X_{4,\beta}/I_{4,\beta}\right) \neq \left(X_{q,\beta}/I_{q,\beta}\right) \neq \left(A_{\beta}/\sum_q I_{q,\beta}\right).$$

6.A2.5. In Section C of Chapter VI it is explained that to avoid the back series step problem, the implied quarterly BI ratios $(X_{q,y}/I_{q,y})$ must differ from quarter to quarter and from the annual BI ratio. Thus, different extrapolation bases will give different estimates when the back series is derived using benchmarking methods that avoid the (back series) step problem associated with pro rata distribution.

C. The Forward Step Problem

6.A2.6. The forward step problem associated with extrapolation bases (b) and (c) above is caused by a discontinuity in the implied quarterly BI ratios. To keep the benchmarked series as proportional as possible to the original quarterly source data, the proportional Denton method generates quarterly BI ratios that for the last year covered by annual data either increase or decrease gradually. Consequently, the quarterly BI ratio for the last quarter of the last benchmark year may differ significantly from the annual BI ratio and even more from the quarterly BI ratio for the first quarter of the last benchmark year. It follows that:
- Extrapolation base (b) introduces an upward step if

$$\left(A_{\beta}/\sum_{q=1}^4 I_{q,\beta}\right) > \left(X_{4,\beta}/I_{4,\beta}\right), \text{ or}$$

a downward step if

$$\left(A_{\beta}/\sum_{q=1}^4 I_{q,\beta}\right) < \left(X_{4,\beta}/I_{4,\beta}\right).$$

- Extrapolation base (c) introduces an upward step if
$$\left(X_{1,b}/I_{1,b}\right) > \left(X_{4,b}/I_{4,b}\right), \text{ or}$$

a downward step if

$$\left(X_{1,b}/I_{1,b}\right) < \left(X_{4,b}/I_{4,b}\right).$$

6.A2.7 It also follows that the step introduced by using the same quarter of the previous year as the extrapolation base (base iii) will always be more severe than the step caused by using the annual average as the extrapolation base (base ii).

D. Annual Rate of Change in the Derived Forward Series

6.A2.8. Using the last quarter of the last benchmark year as the extrapolation base implies adjusting the source data for all subsequent quarters with a factor that systematically differs from the average adjustment in the last benchmark year. This is the cause for the difference between the annual growth rate in the source data and the annual growth rate in the estimates derived by using the basic version of the proportional Denton for the first year of the forward series.[18] It follows that using extrapolation base (a) will result in an annual rate of change for the first year of the forward series that is
- higher than the corresponding change in the source data if

$$\left(A_{\beta}/\sum_{q=1}^4 I_{q,\beta}\right) < \left(X_{4,\beta}/I_{4,\beta}\right), \text{ or}$$

- lower than the corresponding change in the source data if

$$\left(A_{\beta}/\sum_{q=1}^4 I_{q,\beta}\right) > \left(X_{4,\beta}/I_{4,\beta}\right).$$

6.A2.9. The relative difference between the annual changes in the derived QNA estimates and the corresponding changes in the indicator is equal to the relative difference between the quarterly BI ratio for the fourth quarter and the annual average BI ratio of the last benchmark year. This can be shown mathematically as follows:

---

[18]In contrast, it can be shown that the corresponding annual growth rates obtained by using extrapolation base (b) or (c) will for base (b) be identical, and for base (c) approximately identical, to the annual growth rates in the source data. Note that this may not be a desirable property if there is significant bias in the indicator's annual rate of movements.

The ratio of annual change in the derived estimates is equal to

$$\sum_{q=1}^{4} X_{q,y} \Big/ \sum_{q=4}^{4} X_{q,\beta} \, .$$

The ratio of annual change in the indicator is equal to

$$\sum_{q=1}^{4} I_{q,y} \Big/ \sum_{q=1}^{4} I_{q,\beta} \quad (y = \beta + 1).$$

The ratio between these two expressions is equal to the relative difference between the annual changes in the derived estimates and in the indicator, and can be written as

$$\frac{\displaystyle\sum_{q=1}^{4} X_{q,y}}{\displaystyle\sum_{q=1}^{4} X_{q,\beta}} \Bigg/ \frac{\displaystyle\sum_{q=1}^{4} I_{q,y}}{\displaystyle\sum_{q=1}^{4} I_{q,\beta}} = \qquad (6A2.4)$$

$$\frac{\displaystyle\sum_{q=1}^{4} \frac{X_{4,\beta}}{I_{4,\beta}} \cdot I_{q,y}}{A_\beta} \Bigg/ \frac{\displaystyle\sum_{q=1}^{4} I_{q,y}}{\displaystyle\sum_{q=1}^{4} I_{q,\beta}} =$$

$$\frac{X_{4,\beta}}{I_{4,\beta}} \Bigg/ \frac{A_\beta}{\displaystyle\sum_{q=1}^{4} I_{q,\beta}}$$

where we have used that

$$X_{q,y} = \frac{X_{4,\beta}}{I_{4,\beta}} \cdot I_{q,y}$$

(from equation (6.A2.1)) and that

$$\sum_{q=1}^{4} X_{q,\beta} = A_\beta .$$

The last expression in equation (6A2.4) is the relative difference between the BI ratio for the fourth quarter and the annual average BI ratio of the last benchmark year.

6.A2.10. Using the last quarter of the last benchmark year as the extrapolation base will result in the following:[19]

- It will partly adjust for any systematic bias in the annual growth rate of the indicator if the bias is sufficiently large relative to any amount of noise and thus, in those circumstances, give on average relatively smaller revisions in the derived QNA estimates.
- It will create a wagging tail effect with, on average, larger revisions in the derived QNA estimates if the amount of noise is sufficiently large relative to any systematic bias in the annual growth rate of the indicator.

6.A2.11. To see this, consider the case in which the annual rate of change in the indicator is consistently downward biased and in which the amount of noise is zero. Then, by definition, the ratio between the annual rate of change in the annual national accounts (ANA) estimates and the annual rate of change in the indicator will be constant and larger than one:

$$\left(A_y / A_{y-1} \right) \Bigg/ \left(\sum_{q=1}^{4} I_{q,y} \right) = \delta,$$

where δ is a fixed bias parameter.

In that case, the annual BI ratio will be increasing with a constant rate from year to year:

$$\left(A_y \Big/ \sum_{q=1}^{4} I_{q,y} \right) = \delta \cdot \left(A_{y-1} \Big/ \sum_{q=1}^{4} I_{q,y-1} \right).$$

6.A2.12. Quarterizing a time series of annual BI ratios that increases with a constant rate will result in a time series of quarterly BI ratios that also increases steadily from quarter to quarter. In particular, the quarterized BI ratio will be increasing through the last benchmark year,[20] and thus, in this case, the BI ratio for the fourth quarter will always be larger than the annual BI ratio for the last benchmark year:

$$\left(X_{4,\beta} / I_{4,\beta} \right) > \left(A_\beta \Big/ \sum_{q=1}^{4} I_{q,\beta} \right).$$

6.A2.13. Thus, as explained in paragraph 6.A2.8, in this case, using extrapolation base (a) will result in an annual change in the estimated QNA variable that is higher than the corresponding change in the

[19]Note that the enhanced version presented in Section C of Chapter VI provides means for avoiding the potential wagging tail effect and for fully adjusting for any bias.

[20]The increase will taper off toward the end of the series if the series is based on a first difference least-square expression such as equation (6. 4) in Chapter VI.

indicator, as desired. If the rate of change in the indicator is upward biased, then $\delta < 1$ and the line of arguments in paragraphs 6.A2.11 and 6A2.12 applies in the opposite direction.

6.A2.14 The adjustment for bias in the annual growth rate of the indicator will be partial only because, as can be shown, the BI ratio for the fourth quarter will, at the same time, be smaller than the product of the bias parameter and the last annual BI ratio:

$$\left(X_{4,\beta}/I_{4,\beta}\right) < \delta \cdot \left(A_\beta \Big/ \sum_{q=1}^{4} I_{q,\beta}\right).$$

To fully correct for the bias in the indicator, the average adjustment of the indicator for the current years should have been equal to the product of the bias parameter and the last annual BI ratio. The enhanced version of the proportional Denton presented in Chapter VI provides means for fully adjusting for any persistent bias.

6.A2.15. The potential wagging tail effect is caused by erratic variations around the fixed bias parameter in the year-to-year increase of the annual BI ratio. As a consequence:
- The BI ratio for the fourth quarter may sometimes be larger than the product of the bias parameter and the last annual BI ratio, resulting in an annual change in the estimated QNA variable that is higher than the expected change in the annual data.
- The quarterized BI ratio may sometimes be decreasing through the last benchmark year, resulting in an annual change in the estimated QNA variable that is lower than in the indicator and lower than the expected change in the annual data.

The enhanced version of the proportional Denton presented in Chapter VI provides means for avoiding this wagging tail effect.

E. Extrapolation Base and Robustness Toward Errors in the Indicator

6.A2.16. Using a single quarter as the extrapolation base does not make the estimates particularly vulnerable to errors in the source data for that quarter. It is sometimes erroneously argued that using extrapolation base (b) gives more robust estimates than using extrapolation base (a). The idea behind this view is that basing the estimates on just one quarter makes them more vulnerable to errors in the indicator. The difference between the estimates derived by using extrapolation base (a) and (b), however, is solely caused by the movements in the quarterized BI ratio during the last benchmark year, which again is mainly a function of the annual BI ratios for that year and the previous years. In particular, as shown in Example 6.A2.2 below, the BI ratio for the fourth quarter of the last benchmark year is almost totally independent of the indicator value for that quarter.

F. Extrapolation Base and Seasonality

6.A2.17. It should be evident from the above that to preserve the seasonal pattern of the series, the same quarter in the previous year generally should not be used as the extrapolation base. As shown, it can introduce an unintended step problem if used together with benchmarking methods that avoid the back series step problem by keeping the derived series as parallel as possible to the source data. In contrast, extrapolation base (a) transmits to the QNA estimate the indicator's seasonal pattern as unchanged as possible, which is what is generally being sought.

6.A2.18. Use of the same quarter in the previous year as the extrapolation base is only acceptable in the following rare circumstance:
- annual benchmarks are not available for more than one year;
- the indicator and the target variable have different seasonal patterns; and
- initial quarterly estimates are available, with a proper seasonal pattern, for a base year.

Example 6.A2.2.   Extrapolation Base and Robustness Toward Errors in the Indicator

Date	Original Indicator from Example 6.2	Revised Indicator	Annual Data	Annual BI Ratios	Original Estimates from Example 6.2.	Original Quarterized BI Ratios	New Quarterized BI Ratios	Estimates Based on the Revised Indicator	Quarter–to–Quarter Rates of Change		
									Based on the Original Estimates from Example 6.2	Based on the Revised Indicator	Estimates Based on the Revised Indicator
q1 1998	98.2	98.2			969.8	9.876	9.875	969.7			
q2 1998	100.8	100.8			998.4	9.905	9.904	998.4	3.0%	2.6%	3.0%
q3 1998	102.2	102.2			1,018.3	9.964	9.964	1,018.4	2.0%	1.4%	2.0%
q4 1998	100.8	100.8			1,013.4	10.054	10.055	1,013.6	−0.5%	−1.4%	−0.5%
Sum	402.0	402.0	4,000.0	9.950	4,000.0			4,000.0			
q1 1999	99.0	99.0			1,007.2	10.174	10.176	1,007.5	−0.6%	−1.8%	−0.6%
q2 1999	101.6	101.6			1,042.9	10.264	10.268	1,043.2	3.5%	2.6%	3.5%
q3 1999	102.7	132.7			1,060.3	10.325	10.329	1,370.7	1.7%	30.6%	31.4%
q4 1999	101.5	71.5			1,051.0	10.355	10.350	740.1	−0.9%	−46.1%	−46.0%
Sum	404.8	404.8	4,161.4	10.280	4,161.4			4,161.4			
q1 2000	100.5	100.5			1,040.6	10.355	10.350	1,040.2	−1.0%	40.6%	40.6%
q2 2000	103.0	103.0			1,066.5	10.355	10.350	1,066.1	2.5%	2.5%	2.5%
q3 2000	103.5	103.5			1,071.7	10.355	10.350	1,071.2	0.5%	0.5%	0.5%
q4 2000	101.5	101.5			1,051.0	10.355	10.350	1,050.5	−1.9%	−1.9%	−1.9%
Sum	408.5	408.5			4,229.8	10.355	10.350	4,228.0	1.6%	0.9%	1.6%

In this example the following is worth observing:
First, compared with Example 6.2 the values of the indicator for the third and fourth quarter of 1999 have been substantially changed, but the annual sum of the quarterly values of the indicator, and thus the annual BI ratio, for 1999 is not changed. The data for 2000 are also not changed.

Second, in spite of the big changes in the 1999 data, the quarterized BI ratio for the fourth quarter of 1999 is almost the same as in Example 6.2 (10.350 versus 10.355). This demonstrates that the quarterized BI ratio for the fourth quarter of the last benchmark year is almost totally independent of the value of the indicator for that quarter and that it is mainly a function of the annual BI ratios.

Annex 6.3. First-Order Conditions for the Proportional Denton Benchmarking Formula

6.A3.1. The first-order conditions for a minimum of the proportional Denton adjustment formula can be found with the help of the following Lagrange-function:

$$L\left(X_1...X_{4y}\right) = \sum_{t=2}^{4y}\left[\frac{X_t}{I_t} - \frac{X_{t-1}}{I_{t-1}}\right]^2 + 2\lambda_y\left[\sum_{t=4y-3}^{4y} X_t - A_y\right],$$

(6.A3.1)

$$t \in \{1,...(4,\beta),....T\}, \quad y \in \{1,...\beta\}.$$

6.A3.2. Which has the following first order conditions:

$$\frac{\delta L}{\delta X_1} = \frac{1}{I_1^2}\cdot X_1 - \frac{1}{I_1\cdot I_2}\cdot X_2 + \lambda_1 = 0$$

(6.A3.2)

$$\frac{\delta L}{\delta X_2} = -\frac{1}{I_1\cdot I_2}\cdot X_1 + \frac{2}{I_2^2}\cdot X_2 - \frac{1}{I_2\cdot I_3}\cdot X_3 + \lambda_1 = 0$$

.
.

$$\frac{\delta L}{\delta X_5} = -\frac{1}{I_4\cdot I_5}\cdot X_4 + \frac{2}{I_5^2}\cdot X_5 - \frac{1}{I_5\cdot I_6}\cdot X_6 + \lambda_2 = 0$$

.
.
.

$$\frac{\delta L}{\delta X_t} = -\frac{1}{I_{t-1}\cdot I_t}\cdot X_{t-1} + \frac{2}{I_t^2}\cdot X_t - \frac{1}{I_t\cdot I_{t+1}}\cdot X_{t+1} + \lambda_y = 0, \ \text{ for } t \le (4\beta\}$$

$$\frac{\delta L}{\delta X_t} = -\frac{1}{I_{t-1}\cdot I_t}\cdot X_{t-1} + \frac{2}{I_t^2}\cdot X_t - \frac{1}{I_t\cdot I_{t+1}}\cdot X_{t+1} = 0, \ \text{ for } t > (4\beta\}$$

.
.
.

$$\frac{\delta L}{\delta X_T} = -\frac{1}{I_{T-1}\cdot I_T}\cdot X_{T-1} + \frac{1}{I_T^2}\cdot X_T - \frac{1}{I_T\cdot I_{T+1}}\cdot X_{T+1} + \lambda_y = 0, \ \text{ for } T = (4\beta\}$$

$$\frac{\delta L}{\delta X_T} = -\frac{1}{I_{T-1}\cdot I_T}\cdot X_{T-1} + \frac{1}{I_T^2}\cdot X_T = 0, \ \text{ for } t > (4\beta\}$$

6.A3.3. These first-order conditions, together with the benchmark restriction(s)

(in this case, $\displaystyle\sum_{t=4y-3}^{4y} X_t = A_y$),

constitute a system of linear equations. In matrix notation, $I \cdot X = A$, and for a two-year adjustment period with $T = 4\beta = 8$, matrix I and vector X and A are the following:

$$
I = \left[\begin{array}{cccccccc|cc}
\dfrac{1}{I_1^2} & \dfrac{-1}{I_1 \cdot I_2} & 0 & 0 & 0 & 0 & 0 & 0 & 1 & 0 \\[2ex]
\dfrac{-1}{I_1 \cdot I_2} & \dfrac{2}{I_2^2} & \dfrac{-1}{I_1 \cdot I_2} & 0 & 0 & 0 & 0 & 0 & 1 & 0 \\[2ex]
0 & \dfrac{-1}{I_2 \cdot I_3} & \dfrac{2}{I_3^2} & \dfrac{-1}{I_3 \cdot I_4} & 0 & 0 & 0 & 0 & 1 & 0 \\[2ex]
0 & 0 & \dfrac{-1}{I_3 \cdot I_4} & \dfrac{2}{I_4^2} & \dfrac{-1}{I_4 \cdot I_5} & 0 & 0 & 0 & 1 & 0 \\[2ex]
0 & 0 & 0 & \dfrac{-1}{I_4 \cdot I_5} & \dfrac{2}{I_5^2} & \dfrac{-1}{I_5 \cdot I_6} & 0 & 0 & 0 & 1 \\[2ex]
0 & 0 & 0 & 0 & \dfrac{-1}{I_5 \cdot I_6} & \dfrac{2}{I_6^2} & \dfrac{-1}{I_6 \cdot I_7} & 0 & 0 & 1 \\[2ex]
0 & 0 & 0 & 0 & 0 & \dfrac{-1}{I_6 \cdot I_7} & \dfrac{2}{I_7^2} & \dfrac{-1}{I_7 \cdot I_8} & 0 & 1 \\[2ex]
0 & 0 & 0 & 0 & 0 & 0 & \dfrac{-1}{I_7 \cdot I_8} & \dfrac{1}{I_8^2} & 0 & 1 \\[2ex]
\hline
1 & 1 & 1 & 1 & 0 & 0 & 0 & 0 & 0 & 0 \\[1ex]
0 & 0 & 0 & 0 & 1 & 1 & 1 & 1 & 0 & 0
\end{array}\right]
\quad
X = \begin{bmatrix} X_1 \\ X_2 \\ X_3 \\ X_4 \\ X_5 \\ X_6 \\ X_7 \\ X_8 \\ \lambda_1 \\ \lambda_2 \end{bmatrix}
\quad
A = \begin{bmatrix} 0 \\ 0 \\ 0 \\ 0 \\ 0 \\ 0 \\ 0 \\ 0 \\ A_1 \\ A_2 \end{bmatrix}
$$

VII Mechanical Projections

A. Introduction

7.1. This chapter presents some relatively simple techniques that can be used to fill information gaps with synthetic data using mechanical projections based on past trends. Note that this is a fundamentally different situation from the situation described in the previous chapter in that indicators are not available, although there are some similarities in the mathematics. Reliance on mechanical trend projection techniques is only justifiable if the gaps are few and minor because over-reliance on these techniques can easily impart a fictional character to the accounts and does not add any information about current trends. Furthermore, historic trends that are no longer relevant could muffle current trends that would be visible from other components calculated from actual direct or indirect indicators. Thus, as far as possible, quarterly national account (QNA) estimates should be based on direct observations of the relevant detailed accounting item, and QNA compilers should constantly be on the lookout for possibilities to improve the coverage of the economy with relevant source data.

7.2. Although great caution should be used in applying any of these techniques, there may be situations in which they are a last resort solution to covering gaps in the coverage of the economy. Even in the situation of well-established QNA that are underpinned by an extensive set of short-term data, there may be some economic activities for which no timely direct or indirect indicators are available. When that is the case, we can distinguish two situations: (a) no directly relevant short-term source data are available at all, and (b) an indicator becomes available with a time lag that bars its use in the compilation of the QNA. Obviously, the latter situation is more prominent for the first estimates of a quarter than for second or third estimates.

7.3. Compilation of national accounts requires that the whole economy be covered and thus all data gaps be filled, explicitly or implicitly. If QNA data are compiled from both the production and the expenditure side (which is a key recommendation of this manual), the confrontation of supply and demand can help in filling some gaps, and in fact this is recommended for estimating changes in inventories if no direct observations are available. Using the balancing process as an estimation process, however, diminishes the power of the plausibility checks that are such a strong advantage of the commodity flow method. Thus, it is recommended that estimates be generated for all elements of the commodity flow equation, even if some of the estimates are less than satisfactory. Obviously, the less satisfactory estimates are the first choice for making adjustments if the balancing process requires these, but having an estimate in place will support a well-considered decision.

7.4. To ensure control over the estimates, it is preferable to fill the gaps explicitly. Omitting an item from the estimation process means that implicitly the item is assumed either to be zero or to move in line with other parts of the aggregate of which the item is a part. For instance, compiling an output estimate based on the movements in the data for two months without making an explicit estimate of what the third month may look like is the same as forecasting the third month to be equal to an average of the two first months in the quarter. This may not be the most satisfactory way of forecasting (or nowcasting) the missing month. Thus, there is a need to produce an estimate to fill in the gap to ensure a comprehensive total, even if such an estimate is less than satisfactory.

7.5. Deriving estimates using projections based on past trends is particularly undesirable for current price data because, implicitly, current price data also depend on underlying price trends, which tend to be more volatile than volume trends. Thus, if possible, extrapolation based on past trends should be based on volume data combined with available price data. Relevant price data are often available. The timeliness of price statistics generally does not cause any problems, and if price data for the item are not collected, price indices for similar or related products may provide acceptable proxies.

7.6. There are two main QNA uses of projections based on past trends: one based on past trends in annual data and one based on past trends in monthly and quarterly data. Projections based on past trends in annual data are used to fill gaps in cases where no relevant quarterly information is available. Extrapolation based on past trends in monthly or quarterly data is used to mechanically extend indicator series that become available with a time lag that bars direct use.

B. Trend Projections Based on Annual Data

7.7. This section deals with the situation in which no short-term data are available at all and presents techniques that can be used to construct quarterly data based on past trends in annual data. The two main elements of constructing quarterly data based on past trends in annual data are (a) to extend the series of annual data to include forecasts or nowcasts for the current periods and (b) to fit a quarterly series through the annual totals. Extending the series with nowcasts can be achieved by using available forecasts (e.g., crop forecasts, forecasts based on econometrics models) or by simply assuming a continuation of the current trend in the data (e.g., expressed as a simple average of the growth in the series for the past years).

7.8. Fitting a quarterly series through annual totals should ideally be based on some actual information about the seasonal pattern of the series and the timing of any turning points in the series. In cases where data gaps have to be filled by trend projections based on annual data, however, information on the actual timing of possible turning points is normally not available. Although generally unknown, the seasonal pattern of the series may in some cases be broadly known from other information.

7.9. In cases where no information is available about a series' seasonal pattern, the only available option is to use the trend in the annual data to construct a quarterly series without any seasonal pattern that equals the annual totals. Such a series should be as smooth as possible to ensure that its

impact on the period-to-period change in the aggregates is minimized.

7.10. A large number of disaggregation methods, with different degrees of sophistication, have been proposed in the academic literature. In general, most of these methods produce similar results. The main goal in these circumstances is to select a method to fill the gaps that is simple and can be implemented easily.

7.11. It is important to emphasize that quarterly distribution without any related series produces purely synthetic numbers that may not be indicative of the real developments. In particular, such numbers do not contain any information about the precise timing of turning points. Because of this, quarterly distributed data may also deviate substantially from estimates of the underlying trend in subannual data produced by standard seasonal adjustment packages.

7.12. In cases where the seasonal pattern of the series is broadly known, the distribution procedure can be improved by superimposing this known seasonal pattern on the derived quarterly series.

7.13. In this chapter, we look at two methods to construct synthetic quarterly data based on past trends in annual data that are reasonably simple and give similar results, as illustrated in Example 7.1. Both are used by several countries. The first is a purely numerical disaggregation technique proposed by Lisman and Sandee, while the second is based on the least-squares techniques discussed in Chapter VI.[1] The latter can, as will be shown, easily be extended to incorporate a known seasonal pattern into the estimates.

1. The Lisman and Sandee Quarterly Distribution Formula

7.14. Lisman and Sandee (1964) proposed a purely numerical technique for constructing synthetic quarterly data based on past trends in annual data. It works as follows:
(i) Make a forecast of the annual data for the current year $(A_{\beta+1})$ and for the next year $(A_{\beta+2})$.

---

[1] Some of the alternatives to the two methods presented in this chapter include the autoregressive integrated moving average (ARIMA) model-based procedure proposed in Stram and Wei (1986) and Wei and Stram (1990); and the state space modeling procedure proposed in Al-Osh (1989). While generally producing similar results to the two presented in this chapter, these alternative methods are substantially more complicated.

Example 7.1. Quarterly Distribution of Annual Data Without a Related Series

Date	Annual Data	Least-Squares Distribution	Lisman & Sandee Distribution
1994	3,930.0		
q1 1995		967.8	979.2
q2 1995		983.7	967.0
q3 1995		1,015.4	1,001.4
q4 1995	4,030.0	1,063.1	1,082.4
q1 1996		1,126.6	1,163.8
q2 1996		1,204.4	1,226.3
q3 1996		1,296.4	1,288.8
q4 1996	5,030.0	1,402.7	1,351.2
q1 1997		1,523.2	1,466.9
q2 1997		1,565.1	1,581.2
q3 1997		1,528.5	1,564.7
q4 1997	6,030.0	1,413.2	1,417.2
q1 1998		1,219.4	1,225.8
q2 1998		1,104.1	1,088.6
q3 1998		1,067.4	1,056.4
q4 1998	4,500.0	1,109.1	1,129.2
q1 1999		1,229.5	1,234.6
q2 1999		1,285.8	1,296.6
q3 1999		1,278.2	1,281.0
q4 1999	5,000.0	1,206.6	1,187.8
q1 2000		1,071.0	1,062.3
q2 2000		988.3	969.0
q3 2000		958.7	953.4
q4 2000	4,000.0	982.0	1,015.4
q1 2001		1,058.3	1,088.6
q2 2001		1,115.5	1,130.1
q3 2001		1,153.6	1,145.8
q4 2001	4,500.0	1,172.7	1,135.5
2002	4,500.0		

As can be seen, the two alternative procedures for quarterly distribution of annual data without using a related series give very similar results.

Example 7.2. Quarterly Distribution of Annual Data with a Superimposed Seasonal Pattern

Date	Assumed Seasonal Pattern	Annual Data	Least-Squares Distribution
q1 1995		3,930.0	979.2
q1 1995	0.9		870.7
q2 1995	0.8		785.2
q3 1995	1.0		1,008.2
q4 1995	1.3	4,030.0	1,365.9
q1 1996	0.9		1,002.1
q2 1996	0.8		952.0
q3 1996	1.0		1,278.6
q4 1996	1.3	5,030.0	1,797.3
q1 1997	0.9		1,355.5
q2 1997	0.8		1,245.8
q3 1997	1.0		1,543.8
q4 1997	1.3	6,030.0	1,884.9
q1 1998	0.9		1,126.1
q2 1998	0.8		900.3
q3 1998	1.0		1,064.3
q4 1998	1.3	4,500.0	1,409.4
q1 1999	0.9		1,088.4
q2 1999	0.8		1,019.9
q3 1999	1.0		1,287.5
q4 1999	1.3	5,000.0	1,604.2
q1 2000	0.9		985.1
q2 2000	0.8		803.3
q3 2000	1.0		957.2
q4 2000	1.3	4,000.0	254.4
q1 2001	0.9		939.2
q2 2001	0.8		883.5
q3 2001	1.0		1,149.6
q4 2001	1.3		1,527.7

(ii) Derive a smooth continuous quarterly time series from the annual data using the following disaggregation formula:

$$X_{1,y} = 1/4(0.291 \cdot A_{y-1} + 0.793 \cdot A_y - 0.084 \cdot A_{y+1}) \quad (7.1)$$

$$X_{2,y} = 1/4(-0.041 \cdot A_{y-1} + 1.207 \cdot A_y - 0.166 \cdot A_{y+1})$$

$$X_{3,y} = 1/4(-0.166 \cdot A_{y-1} + 1.207 \cdot A_y - 0.041 \cdot A_{y+1})$$

$$X_{4,y} = 1/4(-0.084 \cdot A_{y-1} + 0.793 \cdot A_y + 0.291 \cdot A_{y+1})$$

where
$X_{q,y}$ is the derived quarterly estimate for quarter q in year y,
A_y is the annual estimate for year y, and
β is the last year for which annual data are available.

7.15. The coefficients in the Lisman and Sandee disaggregation formula were derived by imposing a number of restrictions; for example, when the annual data for three consecutive years $y-1$, y, and $y+1$ are not on a straight line, they are assumed to lie on a sine curve.

2. Least-Squares Distribution

7.16. Boot, Feibes, and Lisman (1967) proposed a least-squares-based technique for constructing synthetic quarterly data based on past trends in annual data. It works as follows:

(i) make a forecast of the annual data for the current year ($A_{\beta+1}$).
(ii) Derive a smooth continuous quarterly time series from the annual data using a least-squares minimization technique, as follows:

$$\min_{(x_1,\dots,x_{4y})} \sum_{t=2}^{4y} [X_t - X_{t-1}]^2, \quad (7.2)$$

$$t \in \{1,\dots,(4\beta+1)\} \quad y \in \{1,\dots,(\beta+1)\}$$

under the restriction that

$$\sum_{t=4y-3}^{4y} X_t = A.$$

(that is, the sum of the quarterized data should be equal to the observed annual data)

where
t is used as a generic symbol for time ($t = q,y$) (e.g., $t = 4y - 3$ is equal to the first quarter of year y, and $4y$ the fourth quarter of year y);

X_t is the derived quarterly estimate for quarter t;
A_y is the annual estimate for year y; and
β is the last year for which any annual observations are available.

7.17. This least-squares-based technique can be extended to incorporate a known seasonal pattern into the estimates by replacing the least-squares expression in step (ii) above with the following expression:[2]

$$\min_{(x_1,\dots,x_{4y})} \sum_{t=2}^{4y} \left[\frac{X_t}{SF_t} - \frac{X_{t-1}}{SF_{t-1}} \right]^2, \quad (7.3)$$

$$t \in \{1,\dots,(4\beta+1)\} \quad y \in \{1,\dots,(\beta+1)\}$$

under the restriction that

$$\sum_{t=4y-3}^{4y} X_t = A.$$

(that is, the sum of the quarterized data should be equal to the observed annual data)

where
SF_t is a time series with assumed seasonal factors.

Example 7.2 shows the results of using equation (7.3) to superimpose a seasonal pattern on the annual data used in Example 7.1.

7.18. A small problem with the Boot-Feibes-Lisman method, as well as other methods of distribution that use least squares, is a tendency of the derived series to flatten out at endpoints[3] (as can be seen from Example 7.1). This problem can be alleviated by projecting the annual series for two years in both directions and distributing the extended series.

C. Projection Based on Monthly or Quarterly Data

7.19. This section presents some simple techniques that can be used to mechanically extend data series that are not sufficiently timely to be used when the first QNA estimates for a particular quarter are compiled. The monthly and quarterly source data commonly become available with varying delays. Some quarterly and monthly source data may be available

---

[2]As proposed in for example Cholette (1998a).
[3]This is not a problem for using least squares for benchmarking as discussed in Chapter VI. In that case, the implied flattening out at the endpoints of the quarterly benchmark-indicator (BI) ratios helps reduce the potential wagging tail problem discussed in Annex 6.2.

within the first month after the end of the reference period (e.g., price statistics and industrial production indices), while other data may only be available with a delay of more than three months. Thus, when preparing the first estimates, for some series only data for two months of the last quarter may be available, while for other series data may be missing altogether.

7.20. If no related indicator is available to support an extrapolation, several options can be considered, depending on the strength of the underlying trend in the series and the importance of seasonality in the series. One generally applicable option would be to use ARIMA[4] time-series modeling techniques, which in many cases have proved to produce reasonable forecasts for one or two periods ahead. ARIMA modeling, however, is complicated and time-consuming, and requires sophisticated statistical knowledge. Also, ARIMA models are basically not able to forecast changes in the underlying trend in the series. Their good forecasting reputation stems mainly from their ability to pick up repeated patterns of the series, such as seasonality.

7.21. Thus, if there is strong seasonal variation and trend in the series, a substantially less demanding, and potentially better, solution would be the following three-step procedure:
- First, use standard seasonal adjustment software (e.g., X-11-ARIMA or X-12-ARIMA) to seasonally adjust the series and to estimate the trend component of the series. For this particular purpose, only a basic knowledge of seasonal adjustment is required, and knowledge of ARIMA modeling is not necessary.
- Second, extend the trend component of the series based on judgment, forecasts, or annual data, or by projecting the current trend using the simple trend formula in equation (7.5) below.
- Third, multiply the trend forecast with the seasonal and irregular factors computed by the program.

7.22. In many cases, the following, much simpler, approaches may prove sufficient:
- If there is no clear trend or seasonality in the movements of the series (either in volume or price), one may simply repeat the last observation or set the value for the missing period equal to a simple average of, for example, the last two observations.
- With strong seasonal variation in the series but no clear underlying trend in the series' movements, one may simply repeat the value of the variable in the same period of the previous year or set the value for the missing observation equal to the average for the same period in several of the previous years.
- If there is a clear trend in the series but no pronounced seasonal variation, the past trend may be projected using a weighted average of the period-to-period rates of change for the last observations, for example, by using a weighted average for three last observations as follows:

$$X_{T+t} = X_{T+t-1} \cdot \left[\frac{3}{6} \cdot \frac{X_T}{X_{T-1}} + \frac{2}{6} \cdot \frac{X_{T-1}}{X_{T-2}} + \frac{1}{6} \cdot \frac{X_{T-2}}{X_{T-3}} \right] \quad (7.4)$$

- With both a clear trend and strong seasonal variation in the series, one simple option may be to extrapolate the value of the series in the same period in the previous year, using a weighted average of the rates of change from the same period in the previous year for the last observations as an extrapolator, for example, by using a weighted average for three last observations as follows:

$$X_{T+t} = X_{T+t-s} \cdot \left[\frac{3}{6} \cdot \frac{X_T}{X_{T-s}} + \frac{2}{6} \cdot \frac{X_{T-1}}{X_{T-s-1}} + \frac{1}{6} \cdot \frac{X_{T-2}}{X_{T-s-2}} \right] (7.5)$$

In this formula, s is the periodicity of the series, X_T is the level of the last observation, and t is the number of periods to be projected.

[4]Autoregressive integrated moving average.

VIII   Seasonal Adjustment and Estimation of Trend-Cycles

A. Introduction

8.1. Seasonal adjustment serves to facilitate an understanding of the development of the economy over time, that is, the direction and magnitude of changes that have taken place. Such understanding can be best pursued through the analyses of *time series*.[1] One major reason for compiling high-frequency statistics such as GDP is to allow timely identification of changes in the business cycle, particularly turning points. If observations of, say, quarterly non-seasonally adjusted GDP at constant prices are put together for consecutive quarters covering several years to form a time series and are graphed, however, it is often difficult to identify turning points and the underlying direction of the data. The most obvious pattern in the data may be a recurrent within-a-year pattern, commonly referred to as the seasonal pattern.

8.2. Seasonal adjustment means using analytical techniques to break down a series into its components. The purpose is to identify the different components of the time series and thus provide a better understanding of the behavior of the time series. In seasonally adjusted data, the impact of the regular within-a-year seasonal pattern, the influences of moving holidays such as Easter and Ramadan, and the number of working/trading days and the weekday composition in each period (the trading-day effect, for short) are removed. By removing the repeated impact of these effects, seasonally adjusted data highlight the underlying trends and short-run movements in the series.

8.3. In trend-cycle estimates, the impact of irregular events in addition to seasonal variations is removed.

Adjusting a series for seasonal variations removes the identifiable, regularly repeated influences on the series but not the impact of any irregular events. Consequently, if the impact of irregular events is strong, seasonally adjusted series may not represent a smooth, easily interpretable series. To further highlight the underlying trend-cycle, most standard seasonal adjustment packages provide a smoothed trend line running through the seasonally adjusted data (representing a combined estimate of the underlying long-term trend and the business-cycle movements in the series).

8.4. An apparent solution to get around seasonal patterns would be to look at rates of change from the same quarter of the previous year. This has the disadvantage, however, that turning points are only detected with some delay.[2] Furthermore, these rates of change do not fully exclude all seasonal elements (e.g., Easter may fall in the first or second quarter, and the number of working days of a quarter may differ between succeeding years). Moreover, these year-to-year rates of change will be biased owing to changes in the seasonal pattern caused by institutional or behavioral changes. Finally, these year-to-year rates of change will reflect any irregular events affecting the data for the same period of the previous year in addition to any irregular events affecting the current period. For these reasons, year-to-year rates of change are inadequate for business-cycle analysis.

8.5. Therefore, more sophisticated procedures are needed to remove seasonal patterns from the series. Various well-established techniques are available for this purpose. The most commonly used technique is the Census X-11/X-12 method. Other available seasonal adjustment methods include, among others, TRAMO-SEATS, BV4, SABLE, and STAMP.

---

[1]Paragraph 1.13 defined time series as a series of data obtained through repeated measurement of the same concept over time that allows different periods to be compared.

[2]The delay can be substantial, on average, two quarters. A numerical example illustrating this point is provided in Annex 1.1.

8.6. A short presentation on the basic concept of seasonal adjustment is given in Section B of this chapter, while the basic principles of the Census X-11/X-12 method are outlined in section C. The final section, Section D, addresses a series of related general seasonal adjustment issues, such as revisions to the seasonally adjusted data and the wagging tail problem, and the minimum length of time series for seasonal adjustment. Section D also addresses a set of critical issues on seasonal adjustment of quarterly national accounts (QNA), such as preservation of accounting identities, seasonal adjustment of balancing items and aggregates, and the relationship between annual data and seasonally adjusted quarterly data. Section D also discusses the presentation and status of seasonally adjusted and trend-cycle data.

B. The Main Principles of Seasonal Adjustment

8.7. For the purpose of seasonal adjustment, a time series is generally considered to be made up of three main components—the trend-cycle component, the seasonal component, and the irregular component—each of which may be made up of several subcomponents:

(a) *The trend-cycle (T_t) component* is the underlying path or general direction reflected in the data, that is, the combined long-term trend and the business-cycle movements in the data.

(b) *The seasonal (S_t^c) component* includes seasonal effects narrowly defined and calendar-related systematic effects that are not stable in annual timing, such as trading-day effects and moving holiday effects.

  (i) The seasonal effect narrowly defined (S_t) is an effect that is reasonably stable[3] in terms of annual timing, direction, and magnitude. Possible causes for the effect are natural factors, administrative or legal measures, social/cultural traditions, and calendar-related effects that are stable in annual timing (e.g., public holidays such as Christmas).

  (ii) Calendar-related systematic effects on the time series that are not stable in annual timing are caused by variations in the calendar from year to year. They include the following:

  ▸ The trading-day effect *(TD_t)*, which is the effect of variations from year to year in the number working, or trading, days and the weekday composition for a particular month or quarter relative to the standard for that particular month or quarter.[4,5]

  ▸ The effects of events that occur at regular intervals but not at exactly the same time each year, such as moving holidays (MH_t), or paydays for large groups of employees, pension payments, and so on.

  ▸ Other calendar effects (OC_t), such as leap-year and length-of-quarter effects.

  ▸ Both the seasonal effects narrowly defined and the other calendar-related effects represent systematic, persistent, predictable, and identifiable effects.

(c) *The irregular component (I_t^c)* captures effects that are unpredictable unless additional information is available, in terms of timing, impact, and duration. The irregular component (I_t^c) includes the following:

  (i) Irregular effects narrowly defined (I_t).

  (ii) Outlier[6] effects (OUT_t).

  (iii) Other irregular effects (OI_t) (such as the effects of unseasonable weather, natural disasters, strikes, and irregular sales campaigns).

The irregular effect narrowly defined is assumed to behave as a stochastic variable that is symmetrically distributed around its expected value (0 for an additive model and 1 for a multiplicative model).

---

[3]It may be gradually changing over time (moving seasonality).

[4]The period-to-period variation in the standard, or average, number and type of trading days for each particular month or quarter of the year is part of the seasonal effect narrowly defined.
[5]Trading-day effects are less important in quarterly data than in monthly data but can still be a factor that makes a difference.
[6]That is, an unusually large or small observation, caused by either to errors in the data or special events, which may interfere with estimating the seasonal factors.

8.8. The relationship between the original series and its trend-cycle, seasonal, and irregular components can be modeled as additive or multiplicative.[7] That is, the time-series model can be expressed as

Additive Model

$$X_t = S_t^c + T_t + I_t^c \qquad (8.1.a)$$

or with some subcomponents specified

$$X_t = (S_t + TD_t + MH_t + OC_t) + T_t + (I_t + OUT_t + OI_t) \quad (8.1.b)$$

where

the seasonal component is
$$S_t^c = (S_t + TD_t + MH_t + OC_t)$$

the irregular component is
$$I_t^c = (I_t + OUT_t + OI_t), \text{ and}$$

the seasonally adjusted series is
$$A_t = T_t + I_t^c = T_t + (I_t + OUT_t + OI_t),$$

or as

Multiplicative Model

$$X_t = S_t^c + T_t + I_t^c \qquad (8.2.a)$$

or with some subcomponents specified
$$X_t = (S_t \cdot TD_t \cdot MH_t \cdot OC_t) \cdot T_t \cdot (I_t \cdot OUT_t \cdot OI_t) \qquad (8.2.b)$$

where

the seasonal component is $S_t^c = (S_t \cdot TD_t \cdot MH_t \cdot OC_t)$,

the irregular component is $I_t^c = (I_t \cdot OUT_t \cdot OI_t)$, and

the seasonally adjusted series is
$$A_t = T_t \cdot I_t^c = T_t \cdot (I_t \cdot OUT_t \cdot OI_t).$$

8.9. The multiplicative model is generally taken as the default. The model assumes that the absolute size of the components of the series are dependent on each other and thus that the seasonal oscillation size increases and

---

[7]Other main alternatives exist, in particular, X-12-ARIMA includes a pseudo-additive model $X_t = T_t \cdot (S_t^c + I_t^c - 1)$ tailored to series whose value is zero for some periods. Moreover, within each of the main models, the relationship between some of the subcomponents depends on the exact estimation routine used. For instance, in the multiplicative model, some of the sub-components may be expressed as additive to the irregular effect narrowly defined, e.g., as: $X_t = S_t \cdot T_t \cdot (I_t + OUT_t + OI_t + TR_t + MH_t + OC_t)$.

decreases with the level of the series, a characteristic of most seasonal macroeconomic series. With the multiplicative model, the seasonal and irregular components will be ratios centered around 1. In contrast, the additive model assumes that the absolute size of the components of the series are independent of each other and, in particular, that the size of the seasonal oscillations is independent of the level of the series.

8.10. Seasonal adjustment means using analytical techniques to break down a series into its components. The purpose is to identify the different components of the time series and thus to provide a better understanding of the behavior of the time series for modeling and forecasting purposes, and to remove the regular within-a-year seasonal pattern to highlight the underlying trends and short-run movements in the series. The purpose is not to smooth the series, which is the objective of trend and trend-cycle estimates. A seasonally adjusted series consists of the trend-cycle plus the irregular component and thus, as noted in the introduction, if the irregular component is strong, may not represent a smooth easily interpretable series.

8.11. Example 8.1 presents the last four years of a time series and provides an illustration of what is meant by seasonal adjustment, the trend-cycle component, the seasonal component, and the irregular component.

8.12. Seasonal adjustment and trend-cycle estimation represent an analytical massaging of the original data. As such, the *seasonally adjusted* data and the estimated trend-cycle component complement the original data, but, as explained in Section D of Chapter I, *they can never replace the original* data for the following reasons:
- Unadjusted data are useful in their own right. The non-seasonally adjusted data show the actual economic events that have occurred, while the seasonally adjusted data and the trend-cycle estimate represent an analytical elaboration of the data designed to show the underlying movements that may be hidden by the seasonal variations. Compilation of seasonally adjusted data, exclusively, represents a *loss of information*.
- No unique solution exists on how to conduct seasonal adjustment.
- Seasonally adjusted data are subject to revisions as future data become available, even when the original data *are not* revised.
- When compiling QNA, balancing and reconciling the accounts are better done on the original unadjusted QNA estimates.

Example 8.1. Seasonal Adjustment, Trend-Cycle Component, Seasonal Component, and Irregular Component

Multiplicative Seasonal Model

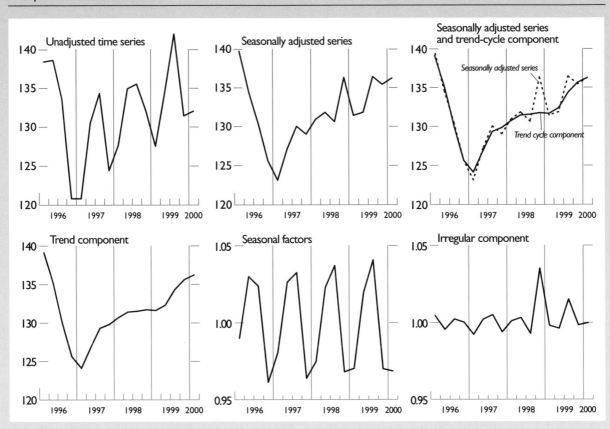

Date	Unadjusted Time Series (X_t) Index 1980 = 100 (1)	Seasonal Factors[1] (S_t) (2)	Irregular Component (I_t) (3)	Seasonally Adjusted Series (X_t/S_t) Index 1980 = 100 (4) = (1)/(2)	Trend-Cycle Component (T_t) Index 1980 = 100 (5) = (4)/(3)
q1 1996	138.5	0.990	1.005	139.8	139.2
q2 1996	138.7	1.030	0.996	134.6	135.2
q3 1996	133.6	1.024	1.003	130.5	130.1
q4 1996	120.9	0.962	1.000	125.7	125.7
q1 1997	120.9	0.981	0.993	123.2	124.2
q2 1998	130.6	1.027	1.002	127.2	126.9
q3 1997	134.4	1.033	1.005	130.1	129.4
q4 1997	124.5	0.964	0.994	129.1	129.9
q1 1998	127.7	0.975	1.001	131.0	130.8
q2 1998	135.0	1.023	1.003	131.9	131.5
q3 1998	135.6	1.037	0.993	130.7	131.6
q4 1998	132.1	0.968	**1.035**	**136.4**	131.8
q1 1999	127.6	0.971	0.998	131.5	131.7
q2 1999	134.6	1.020	0.997	131.9	132.4
q3 1999	142.1	1.041	1.015	136.5	134.4
q4 1999	131.5	0.970	0.999	135.5	135.7
q1 2000	132.1	0.969	1.000	136.3	136.3

With a multiplicative seasonal model, the seasonal factors are ratios centered around 1 and are reasonably stable in terms of annual timing, direction, and magnitude. The irregulars[2] are also centered around 1 but with erratic oscillations.

Observe the particularly strong irregular effect, or outlier, for q4 1998. Examples 8.3 and 8.4 show how an outlier like this causes trouble in early identification of changes in the trend-cycle.

[1]The values of the estimated seasonal component, particularly from the multiplicative model, are often called "seasonal factors."
[2]The irregular component is often referred to as "the irregulars," and the seasonal component is often referred to as "the seasonals."

- While errors in the source data may be more easily detected from seasonally adjusted data, it may be easier to identify the source for the errors and correct the errors working with the unadjusted data.
- Practice has shown that seasonally adjusting the data at the detailed level needed for compiling QNA estimates can leave residual seasonality in the aggregates.

The original unadjusted QNA estimates, the seasonally adjusted estimates, and the trend-cycle component all provide useful information about the economy (see Box 1.1), and, for the major national accounts aggregates, all three sets of data should be presented to the users.

8.13. Seasonal adjustment is normally done using off-the-shelf programs—most commonly worldwide by one of the programs in the X-11 family. Other programs in common use include the TRAMO-SEATS package developed by Bank of Spain and promoted by Eurostat and the German BV4 program. The original X-11 program was developed in the 1960s by the U.S. Bureau of the Census. It has subsequently been updated and improved through the development of X-11-ARIMA[8] by Statistics Canada[9] and X-12-ARIMA by the U.S. Bureau of the Census, which was released in the second half of the 1990s. The core of X-11-ARIMA and X-12-ARIMA is the same basic filtering procedure as in the original X-11.[10]

8.14. For particular series, substantial experience and expertise may be required to determine whether the seasonal adjustment is done properly or to fine-tune the seasonal adjustment. In particularly unstable series with a strong irregular component (e.g., outliers owing to strikes and other special events, breaks, or level shifts), it may be difficult to seasonally adjust properly.

8.15. It is also important to emphasize, however, that many series are well-behaved and easy to seasonally adjust, allowing seasonal adjustment programs to be used without specialized seasonal adjustment expertise.

The X-11 seasonal adjustment procedure has in practice proved to be quite robust, and a large number of the seasonally adjusted series published by different agencies around the world are adjusted by running the programs in their default modes, often without special expertise. Thus, lack of experience in seasonal adjustment or lack of staff with particular expertise in seasonal adjustment should not preclude one from starting to compile and publish seasonally adjusted estimates. When compiling seasonally adjusted estimates for the first time, however, keep in mind that the main focus of compilation and presentation should be on the original unadjusted estimates. Over time, staff will gain experience and expertise in seasonal adjustment.

8.16. It is generally recommended that the statisticians who compile the statistics should also be responsible—either solely or together with seasonal adjustment specialists—for seasonally adjusting the statistics. This arrangement should give them greater insight into the data, make their job more interesting, help them understand the nature of the data better, and lead to improved quality of both the original unadjusted data and the seasonally adjusted data. However, it is advisable in addition to set up a small central group of seasonal adjustment experts, because the in-depth seasonal adjustment expertise required to handle ill-behaved series can only be acquired by hands-on experience with seasonal adjustment of many different types of series.

C. Basic Features of the X-11 Family of Seasonal Adjustment Programs

8.17. The three programs in the X-11 family—X-11, X-11-ARIMA, and X-12-ARIMA— follow an iterative estimation procedure, the core of which is based on a series of moving averages.[11] The programs comprise seven main parts in three main blocks of operations. First (part A), the series may optionally be "preadjusted" for outliers, level shifts in the series, the effect of known irregular events, and calendar-related effects using adjustment factors supplied by the user or estimated using built-in estimation procedures. In addition, the series may be extended by backcasts and forecasts so that less asymmetric filters can be used at the beginning and end of the series. Second (parts B, C, and D), the preadjusted series then goes through three rounds of seasonal filtering and extreme value adjustments, the "B, C, and D iterations" in the X-11/X-12 jargon. Third

---

[8]Autoregressive integrated moving average time-series models. ARIMA modeling represents an optional feature in X-11-ARIMA and X-12-ARIMA to backcast and forecast the series so that less asymmetric filters than in the original X-11 program can be used at the beginning and end of the series (see paragraph. 8.37).
[9]Initially released in 1980, with a major update in 1988, the X-11-ARIMA/88.
[10]The X-12-ARIMA can be obtained by contacting the U.S. Bureau of the Census (as of the time of writing, X-12-ARIMA was available free and could be downloaded with complete documentation and some discussion papers from http://www.census.gov/pub/ts/x12a/). X-11-ARIMA can be obtained by contacting Statistics Canada, and TRAMO-SEATS can be obtained by contacting Eurostat. The original X-11 program is integrated into several commercially available software packages (including among others SAS, AREMOS, and STATSTICA).

[11]Also called "moving average filters" in the seasonal adjustment terminology.

(parts E, F, and G), various diagnostics and quality control statistics are computed, tabulated, and graphed.[12]

8.18. The second block—with the parts B, C, and D seasonal filtering procedure—represents the central (X-11) core of the programs. The filtering procedure is basically the same for all three programs. X-12-ARIMA, however, provides several new adjustment options for the B, C, and D iterations that significantly enhance this part of the program. The main enhancements made in X-12-ARIMA to the central X-11 part of the program include, among others, a pseudo-additive $X_t = T_t \cdot (S_t^c + I_t^c - 1)$ model tailored to series whose value is zero for some periods; new centered seasonal and trend MA filters (see next section); improvements in how trading-day effects and other regression effects—including user-defined effects (a new capability)—are estimated from preliminary estimates of the irregular component (see Subsection 3 below).

8.19. In contrast, the first block, and to some extent the last block (see Subsection 4), differ markedly among the three programs. The original X-11 provided no built-in estimation procedures for preadjustments of the original series besides trading-day adjustments based on regression of tentative irregulars in parts B and C (see Subsection 1), but it provided for user-supplied permanent or temporary adjustment factors. X-11-ARIMA, in addition, provided for built-in procedures for ARIMA-model-based backcasts and forecasts of the series. In contrast, X-12-ARIMA contains an extensive time-series modeling block, the RegARIMA part of the program, that allows the user to preadjust, as well as backcasts and forecasts of the series by modeling the original series. The main components of X-12-ARIMA are shown in Box 8.1.

8.20. The RegARIMA block of the X-12-ARIMA allows the user to conduct regression analysis directly on the original series, taking into account that the non-explained part of the series typically will be autocorrelated, nonstationary, and heteroscedastic. This is done by combining traditional regression techniques with ARIMA modeling into what is labeled RegARIMA modeling.[13] The RegARIMA part of X-12-ARIMA allows the user to provide a set of user-defined

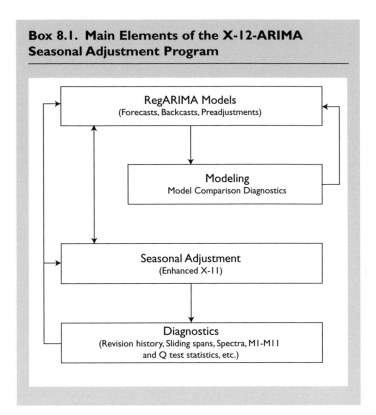

Box 8.1. Main Elements of the X-12-ARIMA Seasonal Adjustment Program

RegARIMA Models
(Forecasts, Backcasts, Preadjustments)

Modeling
Model Comparison Diagnostics

Seasonal Adjustment
(Enhanced X-11)

Diagnostics
(Revision history, Sliding spans, Spectra, M1-M11 and Q test statistics, etc.)

regressor variables. In addition, the program contains a large set of predefined regressor variables to identify, for example, trading-day effects, Easter effects,[14] leap-year effects, length-of-quarter effects, level shifts, point outliers, and ramps in the series. As a simpler alternative to RegARIMA modeling, X-12-ARIMA has retained the traditional X-11 approach of regressing the tentative irregulars on explanatory variables, adding regressors for point outliers and facilities for user-defined regressors to X-11's trading-day and Easter effects (see Subsection 3).

1. Main Aspects of the Core X-11 Moving Average Seasonal Adjustment Filters

8.21. This subsection presents the main elements of the centered moving average filtering procedure in the X-12-ARIMA B, C, and D iterations for estimating the trend-cycle component and the seasonal effects narrowly defined. The moving average filtering procedure implicitly assumes that all effects except the seasonal effects narrowly defined are approximately symmetrically distributed around their expected value (1 for a multiplicative and 0 for an additive model) and thus can be fully eliminated by using the centered moving

---

[12]Test statistics that users should consult regularly are also included in parts A and D.

[13]The standard seasonal ARIMA model is generalized to include regression parameters with the part not explained by the regression parameters following an ARIMA process, that is, $X_t = \beta'Y_t = Z_t$, where X_t is the series to be modeled, β a parameters vector, Y_t a vector of fixed regressors, and Z_t a pure seasonal ARIMA model.

[14]The user can select from different Easter-effect models.

average filter instead of ending up polluting the estimated trend-cycle component and the seasonal effects narrowly defined. Ideally, all effects that are not approximately symmetrically distributed around the expected value of 1 or 0 should have been removed in the preadjustment part (part A).

8.22. The centered moving average filtering procedure described below only provides estimates of the seasonal effects narrowly defined (S_t), not the other parts of the seasonal component (S_t^c). Subsection 3 briefly discusses the procedures available for estimating the not-captured impact of trading-day effects and other calendar-related systematic effects. It includes, namely, the traditional X-11 approach of regressing the tentative irregulars on explanatory trading-day and other calendar-related variables as part of the B and C iterations, and the X-12-ARIMA option of estimating these effects as part of the RegARIMA-based preadjustment of the series.

8.23. The main steps of the multiplicative version of the filtering procedure for quarterly data in the B, C, and D iterations, assuming preadjusted data, are as follows:[15]

Stage 1. Initial Estimates

(a) Initial trend-cycle. The series is smoothed using a weighted 5-term (2 x 4)[16] centered moving average to produce a first estimate of the trend-cycle. $T_t^1 = {}^1\!/_8 X_{t-2} + {}^1\!/_4 X_{t-1} + {}^1\!/_4 X_t + {}^1\!/_4 X_{t+1} + {}^1\!/_8 X_{t+2}$.

(b) *Initial SI ratios.* The "original"[17] series is divided by the smoothed series (T_t^1) to give an initial estimate of the seasonal and irregular component $S_t I_t^1$.

(c) *Initial preliminary seasonal factors.* A time series of initial preliminary seasonal factors is then

derived as a weighted 5-term (3 x 3) centered seasonal[18] moving average[19] of the initial SI ratios ($S_t I_t^1$). This method implicitly assumes that I_t behaves as a stochastic variable that is symmetrically distributed around its expected value (1 for a multiplicative model) and therefore can be eliminated by averaging.

$\hat{S}_t^1 = {}^1\!/_9 SI_{t-8} + {}^2\!/_9 SI_{t-4} + {}^3\!/_9 SI_t + {}^2\!/_9 SI_{t+4} + {}^1\!/_9 SI_{t+8}$

(d) *Initial seasonal factors.* A time series of initial seasonal factors is then derived by normalizing the initial preliminary seasonal factors.

$$S_t^1 = \frac{\hat{S}_t^1}{{}^1\!/_8 \hat{S}_{t-2}^1 + {}^1\!/_4 \hat{S}_{t-1}^1 + {}^1\!/_4 \hat{S}_t^1 + {}^1\!/_4 \hat{S}_{t+1}^1 + {}^1\!/_8 \hat{S}_{t+2}^1}$$

This step is done to ensure that the annual average of the seasonal factors is close to 1.

(e) *Initial seasonal adjustment.* An initial estimate of the seasonally adjusted series is then derived as $A_t^1 = X_t / S_t^1 = T_t \cdot S_t \cdot I_t / S_t = T_t^1 \cdot I_t$.

Stage 2. Revised Estimates

(a) *Intermediate trend-cycle.* A revised estimate of the trend-cycle (T_t^2) is then derived by applying a Henderson moving average[20] to the initial seasonally adjusted series (A_t^1).

(b) *Revised SI ratios,* are then derived by dividing the "original" series by the intermediate trend-cycle estimate (T_t^2).

(c) *Revised preliminary seasonal factors* are then derived by applying a 3 x 5 centered seasonal moving average[21] to the revised SI ratios.

---

[15]Adapted from Findley and others (1996), which presents the filters assuming monthly data.

[16]A 2 x 4 moving average

$\left(\overline{X}_t^{2x4} = {}^1\!/_2 \left(\overline{X}_t^{1x4} + \overline{X}_{t+1}^{1x4} \right) \right)$

is a 2-term moving average

$\left(\overline{X}_t^{1x4} + \overline{X}_{t+1}^{1x4} \right)$

of a 4-term moving average.

$\left(\overline{X}_t^{1x4} = {}^1\!/_4 \left(X_{t-2} + X_{t-2} + X_t + X_{t+2} \right) \right)$.

[17]The series may be pre-adjusted, and, for the C and D iterations, extreme value adjusted (see below).

[18]A seasonal moving average is a moving average that is applied to each quarter separately, that is, as moving averages of neighboring q1s, q2s, etc.

[19]The 3 x 3 seasonal moving average filter is the default. In addition, users can select a 3 x 5 or 3 x 9 moving average filter (X-12-ARIMA also contains an optional 3 x 15 seasonal moving average filter). The user-selected filter will then be used in both stage 1 and stage 2.

[20]A Henderson moving average is a particular type of weighted moving average in which the weights are determined to produce the smoothest possible trend-cycle estimate. In X-11 and X-11-ARIMA, for quarterly series, Henderson filters of length 5, and 7 quarters could be automatically chosen or user-determined. In X-12-ARIMA, the users can also specify Henderson filters of any odd-number length.

[21]The 3 x 5 seasonal moving average filter is the default. In the D iteration, X-11-ARIMA, and X-12-ARIMA automatically select from among the four seasonal moving average filters (3 x 3, 3 x 5, 3 x 9, and the average of all SI ratios for each calendar quarter (the stable seasonal average)), unless the user has specified that the program should use a particular moving average filter.

(d) *Revised seasonal factors.* A revised time series of initial seasonal factors is then derived by normalizing the initial preliminary seasonal factors as in stage 1.

(e) *Revised seasonal adjustment.* A revised estimate of the seasonally adjusted series is then derived as $A_t^2 = X_t/S_t^2 = T_t^2 \cdot I_t$.

(f) *Tentative irregular.* A tentative estimate of the irregular component is then derived by de-trending the revised seasonally adjusted series: $I_t^2 = A_t^2/T_t^3$.

Stage 3. Final Estimates (D iteration only)

(a) *Final trend-cycle.* A final estimate of the trend-cycle component (T_t^3) is derived by applying a Henderson moving average to the revised and final seasonally adjusted series (A_t^2).

(b) *Final irregular.* A final estimate of the irregular component is derived by de-trending the revised and final seasonally adjusted series $I_t^3 = A_t^2/T_t^3$.

8.24. The filtering procedure is made more robust by a series of identifications and adjustments for extreme values. First, for the B and D iterations, when estimating the seasonal factors in steps (b) to (d) (stages 1 and 2) based on analyses of implied irregulars, extreme SI ratios are identified and temporarily replaced. For the B iteration, this is done in both stages 1 and 2, while for the D iteration it is done only at stage 2. Second, after the B and C iterations and before the next round of filtering, based on analyses of the tentative irregular component (I_t^2) derived in step (f) of stage 2, extreme values are identified and temporarily removed from the original (or preadjusted) series (that is, before the C and D iterations, respectively).

2. Preadjustments

8.25. The series may have to be preadjusted before entering the filtering procedure. For the seasonal moving average in step (c) (stages 1 and 2) above to fully isolate the seasonal factors narrowly defined, the series may have to be preadjusted to temporarily remove the following effects:
- outliers;
- level-shifts (including ramps);
- some calendar-related effects, particularly moving holidays, and leap-years;
- unseasonable weather changes and natural disasters; and
- strikes and irregular sale campaigns.

The extreme value adjustments described in paragraph 8.24 will to some extent take care of the distortions caused by point outliers but generally not the other effects. Furthermore, because outliers and the other effects listed cannot be expected to behave as a stochastic variable that is approximately symmetrically distributed around its expected value (1 for a multiplicative model), they will not be fully eliminated by the seasonal moving average filter used in step (c) (stages 1 and 2), and may end up polluting the estimated seasonal factors narrowly defined. For that reason, the impact of these effects cannot be fully identified from the estimated irregular component. Preadjustment can be conducted in a multitude of ways. The user may adjust the data directly based on particular knowledge about the data before feeding them to the program, or, in the case of X-12-ARIMA, use the estimation procedures built into the program.

3. Estimation of Other Parts of the Seasonal Component Remaining Trading-Day and Other Calendar-Related Effects

8.26. The moving average filtering procedure in paragraph 8.23 provides estimates of the seasonal effects narrowly defined (S_t), but not of the other parts of the overall seasonal component (S_t^c). Variations in the number of working/trading days and the weekday composition in each period, as well as the timing of moving holidays and other events that occur at regular calendar-related intervals, can have a significant impact on the series. Parts of these calendar effects will occur on average at the same time each year and affect the series in the same direction and with the same magnitude. Thus, parts of these calendar effects will be included in the (estimated) seasonal effects narrowly defined. Important parts of these systemic calendar effects will not be included in the seasonal effect narrowly defined, however, because (a) moving holidays and other regular calendar-related events may not fall in the same quarter each year and (b) the number of trading days and the weekday composition in each period varies from year to year.

8.27. Seasonally adjusted data should be adjusted for all seasonal variations, not only the seasonal effect narrowly defined. Leaving parts of the overall seasonal component in the adjusted series can be misleading and seriously reduce the usefulness of the seasonally adjusted data. Partly seasonally adjusted series, where the remaining identifiable calendar-related effects have not been removed, can give false signals of what's happening in the economy. For instance, such series may indicate that the economy declined in a particular quarter when it actually increased. Both the seasonal effects narrowly defined and the other calendar-related effects represent systematic, persistent, predictable, and identifiable seasonal effects, and all should be removed when compiling seasonally adjusted data.

8.28. Separate procedures are needed to estimate the remaining impact of the calendar-related systematic effects. X-11 and X-11-ARIMA contain built-in models for estimation of trading-day and Easter effects based on ordinary least-square (OLS) regression analysis of the tentative irregular component (I_t^2). When requested, the program derives preliminary estimates and adjustments for trading days and Easter effects at the end of the B iteration and final estimates and adjustments for trading days and Easter[22] effects at the end of the C iteration. X-12-ARIMA, in addition, provides an option for estimating these effects and others directly from the original data as part of the RegARIMA block of the program.

8.29. X-12-ARIMA's options for supplying user-defined regressors make it possible for users to construct custom-made moving holiday adjustment procedures. This option makes it easier to take into account holidays particular to each country or region, or country-specific effects of common holidays. Typical examples of such regional specific effects are regional moving holidays such as Chinese new year[23] and Ramadan, and the differences in timing and impact of Easter. Regarding the latter, while in some countries Easter is mainly a big shopping weekend creating a peak in retail trade, in other countries most shops are closed for more than a week creating a big drop in retail trade during the holiday combined with a peak in retail trade before the holiday. Also, Easter may fall on different dates in different countries, depending on what calendar they follow.

8.30. Some countries publish as *"non-seasonally adjusted data"* data that have been adjusted for some seasonal effects, particularly the number of working days. It is recommended that this approach not be adopted for two main reasons. First, data presented as non-seasonally adjusted should be fully unadjusted, showing what actually has happened, not partly adjusted for some seasonal effects.

Working/trading-day effects are part of the overall seasonal variation in the series, and adjustment for these effects should be treated as an integral part of the seasonal adjustment process, not as a separate process. Partly adjusted data can be misleading and are of limited analytical usefulness. Second, working-day adjustments made outside the seasonal adjustment context are often conducted in a rather primitive manner, using fixed coefficients based on the ratio of the number of working days in the month or quarter to the number of working days in a standard month or quarter. Moreover, it has been shown that the simple proportional method overstates the effect of working days on the series and may render it more difficult to seasonally adjust the series. Parts of these calendar effects will be captured as part of the seasonal effect narrowly defined, and X-11/X-12's trading-days adjustment procedures are able to handle the remaining part of these calendar effects in a much more sophisticated and realistic manner.

4. Seasonal Adjustment Diagnostics

8.31. X-11-ARIMA and, especially, X-12-ARIMA provide a set of diagnostics to assess the outcome, both from the modeling and the seasonal adjustment parts of the programs. These diagnostics range from advanced tests targeted for the expert attempting to fine-tune the treatment of complex series to simple tests that as a minimum should be looked at by all users of the programs. While the programs sometimes are used as a black box without the diagnostics, they should not (and need not be) used that way, because many tests can be readily understood.

8.32. Basic tests that as a minimum should be looked at include F-tests for existence of seasonality and the M- and Q-test statistics introduced with X-11-ARIMA. Other useful tests include tests for residual seasonality (shown in Box 8.2), existence of trading-day effects, other calendar-related effects, extreme values, and tests for fitting an ARIMA model to the series. Box 8.2 shows the parts of the output from X-12-ARIMA for the illustrative series in Example 8.1 regarding the F-tests for existence of seasonality. Similarly, Box 8.3 shows the M- and Q-test statistics for the same illustrative series. Series for which the program cannot find any identifiable seasonality or that fail the M- and Q-test statistics should be left unadjusted. Unfortunately, in these cases, the programs will not abort with a message that the series cannot

---

[22]Custom-making may be needed to account for country-specific factors (see paragraph 8.29).

[23]The Chinese new year represents a moving holiday effect in monthly data but not in quarterly data, because it always occurs within the same quarter.

Box 8.2. X-11/X-11-ARIMA/X-12-ARIMA Tests for Existence of Seasonality

The following is an edited copy of the relevant parts of X-12-ARIMA's main output file with the basic F-tests for existence of seasonality. The test statistics values are for the full 21 years of the illustrative series, of which the last four years of data were presented in Example 8.1. The D 8.A and D 11 codes refer to the various "output tables" in the main output file from the different programs in the X-11 family, documenting the various steps in the A, B, C, D, E, F, and G parts of the program.

As a minimum, Table D 8.A should be checked to make sure that the program returns an IDENTIFIABLE SEASONALITY PRESENT and not an IDENTIFIABLE SEASONALITY NOT PRESENT statement. The series should generally be left unadjusted if the F-tests indicate that identifiable seasonality is not present.

D8.A F-Tests for Seasonality

Test for the Presence of Seasonality Assuming Stability

	Sum of Squares	Degrees of Freedom	Mean Square	F-Value
Between quarters	809.1996	3	269.73319	43.946**
Residual	497.1645	81	6.13783	
Total	1306.3640	84		

Seasonality present at the 0.1 percent level.

Nonparametric Test for the Presence of Seasonality Assuming Stability

Kruskal-Wallis Statistic	Degrees of Freedom	Probability Level
53.2410	3	0.000%

Seasonality present at the 1 percent level.

Moving Seasonality Test

	Sum of Squares	Degrees of Freedom	Mean Square	F-Value
Between Years	85.8291	20	4.291454	1.857
Error	138.6635	60	2.311058	

Moving seasonality present at the 5 percent level.

COMBINED TEST FOR THE PRESENCE OF IDENTIFIABLE SEASONALITY
IDENTIFIABLE SEASONALITY PRESENT

D 11 Final Seasonally Adjusted Data

Test for the Presence of Residual Seasonality.
No evidence of residual seasonality in the entire series at the 1 percent level. F = 0.03
No evidence of residual seasonality in the last 3 years at the 1 percent level. F = 0.48
No evidence of residual seasonality in the last 3 years at the 5 percent level.

be properly adjusted. Instead, they will produce "adjusted" data. The only way to detect that these adjusted data should not be used is to look at the diagnostics.

8.33. X-12-ARIMA provides, in addition, a large set of new diagnostic tools to further gauge the quality of the seasonal adjustment and the appropriateness of the seasonal adjustment and modeling options chosen. These new diagnostic tools include features such as sliding span and frequency spectrum estimates, revision history[24] simulations, and options for comparing direct and indirect seasonal adjustments of aggregates.[25] Sliding spans can be used to evaluate the overall quality of the seasonal adjustment in competition with the Q statistics. They can also be used to assess the stability of trading-day estimates, to assess the adequateness of the length of the filters chosen, and to decide between direct and indirect adjustment. Frequency spectrum estimates from the irregular component can help identify residual seasonality narrowly defined and residual trading-day effects in different parts of the series. Revision history simulations can help decide between direct and indirect adjustment, selection of competing RegARIMA models, and identification of optimal length of forecast extension before filtering. The RegARIMA part of X-12-ARIMA also contains a large set of test statistics for model selection and outlier detection.

D. Issues in Seasonality

8.34. This section addresses a series of general and more QNA-specific issues related to seasonal adjustment.

- Subsection 1 explains how changes in the seasonal patterns cause revisions to the seasonally adjusted and trend-cycle estimates—the wagging tail problem. The subsection explains why trend-cycle estimates at the end of the series are particularly prone to revisions and why turning points can be identified only after a lag of several observations, because it is logically impossible to distinguish an outlier from a change in the trend-cycle based on one observation.
- Subsection 2 discusses the minimum length of time-series data required for obtaining seasonally adjusted estimates.

---

[24]See Section D.1 of this chapter for a discussion of revisions to seasonally adjusted data, and the wagging tail effect.
[25]See Section D.3.a of this chapter for a discussion of direct-versus-indirect seasonal adjustment of balancing items and aggregates.

- Subsection 3 addresses a series of issues related particularly to seasonal adjustment and trend-cycle estimation of QNA data, such as preservation of accounting identities, seasonal adjustment of balancing items and aggregates, and the relationship between annual data and seasonally adjusted quarterly data.

- Finally, Subsection 4 discusses the status and presentation of seasonally adjusted and trend-cycle QNA estimates.

1. Changes in Seasonal Patterns, Revisions, and the Wagging Tail Problem

8.35. Seasonal effects may change over time. The seasonal pattern may gradually evolve as economic behavior, economic structures, and institutional and social arrangements change. The seasonal pattern may also change abruptly because of sudden institutional changes.

8.36. Seasonal filters estimated using centered moving averages allow the seasonal pattern of the series to change over time and allow for a gradual update of the seasonal pattern, as illustrated in Example 8.2. This results in a more correct identification of the seasonal effects influencing different parts of the series.

8.37. Centered moving average seasonal filters also imply, however, that the final seasonally adjusted values depend on both past and future values of the series. Thus, to be able to seasonally adjust the earliest and latest observations of the series, either asymmetric filters have to be used for the earliest and the latest observations of the series or the series has to be extended by use of backcasts and forecasts based on the pattern of the time series. While the original X-11 program used asymmetric filters at the beginning and end of the series, X-12-ARIMA and X-11-ARIMA use ARIMA modeling techniques to extend the series so that less asymmetric filters can be used at the beginning and end.

8.38. Consequently, new observations may result in changes in the estimated seasonal pattern for the latest part of the series and subject seasonally adjusted data to more frequent revisions than the original non-seasonally adjusted series. This is illustrated in Example 8.3 below. Estimates of the underlying trend-cycle component for the most recent parts of the time series in particular may be subject to relatively large revisions at the first updates,[26] however,

theoretical and empirical studies indicate that the trend-cycle converges much faster to its final value than the seasonally adjusted series. In contrast, the seasonally adjusted series may be subject to lower revisions at the first updates but not-negligible revisions even after one to two years. There are two main reasons for slower convergence of the seasonal estimates. First, the seasonal moving average filters are significantly longer than the trend-cycle filters.[27] Second, revisions to the estimated regression parameters for calendar-related systematic effects may affect the complete time series. These revisions to the seasonally adjusted and trend-cycle estimates, owing to new observations, are commonly referred to as the "wagging tail problem."

8.39. Estimates of the underlying trend-cycle component for the most recent parts of the series should be interpreted with care, because signals of a change in the trend-cycle at the end of the series may be false. There are two main reasons why these signals may be false. First, outliers may cause significant revisions to the trend-cycle end-point estimates. It is usually not possible from a single observation to distinguish between an outlier and a change in the underlying trend-cycle, unless a particular event from other sources generating an outlier is known to have occurred. In general, several observations verifying the change in the trend-cycle indicated by the first observation are needed. Second, the moving average trend filters used at the end of the series (asymmetric moving average filters with or without ARIMA extension of the series) implicitly assume that the most recent basic trend of the series will persist. Consequently, when a turning point appears at the current end of the series, the estimated trend values at first present a systematically distorted picture, continuing to point in the direction of the former, now invalidated, trend. It is only after a lag of several observations that the change in the trend comes to light. While the trend-cycle component may be subject to large revisions at the first updates, however, it typically converges relatively fast to its final value.[28] An illustration of this can be found by comparing the data presented in Example 8.3 (seasonally adjusted estimates) with that in Example 8.4 (trend-cycle estimates).

---

[26]Illustrated in Example 8.4.

[27]For instance, the seasonal factors will be final after 2 years with the default 5-term (3 x 3) moving average seasonal filter (as long as any adjustments for calendar effects and outliers are not revised). In contrast, the trend-cycle estimates will be final after 2 quarters with the 5-term Henderson moving average trend-cycle filter (as long as the underlying seasonally adjusted series is not revised).

[32]The trend-cycle estimates will be final after 2 quarters with a 5-term Henderson moving average filter and after 3 quarters with a 7-term filter as long as the underlying seasonally adjusted series is not revised.

Box 8.3. X-11-ARIMA/X-12-ARIMA M- and Q-Test Statistics

The first and third column below are from the F 3 table of X-12-ARIMA's main output file with the M- and Q-test statistics. The test statistic values are for the full 21 years of the illustrative series, of which the last four years of data were presented in Example 8.1. The F 3 and F 2.B codes refer to the various "output tables" in the program's main output file.

The Q-test statistic at the bottom is a weighted average of the M-test statistics.

F 3. Monitoring and Quality Assessment Statistics

All the measures below are in the range from 0 to 3 with an acceptance region from 0 to 1.

Statistics	Weight in Q	Value
1. The relative contribution of the irregular component over a one-quarter span (from Table F 2.B).	13	M1 = 0.245
2. The relative contribution of the irregular component to the stationary portion of the variance (from Table F 2.F).	13	M2 = 0.037
3. The amount of quarter-to-quarter change in the irregular component compared with the amount of quarter-to-quarter change in the trend-cycle (from Table F2.H).	10	M3 = 0.048
4. The amount of auto-correlation in the irregular as described by the average duration of run (Table F 2.D).	5	M4 = 0.875
5. The number of quarters it takes the change in the trend-cycle to surpass the amount of change in the irregular (from Table F 2.E).	11	M5 = 0.200
6. The amount of year-to-year change in the irregular compared with the amount of year-to-year change in the seasonal (from Table F 2.H).	10	M6 = 0.972
7. The amount of moving seasonality present relative to the amount of stable seasonality (from Table F 2.I).	16	M7 = 0.378
8. The size of the fluctuations in the seasonal component throughout the whole series.	7	M8 = 1.472
9. The average linear movement in the seasonal component throughout the whole series.	7	M9 = 0.240
10. Same as 8, calculated for recent years only.	4	M10= 1.935
11. Same as 9, calculated for recent years only.	4	M11= 1.935

ACCEPTED at the level 0.52 Check the three above measures that failed. Q (without M2) = 0.59 ACCEPTED.

[1] Based on Eurostat (1998).
[2] Based on Statistics Canada's seasonal adjustment course material.

Motivation[1]	Diagnose and Remedy if Fails[2]
The seasonal and irregular components cannot be separated sufficiently if the irregular variation is too high compared with the variation in the seasonal component. M1 and M2 test this property by using two different trend removers.	Series too irregular. Try to preadjust the series.
If the quarter-to-quarter movement in the irregular is too important in the SI component compared with the trend-cycle, the separation of these component can be of low quality.	Irregular too strong compared to trend-cycle. Try to preadjust the series.
Test of randomness of the irregular component. (Be careful, because the estimator of the irregular is not white noise and the statistics can be misleading.)	Irregulars are autocorrelated. Try to change length of the trend filter and (different) preadjustment for trading-day effects. There may be residual trading-day effects in the series.
Similar to M3.	Irregular too strong compared to trend-cycle. Try to preadjust the series.
In one step of the X-11 filtering procedure, the irregular is separated from the seasonal by a 3x5 seasonal moving average. Sometimes, this can be too flexible (I/S ratio is very high) or too restrictive (I/S ratio is very low). If M6 fails, you can try to use the 3x1 or the stable option to adjust for this problem.	Irregular too strong compared with seasonality. Try to change length of seasonal MA filter.
Combined F-test to measure the stable seasonality and the moving seasonality in the final SI ratios. Important test statistics for indicating whether seasonality is identifiable by the program.	Do not seasonally adjust the series. Indicates absence of Seasonality.
Measurement of the random fluctuations in the seasonal factors. A high value can indicate a high distortion in the estimate of the seasonal factors.	Change seasonal moving average filter. Seasonality may be moving too fast.
Because one is normally interested in the recent data, these statistics give insights into the quality of the recent estimates of the seasonal factors. Watch these statistics carefully if you use forecasts of the seasonal factors and not concurrent adjustment.	Look at ARIMA extrapolation. Indicate that the seasonality may be moving too fast at the end of the series

Example 8.2. Moving Seasonality

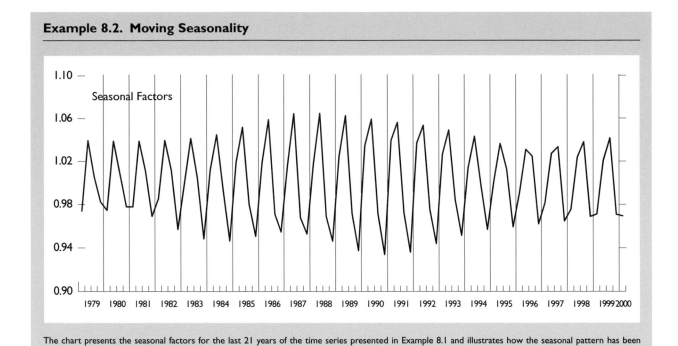

The chart presents the seasonal factors for the last 21 years of the time series presented in Example 8.1 and illustrates how the seasonal pattern has been changing gradually over time, as estimated by X-12-ARIMA.

8.40. Studies have shown that using ARIMA models to extend the series before filtering generally signifi cantly reduces the size of these revisions compared with using asymmetric filters.[29] These studies have shown that, typically, revisions to the level of the series as well as to the period-to-period rate of change are reduced. Use of RegARIMA models, as offered by X-12-ARIMA, may make the backcasts and forecasts more robust and thus further reduces the size of these revisions compared with using pure ARIMA models. The reason for this is that RegARIMA models allow trading-day effects and other effects captured by the regressors to be taken into account in the forecasts in a consistent way. Availability of longer time series should result in a more precise identification of the regular pattern of the series (the seasonal pattern and the ARIMA model) and, in general, also reduce the size of the revisions.

8.41. Revisions to the seasonally adjusted data can be carried out as soon as new observations become available—concurrent revisions—or at longer intervals. The latter requires use of the one-year-ahead forecasted seasonal factors offered by X-11, X-11-ARIMA, and X-12-ARIMA to compute seasonally adjusted estimates for more recent periods not covered by the last

revision. Use of one-year-ahead forecast of seasonal factors was common in the early days of seasonal adjustment with X-11 but is less common today. Besides full concurrent revisions and use of forecasts of seasonal factors, a third alternative is to use period-to-period rates of change from estimates based on concurrent adjustments to update previously released data and only revise data for past periods once a year.

8.42. From a purely theoretical point of view, and excluding the effects of outliers and revisions to the original unadjusted data, concurrent adjustment is always preferable. New data contribute new information about changes in the seasonal pattern that preferably should be incorporated into the estimates as early as possible. Consequently, use of one-year-ahead forecasts of seasonal factors results in loss of information and, as empirical studies[30] have shown and as illustrated in Example 8.5, often in larger, albeit less frequent, revisions to the levels as well as the period-to-period rates of change in the seasonally adjusted data. Theoretical studies[31] support this finding.

8.43. The potential gains from concurrent adjustment can be significant but are not always. In general

[29]See among others Bobitt and Otto (1990), Dagum (1987), Dagum and Morry (1984), Hout et al. (1986).

[30]See among others Dagum and Morry (1984), Hout and others. (1986), Kenny and Durbin (1982), and McKenzie (1984).
[31]See among others Dagum (1981 and 1982) and Wallis (1982).

Example 8.3. Changes in Seasonal Patterns, Revisions of the Seasonally Adjusted Series, and the Wagging Tail Problem

Revisions to the Seasonally Adjusted Estimates by Adding New Observations

(Original unadjusted data in Example 8.1.)

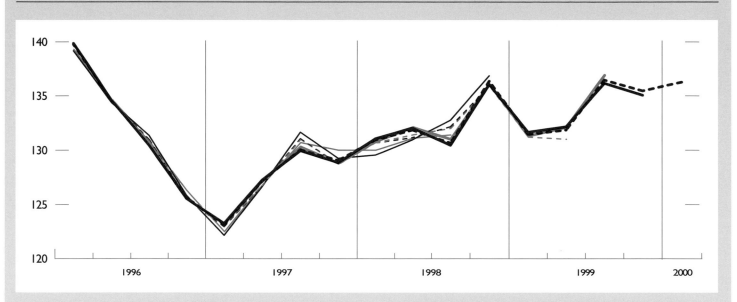

Date	Data until q1 00 Index	Period-to-Period Rate of Change	Data until q4 99 Index	Period-to-Period Rate of Change	Data until q3 99 Index	Period-to-Period Rate of Change	Data until q2 99 Index	Period-to-Period Rate of Change	Data until q1 99 Index	Period-to-Period Rate of Change	Data until q4 98 Index	Period-to-Period Rate of Change	Data until q3 98 Index	Period-to-Period Rate of Change
q1 1996	139.8		139.9		139.8		139.7		139.7		139.2		139.3	
q2 1996	134.6	–3.7%	134.6	–3.7%	134.6	–3.7%	134.5	–3.7%	134.5	–3.7%	134.4	–3.4%	134.5	–3.5%
q3 1996	130.5	–3.1%	130.5	–3.1%	130.6	–3.0%	130.9	–2.7%	131.0	–2.6%	131.4	–2.2%	130.8	–2.7%
q4 1996	125.7	–3.7%	125.6	–3.7%	125.6	–3.8%	125.6	–4.1%	125.6	–4.1%	125.9	–4.2%	126.3	–3.5%
q1 1997	123.2	–2.0%	123.3	–1.9%	123.2	–2.0%	123.1	–2.0%	123.0	–2.0%	122.2	–2.9%	122.5	–3.0%
q2 1997	127.2	3.2%	127.3	3.2%	127.2	3.3%	126.8	3.1%	126.8	3.0%	126.7	3.7%	126.8	3.5%
q3 1997	130.1	**2.3%**	130.0	2.2%	130.3	2.4%	131.0	3.3%	131.1	3.5%	131.7	3.9%	130.7	**3.1%**
q4 1997	129.1	–0.7%	128.9	–0.8%	128.8	–1.1%	128.7	–1.7%	128.7	–1.8%	129.3	–1.8%	130.0	–0.5%
q1 1998	131.0	**1.4%**	131.1	1.7%	130.8	1.6%	130.7	1.6%	130.7	1.5%	129.6	0.2%	130.0	**0.0%**
q2 1998	131.9	0.7%	132.1	0.8%	132.1	0.9%	131.4	0.5%	131.2	0.4%	131.0	1.1%	131.1	0.8%
q3 1998	130.7	–1.0%	130.5	–1.2%	131.0	–0.8%	132.0	0.5%	132.2	0.7%	132.8	1.3%	131.4	0.2%
q4 1998	136.4	4.4%	136.1	4.3%	136.1	3.9%	135.9	3.0%	135.9	2.8%	136.9	3.0%		
q1 1999	131.5	–3.6%	131.7	–3.2%	131.3	–3.5%	131.2	–3.4%	131.2	–3.5%				
q2 1999	131.9	0.3%	132.2	0.4%	132.1	**0.6%**	131.0	**–0.2%**						
q3 1999	136.5	3.4%	136.2	**3.0%**	136.9	**3.6%**								
q4 1999	135.5	–0.7%	135.1	–0.8%										
q1 2000	136.3	0.6%												

Note how the seasonally adjusted data (like the trend-cycle data presented in Example 8.4 but less so) for a particular period are revised as later data become available, even when the *unadjusted data for that period were not revised.* In this example, adding q1 2000 results in an upward adjustment of the growth from q2 1999 to q3 1999 in the seasonally adjusted series from an estimate of 3.0 percent to a revised estimate of 3.4 percent. Minor effects on the seasonally adjusted series of adding q1 2000 can be traced all the way back to 1993.

Example 8.4. Changes in Seasonal Patterns, Revisions and the Wagging Tail Problem
Revisions to Trend-Cycle Estimates
(Original unadjusted data in Example 8.1, seasonally adjusted in Example 8.3.)

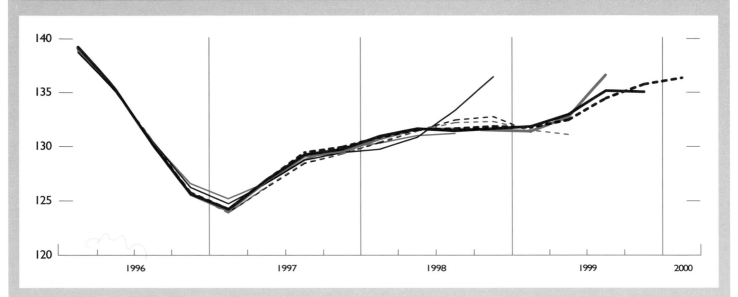

Date	Data until q1 00 Index	Period-to-Period Rate of Change	Data until q4 99 Index	Period-to-Period Rate of Change	Data until q3 99 Index	Period-to-Period Rate of Change	Data until q2 99 Index	Period-to-Period Rate of Change	Data until q1 99 Index	Period-to-Period Rate of Change	Data until q4 98 Index	Period-to-Period Rate of Change	Data until q3 98 Index	Period-to-Period Rate of Change
q1 1996	139.8		139.9		139.8		139.7		139.7		139.2		139.3	
q1 1996	139.2		139.2		139.1		139.0		139.0		138.7		138.9	
q2 1996	135.2	−2.9%	135.2	−2.9%	135.2	−2.8%	135.2	−2.7%	135.2	−2.7%	135.0	−2.7%	135.0	−2.8%
q3 1996	130.1	−3.7%	130.1	−3.8%	130.2	−3.7%	130.3	−3.6%	130.4	−3.6%	130.4	−3.4%	130.4	−3.4%
q4 1996	125.7	−3.4%	125.6	−3.5%	125.6	−3.5%	125.7	−3.6%	125.7	−3.6%	126.2	−3.2%	126.6	−2.9%
q1 1997	124.2	−1.2%	124.2	−1.1%	124.1	−1.2%	123.9	−1.4%	123.9	−1.4%	124.7	−1.2%	125.2	−1.1%
q2 1997	126.9	2.2%	126.9	2.2%	126.8	2.1%	126.3	1.9%	126.2	1.9%	126.6	1.5%	126.7	1.2%
q3 1997	129.4	2.0%	129.2	1.8%	129.1	1.8%	128.5	1.8%	128.4	1.8%	128.7	1.7%	128.8	1.7%
q4 1997	129.9	0.4%	129.7	0.4%	129.5	0.4%	129.3	0.6%	129.3	0.7%	129.4	0.5%	129.9	0.8%
q1 1998	130.8	0.7%	130.9	0.9%	130.7	0.9%	130.4	0.8%	130.3	0.8%	129.7	0.3%	130.3	0.4%
q2 1998	131.5	0.5%	131.6	0.5%	131.6	0.7%	131.4	0.8%	131.4	**0.8%**	130.8	**0.9%**	131.0	0.5%
q3 1998	131.6	0.1%	131.4	−0.2%	131.6	0.0%	132.2	0.5%	132.4	**0.8%**	133.3	**1.9%**	131.2	**0.2%**
q4 1998	131.8	0.2%	131.6	0.2%	131.5	−0.1%	132.3	0.1%	132.7	**0.3%**	136.4	**2.3%**		
q1 1999	131.7	−0.1%	131.8	0.2%	131.4	−0.1%	131.5	−0.6%	131.3	**−1.1%**				
q2 1999	132.4	0.5%	132.9	0.8%	132.7	1.0%	131.1	−0.3%						
q3 1999	134.4	1.5%	135.1	1.6%	136.6	2.9%								
q4 1999	135.7	**1.0%**	135.0	**−0.1%**										
q1 2000	136.3	0.4%												

The chart and table demonstrate how the trend-cycle estimates for a particular period may be subject to relatively large revisions as data for new periods become available, even when *the unadjusted data for that period were not revised*. In this example, adding q1 2000 results in an upward adjustment of the change in the estimated trend-cycle component from q3 1999 to q4 1999, from an initial estimate of –0.1 percent to a revised estimate of 1.0 percent.

Also, observe how the strong irregular effect that occurred in q4 1998—an upward turn that disappears in the later trend-cycle estimates—wrongly resulted in an initial estimated strong growth from mid-1998 and onward in the earlier trend-cycle estimates.

Example 8.5. Changes in Seasonal Patterns, Revisions, and the Wagging Tail Problem

Concurrent Adjustment Versus Use of One-Year-Ahead Forecast of Seasonal Factors

(Original unadjusted data in Example 8.1, revisions of last seven quarters with concurrent seasonally adjusted data in Example 8.3.)

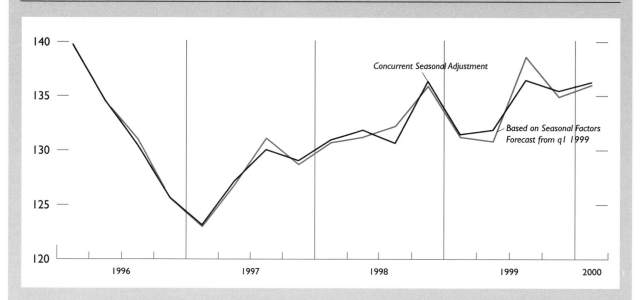

Date	Concurrent Seasonal Adjustment	Period-to-Period Rate of Change	Based on Seasonal Factors Forecast from q1 1999	Period-to-Period Rate of Change
q1 1996	139.8		139.7	
q2 1996	134.6	−3.7%	134.5	−3.7%
q3 1996	130.5	−3.1%	131.0	−2.6%
q4 1997	125.7	−3.7%	125.6	−4.1%
q1 1997	123.2	−2.0%	123.0	−2.0%
q2 1997	127.2	3.2%	126.8	3.0%
q3 1997	130.1	2.3%	131.1	3.5%
q4 1997	129.1	−0.7%	128.7	−1.8%
q1 1998	131.0	1.4%	130.7	1.5%
q2 1998	131.9	0.7%	131.2	0.4%
q3 1998	130.7	−1.0%	132.2	0.7%
q4 1998	136.4	4.4%	135.9	2.8%
q1 1999	131.5	−3.6%	131.2	−3.5%
q2 1999	131.9	**0.3%**	130.8	**−0.3%**
q3 1999	136.5	**3.4%**	138.6	**6.0%**
q4 1999	135.5	**−0.7%**	134.9	**−2.7%**
q1 2000	136.3	**0.6%**	136.0	**0.8%**

The chart and table demonstrate the effect of current update (concurrent adjustment) versus use of one-year-ahead forecast seasonal factors. As can be seen by comparing with Example 8.3, use of one-year-ahead forecasts of the seasonal factors results in loss of information and larger, but less frequent, revisions. In particular, in this example, using one-year-ahead forecasts of the seasonal factors gave an initial estimated decline from q3 to q4 1999 in the seasonally adjusted series of −2.7 percent, which is substantially larger compared with the initial estimate of −0.8 percent with current update of the seasonal factors (see Example 8.3).

the potential gains depend on, among other things, the following factors:
- The stability of the seasonal component. A high degree of stability in the seasonal factors implies that the information gain from concurrent adjustment is limited and makes it easier to forecast the seasonal factors. On the contrary, rapidly moving seasonality implies that the information gain can be significant.

- The size of the irregular component. A high irregular component may reduce the gain from concurrent adjustment because there is a higher likelihood for the signals from the new observations about changes in the seasonal pattern to be false, reflecting an irregular effect and not a change in the seasonal pattern.
- The size of revisions to the original unadjusted data. Large revisions to the unadjusted data may

reduce the gain from concurrent adjustment because there is a higher likelihood for the signals from the new observations about changes in the seasonal pattern to be false.

2. Minimum Length of the Time Series for Seasonal Adjustment

8.44. Five years of data and relatively stable seasonality are required in general as a minimum length to obtain properly seasonally adjusted estimates. For series that show particularly strong and stable seasonal movements, it may be possible to obtain seasonally adjusted estimates based on only three years of data.

8.45. A longer time series, however, is required to identify more precisely the seasonal pattern and to adjust the series for calendar variations (i.e., trading days and moving holidays), breaks in the series, outliers, and particular events that may have affected the series and may cause difficulties in properly identifying the seasonal pattern of the series.

8.46. For countries that are setting up a new QNA system, at least five years of retrospective calculations are recommended to conduct seasonal adjustment.

8.47. If a country has gone through severe structural changes resulting in radical changes in the seasonal patterns, it may not be possible to seasonally adjust its data until several years after the break in the series. In such cases, it may be necessary to seasonally adjust the pre-break and post-break part of the series separately.

3. Critical Issues in Seasonal Adjustment of QNA

8.48. When producing seasonally adjusted national account estimates, four critical issues must be decided:
(a) Should balancing items and aggregates be seasonally adjusted directly or derived residually, and should accounting and aggregation relationships be maintained?
(b) Should the relationship among current price value, price indices, and volume estimates be maintained, and, if so, which component should be derived residually?
(c) Should supply and use and other accounting identities be maintained, and, if so, what are the practical implications?
(d) Should the relationship to the annual accounts be strictly preserved?

a. Compilation levels and seasonal adjustment of balancing items and aggregates

8.49. Seasonally adjusted estimates for balancing items and aggregates can be derived directly or indirectly from seasonally adjusted estimates for the different components; generally the results will differ, sometimes significantly. For instance, a seasonally adjusted estimate for value added in manufacturing at current prices can be derived either by seasonally adjusting value added directly or as the difference between seasonally adjusted estimates for output and intermediate consumption at current prices. Similarly, a seasonally adjusted estimate for GDP at current prices can be derived either by seasonally adjusting GDP directly or as the sum of seasonally adjusted estimates for value added by activity (plus taxes on products). Alternatively, a seasonally adjusted estimate for GDP can be derived as the sum of seasonally adjusted estimates for the expenditure components.

8.50. Conceptually, neither the direct approach nor the indirect approach is optimal. There are arguments in favor of both approaches. It is convenient, and for some uses crucial, that accounting and aggregation relationships are preserved.[32] Studies[33] and practice, however, have shown that the quality of the seasonally adjusted series, and especially estimates of the trend-cycle component, may be improved, sometimes significantly, by seasonally adjusting aggregates directly or at least at a more aggregated level. Practice has shown that seasonally adjusting the data at a detailed level can leave residual seasonality in the aggregates, may result in less smooth seasonally adjusted series, and may result in series more subject to revisions. Which compilation level for seasonal adjustment gives the best results varies from case to case and depends on the properties of the particular series.

8.51. For aggregates, the direct approach may give the best results if the component series shows the same seasonal pattern or if the trend-cycles of the series are highly correlated. If the component series shows the same seasonal pattern, aggregation often reduces the impact of the irregular components of the component series, which at the most detailed level (the level of the source data) may be too dominant for

---

[32] However, for time series of chain-linked price indices and volume data, these accounting relationships are already broken (see Section D.4 of Chapter IX for a discussion of the non-additivity feature of chain-linked measures).
[33] See, among others, Dagum and Morry (1984).

proper seasonal adjustment. This effect may be particularly important for small countries where irregular events have a stronger impact on the data. Similarly, if the component series do not show the same seasonal pattern but their trend-cycles are highly correlated, aggregation reduces the impact of both the seasonal and irregular components of the component series.

8.52. In other cases, the indirect approach may give the best results. For instance, if the component series show very different seasonal patterns and the trend-cycles of the series are uncorrelated, aggregation may increase the appearance of irregular movements in the aggregate. Similarly, aggregation may cause large, highly volatile nonseasonal component series to overshadow seasonal component series, making it difficult or impossible to identify any seasonality that is present in the aggregate series. Moreover, it may be easier to identify breaks, outliers, calendar effects, the seasonal effect narrowly defined, and so on in detailed series with low to moderate irregular components than directly from the aggregates, because at the detailed level these effects may display a simpler pattern.

8.53. For balancing items, there is reason to believe that the indirect approach more often gives better results. Because balancing items are derived as the difference between two groups of component series, in the balancing item, the impact of the irregular components of the component series is more likely to be compounded. In contrast, because aggregates are derived by summation, opposite irregular movements in the component series will cancel each other out.

8.54. Some seasonal adjustment programs, including the X-11-ARIMA and the X-12-ARIMA, offer the possibility of adjusting aggregates using the direct and indirect approach simultaneously and comparing the results. For instance, the X-12-ARIMA, using the Composite series specifications command, adjusts aggregates simultaneously using the direct and indirect approach and provides users with a set of test statistics to compare the results. These test statistics are primarily the M and Q statistics presented in Example 8.4, measures of smoothness, and frequency spectrum estimates from the directly and indirectly estimated irregular component. In addition, sliding span and revision history simulation tests for both the direct and the indirect estimates are available to assess which approach results in estimates less subject to revisions.

8.55. In practice, the choice between direct and indirect seasonal adjustment should be based on the main intended use of the estimates and the relative smoothness and stability of the derived estimates. For some uses, preserved accounting and aggregation relationships in the data may be crucial, and the smoothness and stability of the derived estimates secondary. For other uses, the time-series properties of the derived estimates may be crucial, while accounting and aggregation relationships may be of no importance. If the difference is insignificant, representing a minor annoyance rather than adding any useful information, most compilers will opt for preserving accounting and aggregation relationships between published data.

8.56. Consequently, international practice varies with respect to the choice between direct and indirect seasonal adjustment. Many countries obtain the seasonally adjusted QNA aggregates as the sum of adjusted components, while some also adjust the totals independently, with discrepancies between the seasonally adjusted total and the sum of the component series as a result. Finally, some countries only publish seasonally adjusted estimates for main aggregates and typically seasonally adjust these directly or derive them indirectly by adjusting rather aggregated component series.

b. Seasonal adjustment and the relationship among price, volume, and value

8.57. As for balancing items and aggregates, seasonally adjusted estimates for national accounts price indices, volume measures, and current price data can be derived either by seasonally adjusting the three series independently or by seasonally adjusting two of them and deriving the third as a residual, if all three show seasonal variations.[34] Again, because of nonlinearities in the seasonal adjustment procedures, the alternative methods will give different results; however, the differences may be minor. Preserving the relationship among the price indices, volume measures, and the current price data is convenient for users.[35] Thus, it seems reasonable to seasonally adjust two of them and derive a seasonally adjusted estimate for the third residually. Choosing which series to derive residually must be determined on a case-by-case basis, depending on which alternative seems to produce the most reasonable result.

---

[34]Experience has shown that the price data may not always show identifiable seasonal variations.
[35]Note that chain-linking preserves this relationship $(V = P \cdot Q)$.

c. Seasonal adjustment and supply and use and other accounting identities

8.58. Seasonal adjustment may cause additional statistical discrepancies in seasonally adjusted data between supply and use, GDP estimated from alternative sides, and between the different sides of other accounting identities. These statistical discrepancies are caused by nonlinearities in the seasonal filters, as well as use of different filter length, use of different pre-adjustments, and differences in estimated calendar effects on the various sides of the accounting identity. The statistical discrepancies may be reduced by forcing the programs to choose the same filter length and use the same pre-adjustment factors and calendar-effect factors for all series. This may, however, reduce the smoothness and stability of the individual seasonally adjusted series.

d. Seasonal adjustment and consistency with annual accounts

8.59. Annual totals based on the seasonally adjusted data will not automatically—and often should not conceptually—be equal to the corresponding annual totals based on the original unadjusted data. The number of working days, the impact of moving holidays, and other calendar-related effects vary from year to year. Similarly, moving seasonality implies that the impact of the seasonal effect narrowly defined will vary from year to year. Thus, conceptually, for series with significant calendar-related effects or moving seasonality effects, the annual totals of a seasonally adjusted series *should differ* from the unadjusted series.

8.60. For series without any significant calendar-related or moving seasonality effects, X-11/X-12 will produce seasonally adjusted data that automatically add up to the corresponding unadjusted annual totals if the seasonal components are additive (equation 8.1) but not if the seasonals are multiplicative (equation 8.2). Multiplicative seasonal factors require that a current-period weighted average of the seasonal factors averages to 1 and for the seasonally adjusted data to automatically add up to the corresponding unadjusted annual totals. However, the normalization of the seasonal factors in step (d) of the filtering procedure in stages 1 and 2 described in paragraph 8.23 only ensures that the unweighted, and not the weighted, annual average of the seasonal factors averages 1. It follows that,

for series with multiplicative seasonal factors and no significant calendar-related or moving seasonality effects, the difference between the annual totals of the adjusted and unadjusted series will depend on the amplitude of the seasonal variation narrowly defined, the volatility of the seasonally adjusted series, and the pace of the change in the underlying trend-cycle. The difference will be small, and often insignificant, for series with moderate to low seasonal amplitudes and for series with little volatility and trend-cycle change.

8.61. X-11-ARIMA and X-12-ARIMA provide options for forcing the annual totals from the seasonally adjusted data to be equal to the original totals. Seasonal adjustment experts, however, generally recommend not using the forcing option[36] if the series show significant[37] trading-day, other calendar-related, or moving seasonality effects and trading-day or other calendar adjustments are performed. In such cases, consistency with the annual series would be achieved at the expense of the quality of the seasonal adjustment and would be conceptually wrong.

4. Status and Presentation of Seasonally Adjusted and Trend-Cycle QNA Estimates

8.62. The status and presentation of seasonally adjusted and trend-cycle QNA estimates vary. Some countries publish seasonally adjusted estimates for only a few main aggregates and present them as additional (sometimes unofficial) analytical elaborations of the official data. Other countries focus on the seasonally adjusted and trend-cycle estimates and publish an almost complete set of seasonally adjusted and trend-cycle QNA estimates in a reconciled accounting format. They may present the original unadjusted data as supplementary information.

8.63. The mode of presentation also varies substantially. Seasonally adjusted and trend-cycle data can be presented as charts; as tables with the actual data, either in money values or as index series; and as tables with derived measures of quarter-to-quarter rates of change. The last may be presented as the actual rates of change or as annualized rates (see Box 8.4).

---

[36]The X-12-ARIMA manual explicitly recommends against using the forcing option if trading-day adjustment is performed or if the seasonal pattern is changing rapidly.
[37]Relative to the "adding-up error" introduced by the unweighted, and not the weighted, annual average of the seasonal factors averaging to 1 for multiplicative seasonal adjustment.

8.64. The rates of change are sometimes annualized to make it easier for the layman to interpret the data. Most users have a feel for the size of annual growth rates but not for monthly or quarterly rates. Annualizing growth rates, however, also means that the irregular effects are compounded. Irrespectively of whether the actual or annualized quarterly rates of change are presented, it is important to indicate clearly what the data represent.

8.65. Growth rates representing different measures of change can easily be confused unless it is clearly indicated what the data represent. For instance, terms like "annual percentage change" or "annual rate of growth" can mean (a) the rate of change from one quarter to the next annualized (at annual rate); (b) the change from the same period of the previous year; (c) the change from one year to the next in annual data, or, equivalently, the change from the average of one year to the average of the next year; or (d) the change from the end of one year to the end of the next year.

8.66. Some countries also present the level of quarterly current and constant price data at annualized levels by multiplying the actual data by four. This seems artificial, does not make the data easier to interpret, and may be confusing because annual flow data in monetary terms no longer can be derived as the sum of the quarters. Users not familiar with the practice of annualizing levels of current and constant price data by multiplying the actual data by four may confuse annualized levels with forecast annual data. For these reasons, this practice is not recommended.

8.67. Finally, whether to present seasonally adjusted data or estimates of the trend-cycle component is still the subject of debate between experts in this area. In this manual, it is recommended to present both, preferably in the form of graphs incorporated into the same chart, as illustrated in Example 8.6.

8.68. An integrated graphical presentation highlights the overall development in the two series over time, including the uncertainties represented by the irregular component. In contrast, measures of quarter-to-quarter rates of change (in particular, annualized rates) may result in an overemphasis on the short-term movements in the latest and most uncertain observations at the expense of the general trend in the series. The underlying data and derived measures of quarter-to-quarter rates of change, however, should be provided as supplementary information.

8.69. The presentation should highlight the lower reliability, particularly for the trend-cycle component, of the estimates for the latest observations as discussed in this section. Means of highlighting the lower quality of the end-point estimates include (a) noting past revisions to these estimates; (b) suppressing estimates of the trend-cycle component for the latest observations in graphical presentations, as in Example 8.6; and (c) showing estimates for the latest observations with a trumpet on graphical presentations and with an estimated confidence interval in tabular presentations.

Box 8.4. Annualizing, or Compounding, Growth Rates

Period-to-period rates of change in quarterly data can be annualized using the following compounding formula:

$$ar_{q,y} = (1 + r_{q,y})^4 - 1, \qquad r_{q,y} = (X_{q,y}/X_{q-1,y} - 1)$$

where:

$ar_{q,y}$ Annualized quarter-to-quarter rate of change for quarter q of year y.

$r_{q,y}$ Original quarter-to-quarter rate of change for quarter q of year y in time series $X_{q,y}$.

The purpose of annualizing the rates of change is to present period-to-period rates of change for different period lengths on the same scale and thus to make it easier for the layman to interpret the data. For instance, annualizing the rates of change may help to clarify that a 0.8 per-cent growth from one month to the next is equivalent to:

- 2.4 percent growth from one quarter to the next ($2.4\% = [(1 + 0.008)^3 - 1] \cdot 100$), or
- 10.0 percent growth from one year to the next ($10.0\% = [(1 + 0.024)^4 - 1] \cdot 100 = [(1 + 0.008)^{12} - 1] \cdot 100$).

Most users have a feel for annual growth rates and immediately recognize that a 10.0 percent annual growth in, for example, constant price household consumption expenditures is a lot, while 0.8 percent from one month to the next appears meager.

Annualized quarterly growth rates do not indicate what the annual growth will be and are not intended to be simple forecasts of what the annual growth rate would be if this growth continues for four quarters. The quarterly growth rate has to be constant for eight quarters for the annualized quarterly growth rate to be equal to the annual growth rate.

Example 8.6. Presentation of Seasonally Adjusted Series and the Corresponding Trend-Cycle Component

(Based on data from Example 8.1.)

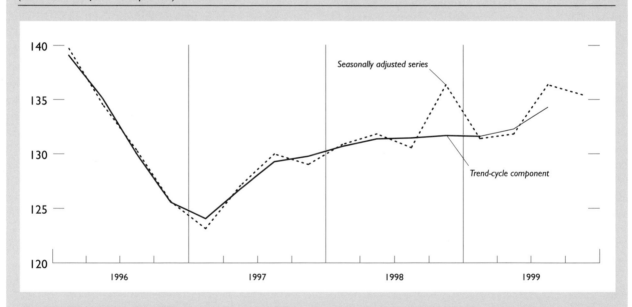

Presenting the seasonally adjusted series and estimates of the trend-cycle components in the same chart highlights the overall development in the two series over time, including the uncertainties represented by the irregular component. Suppressing in the chart the estimates of the trend-cycle component at the end of the series or showing the trend-cycle estimates at the end with a trumpet based on estimated confidence intervals further highlights the added uncertainties at the end of the series.

IX Price and Volume Measures: Specific QNA-ANA Issues

A. Introduction

9.1. This chapter addresses a selected set of issues for constructing time series of price and volume measures that are of specific importance for the quarterly national accounts (QNA). In particular, it discusses the relationship between price and volume measures in the QNA and in the annual national accounts (ANA): namely, (1) how to aggregate price and volume measures over time; (2) how to choose the base period in the QNA; (3) the frequency of chain-linking; and (4) the techniques for annual chain-linking of quarterly data. In addition, the chapter addresses how to deal with nonadditivity and presentation of chain-linked volume measures in the QNA.

9.2. The *1993 SNA* does not contain specific recommendations for price and volume measures for the QNA or the relationship between price and volume measures in the QNA and the ANA. The basic principles for quarterly price and volume measures in the QNA and the ANA are the same, including the *1993 SNA* recommendation of moving away from the traditional constant-price measures[1] to annually chain-linked measures, preferably using superlative index number formulas such as the Fisher and Tornquist formulas. The issues listed above raise new problems, however, many of which have not satisfactorily been dealt with to date in the literature. Conventional intertemporal index number theory has mainly been concerned with price and quantity comparisons between separate pairs of *points in time* and not with price and volume measures in a time-series context. In particular, conventional index number theory has not been concerned with price and quantity comparisons between *periods of time of different duration* (e.g., years and quarters) and the relationship among

these price and volume measures for longer time periods, the corresponding measures for the subperiods, and the point-to-point measures.

9.3. QNA price and volume measures should be in the form of time series and should be consistent with corresponding ANA estimates. For QNA price and volume measures to constitute a time series, they must meet the following four requirements:
(a) The data should reflect both the *short- and long-term* movements in the series, particularly the timing of any turning points.
(b) The data should allow different *periods* to be compared in a consistent manner. That is, based on the underlying time series, the data should allow measures of change to be derived between any period (i.e., from the previous period, the same period in the previous year, and a particular period several years earlier).
(c) The data should allow *periods of different duration* to be compared in a consistent manner. That is, based on the underlying time series, the data should allow measures of change to be derived between any periods of any length (e.g., between the average of the last two quarters and of the previous two quarters or the same two quarters several years earlier, from the average of the previous year and of a year several years earlier).
(d) The data should allow *subperiods and periods* to be compared in a consistent manner (e.g., quarters with years).

9.4. Consistency between QNA and ANA price and volume measures, in principle, requires either that the ANA measures are derived from quarterly measures or that consistency is forced on the QNA data using benchmarking techniques. This is true even if the basic requirement that the QNA and ANA measures are based on the same methods of compilation and presentation (i.e., same index formula, base year(s), and reference period) is met. Strict consistency

---

[1]Constant price measures are fixed-base Laspeyres-type volume measures (fixed-price weights) and the corresponding price deflators are Paasche price indices.

between QNA and direct ANA price and volume measures is generally not possible because quarterly indices based on most index formulas, including Paasche and Fisher, do not aggregate exactly to their corresponding direct annual indices. For fixed-base Laspeyres volume indices, or traditional constant price estimates, consistency requires that the estimates are derived by explicitly or implicitly valuing the quantities at the annual quantity-weighted average of the prices charged in different time periods of the base year,[2] effectively implying that the annual volume data are derived from the quarterly data[3] (see Section B) and not directly. Finally, for annually chain-linked Laspeyres volume indices, strict consistency can only be achieved by use of an annual linking technique that can result in a break[4] in the estimates between the fourth quarter of one year and the first quarter of the next year (see Section D).

9.5. Consistency between QNA and ANA price and volume measures also requires that new methods, like chain-linking, are implemented simultaneously in both the QNA and ANA. Although the *1993 SNA* recommends moving to chain-linked volume measures, for countries currently compiling traditional constant price estimates, it would generally be undesirable to complicate the introduction of QNA by also introducing new techniques for constructing and presenting volume measures at the same time. It is recommended for these countries to introduce chaining in a second phase, concurrent with the introduction of chain-linking in the ANA. Thus, for countries currently compiling traditional constant price estimates, only the discussion in Section B of aggregating price and volume measures over time is of immediate importance.

B. Aggregating Price and Volume Measures Over Time

9.6. Aggregation over time means deriving less frequent data (e.g., annual) from more frequent data (e.g., quarterly). Incorrect aggregation of prices, or price indices, over time to derive annual deflators can introduce errors in independently compiled annual estimates and thus can cause inconsistency between QNA and ANA estimates, even when they are derived from the same underlying data. When deriving annual constant price estimates by deflating annual current price data, a common practice is to compute the annual price deflators as a simple unweighted average of monthly or quarterly price indices. This practice may introduce substantial errors in the derived annual constant price estimates, even when inflation is low. This may happen when

- there are seasonal or other within-year variations in prices or quantities, and
- the within-year pattern of variation in either prices or quantities is unstable.

9.7. Volume measures for aggregated periods of time should conceptually be constructed from period-total quantities for each individual homogenous product. The corresponding implicit price measures would be quantity-weighted period-average price measures. For example, annual volume measures for single homogenous products[5] should be constructed as sums of the quantities in each subperiod. The corresponding implicit annual average price, derived as the annual current price value divided by the annual quantity, would therefore be a quantity-weighted average of the prices in each quarter. As shown in Example 9.1, the quantity-weighted average price will generally differ, sometimes significantly, from the unweighted average price. Similarly, for groups of products, conceptually, annual volume measures can be constructed as a weighted aggregate of the annual quantities for each individual product. The corresponding implicit annual price deflator for the group would be a weighted aggregate of the quantity-weighted annual average prices for the individual products. This annual price deflator for the group based on the quantity-weighted annual average prices would generally differ, sometimes significantly, from the annual price deflators derived as a simple unweighted average of monthly or quarterly price indices often used in ANA systems—deflation by the latter may introduce substantial errors in the derived annual constant price estimates.

---

[2]The corresponding explicit or implicit annual deflators should be derived as current-year quantity-weighted averages of monthly or quarterly fixed-based Paasche price indices.

[3]This is particularly an issue under high inflation and for highly volatile items.

[4]This can occur if there are strong changes in relative quantities and relative prices.

[5]Homogenous products are identical in physical and economic terms to other items in that product group and over time. In contrast, when there are significant variations among items or over time in the physical or economic characteristic of the product group, each version should be treated as a separate product (e.g., out-of-season fruit and vegetables such as old potatoes may be regarded as different products than in-season fruit and vegetables such as new potatoes).

Example 9.1. Weighted and Unweighted Annual Averages of Prices (or Price Indices) When Sales and Price Patterns Through the Year are Uneven

	Quantity (1)	Price (2)	Current Price Value (3)	Unweighted Average Price (4)	Unit Value Weighted Average Price (5) = (3)/(1)	Constant Price Value	
						At Unweighted Average 1999 Prices (6) = (4)·(1)	At Weighted Average 1999 Prices (7) = (5)·(1)
q1	0	80	0			0	0
q2	150	50	7,500			7,500	6,750
q3	50	30	1,500			2,500	2,250
q4	0	40	0			0	0
1999	**200**		**9,000**	**50**	**45**	**10,000**	**9,000**
q1	0	40	0			0	0
q2	180	50	9,000			9,000	8,100
q3	20	30	600			1,000	900
q4	0	40	0			0	0
2000	**200**		**9,600**	**40**	**48**	**10,000**	**9,000**
% Change from 1999 to 2000	0.00%		6.70%	−20.00%	6.70%	0.00%	0.00%

Direct Deflation of Annual Current Price Data

2000 at 1999 prices	9600/(40/50) = 9600/0.8	= 12,000
% change from 1999	(12000/9000−1) · 100	= 33.3%

This example highlights the case of an unweighted annual average of prices (or price indices) being misleading when sales and price patterns through the year are uneven for a single homogenous product. The products sold in the different quarters are assumed to be identical in all economic aspects.

In the example, the annual quantities and the quarterly prices in quarters with nonzero sales are the same in both years, but the pattern of sales shifts toward the second quarter in 1998. As a result, the total annual current price value increases by 6.7 percent.

If the annual deflator is based on a simple average of quarterly prices then the deflator appears to have dropped by 20 percent. As a result, the annual constant price estimates will wrongly show an increase in volume of 33.3 percent.

Consistent with the quantity data, the annual sum of the quarterly constant price estimates for 1999 and 2000, derived by valuing the quantities using their quantity-weighted average 1999 price, shows no increase in volumes (column 7). The change in annual current price value shows up as an increase in the implicit annual deflator, which would be implicitly weighted by each quarter's proportion of annual sales at constant prices.

Price indices typically use unweighted averages as the price base, which corresponds to valuing the quantities using their unweighted average price. As shown in column 6, this results in an annual sum of the quarterly constant price estimates in the base year (1999) that differs from the current price data, which it should not. This difference, however, can easily be removed by a multiplicative adjustment of the complete constant price time series, leaving the period-to-period rate of change unchanged. The adjustment factor is the ratio between the annual current price data and sum of the quarterly constant price data in the base year (9000/10000).

9.8. Consequently, to obtain correct volume measures for aggregated periods of time, deflators should take into account variations in quantities as well as prices within the period. For example, annual deflators could be derived implicitly from annual volume measures derived from the sum of quarterly volume estimates obtained using the following two-step procedure:
(a) Benchmark the quarterly current price data/ indicator(s) to the corresponding annual current price data.
(b) Construct quarterly constant price data by deflating the benchmarked quarterly current price data. Equivalently, the annual volume measure could be obtained by deflating using an annual deflator that weights the quarterly price indices by the constant price values of that item for each quarter.

Either way of calculation achieves annual deflators that are quantity-weighted average annual price measures.[6]

9.9. A more difficult case occurs when the annual estimates are based on more detailed price and value information than is available quarterly. In those cases, if seasonal volatility is significant, it would be possible to approximate the correct procedure using weights derived from more aggregated, but closely related, quarterly data.

9.10. The issue of price and quantity variations also apply within quarters. Accordingly, when monthly data are available, quarterly data will better take into

_____
[6] The corresponding formulas are provided in Annex 9.1.

account variations within the period if they are built up from the monthly data.

9.11. In many cases, variation in prices and quantities within years and quarters will be so insignificant that it will not substantially affect the estimates. Primary products and high-inflation countries are cases where the variation can be particularly significant. Of course, there are many cases in which there are no data to measure variations within the period.

9.12. A related problem that can be observed in quarterly data is the annual sum of the quarterly constant price estimates in the base year differing from the annual sum of the current price data, which should not be the case. This difference can be caused by the use of unweighted annual average prices as the price base when constructing monthly and quarterly price indices. As shown in Annex 9.1, deflating quarterly data with deflators constructed with unweighted average prices as the price base corresponds to valuing the quantities using their unweighted annual average price rather than their weighted annual average price. This difference in the base year between the annual sum of the quarterly constant price estimates and the annual sum of the current price data can easily be removed by a multiplicative adjustment of the complete constant price time series, leaving the period-to-period rate of change unchanged. The adjustment factor is the ratio between the annual current price data and the sum of the initial quarterly constant price data based on the unweighted annual average prices in the base year, which, for a single product, is identical to the ratio of the weighted and unweighted average price.

9.13. Two different concepts and measures of annual change in prices are illustrated in Example 9.1, which both are valid measures of economic interest. The first—showing a decline in prices of 20 percent based on unweighted annual average prices—corresponds to a measure of the *average change in prices*. The second—showing an increase in prices of 6.7 percent based on weighted annual average prices—corresponds to *change in average prices*. As shown in Example 9.1, only the latter fits in a value/volume/price measurement framework for *time periods*, as required by the national accounts, in contrast to the measurement framework for *points in time* addressed in conventional index number theory. In Example 9.1, the annual value change is 6.7 percent, and the correct annual volume

change is an undisputable 0.0 percent, because the annual sum of the quantities is unchanged and the quantities refer to a single homogenous product.

9.14. An apparent difficulty is that the changes shown by the weighted annual average price measure fail the fundamental index number axiom that the measures should reflect only changes in prices and not changes in quantities. Thus, the weighted annual average price measure appears to be invalid as a measure of price change. The 6.7 increase in *average prices* from 1997 to 1998 results from changes in the quantities transacted at each price and not from increases in the prices, and therefore does not satisfy basic index number tests such as the identity and proportionality tests. For that reason, it can be argued that Example 9.1 shows that, in principle, it is not possible to factor changes in values for time periods into measures of price and quantity changes that are each acceptable as index numbers in their own right. The basic index number tests and conventional index number theory, however, are concerned with price and quantity comparisons between separate pairs of *points in time* rather than with price and quantity comparisons between *time periods* and, consequently, not with measures of the change in average prices from one period to another. To measure the *change in average prices,* for a single homogenous product, each period's average price should be defined as the total value divided by the corresponding quantities within that period; that is, they should be unit values. From Example 9.1, it is clear that annual average prices for national accounting purposes cannot be realistically defined without reference to the corresponding quantities and therefore should be calculated using a weighted average with quarterly/subannual quantities as weights.

C. Choice of Price Weights for QNA Volume Measures

1. Laspeyres-Type Volume Measures

9.15. The time-series requirements and the QNA-ANA consistency requirement imply that the quantity-weighted average prices of a whole year should be used as price weights for ANA and QNA Laspeyres-type volume measures.[7] Use of the prices of one

---
[7]The term "Laspeyres-type" is used to cover the traditional constant price measures, fixed-base Laspeyres volume indices, and chain-linked Laspeyres volume indices.

particular quarter, the prices of the corresponding quarter of the previous year, the prices of the corresponding quarter of a fixed "base year," or the prices of the previous quarter are not appropriate for time series of Laspeyres-type volume measures in the national accounts for the following reasons:

- Consistency between directly derived ANA and QNA Laspeyres-type volume measures requires that the same price weights are used in the ANA and the QNA, and that the same price weights are used for all quarters of the year.
- The prices of one particular quarter are not suitable as price weights for volume measures in the ANA, and thus in the QNA, because of seasonal fluctuations and other short-term volatilities in relative prices. Use of weighted annual average prices reduces these effects. Therefore, weighted annual average prices are more representative for the other quarters of the year as well as for the year as a whole.
- The prices of the corresponding quarter of the previous year or the corresponding quarter of a fixed "base year" are not suitable as price weights for volume measures in the QNA because the derived volume measures only allow the current quarter to be compared with the same quarter of the previous year or years. Series of year-to-year changes do not constitute time series that allow different periods to be compared and cannot be linked together to form such time series. In particular, because they involve using different prices for each quarter of the year, they do not allow different quarters within the same year to be compared. For the same reason, they do not allow the quarters within the same year to be aggregated and compared with their corresponding direct annual estimates. Furthermore, as shown in Annex 1.1, changes from the same period in the previous year can introduce significant lags in identifying the current trend in economic activity.
- The prices of the previous quarter are not suitable as price weights for Laspeyres-type volume measures for two reasons:
  (a) The use of different price weights for each quarter of the year does not allow the quarters within the same year to be aggregated and compared with their corresponding direct annual estimates.
  (b) If the quarter-to-quarter changes are linked together to form a time series, short-term volatility in relative prices may cause the quarterly chain-linked measures to show substantial drift compared to corresponding direct measures. This is illustrated in Example 9.3.

9.16. Quarterly Laspeyres-type volume measures with two different base-period[8] price weights may be used:

(a) The annual average of a fixed-base year, resulting in the traditional constant price measures, which is equivalent to a fixed-based Laspeyres volume index.
(b) The annual average of the previous year, resulting in the annually chain-linked quarterly Laspeyres volume index.

9.17. The traditional volume measures at the constant price of a fixed base year, the fixed-based quarterly Laspeyres volume index, and the short-term link in the annually chain-linked quarterly Laspeyres volume index can be expressed in mathematical terms as the following:

- At the constant "average" prices of a fixed base year:

$$CP_{q,y_{\bar{0}}} = \sum_i \bar{p}_{i,0} \cdot q_{i,q,y} \qquad (9.1.a)$$

- The fixed-based quarterly Laspeyres:

$$LQ_{0 \to (q,y)} = \frac{\sum_i \bar{p}_{i,0} \cdot q_{i,q,y}}{\sum_i \bar{p}_{i,0} \cdot \bar{q}_{i,0}} \qquad (9.1.b)$$

- Short-term link in the annually chain-linked quarterly Laspeyres:

$$LQ_{\overline{(y-1)} \to (q,y)} = \frac{\sum_i \bar{p}_{i,y-1} \cdot q_{i,q,y}}{\sum_i \bar{p}_{i,y-1} \cdot \bar{q}_{i,y-1}} \qquad (9.1.c)$$

where

$CP_{q,y_{\bar{0}}}$ is the total value in quarter q of year y measured at the annual average prices of year 0.

$LQ_{0 \to (q,y)}$ represents a Laspeyres volume index measuring the volume change from the average of year 0 to quarter q in year y with average of year 0 as base and reference period;[9]

$LQ_{\overline{(y-1)} \to (q,y)}$ represents a Laspeyres volume index measuring the volume change from the average of year $y-1$ to quarter q in year

---

[8]The term "base period" is defined in paragraph 9.22 as meaning (1) the base of the price or quantity ratios being weighted together (e.g., period 0 is the base for the quantity ratio), and (2) the pricing year (the base year) for constant price data.
[9]The term "Reference period" is defined in paragraph 9.22 as meaning the period for which the index series is expressed as equal to 100.

y with the average of year $y - 1$ as base and reference period;

$p_{i,q,y}$ is the price of item i in quarter q of year y;

$\overline{p}_{i,y-1}$ is the quantity-weighted arithmetic average of the price of item i in the quarters of year $y - 1$;

$\overline{p}_{i,0}$ is the quantity-weighted arithmetic average of the price of item i in the quarters of year 0

$$\overline{p}_{i,0} = \frac{\sum_q p_{i,q,0} \cdot q_{i,q,0}}{\sum_q q_{i,q,0}};$$

$q_{i,q,y}$ is the quantity of item i in quarter q of year y;

$\overline{q}_{i,y-1}$ is the simple arithmetic average of the quantities of item i in the quarters of $y - 1$; and

$\overline{q}_{i,0}$ is the simple arithmetic average of the quantities of item i in the quarters of year 0.

2. Fisher-Type Volume Indices

9.18. The Fisher volume index, being the geometric average of a Laspeyres and a Paasche volume index, uses price weights from two periods—the base period and the current period. Quarterly Fisher indices with three different base-period weights may be used:

(a) The annual average of a fixed-base year, resulting in the fixed-based quarterly Fisher index.

(b) The annual average of the previous year, resulting in the annually chain-linked quarterly Fisher index.

(c) The average of the previous quarter, resulting in the quarterly chain-linked quarterly Fisher index.

9.19. The fixed-based quarterly Fisher volume index and the short-term links in the annually and quarterly chain-linked quarterly Fisher volume index can be expressed in mathematical terms as the following:

• Fixed-based quarterly Fisher:

$$FQ_{0\to(q,y)} = \sqrt{LQ_{0\to(q,y)} \cdot PQ_{0\to(q,y)}} \qquad (9.2.a)$$

$$\equiv \sqrt{\frac{\sum_i \overline{p}_{i,0} \cdot q_{i,q,y}}{\sum_i \overline{p}_{i,0} \cdot \overline{q}_{i,0}} \cdot \frac{\sum_i p_{i,q,y} \cdot q_{i,q,y}}{\sum_i p_{i,q,y} \cdot \overline{q}_{i,0}}}$$

• Short-term link in the annually chain-linked quarterly Fisher:

$$FQ_{\overline{(y-1)}\to(q,y)} = \sqrt{LQ_{\overline{(y-1)}\to(q,y)} \cdot PQ_{\overline{(y-1)}\to(q,y)}} \qquad (9.2.b)$$

$$\equiv \sqrt{\frac{\sum_i \overline{p}_{i,y-1} \cdot q_{i,q,y}}{\sum_i \overline{p}_{i,y-1} \cdot \overline{q}_{i,y-1}} \cdot \frac{\sum_i p_{i,q,y} \cdot q_{i,q,y}}{\sum_i p_{i,q,y} \cdot \overline{q}_{i,y-1}}}$$

• Short-term link in the quarterly chain-linked quarterly Fisher:

$$FQ_{(t-1)\to1} = \sqrt{LQ_{(t-1)\to(t)} \cdot PQ_{(t-1)\to(t)}} \qquad (9.2.c)$$

$$\equiv \sqrt{\frac{\sum_i p_{i,t-1} \cdot q_{i,t}}{\sum_i p_{i,t-1} \cdot q_{i,t-1}} \cdot \frac{\sum_i p_{i,t} \cdot q_{i,t}}{\sum_i p_{i,t} \cdot q_{i,t-1}}}$$

where

t is a generic symbol for time, which is more convenient to use for period-to period measures than the quarter q in year y notation used for most formulas in this chapter;

$FQ_{A\to(q,y)}$ represents a Fisher volume index measuring the volume change from period A to quarter q in year y with period A as base and reference period;

$LQ_{A\to(q,y)}$ represents a Laspeyres volume index measuring the volume change from period A to quarter q in year y with period A as base and reference period;

$PQ_{A\to(q,y)}$ represents a Paasche volume index measuring the volume change from period A to quarter q in year y with period A as base and reference period; and

$p_{i,A}$ is the price of item i in period A.

Period A is equal to the average of year 0 for the fixed-based Fisher, to the average of the previous year for the annually chain-linked Fisher, and to the previous quarter for the quarterly chain-linked Fisher.

9.20. For the same reasons as for Laspeyres-type volume measures, the following alternative periods are not suitable as base periods for time series of Fisher-type volume indices:
• One particular fixed quarter.
• The corresponding quarter of the previous year.
• The corresponding quarter of a fixed "base year."

D. Chain-Linking in the QNA

1. General

9.21. The *1993 SNA* recommends moving away from the traditional fixed-base year constant price estimates to chain-linked volume measures. Constant price estimates use the average prices of a particular period,[10] the base period, to weight together the corresponding quantities. Constant price data have the advantage for the users of the component series being additive, unlike alternative volume measures. The pattern of relative prices in the base year, however, is less representative of the economic conditions for periods farther away from the base year. Therefore, from time to time it is necessary to update the base period to adopt weights that better reflect the current conditions (i.e., with respect to production technology and user preferences). Different base periods, and thus different sets of price weights, give different perspectives. When the base period is changed, data for the distant past should not be recalculated (rebased). Instead, to form a consistent time series, data on the old base should be linked to data on the new base.[11] Change of base period and chain-linking can be done with different frequencies; every 10 years, every 5 years, every year, or every quarter/month. The *1993 SNA* recommends changing the base period, and thus conducting the chain-linking, annually.

9.22. The concepts of base, weight, and reference period should be clearly distinguished. Index number terminology is not well established internationally, which can lead to confusion. In particular, the term "base period" is sometimes used for different concepts. Similarly, the terms "base period," "weight period," and "reference period" are sometimes used interchangeably. In this manual, following *1993 SNA* and the current dominant national accounts practice, the following terminology is used:
- *Base period* for (1) the base of the price or quantity ratios being weighted together (e.g., period 0 is the base for the quantity ratio $q_{i,t}/q_{i,0}$), and (2) the pricing year (the base year) for the constant price data.

- *Weight period* for the period(s) from which the weights are taken. The weight period is equal to the base period for a fixed-base Laspeyres index and to the current period for a fixed-base Paasche index. Symmetric fixed-base index formulas like Fisher and Tornquist have two weight periods—the base and the current period.
- *Reference period* for the period for which the index series is expressed as equal to 100. The reference period can be changed by simply dividing the index series with its level in any period chosen as the new reference period.

9.23. Chain-linking means constructing long-run price or volume measures by cumulating movements in short-term indices with different base periods. For example, a period-to-period chain-linked index measuring the changes from period 0 to t (i.e., $CI_{0 \to t}$) can be constructed by multiplying a series of short-term indices measuring the change from one period to the next as follows:

$$CI_{0 \to t} = I_{0 \to 1} \cdot I_{1 \to 2} \cdot I_{2 \to 3} \cdot I_{3 \to 4} \cdot \ldots \ldots I_{(t-1) \to t} \quad (9.3)$$

$$\equiv \prod_{\tau=1}^{t} I_{(\tau-1) \to \tau}$$

where $I_{(t-1) \to \tau}$ represents a price or volume index measuring the change from period $t - 1$ to t, with period $t - 1$ as base and reference period.

9.24. The corresponding run, or time series, of chain-linked index numbers where the links are chained together so as to express the full time series on a fixed reference period is given by

$$\begin{cases} CI_{0 \to 0} = 1 & (9.4.a) \\ CI_{0 \to 1} = I_{0 \to 1} \\ CI_{0 \to 2} = I_{0 \to 1} \cdot I_{1 \to 2} \\ CI_{0 \to 3} = I_{0 \to 1} \cdot I_{1 \to 2} \cdot I_{2 \to 3} \\ \quad \cdots \\ CI_{0 \to t} = \prod_{\tau=1}^{t} I_{(\tau-1) \to \tau} \end{cases}$$

9.25. Chain-linked indices do not have a *particular base or weight period*. Each link ($I_{(t-1) \to t}$) of the chain-linked index in equation (9.4.a) has a base period and one or two weight periods, and the base and weight period(s) are changing from link to link. By the same token, the full run of index numbers in

---

[10]The period length should be a year, as recommended in the previous section.

[11]This should be done for each series, aggregates as well as subcomponents of the aggregates, independently of any aggregation or accounting relationship between the series. As a consequence, the chain-linked components will not aggregate to the corresponding aggregates. No attempts should be made to remove this "chain discrepancy," because any such attempt implies distorting the movements in one or several of the series.

equation (9.4.a) derived by chaining each link together does not have a particular base period—it has a fixed reference period.

9.26. The *reference period* can be chosen freely without altering the rates of change in the series. For the chain-linked index time series in equation (9.4.a), period 0 is referred to as the index's reference period and is conventionally expressed as equal to 100. The reference period can be changed simply by dividing the index series with its level in any period chosen as a new reference period. For instance, the reference period for the run of index numbers in equation (9.4.a) can be changed from period 0 to period 2 by dividing all elements of the run by the constant $CI_{0\to2}$ as follows:

$$
\begin{cases}
CI_{2\to0} = CI_{0\to0}/CI_{0\to2} = 1/I_{0\to1}I_{1\to2} \\
CI_{2\to1} = CI_{0\to1}/CI_{0\to2} = 1/I_{1\to2} \\
CI_{2\to2} = CI_{0\to2}/CI_{0\to2} = 1 \\
CI_{2\to3} = CI_{0\to3}/CI_{0\to2} = I_{1\to2} \\
\quad \ldots \\
CI_{2\to t} = CI_{0\to t}/CI_{0\to2} = \prod_{\tau=1}^{t} I_{(\tau-1)\to\tau}
\end{cases}
\qquad (9.4.b)
$$

9.27. The chain-linked index series in equation (9.3) and equations (9.4.a) and (9.4.b) will constitute a period-to-period chain-linked Laspeyres volume index series if, for each link, the short-term indices ($I_{(t-1)\to t}$) are constructed as Laspeyres volume indices with the previous period as base and reference period. That is, if

$$
I_{(t-1)\to t} = LQ_{(t-1)\to t} = \sum_i \frac{q_{i,t}}{q_{i,t-1}} \cdot w_{i,t-1} \qquad (9.5.)
$$

$$
\equiv \frac{\sum_i p_{i,t-1} \cdot q_{i,t}}{\sum_i p_{i,t-1} \cdot q_{i,t-1}} \equiv \frac{\sum_i p_{i,t-1} \cdot q_{i,t}}{V_{t-1}}
$$

where
$LQ_{(t-1)\to t}$ represents a Laspeyres volume index measuring the volume change from period $t-1$ to t, with period $t-1$ as base and reference period;

$p_{i,t-1}$ is the price of item i in period $t-1$ (the "price weights");

$q_{i,t}$ is the quantity of item i in period t;

$w_{i,t-1}$ is the base period "share weight," that is, the item's share in the total value of period $t-1$; and

V_{t-1} is the total value at current prices in period $t-1$.

9.28. Similarly, the chain-linked index series in equation (9.3) and equations (9.4.a) and (9.4.b) will constitute a period-to-period chain-linked Fisher volume index series if, for each link, the short-term indices ($I_{(t-1)\to t}$) are constructed as Fisher volume indices with the previous period as base and reference period as in equation (9.2.c).

9.29. Any two index series with different base and reference periods can be linked to measure the change from the first to the last year[12] as follows:

$$
CI_{0\to t} = I_{0\to(t-h)} \cdot I_{(t-h)\to t} \qquad (9.6)
$$

That is, each link may cover any number of periods.

9.30. For instance, if in equation (9.6) $t = 10$ and $h = 5$, the resulting linked index ($CI_{0\to10}$) constitutes a 5-year chain-linked annual index measuring the change from year 0 to year 10. Example 9.2 provides an illustration of the basic chain-linking technique for annual data with $t = 15$ and $h = 10$.

9.31. Growth rates and index numbers computed for series that contain negatives or zeroes—such as changes in inventories and crop harvest data—generally are misleading and meaningless. For instance, consider a series for changes in inventories at constant prices that is −10 in period one and +20 in period two. The corresponding growth rate between these two periods is −300 percent (= ((20/−10) − 1) · 100), which obviously is both misleading and meaningless. Similarly, for a series that is 1 in period one and 10 in period two, the corresponding growth rate from period one to two would be 900 percent. Consequently, for such series, only measures of contribution to percentage change in the aggregates they belong to can be made (see Section D.7. for a discussion of measure of contribution to percentage change in index numbers).

2. Frequency of Chain-Linking in the QNA

9.32. The *1993 SNA* recommends that chain-linking should not be done more frequently than annually. This is mainly because short-term volatility in relative prices (e.g., caused by sampling errors and seasonal effects) can cause volume measures that are chain-linked more frequently than annually to show substantial drift—particularly so

---

[12]As long as they have one period in common, that is, there is at least one overlapping period. For instance, in equation (9.6) with $t = 10$ and $h = 5$, year 5 represents the overlap. Similarly, in Example 9.2, year 10 represents the overlap.

Example 9.2. Basic Chain-Linking of Annual Data

The 1993 SNA Example

The example is an elaborated version of the illustration provided in the 1993 SNA.
(1993 SNA Table 16.1, pages 386–387.)

Basic Data

	Year 0			Year 10			Year 15		
	p_0	q_0	v_0	p_{10}	q_{10}	v_{10}	p_{15}	q_{15}	v_{15}
Item A	6	5	30	9	12	108	11	15	165
Item B	4	8	32	10	11	110	14	11	154
Total			62			218			319

Constant price Data

	Base Year 0				Base Year 10		
	Year 0	Year 10	Year 15		Year 0	Year 10	Year 15
	$p_0 \cdot q_0$	$p_0 \cdot q_{10}$	$p_0 \cdot q_{15}$		$p_{10} \cdot q_0$	$p_{10} \cdot q_{10}$	$p_{10} \cdot q_{15}$
Item A	30	72	90		45	108	135
Item B	32	44	44		80	110	110
Total	62	116	134		125	218	245

Laspeyres Volume Indices for the Total

	Year 0	Year 10	Year 15
Fixed-Based			
Year 0 as base and reference	100	187.1	216.1
Period-to-period rate of change		87.1%	15.5%
Year 10 as base and reference	57.3	100	112.4
Period-to-period rate of change		74.4%	12.4%
Re-referenced to year 0 (year 10 as base)	100	174.4	196.0
Chain-Linked Index			
Year 0 = 100	100	187.1	210.3= 112.4 · 1.871
Period-to-period rate of change		87.1%	12.4%
Year 10 = 100	100/1.871 = 53.4	100	112.4
Period-to-period rate of change		87.1%	12.4%

The Laspeyres fixed-base volume index for the total with year 0 as base and reference period was derived as
   62/62 · 100 = 100,   116/62 · 100 = 187.1,   134/62 · 100 = 216.1
Similarly, the Laspeyres fixed-base volume index for the total year with 10 as base and reference period was derived as
 125/218 · 100 = 57.3,   218/218 · 100 = 100,   245/218 · 100 = 112.4
And the Laspeyres fixed-base volume index for the total with year 10 as base and year 0 as reference period was derived as
 57.3/57.3 · 100 = 100,   100/57.3 · 100 = 174.4,   112.4/57.3 · 100 = 196.0

for nonsuperlative index formulas like Laspeyres and Paasche—as illustrated in Example 9.3. Similarly, short-term volatility in relative quantities can cause price measures that are chain-linked more frequently than annually to show substantial drift. The purpose of chain-linking is to take into account long-term trends in changes in relative prices, not temporary short-term variations.

9.33. Superlative index formulas, such as the Fisher index formula, are more robust against the drift problem than the other index formulas—as illustrated in Example 9.3. For this reason, a quarterly chain-linked Fisher index may be a feasible alternative to annually chain-linked Fisher or Laspeyres indices for quarterly data that show little or no short-term volatility. The quarterly chain-linked Fisher index does not aggregate exactly to the corresponding direct annual Fisher index.[13] For chain-linked Fisher indices, consistency between QNA and ANA price and volume measures can only be achieved by deriving the ANA measures from the quarterly measures or by forcing consistency on the data with the help of benchmarking techniques. There is no reason to believe that for nonvolatile series the average of an annually chain-linked Fisher will be closer to a direct annual Fisher index than the average of a quarterly chain-linked Fisher.

---

[13]Neither does the annually-linked, nor the fixed-based, Fisher index.

Example 9.3. Frequency of Chain-Linking and the Problem of "Drift"[1] in the Case of Price and Quantity Oscillation

Observation/Quarter	Quarter 1	Quarter 2	Quarter 3	Quarter 4
Price item A (pA)	2	3	4	2
Price item B (pB)	5	4	2	5
Quantities item A (qA,t)	50	40	60	50
Quantities item B (qB,t)	60	70	30	60
Total value (Vt)	400	400	300	400
Volume Indices	q1	q2	q3	q4
Fixed-based Laspeyres (q1-based)	100.0	107.5	67.5	100.0
Fixed-based Paasche (q1-based)	100.0	102.6	93.8	100.0
Fixed-based Fisher (q1-based)	100.0	105.0	79.6	100.0
Quarterly chain-linked Laspeyres	100.0	107.5	80.6	86.0
Quarterly chain-linked Paasche	100.0	102.6	102.6	151.9
Quarterly chain-linked Fisher	100.0	105.0	90.9	114.3

Fixed-Based Laspeyres Index:

$$I_{0 \to t} = \frac{\sum_i p_{i,0} \cdot q_{i,t}}{\sum_i p_{i,0} \cdot q_{i,0}} \equiv \frac{\sum_i p_{i,0} \cdot q_{i,t}}{V_0}$$

$$I_{t \to 2} = [2 \cdot 40 + 5 \cdot 70]/400 \cdot 100 = 107.5$$
$$I_{t \to 2} = [2 \cdot 60 + 5 \cdot 30]/400 \cdot 100 = 67.5$$
$$I_{t \to 4} = [2 \cdot 50 + 5 \cdot 60]/400 \cdot 100 = 100.0$$

Fixed-Based Paasche Index:

$$I_{0 \to t} = \frac{\sum_i p_{i,t} \cdot q_{i,t}}{\sum_i p_{i,t} \cdot q_{i,0}} \equiv \frac{V_t}{\sum_i p_{i,t} \cdot q_{i,0}}$$

$$I_{t \to 2} = [400/(3 \cdot 50 + 4 \cdot 60] \cdot 100 = 102.6$$
$$I_{t \to 3} = [300/(4 \cdot 50 + 2 \cdot 60] \cdot 100 = 93.8$$
$$I_{t \to 4} = [400/(2 \cdot 50 + 5 \cdot 60] \cdot 100 = 100.0$$

Quarterly Chain-Linked Laspeyres Index:

$$CL_{0,t} = \prod_{\tau=1}^{t} I_{(\tau-1) \to \tau} = \prod_{\tau=1}^{t} \frac{\sum_i p_{i,\tau-1} \cdot q_{i,\tau}}{\sum_i p_{i,\tau-1} \cdot q_{i,\tau-1}}$$

$$I_{t \to 3} = I_{t \to 2} \cdot [3 \cdot 60 + 4 \cdot 30]/400] = 80.6$$
$$I_{t \to 4} = I_{t \to 3} \cdot [4 \cdot 50 + 2 \cdot 60]/400] = 86.0$$

Quarterly Chain-Linked Paasche Index:

$$CL_{0,t} = \prod_{\tau=1}^{t} I_{(\tau-1) \to \tau} = \prod_{\tau=1}^{t} \frac{\sum_i p_{i,\tau-1} \cdot q_{i,\tau}}{\sum_i p_{i,\tau-1} \cdot q_{i,\tau-1}}$$

$$I_{t \to 3} = I_{t \to 2} \cdot [300/(4 \cdot 40 + 2 \cdot 70] = 102.6$$
$$I_{t \to 2} = I_{t \to 3} \cdot [400/(2 \cdot 60 + 5 \cdot 30] = 151.9$$

In this example, the prices and quantities in quarter 4 are the same as those in quarter 1, that is, the prices and quantities oscillate rather than move as a trend. The fixed-base indices correspondingly show identical values for q1 and q4, but the chain-linked indices show completely different values. This problem can also occur in annual data if prices and quantities oscillate and may make annual chaining inappropriate in some cases. It is more likely to occur in data for shorter periods, however, because seasonal and irregular effects cause those data to be more volatile.

Furthermore, observe that the differences between the q1 and q4 data for the quarterly chain-linked Laspeyres and the quarterly chain-linked Paasche indices are in opposite directions; and, correspondingly, that the quarterly chain-linked Fisher index drifts less. This is a universal result.

[1]The example is based on Szultc (1983).

9.34. For Laspeyres-type volume measures, consistency between QNA and ANA provides an additional reason for not chain-linking more frequently than annually. Consistency between quarterly data and corresponding direct annual indices requires that the same price weights are used in the ANA and the QNA, and consequently that the QNA should follow the same change of base year/chain-linking practice as in the ANA. Under those circumstances, the annual overlap linking technique presented in the next section will ensure that the quarterly data aggregate exactly to the corresponding direct index.

Moreover, under the same circumstances, any difference between the average of the quarterly data and the direct annual index caused by the preferred one-quarter overlap technique will be minimized.

9.35. Thus, in the QNA, chain-linked Laspeyres-type volume measures should be derived by compiling quarterly estimates at the average prices of the previous year. These quarterly volume measures for each year should then be linked to form long, consistent time series—the result constitutes an annually chain-linked quarterly Laspeyres index. Alternative linking techniques for such series are discussed in the next section.

3. Choice of Index Number Formulas for Annually Chain-Linked QNA Data

9.36. The *1993 SNA* recommends compiling annually chain-linked price and volume measures, preferably using superlative index number formulas such as the Fisher and Tornquist formulas. The rationale for this recommendation is that index number theory shows that annually chain-linked Fisher and Tornquist indices will most closely approximate the theoretically ideal index. Fisher and Tornquist indices will, in practice, yield almost the same results, and Fisher, being the geometric average of a Laspeyres and a Paasche index, will be within the upper and lower bounds provided by those two index formulas. Most countries[14] that have implemented chain-linking in their national accounts, however, have adopted the annually chain-linked Laspeyres formula for volume measures with the corresponding annually chain-linked Paasche formula for price measures,[15] and the European Union's statistical office (Eurostat) is requiring member states to provide annually chain-linked volume measures using the Laspeyres formula.[16]

9.37. Annual chain-linking of quarterly data implies that each link in the chain is constructed using the chosen index number formula with the average of the previous year $(y-1)$ as base and reference period. The resulting short-term quarterly indices must subsequently be linked to form long, consistent time series expressed on a fixed reference period. Alternative annual linking techniques for such series will be discussed in Section D.3. While the discussion in Section D.3 focuses on Laspeyres indices, the techniques illustrated and

the issues discussed are applicable to all annually chain-linked index formulas. The Laspeyres, Paasche, and Fisher annually chain-linked quarterly volume index formulas for each short-term link in the chain are given as

- Short-term link in annually chain-linked Laspeyres:

$$LQ_{\overline{(y-1)}\to(q,y)} = \frac{\sum_i \overline{p}_{i,y-1} \cdot q_{i,q,y}}{\sum_i \overline{p}_{i,y-1} \cdot \overline{q}_{i,y-1}} \quad (9.7.a)$$

$$\equiv \sum_i \frac{q_{i,q,y}}{\overline{q}_{i,y-1}} \cdot w_{i,y-1}$$

- Short-term link in annually chain-linked Paasche:

$$PQ_{\overline{(y-1)}\to(q,y)} = \frac{\sum_i p_{i,q,y} \cdot q_{i,q,y}}{\sum_i p_{i,q,y} \cdot \overline{q}_{i,y-1}} \quad (9.7.b)$$

- Short-term link in annually chain-linked Fisher:

$$FQ_{\overline{(y-1)}\to(q,y)} = \sqrt{LQ_{\overline{(y-1)}\to(q,y)} \cdot PQ_{\overline{(y-1)}\to(q,y)}} \quad (9.7.c)$$

$$= \sqrt{\frac{\sum_i \overline{p}_{i,y-1} \cdot q_{i,q,y}}{\sum_i \overline{p}_{i,y-1} \cdot \overline{q}_{i,y-1}} \cdot \frac{\sum_i p_{i,q,y} \cdot q_{i,q,y}}{\sum_i p_{i,q,y} \cdot \overline{q}_{i,y-1}}}$$

where

$$w_{i,y-1} = \frac{\overline{p}_{i,y-1} \cdot \overline{q}_{i,y-1}}{\sum_i \overline{p}_{i,y-1} \cdot \overline{q}_{i,y-1}}$$

$$\equiv \frac{\sum_q p_{i,q,y-1} \cdot q_{i,q,y-1}}{\sum_i \sum_q p_{i,q,y-1} \cdot q_{i,q,y-1}}$$

is the base period "share weight," that is, the item's share in the total value in year $y-1$; and $p_{i,q,y-1}$ is the price of item i in quarter q of year $y-1$.

9.38. Countries have opted for the annually chain-linked Laspeyres formula instead of the annually chain-linked Fisher formula for volume measures mainly for the following reasons:

- Experience and theoretical studies indicate that annual chain-linking tends to reduce the index number spread to the degree that the exact choice of index number formula assumes less significance (see, for example, *1993 SNA*, paragraph 16.51).
- The annually chain-linked quarterly Fisher index does not aggregate to the corresponding direct

---

[14]The use of chain-linked measures for official national accounts data was pioneered by the Netherlands (1985) and Norway (1990). Subsequently, a large number of countries have adopted, or are in the process of adopting, chain-linking for their official measures. Currently, only the United States has opted for a chain-linked Fisher index formula instead of the chain-linked Laspeyres formula. The United States adopted in 1996 an annually chain-linked quarterly "Fisher-like" formula using annual weights in both the Laspeyres and the Paasche part of the index but changed to a standard quarterly chain-linked Fisher index in 1999.

[15]Laspeyres volume measures require that the corresponding price measures are based on the Paasche formula so that the product of the volume and price indices is equal to the corresponding value index.

[16]European Commission Decision of November 30, 1998, clarifying the *European System of Accounts 1995* principles for price and volume measures, and Eurostat (1999) paragraph 3.186.

annual index;[17] the annually chain-linked Laspeyres index linked, using the annually overlap technique presented in Example 9.4.a, does.[18]

- Chain volume measures in monetary terms[19] based on the annually chain-linked Laspeyres formula will be additive in the reference year and the subsequent year,[20] while volume measures based on the Fisher index will not.
- The Laspeyres formula is simpler to work with and to explain to users than the Fisher index. For instance, time series of annually chain-linked Laspeyres indices easily can be converted into series of data valued at the constant average prices of the previous year that are additive if corresponding current price data are made available. This feature makes it easy for users to construct their own aggregates from published data.
- The formulas for computing contribution to percentage change are easier for data based on the chain-linked Laspeyres formula than for data based on the Fisher index.
- The Fisher formula is not consistent in aggregation within each link; it is only approximately consistent in aggregation.
- The Laspeyres formula, in contrast, is additive within each link. This makes it easier to combine chain-linking with compilation analytical tools like supply and use (SU) tables and input-output tables that require additivity of components.[21]

4. Techniques for Annual Chain-Linking of Quarterly Data

9.39. Two alternative techniques for annual chain-linking of quarterly data are usually applied: annual overlaps and one-quarter overlaps. In addition to these two conventional chain-linking techniques, a third technique sometimes is used based on changes from the same period in the previous year (the "over-the-year technique"). While, in many cases, all three techniques give similar results, in situations with strong changes in relative quantities and relative prices, the over-the-year technique can result in distorted seasonal patterns in the linked series. While standard price statistics compilation exclusively uses the one-quarter overlap technique, the annual overlap technique may be more practical for Laspeyres-type volume measures in the national accounts because it results in data that aggregate exactly to the corresponding direct annual index. In contrast, the one-quarter overlap technique and the over-the-year technique do not result in data that aggregate exactly to the corresponding direct annual index. The one-quarter overlap provides the smoothest transition between each link, however, in contrast to the annual overlap technique that may introduce a step between each link. Examples 9.4.a, 9.4.b, 9.4.c, and Chart 9.1 provide an illustration of these three chain-linking techniques. (A formal presentation of the two first methods is given in Annex 9.2.)

9.40. The technique of using annual overlaps implies compiling estimates for each quarter at the weighted annual average prices of the previous year, with subsequent linking using the corresponding annual data to provide linking factors to scale the quarterly data upward or downward. The technique of one-quarter overlaps requires compiling estimates for the overlap quarter at the weighted annual average prices of the current year in addition to estimates at the average prices of the previous year. The ratio between the estimates for the linking quarter at the average prices of the current year and at the average prices of the previous year then provides the linking factor to scale the quarterly data up or down. The over-the-year technique requires compiling estimates for each quarter at the weighted annual average prices of the current year in addition to estimates at the average prices of the previous year. The year-on-year changes in these constant price data are then used to extrapolate the quarterly constant price data of the chosen reference period.

9.41. To conclude, there are no established standards with respect to techniques for annually chain-linking of QNA data, but chain-linking using the one-quarter overlap technique, combined with benchmarking to remove any resulting discrepancies between the quarterly and annual data, gives the best result. In many circumstances, however, the annual overlap technique may give similar results. The over-the-year technique should be avoided.

---

[17]Neither does the quarterly-chain linked, nor the fixed-based, quarterly Fisher index.

[18]However, this may not be a decisive argument for two reasons. First, simulations indicate that, in practice, the difference between a direct annual Fisher and the average of a quarterly Fisher may often not be significant and may easily be removed using benchmarking techniques. Second, the preferred quarterly overlap technique presented in Section D.3., even when used for Laspeyres indices, also introduces differences between direct annual indices and the average of quarterly indices.

[19]See Section D.7. and particularly paragraph 9.48 for a discussion of chain volume measures in monetary terms.

[20]See Example 9.5.a for an illustration of this and Section D.5. for a discussion of the nonadditivity property of most index number formulas besides the fixed-based Laspeyres formula.

[21]The first two countries to adopt chain-linking for their official national accounts price and volume measures both did it within an SU compilation framework.

Example 9.4.a. Quarterly Data and Annual Chain-Linking
Annual Overlap
Laspeyres Volume Index
Annual sums and averages in bold.

Basic data	Quanti-ties A	Quanti-ties B	Price A	Price B	Total at current prices	At Constant Prices of: 1997 Level	Index 1997 =100	1998 Level	Index 1998 = 100	1999 Level	Index 1999 =100	Chain-Linked Index 1997=100 Level	q-q Rate of Change
1997	**251.0**	**236.0**	**7.0**	**6.0**	**3,173.00**	3,173.00	100.00					100.00	
q1	67.4	57.6	6.1	8.0	871.94	817.40	103.04					103.04	3.0%
q2	69.4	57.1	5.7	8.6	885.51	828.40	104.43					104.43	1.3%
q3	71.5	56.5	5.3	9.4	910.05	839.50	105.83					105.83	1.3%
q4	73.7	55.8	5.0	10.0	926.50	850.70	107.24					107.24	1.3%
1998	**282.0**	**227.0**	**5.5**	**9.0**	**3,594.00**	3,336.00	105.14	3,594.00	100.00			**105.14**	
q1	76.0	55.4	4.5	10.7	934.78			916.60	102.01			107.26	0.0%
q2	78.3	54.8	4.3	11.5	963.07			923.85	102.82			108.10	0.8%
q3	80.6	54.2	3.8	11.7	940.42			931.10	103.63			108.95	0.8%
q4	83.1	53.6	3.5	12.1	940.73			939.45	104.56			109.93	0.9%
1999	**318.0**	**218.0**	**4.0**	**11.5**	**3,779.00**			3,711.00	103.26	3,779.00	100.00	**108.56**	
q1	85.5	53.2	3.4	12.5	955.70					953.80	100.96	109.60	−0.3%
q2	88.2	52.7	3.1	13.0	961.70					958.85	101.49	110.18	0.5%
q3	90.8	52.1	2.8	13.8	973.22					962.35	101.86	110.58	0.4%
q4	93.5	52.0	2.7	14.7	1018.36					972.00	102.88	111.69	1.0%
2000	**358.0**	**210.0**	**3.0**	**13.5**	**3,908.97**					3,847.00	101.80	**110.51**	−1.1%

Independently chain-linked annuals													
1997						3,173.0						**100.00**	
1998						3,336.0	105.1	3,594.0				**105.14**	
1999								3,711.0	103.3	3,779.0		**108.56**	
2000										3,847.0	101.8	**110.51**	

Step 1: Compile estimates for each quarter at the annual average prices of the previous year; the annual data being the sum of the four quarters.

e.g.: q1 1998 $7.0 \cdot 67.4 + 6.0 \cdot 57.6 = 817.00$

q4 1998 $7.0 \cdot 73.7 + 6.0 \cdot 55.8 = 850.70$

1998 $817.0 + 828.4 + 839.5 + 850.7 = 3336.00$

Step 2: Convert the constant price estimates for each quarter into a volume index with the average of last year = 100.

e.g.: q1 1998 $[817.0/(3173.0/4)] \cdot 100 = 103.00$

q4 1998 $[850.7/(3173.0/4)] \cdot 100 = 107.20$

1998 $3336.0/3173.0 \cdot 100 = 105.10$

Step 3: Link the quarterly volume indices with shifting base and reference year using the annual indices as linking factors (using 1997 as the reference period for the chain-linked index).

e.g.: q1 1999 $102.01 \cdot 1.051 = 107.26$

q4 1999 $104.56 \cdot 1.051 = 109.93$

q1 2000 $100.9 \cdot 1.0326 \cdot 1.051 = 109.60$

Observe that the unweighted annual average of the derived chain-linked quarterly index series is equal to the independently derived chain-linked annual data.

e.g.: 2000 $[109.6 + 110.18 + 110.58 + 111.69]/4 = 110.51$

Finally, observe that the change from, e.g., q4 1999 to q1 2000, in the chain-linked series based on annual overlap differs from the corresponding change in the chain-linked index based on a one-quarter overlap in the next example.

e.g.: q1 2000/q 4 1999 based on annual overlap −0.3%

≠ q1 1999/q 4 1998 based on one quarter overlap (and 1999 prices) 0.5%

This is the step in the series introduced by the annual overlap technique.

Example 9.4.b. Quarterly Data and Annual Chain-Linking
One-quarter overlap
Annual sums and averages in bold.

Basic data	q1	q2	p1	p2	Total at current prices	At Constant Prices of: 1997 Level	Index 1997 =100	At Constant Prices of: 1998 Level	Index q4 1998 = 100	At Constant Prices of: 1999 Level	Index q4 1999 = 100	Chain-linked index 1997=100 Level	q-q Rate of Change
1997	**251.0**	**236.0**	**7.0**	**6.0**	**3,173.00**	**3,173.00**	*100.00*					**100.00**	
q1	67.4	57.6				817.40	103.04					103.04	
q2	69.4	57.1				828.40	104.43					104.43	1.3%
q3	71.5	56.5				839.50	105.83					105.83	1.3%
q4	73.7	55.8				850.70	107.24		907.55	100.00			107.24	1.3%
1998	**282.0**	**227.0**	**5.5**	**9.0**	**3,594.00**	**3,336.00**	**105.14**	**3,594.00**				**105.14**	
q1	76.0	55.4							916.60	101.00		108.31	*1.0%*
q2	78.3	54.8							923.85	101.80		109.17	0.8%
q3	80.6	54.2							931.10	102.59		110.03	0.8%
q4	83.1	53.6						939.45	103.51	948.80	100.00	111.01	0.9%
1999	**318.0**	**218.0**	**4.0**	**11.5**	**3,779.00**			**3,711.00**		**3,779.00**		**109.63**	
q1	85.5	53.2								953.80	100.53	111.60	*0.5%*
q2	88.2	52.7								958.85	101.06	112.19	0.5%
q3	90.8	52.1								962.35	101.43	112.60	0.4%
q4	93.5	52.0								972.00	102.45	113.73	1.0%
2000	**358.0**	**210.0**	**3.0**	**13.5**	**3,908.97**					**3,847.00**		**112.53**	

Step 1:   Compile estimates for each quarter at the annual average prices of the previous year; the annual data being the sum of the four quarters.
Step 2:   Compile estimates for the fourth quarter of each year at the annual average prices of the same year.
    e.g.:   q4 1998 $5.5 \cdot 73.7 + 9.0 \cdot 55.8 = 907.55$
Step 3:   Convert the constant price estimates for the quarters of the first year after the chosen reference year (1997) into a volume index with the average of the reference year = 100
    e.g.:   q1 1998 $[817.4/(3173.0/4)] \cdot 100 = 103.04$
               q4 1998 $[850.7/(3173.0/4)] \cdot 100 = 107.24$
Step 4:   Convert the constant price estimates for each of the other quarters into a volume index with the fourth quarter of last year = 100
    e.g.:   q1 1999 $[916.60/907.55] \cdot 100 = 101.00$
               q4 1999 $[936.45/907.55] \cdot 100 = 103.51$
Step 5:   Link together the quarterly volume indices with shifting base using the fourth quarter of each year as link.
    e.g.:   q1 1999 $101.00 \cdot 1.0724 = 108.31$
               q4 1999 $103.51 \cdot 1.0724 = 111.01$
               q1 2000 $100.53 \cdot 1.1101 = 111.60$
The resulting linked series is referenced to average 1997 = 100.

Finally, observe that the unweighted annual average of the derived chain-linked quarterly index series differs from the independently derived chain-linked annuals in example 9.4.a.
    e.g.:   2000 $[111.6+112.19+112.6+113.73]/4 = 112.53 \neq 110.51$

5. Chain-Linked Measures and Nonadditivity

9.42. In contrast to constant price data, chain-linked volume measures are nonadditive. To preserve the correct volume changes, related series should be linked independently of any aggregation or accounting relationships that exist between them; as a result, additivity is lost. Additivity is a specific version of the *consistency in aggregation* property for index numbers. Consistency in aggregation means that an aggregate can be constructed both directly by aggregating the detailed items and indirectly by aggregating subaggregates using the same aggregation formula. Additivity, in particular, implies that at each level of aggregation the volume index for an aggregate takes the form of a weighted arithmetic average of the volume indices for its components with the base-period values as weights (*1993 SNA*, paragraph 6.55). That is the same as requiring that the aggregate be equal to the sum of its components when the current price value of the aggregate and the components in some reference period are multiplied, or extrapolated, with the aggregate index and the component indices, respectively, resulting in *chain volume measures expressed in monetary terms*. It follows that, at the most detailed level, additivity is the same as requiring that the value obtained by extrapolating the aggregate is equal to the sum of the components valued at the reference period's prices. Thus, the additivity requirement effectively defines the fixed-base Laspeyres index and standard constant price data.

Example 9.4.c. Quarterly Data and Annual Chain-Linking
The Over-the-Year Technique
Laspeyres Volume Index

(i) Pair of years at the same prices.

(ii) Chain-linking using changes from the same quarter in the previous year.

Annual sums and averages in bold.

Basic Data	Quanti-ties A	Quanti-ties B	Price A	Price B	Total at Current Prices	At Constant Prices of: 1997 Level	Index 1997 =100	1998 Level	q-4 =1	1999 Level	q-4 =1	Chain-Linked Index 1997=100 Level	q-q- Rate of Change
1997	**251.0**	**236.0**	**7.0**	**6.0**	**3,173.00**	**3,173.00**	*100.00*					**100.00**	
q1	67.4	57.6				817.40	103.04	889.10				103.04	1.3%
q2	69.4	57.1				828.40	104.43	895.60				104.43	1.3%
q3	71.5	56.5				839.50	105.83	901.75				105.83	1.3%
q4	73.7	55.8				850.70	107.24	907.55		936.50		107.24	1.3%
1998	**282.0**	**227.0**	**5.5**	**9.0**	**3,594.00**	**3,336.00**	**105.14**	**3,594.00**				**105.14**	
q1	76.0	55.4						916.60	1.0309	941.10		106.23	**−0.9%**
q2	78.3	54.8						923.85	1.0315	943.40		107.73	1.4%
q3	80.6	54.2						931.10	1.0325	945.70		109.28	1.4%
q4	83.1	53.6						939.45	1.0451	948.80		111.01	1.6%
1999	**318.0**	**218.0**	**4.0**	**11.5**	**3,779.00**			**3,711.00**		**3,779.00**		**108.56**	
q1	85.5	53.2								953.80	1.0135	107.67	−3.0%
q2	88.2	52.7								958.85	1.0164	109.49	1.7%
2													
q3	90.8	52.1								962.35	1.0176	111.20	1.6%
q4	93.5	52.0								972.00	1.0245	113.73	2.3%
2000	**358.0**	**210.0**	**3.0**	**13.5**	**3,908.97**					**3,847.00**		**110.52**	

Step 1: Compile estimates for each quarter at the annual average prices of the previous year.

      e.g.:   q1 1998 $7.0 \cdot 67.4 + 6.0 \cdot 57.6 = 817.00$

              q4 1998 $7.0 \cdot 73.7 + 6.0 \cdot 55.8 = 850.70$

Step 2: Compile estimates for each quarter at the annual average prices of the same year.

      e.g.:   q1 1998 $5.5 \cdot 67.4 + 9.0 \cdot 57.6 = 889.10$

              q4 1998 $5.5 \cdot 73.7 + 9.0 \cdot 55.8 = 895.60$

Step 3: Convert the constant price estimates for each quarter of the first year after the chosen reference year (1997) into a volume index with the average of the previous year = 100

      e.g.:   q1 1998 $[817.4/(3173.0/4)] \cdot 100 = 103.04$

              q4 1998 $[850.7/(3173.0/4)] \cdot 100 = 107.24$

Step 4: For the other years, based on the constant price estimates derived in steps 1 and 2, calculate the volume change from the same quarter of the proceeding year as the following:

      e.g.:   q1 1999/q1 1998 $916.60 / 889.10 = 1.0309$

              q4 1999/q4 1998 $939.45 / 907.55 = 1.0451$

Step 5: Link the quarterly volume indices with shifting base and reference year using the changes from the same period of the previous year as linking factors (extrapolators).

      e.g.:   q1 1999 $1.0309 \cdot 103.04 = 106.23$

              q4 1999 $1.0451 \cdot 107.24 = 111.07$

              q1 2000 $1.0135 \cdot 106.23 = 107.67$

Observe that the unweighted annual average of the derived chain-linked quarterly index series is only approximately equal to the independently derived chain-linked annuals.

      e.g.:   2000 $[107.67+109.49+111.20+113.73]/4 = 110.52 \neq 110.51$

Finally, observe that the rate of change from q4 in one year to q1 in the next year in the chain-linked series based on the over-the-year technique differs substantially from the corresponding changes in chain-linked index based on a one-quarter overlap in the previous example.

      e.g.:   q1 1999/q 4 1998 based on the over-the-year technique $(106.23/107.24-1) \cdot 100 = -0.9\%$

           $\neq$ q1 1999/q 4 1998 based on one-quarter overlap (and 1998 prices): $(108.31/107.24-1) \cdot 100 = 1.0\%$

           q1 2000/q 4 1999 based on the over-the-year technique $(107.67/111.01-1) \cdot 100 = -3.0\%$

           $\neq$ q1 2000/q 4 1999 based on one-quarter overlap (and 1999 prices): $(111.60/111.01-1) \cdot 100 = 0.5\%$

Observe also that the rate of change from q4 in one year to q1 in the next year in the chain-linked series based on the over-the-year technique differs substantially from the corresponding changes in the constant price measures based on the average prices of the current year. That is, q1 1999/q 4 1998 based on average 1999 prices $(953.8/936.50-1) \cdot 100 = 0.5\%$

These differences between the q4-to-q1 rate of change in the chain-linked series based on the over-the-year technique and the corresponding rate of change based on direct measurements are the steps in the series introduced by the technique. Notice also that, in this example, the break appears to increase over time, that is, the breaks are cumulative. The breaks will be cumulative if there is a trend-wise change in relative prices and relative quantities, as in this example.

Chart 9.1 Chain-Linking of QNA Data

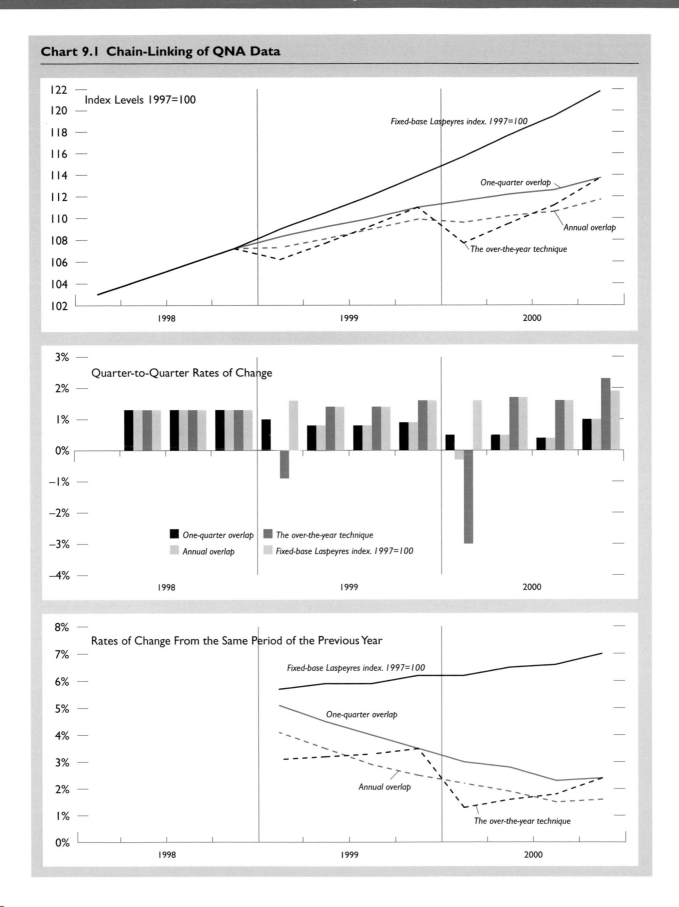

Example 9.5.a. Chain-Linking and Nonadditivity

This example illustrates the difference between constant price data and chain volume measures presented in monetary terms and shows the loss of additivity stemming from chain-linking.

The basic data are the same as in Examples 9.4.a, b, and c.

| | Basic Data | | | | At Constant 1997 Prices | | | Chain-Linked Index | Chain Volume Measures for the Total Referenced to its Average Current price Level in 1997 | Chain Discre-pancy |
| | Quanti-ties A | Quanti-ties B | Price A | Price B | Item A | Item B | Total | | | |
	(1)	(2)	(3)	(4)	(5)=(1)·(3)	(6)=(2)·(4)	(7)=(6)+(6)	(8)	(9)=(8)·3173.0/4	(10)= (7)−(8)
1997	**251.0**	**236.0**	**7.0**	**6.0**	**1,757.0**	**1,416.0**	**3,173.0**	**100.00**	**3,173.0**	**0.0**
q1 1998	67.4	57.6			471.8	345.6	817.4	103.04	817.4	0.0
q2 1998	69.4	57.1			485.8	342.6	828.4	104.43	828.4	0.0
q3 1998	71.5	56.5			500.5	339.0	839.5	105.83	839.5	0.0
q4 1998	73.7	55.8			515.9	334.8	850.7	107.24	850.7	0.0
q1 1999	76.0	55.4			532.0	332.4	864.4	107.26	850.8	13.6
q2 1999	78.3	54.8			548.1	328.8	876.9	108.10	857.5	19.4
q3 1999	80.6	54.2			564.2	325.2	889.4	108.95	864.3	25.1
q4 1999	83.1	53.6			581.7	321.6	903.3	109.93	872.0	31.3
q1 2000	85.5	53.2			598.5	319.2	917.7	109.60	869.4	48.3
q2 2000	88.2	52.7			617.4	316.2	933.6	110.18	874.0	59.6
q3 2000	90.8	52.1			635.6	312.6	948.2	110.58	877.2	71.0
q4 2000	93.5	52.0			654.5	312.0	966.5	111.69	886.0	80.5

The chain-linked Laspeyres volume index in column 8 was derived in Example 9.4.a.

The chain discrepancies are zero for all quarters in 1998 because the 1998 link in the chain-linked Laspeyres index in column 8 is based on 1997 weights.

Finally, observe that the chain discrepancies for 2000 are substantially larger than for 1999. This is a general result. The chain discrepancies increase the more distant the reference period is if the weight changes are trend-wise and not cyclical.

All other indices in common use are nonadditive.[22] Example 9.5.a. illustrates the difference between constant price data and chain volume measures presented in monetary terms and shows the loss of additivity stemming from chain-linking.

6. Chain-Linking, Benchmarking, Seasonal Adjustment, and Compilation Procedures Requiring Additivity

9.43. Benchmarking and seasonal adjustment require long consistent time series with a fixed reference period at a detailed level, while many standard national accounts compilation methods require additive data. Examples of national accounts compilation methods requiring additive data include estimating

value added as the difference between output and intermediate consumption, commodity flow techniques, and use of SU tables as a integrating framework. Both requirements may appear inconsistent with chain-linking, but they may not be.

9.44. In practice, the problem of nonadditivity can in most cases be circumvented by using the following multistep procedure (or its permutations):

Step 1

At the most detailed compilation level, construct long time series of non-seasonally adjusted traditional constant price data with a fixed-base year and corresponding Paasche price deflators using benchmarking, commodity flow, and other standard national accounts compilation techniques. These constant price data may be reconciled within an SU-table framework, if desired.

---

[22]The reason for non-additivity is that different weights are used for different annual periods, and therefore, will not yield the same results unless there have been no shifts in the weights.

Step 2

Aggregate these detailed constant price data using one of the following two alternative procedures:

A. Annual chain-linked Laspeyres framework

(i)   For each year, revalue all detailed constant price data to the constant average prices of the previous year.

(ii) Add together these revalued data measured at the average prices of the previous year to construct the various aggregates and subaggregates at the constant average prices of the previous year.

(iii) Construct long time series with a fixed reference year by chain-linking the aggregates and subaggregates at the constant average prices of the previous year, using the annual overlap technique in Example 9.4.a or the one-quarter overlap technique in Example 9.4.b (preferred).

B. All index formulas

Use the price-quantity version of the relevant index formula,[23] and treat in the formula the detailed constant price data as if they were quantities and the detailed price deflators as if they were prices.

Aggregation procedures A and B in step 2 will give the same results for annually chain-linked Laspeyres indices.

9.45. The multistep procedure outlined above also can be used for indirect seasonal adjustment of aggregates. In that case, to obtain the best seasonally adjusted estimates, aggregation to an intermediate level before seasonally adjusting the various components may be required for the reasons given in Chapter VIII, Section D.3.a, which discusses the pros and cons of direct versus indirect seasonal adjustment of aggregates.

7. Presentation of Chain-Linked Measures

9.46. There are some important aspects to consider in presenting chain-linked measures in publications:
- Whether to present measures of percentage change or time series with a fixed reference period.
- Whether to present time series as index numbers or in monetary terms.
- Terminology to avoid confusing chain-linked measures in monetary terms for constant price data (fixed-based measures).

---

[23]For value added, the "double indicator" version of the formulas should be used.

- Choice of reference year and frequency of reference year change—among others, as a means to reduce the inconvenience of nonadditivity associated with chain-linked measures.
- Whether to present supplementary measures of contribution of components to percentage change in aggregates.

9.47. Chain-linked price and volume measures must, at the minimum, be made available *as time series with a fixed reference period*. The main reason is that data presented with a fixed reference period allow different periods and periods of different duration to be compared and provide measures of long-run changes. Thus, presentation of price and volume measures should not be restricted to presenting only tables with period-to-period or year-on-year percentage change nor tables with each quarter presented as a percentage of a previous quarter. For users, tables with percentage changes derived from the time series may represent a useful supplement to the time series with a fixed reference period and may be best suited for presentation of headline measures. Tables with such data cannot replace the time-series data with a fixed reference period, however, because such tables do not provide the same user flexibility. Tables with each quarter presented as a percentage of a previous quarter (e.g., the previous quarter or the same quarter in the previous year) should be avoided because they are less useful and can result in users confusing the original index with the derived changes. Restricting the presentation of price and volume measures to presenting changes only runs counter to the core idea behind chain-linking, which is to construct long-run measures of change by cumulating a chain of short-term measures.

9.48. Chain-linked volume measures can be presented either as *index numbers* or in *monetary terms*. The difference between the two presentations is in how the reference period is expressed. As explained in paragraph 9.26, the reference period and level can be chosen freely without altering the rates of change in the series. The *index number* presentation shows the series with a fixed reference period that is set to 100, as shown in Examples 9.4.a, b, and c. The presentation is in line with usual index practice. It emphasizes that volume measures fundamentally are measures of relative change and that the choice and form of the reference point, and thus the level of the series, is arbitrary. It also highlights the differences of chain-linked measures from constant price estimates and prevents users from treating components as additive. Alternatively, the time series of chain-linked volume measures can be presented in *monetary terms* by multiplying the series by a constant to equal the constant price value in a particular reference period, usually a recent year. While this presentation has the advantage of showing the relative importance of the series, the indication of relative importance can be highly sensitive to the choice of reference year and may thus be misleading.[24] Because relative prices are changing over time, different reference years may give very different measures of relative importance. In addition, volume data expressed in monetary terms may wrongly suggest additivity to users who are not aware of the nature of chain-linked measures. On the other hand, they make it easier for users to gauge the extent of nonadditivity. Both presentations show the same underlying growth rates and both are used in practice.

9.49. Annually chain-linked Laspeyres volume measures in monetary terms are additive in the reference period. The nonadditivity inconvenience of chain volume measures in monetary terms may further be reduced by simultaneously doing the following:
- Using the average of a year and not the level of a particular quarter as reference period.
- Choosing the last complete year as reference year.
- Moving the reference year forward annually.

This procedure may give chain volume measures presented in monetary terms that are approximately additive for the last two years of the series. As illustrated in Example 9.5.a, the chain discrepancy increases (unless the weight changes are cyclical or noise) the more distant the reference year is. Thus, as illustrated in Example 9.5.b, moving the reference year forward can reduce the chain discrepancies significantly for the most recent section of the time series (at the expense of increased nonadditivity at the beginning of the series). For most users, additivity at the end of the series is more important than additivity at the beginning of the series.

9.50. To avoid chain discrepancies completely for the last two years of the series, some countries have adopted a practice of compiling and presenting data for the quarters of the last two years as the weighted annual average prices of the first of these two years. That second-to-last year of the series is also used as reference year for the complete time series. Again the reference year is moved forward annually. This approach has the advantage of providing absolute additivity for the last two years. The disadvantage, however, is that it also involves a series of back-and-forth changes in the price weights for the last two years, with added revisions to the growth rates as a result.

9.51. Chain-linked volume measures presented in monetary terms are *not* constant price measures and should not be labeled as measures at "*Constant xxxx Prices.*" Constant prices means estimates based on fixed-price weights, and thus the term should not be used for anything other than true constant price data based on fixed-price weights. Instead, chain-volume measures presented in monetary terms can be referred to as "chain-volume measures referenced to their nominal level in xxxx."

9.52. The inconvenience for users of chain-linked measures being nonadditive can be reduced somewhat by presenting measures of the components' contribution to percentage change in the aggregate. Contributions to percentage change measures are additive and thus allow cross-sectional analysis such as explaining the relative importance of GDP components to overall GDP volume growth. The exact formula for calculating contribution to percentage change depends on the aggregation formula used in constructing the aggregate series considered and the time span the percentage change covers. The following provides a sample of the most common cases:

- Contribution to percentage change from period $t-n$ to t in current and constant price data:

$$\%\Delta_{i,(t-n)\to t} = 100 \cdot \left(X_{i,t} - X_{i,t-n}\right)\Big/\sum_i X_{i,t-n} \qquad (9.9)$$
$$n \in \{1,2..\}$$

- Contribution to percentage change from period $t-1$ to t in a period-to-period as well as in an annually chain-linked[25] Laspeyres index series:

$$\%\Delta_{i,(t-1)\to t} = 100 \cdot w_{i,t-1} \cdot \left(I_{i,t} - I_{i,t-1}\right)\Big/\sum_i w_i \cdot I_{i,t-1} \quad (9.8)$$

Where $w_{i,t-1}$ is the base period "share weight," that is, the item's share in the total value of period $t-1$.

---

[24]For the same reason, measuring relative importance from constant price data can be grossly misleading. For most purposes, it is better to make comparisons of relative importance based on data at current prices—these are the prices that are most relevant for the period for which the comparisons are done, and restating the aggregates relative to prices for a different period detracts from the comparison.

[25]The formula assumes that the series is linked using the one-quarter overlap technique.

Example 9.5.b. Choice of Reference Period and Size of the Chain Discrepancy

This example illustrates how moving the reference period forward may reduce the nonadditivity inconvenience of chain volume measures.

The basic data are the same as in Examples 9.4 and 9.5.a.

	Basic Data				At Constant 1999 Prices			Chain Linked-Index 1999=100	Chain Volume Measures for the Total Referenced to its Average Current price Level in 1999	Chain Discre-pancy
	Quanti-ties A (1)	Quanti-ties B (2)	Price A (3)	Price B (4)	Item A (5)=(1)·(3)	Item B (6)=(2)·(4)	Total (7)=(5)+(6)	(8)	(9)=(8)·3394.2/4	(10)= (7)−(8)
q1 1998	67.4	57.6			269.6	662.4	932.0	94.92	896.8	35.2
q2 1998	69.4	57.1			277.6	656.6	934.2	96.20	908.8	25.4
q3 1998	71.5	56.5			286.0	649.7	935.7	97.49	921.0	14.8
q4 1998	73.7	55.8			294.8	641.7	936.5	98.79	933.3	3.2
q1 1999	76.0	55.4			304.0	637.1	941.1	98.80	933.4	7.7
q2 1999	78.3	54.8			313.2	630.2	943.4	99.68	940.8	2.6
q3 1999	80.6	54.2			322.4	623.3	945.7	100.36	948.2	−2.5
q4 1999	83.1	53.6			332.4	616.4	948.8	101.26	956.7	−7.9
1999	**318.0**	**218.0**	**4.0**	**11.5**	**1,272.0**	**2,507.0**	**3,779.0**	**100.00**	**3,779.0**	**0.0**
q1 2000	85.5	53.2			342.0	611.8	953.8	100.96	953.8	0.0
q2 2000	88.2	52.7			352.8	606.0	958.8	101.49	958.8	0.0
q3 2000	90.8	52.1			363.2	599.1	962.3	101.86	962.3	0.0
q4 2000	93.5	52.0			374.0	598.0	972.0	102.88	972.0	0.0

First, the chain-linked index in column 8 is obtained by re-referencing the chain-linked index derived in Example 9.4.a, to average 1999 = 100. The original index series derived in Example 9.4.a was expressed with 1997 = 100. Changing the reference period to 1999 simply means dividing the original index series by its average level in 1999 (102.5).

e.g.:

q1 1998	103.04 / 1.0856 =	94.92
q3 1998	105.83 / 1.0856 =	97.49
q1 1999	107.26 / 1.0856 =	98.80
q4 1999	109.93 / 1.0856 =	101.26
q4 2000	111.69 / 1.0856 =	102.88

The chain discrepancies are zero for all quarters in 2000 because the 2000 link in the original chain-linked Laspeyres index derived in Example 9.4.a is based on 1999 weights.

Finally, observe that the chain discrepancies for 1998 are substantially larger than for 1999. Again, we see that the chain discrepancies increase the more distant the reference period is.

For a period-to-period chain-linked Laspeyres index series, as equation (9.5), the share weights are

$$w_{i,t-1} = p_{i,t-1} \cdot q_{i,t} \Big/ \sum_i p_{i,t-1} \cdot q_{i,t-1}.$$

Correspondingly, for an annually chain-linked Laspeyres index series the share weights are

$$w_{i,y-1} = \bar{p}_{i,y-1} \cdot \bar{q}_{i,y-1} \Big/ \sum_i \bar{p}_{i,y-1} \cdot \bar{q}_{i,y-1},$$

where year $y - 1$ is the base year for each short-term link in the index as given by equation (9.7.a).

• Contribution to percentage change from period $t-1$ to t in a period-to-period chain-linked Fisher volume index series:

$$\%\Delta_{i,(t-1)\to t} = 100 \cdot \frac{\left(p_{i,t}\big/P_t^F + p_{i,t-1}\right) \cdot \left(q_{i,t} - q_{i,t-1}\right)}{\sum_i \left(p_{i,t}\big/P_t^F + p_{i,t-1}\right) \cdot q_{i,t-1}} \quad (9.9)$$

where P_t^F is the Fisher price index for the aggregate in period t with period $t - 1$ as base and reference period.

9.53. The nonadditivity inconvenience of chain-linking often can be circumvented by simply noting that chain Laspeyres volume measures are additive within each link. For that reason, chain-linked Laspeyres volume measures, for instance, can be combined with analytical tools like constant price SU and IO tables/models that require additivity.[26]

---

[26]In fact, the first countries to adopt annually chain-linked volume measures as their official national accounts volume measures used SU tables as their integrating GDP compilation framework.

Annex 9.1. Aggregation Over Time and Consistency Between Annual and Quarterly Estimates

A. Introduction

9A1.1. This annex provides a formal presentation of the following conclusions about annual and quarterly Laspeyres-type volume measures with corresponding Paasche deflators reached in Section B of the chapter and illustrated in Example 9.1:

(a) To ensure consistency between quarterly and annual data, annual Paasche deflators should in principle be derived as current period weighted averages of monthly or quarterly price deflators, where the weights represent constant price data.

(b) These annual deflators correspond to quantity-weighted period-average price measures and, equivalently to being derived as in conclusion (a), can be constructed directly from current period quantity-weighted average annual prices.

(c) Quarterly Paasche price indices should be based on the quantity-weighted average of each item's prices in the quarters of the base year and not on unweighted averages as typically used in price index compilations, to ensure that in the base year the annual sum of the quarterly constant price estimates is equal to the annual sum of the current price data.

(d) Deflating quarterly data with deflators constructed with unweighted average prices as the price base corresponds to valuing the quantities using their unweighted annual average price rather than their weighted annual average price.

(e) Valuing the quantities using their unweighted annual average price rather than heir weighted annual average price causes the annual sum of the quarterly constant price estimates in the base year to differ from the annual sum of the current price data.

(f) The error in conclusion (e) can be removed by a multiplicative adjustment of the complete constant price time series. The adjustment factor is the ratio of the annual current price data to the sum of the initial quarterly constant price data based on the unweighted annual average prices in the base year, which, for a single product, is identical to the ratio of the weighted to the unweighted average price.

The two first conclusions are formally shown in Section B and the last four conclusions in Section C of this annex.

B. Relationship Between Quarterly and Annual Deflators

9.A1.2. Quarterly data at current prices, at the "average" prices of the base year (year 0), and the corresponding (implicit) quarterly deflator with the average of year 0 as base and reference period can be expressed mathematically as the following:

• At current prices:

$$V_{q,y} = \sum_i p_{i,q,y} \cdot q_{i,q,y} \qquad (9.\text{A}1.1)$$

• At the "average" prices of the base year:

$$CP_{q,y_{\bar{0}}} = \sum_i \bar{p}_{i,0} \cdot q_{i,q,y}, \qquad (9.\text{A}1.2)$$

$$\bar{p}_{i,0} = \frac{\sum_q p_{i,q,0} \cdot q_{i,q,0}}{\sum_q q_{i,q,0}}$$

$$\equiv \sum_q p_{i,q,0} \cdot \left(\frac{q_{i,q,0}}{\sum_q q_{i,q,0}} \right)$$

• Quarterly deflator (quarterly fixed-base Paasche index):[27]

$$PP_{\bar{0} \to (q,y)_{\bar{0}}} = \frac{V_{q,y}}{CP_{q,y_{\bar{0}}}} \qquad (9.\text{A}1.3)$$

$$\equiv \frac{\sum_i p_{i,q,y} \cdot q_{i,q,y}}{\sum_i \bar{p}_0 \cdot q_{i,q,y}}$$

where

$p_{i,q,y}$ is the price of item i in quarter q of year y;

$q_{i,q,y}$ is the quantity of item i in quarter q of year y;

---

[27] In the remainder of this annex, index numbers are presented with the following syntax: *Type of index (Reference period)→(Current period)(base period)*. Using the following codes for the elements of the syntax: *LQ* for a Laspeyres volume index, *PP* for a Paasche price index, *y–1* for average year *y–1*, and *(q,y)* for quarter *q* of year *y*.

$V_{q,y}$ is the total value at current prices in quarter q of year y;

$\bar{p}_{i,0}$ is the quantity-weighted annual arithmetic average of the price of item i in each quarter of year 0; and

$CP_{q,y_{\bar{0}}}$ is the total value in quarter q of year y measured at the annual average prices of year 0.

The quarterly deflator can either be implicitly derived as the current price value divided by the constant price value ($V_{q,y}/CP_{q,y_{\bar{0}}}$) or explicitly as a quarterly fixed-base Paasche index with the weighted average prices in year 0 ($\bar{p}_{i,0}$) as the price base.

9.A1.3. Similarly, annual data at current prices, at the "average" prices of the base year (year *0*), and the corresponding (implicit) annual deflator with the average of year 0 as base and reference period can be expressed mathematically as the following:

• At current prices:

$$V_y = \sum_q \sum_i v_{i,q,y} \qquad (9.\text{A}1.4)$$

$$\equiv \sum_q \sum_i p_{i,q,y} \cdot q_{i,q,y}$$

• At the "average" prices of the base year:

$$CP_{y_{\bar{0}}} = \sum_q CP_{q,y_{\bar{0}}} \qquad (9.\text{A}1.5)$$

$$= \sum_q \sum_i \bar{p}_{i,0} \cdot q_{i,q,y}$$

• Annual deflator (annual fixed-base Paasche index):

$$PP_{\bar{0} \to \bar{y}_{\bar{0}}} = \frac{\sum_q V_{q,y}}{\sum_q CP_{q,y_{\bar{0}}}} \qquad (9.\text{A}1.6\text{a})$$

$$= \sum_q PP_{(\bar{0}) \to (q,y)_{\bar{0}}} \cdot \left[\frac{CP_{q,y_{\bar{0}}}}{\sum_q CP_{q,y_{\bar{0}}}} \right]$$

where

$v_{i,q,y}$ is the value of item i at current prices in quarter q of year y; and

$CP_{y_{\bar{0}}}$ is the total annual value for year y measured at the annual average prices of year 0.

9.A1.4. Equations (9.A1.1) to (9.A1.6a) show that to ensure consistency between quarterly and annual

data, annual Paasche deflators should in principle be current period weighted averages of the quarterly price deflators ($PP_{\bar{0} \to (q,y)\bar{0}}$), where the weights ($CP_{q,y_{\bar{0}}}/\sum_q CP_{q,y_{\bar{0}}}$) are based on current period constant price data, as stated in paragraph 9.A1.1 conclusion (a) above. These current period weighted averages of the quarterly price deflators can either be implicitly derived as the annual sum of the quarterly current price data divided by the annual sum of the quarterly constant price data, or explicitly as a weighted average of monthly or quarterly price indices.

9.A1.5. The implicit annual deflator in equation (9.A1.6a) can, as stated in paragraph 9.A1.1 conclusion (b), equivalently be constructed directly from current period quantity-weighted average annual prices as evident from the following:

$$PP_{\bar{0} \to \bar{y}_{\bar{0}}} = \frac{\sum_q V_{q,y}}{\sum_q CP_{q,y_{\bar{0}}}} \qquad (9.\text{A}1.6\text{b})$$

$$= \frac{\sum_q \sum_i p_{i,q,y} \cdot q_{i,q,y}}{\sum_q \sum_i \bar{p}_{i,0} \cdot q_{i,q,y}} = \frac{\sum_i \bar{p}_{i,y} \cdot \bar{q}_{i,y}}{\sum_i \bar{p}_{i,0} \cdot \bar{q}_{i,y}}$$

when $\bar{p}_{i,y} = \dfrac{\sum_q p_{i,q,y} \cdot q_{i,q,y}}{\sum_q q_{i,q,y}}$, $\bar{q}_{i,y} = \sum_q q_{i,q,y}$

where

$\bar{p}_{i,y}$ is the quantity-weighted annual arithmetic average of the price of item i in each quarter of year y; and

$\bar{q}_{i,y}$ is the total annual quantity of item i in year y.

C. Annual Average Prices as Price Base

9.A1.6. In the base year 0, the annual sum of the quarterly constant price data is given by the following:

$$CP_{0_{\bar{0}}} = \sum_q CP_{q,0_{\bar{0}}} = \sum_q \sum_i \bar{p}_{i,0} \cdot q_{i,q,0} \qquad (9.\text{A}1.7\text{a})$$

9.A1.7. It follows that the annual sum of the quarterly constant price data is equal to the annual sum of the current price data in the base year, if, for each item, the base price is the quantity-weighted average of the item's prices in each quarter of the base year. That is, the base price is derived as $\bar{p}_{i,0} = \sum_q p_{i,q,0} \cdot q_{i,q,0} / \sum_q q_{i,q,0}$. This conclusion is evident from the following:

$$CP_{0_{\bar{0}}} = \sum_i \left(\bar{p}_{i,0} \cdot \sum_q q_{i,q,0} \right) \qquad (9.A1.7b)$$

$$= \sum_i \left(\frac{\sum_i p_{i,q,0} \cdot q_{i,q,0}}{\sum_q q_{i,q,0}} \cdot \sum_q q_{i,q,0} \right)$$

$$\equiv \sum_i \sum_q p_{i,q,0} \cdot q_{i,q,0} \equiv V_0$$

9.A1.8. It follows furthermore, as stated in paragraph 9.A1.1 conclusion (c), that the quarterly deflators should be constructed with quantity-weighted average prices as the price base—as in equation (9.A1.3)—to ensure that in the base year the annual sum of the quarterly constant price estimates is equal to the annual sum of the current price data. This conclusion is evident from the following in combination with equation (9.A1.7b):

$$CP_{q,0_{\bar{0}}} = \frac{V_{q,0}}{PP_{\bar{0} \to (q,0)_{\bar{0}}}} \qquad (9.A1.7c)$$

$$= \sum_i p_{i,q,0} \cdot q_{i,q,0} \Big/ \frac{\sum_i p_{i,q,0} \cdot q_{i,q,0}}{\sum_i \bar{p}_0 \cdot q_{i,q,0}}$$

$$\equiv \sum_i \bar{p}_0 \cdot q_{i,q,0}$$

9.A1.9. Deflating quarterly data with deflators constructed with unweighted average prices as the price base, corresponds, as stated in paragraph 9.A1.1 conclusion (d), to valuing the quantities using their unweighted annual average price. This result is evident from the following:

$$CP_{q,y_{\bar{0}}} = V_{q,y} \Big/ \frac{\sum_i p_{i,q,y} \cdot q_{i,q,y}}{\sum_i \hat{p}_{i,q,0} \cdot q_{i,q,y}} \qquad (9.A1.8)$$

$$\equiv \sum_i p_{i,q,y} \cdot q_{i,q,y} \Big/ \frac{\sum_i p_{i,q,y} \cdot q_{i,q,y}}{\sum_i \hat{p}_{i,q,0} \cdot q_{i,q,y}}$$

$$\equiv \sum_i \hat{p}_{i,0} \cdot q_{i,q,y}$$

where

$p_{i,0} = 1/4 \sum_q p_{i,q,0}$ is the unweighted annual arithmetic average of the price of item i in each quarter of year 0; and

$\dfrac{\sum_i p_{i,q,y} \cdot q_{i,q,y}}{\sum_i \hat{p}_{i,q,0} \cdot q_{i,q,y}}$ is a Paasche index (deflator) constructed with unweighted average prices as price base.

9.A1.10. As stated in paragraph 9.A1.1 conclusion (e) above, in the base year, the constant price data derived in equation (9.A1.8), in contrast to the constant price data derived in equation (9.A1.7), do not sum to the annual sum of the current price data. However, as stated in paragraph 9.A1.1 conclusion (f), this error can be removed by a multiplicative adjustment, using the following adjustment factor:

$$\frac{\sum_q CP_{q,0_{\bar{0}}}}{\sum_q CP_{q,0_{\bar{0}}}} = \frac{\sum_q \sum_i \bar{p}_{i,0} \cdot q_{i,q,0}}{\sum_q \sum_i \hat{p}_{i,0} \cdot q_{i,q,0}} \qquad (9.A1.9a)$$

$$\equiv \frac{\sum_i \sum_q p_{i,q,0} \cdot q_{i,q,0}}{\sum_i \sum_q \hat{p}_{i,0} \cdot q_{i,q,0}} \equiv \frac{\sum_q V_{q,0}}{\sum_q CP_{q,0_{\bar{0}}}}$$

That is, the ratio of the annual current price data to the sum of the initial quarterly constant price data based on the unweighted annual average prices in the base year. This factor, for a single product, is identical to the ratio of the weighted and unweighted average price:

$$\frac{\sum_q \bar{p}_{i,0} \cdot q_{i,q,0}}{\sum_q \hat{p}_{i,0} \cdot q_{i,q,0}} = \frac{\sum_q \bar{p}_{i,0} \cdot q_{i,q,0} \big/ \sum_q q_{i,q,0}}{\hat{p}_{i,0}} \qquad (9.A1.9b)$$

$$\equiv \frac{\bar{p}_{i,0}}{\hat{p}_{i,0}}$$

Annex 9.2. Annual Chain-Linking of Quarterly Laspeyres Volume Measures: A Formal Presentation of the Annual and One-Quarter Overlap Techniques

A. The Annual Overlap Technique

9.A2.1. Quarterly estimates at the quantity-weighted average prices of the previous year (year $y-1$) are given as

$$CP_{q,y\overline{-1}} = \sum_i \overline{p}_{i,y-1} \cdot q_{i,q,y}, \qquad (9.A2.1)$$

$$\overline{p}_{i,y-1} = \frac{\sum_q p_{i,q,y-1} \cdot q_{i,q,y-1}}{\sum_q q_{i,q,y-1}}$$

where

$p_{i,q,y-1}$ is the price of item i in quarter q of year $y-1$;

$q_{i,q,y}$ is the quantity of item i in quarter q in year y;

$\overline{q}_{i,y-1}$ is the simple arithmetic average of the quantities of item i in the quarters of year $y-1$;

$\overline{p}_{i,y-1}$ is the quantity weighted arithmetic average of the price of item i in the quarters of year $y-1$; and

$CP_{q,y\overline{-1}}$ is the total value in quarter q of year y measured at the average prices of year $y-1$.

9.A2.2. The corresponding short-term quarterly Laspeyres volume index and (implicit) Paasche deflator series with the average of the previous year as base and reference period are given as the following:[28]

- Short-term quarterly Laspeyres volume index:

$$LQ_{\overline{y-1}\to(q,y)\overline{y-1}} = \frac{CP_{q,y\overline{-1}}}{\tfrac{1}{4}\sum_q V_{q,y-1}} \qquad (9.A2.2)$$

$$\equiv \frac{\sum_i \overline{p}_{i,y-1} \cdot q_{i,q,y}}{\tfrac{1}{4}\sum_q \sum_i \overline{p}_{i,y-1} \cdot q_{i,q,y-1}}$$

$$\equiv \frac{\sum_i \overline{p}_{i,y-1} \cdot q_{i,q,y}}{\sum_i \overline{p}_{i,y-1} \cdot \tfrac{1}{4}\sum_q q_{i,q,y-1}}$$

$$\equiv \frac{\sum_i \overline{p}_{i,y-1} \cdot q_{i,q,y}}{\sum_i \overline{p}_{i,y-1} \cdot \overline{q}_{i,q,y-1}}$$

$$\equiv \sum_i \left(\frac{q_{i,q,y}}{\overline{q}_{i,y-1}}\right) \cdot \frac{\overline{p}_{i,y-1} \cdot \overline{q}_{i,y-1}}{\sum \overline{p}_{i,y-1} \cdot \overline{q}_{i,q,y-1}}$$

$$= \sum_i \frac{q_{i,q,y}}{\overline{q}_{i,y-1}} \cdot w_{i,y-1}$$

- Short-term (implicit) quarterly Paasche deflator:

$$PP_{\overline{y-1}\to(q,y)\overline{y-1}} = \frac{V_{q,y}}{CP_{q,y_{y-1}}} \qquad (9.A2.3)$$

$$= \frac{\sum_i p_{i,q,y} \cdot q_{i,q,y}}{\sum_i \overline{p}_{i,y-1} \cdot q_{i,q,y}}$$

where

$w_{i,y-1}$ is the base-period weight, that is, item i's share of the total value in period $y-1$ at current prices;

$V_{q,y-1}$ is the total value at current prices in quarter q of year y;

$LQ_{(\overline{y-1})\to(q,y)(\overline{y-1})}$ is a Laspeyres volume index for quarter q of year y with average year $y-1$ as base and reference period; and

$PP_{(\overline{y-1})\to(q,y)(\overline{y-1})}$ is a Paasche price index (deflator) for quarter q of year y with average year $y-1$ as base and reference period.

---

[28]In the remainder of this annex, index numbers are presented with the following syntax: *Type of index* (Reference period)→(Current period)(base period). Using the following codes for the elements of the syntax: *LQ* for a Laspeyres volume index, *CLQ* for a chain-linked Laspeyres volume index, *PP* for a Paasche price index, *CPP* for a chain-linked Paasche Price index, $\overline{y-1}$ for average year $y-1$, and (q,y) for quarter q of year y.

9.A2.3. Similarly, the short-term annual Laspeyres volume index and Paasche deflator series with the average of the previous year as base and reference period are given as the following:

- Short-term annual Laspeyres volume index:

$$LQ_{\overline{y-1} \to \overline{y}_{\overline{y-1}}} = \frac{\sum_q CP_{q,y_{\overline{y-1}}}}{\sum_q V_{q,y-1}} \tag{9.A2.4}$$

$$\equiv \frac{\sum_q \sum_i \overline{p}_{i,y-1} \cdot q_{i,q,y}}{\sum_q \sum_i \overline{p}_{i,y-1} \cdot q_{i,q,y-1}}$$

$$\equiv \frac{\sum_i \overline{p}_{i,y-1} \cdot \sum_q q_{i,q,y}}{\sum_i \overline{p}_{i,y-1} \cdot \sum_q q_{i,q,y-1}}$$

$$\equiv \frac{\sum_i \overline{p}_{i,y-1} \cdot \overline{q}_{i,q,y}}{\sum_i \overline{p}_{i,y-1} \cdot \overline{q}_{i,q,y-1}}$$

$$= \sum_i \frac{\sum_q q_{i,q,y}}{\sum_q q_{i,q,y-1}} \cdot w_{i,y-1}$$

$$\equiv \sum_i \frac{\overline{q}_{i,y}}{\overline{q}_{i,y-1}} \cdot w_{i,y-1}$$

- Short-term annual Paasche deflator:

$$PP_{\overline{y-1} \to \overline{y}_{\overline{y-1}}} = \frac{\sum_q \sum_i p_{i,q,y} \cdot p_{i,q,y}}{\sum_q \sum_i \overline{p}_{i,y-1} \cdot q_{i,q,y}} \tag{9.A2.5}$$

$$\equiv \frac{\sum_i \overline{p}_{i,y} \cdot \overline{q}_{i,y}}{\sum_i \overline{p}_{i,y-1} \cdot \overline{q}_{i,y}}$$

9.A2.4. Thus, the long-term annually chain-linked quarterly Laspeyres volume index and Paasche deflator can be constructed as the following:

- Long-term annually chain-linked quarterly Laspeyres volume index:

For measuring the overall change from the average of year 0 (the reference year) to quarter q of year 2:

$$CLQ_{(\overline{0}) \to (q,2)} = \frac{\sum_i \overline{p}_{i,0} \cdot \overline{q}_{i,1}}{\sum_i \overline{p}_{i,0} \cdot \overline{q}_{i,0}} \cdot \frac{\sum_i \overline{p}_{i,1} \cdot \overline{q}_{i,q,2}}{\sum_i \overline{p}_{i,1} \cdot \overline{q}_{i,1}} \tag{9.A2.6a}$$

For measuring overall change from the average of year 0 (the reference year) to quarter q of year Y:

$$CLQ_{(\overline{0}) \to (q,Y)} = \left[\prod_{y=1}^{Y-1} \frac{\sum_i \overline{p}_{i,y-1} \cdot \overline{q}_{i,y}}{\sum_i \overline{p}_{i,y-1} \cdot \overline{q}_{i,y-1}} \right] \cdot \frac{\sum_i \overline{p}_{i,Y-1} \cdot \overline{q}_{i,q,Y}}{\sum_i \overline{p}_{i,Y-1} \cdot \overline{q}_{i,Y-1}} \tag{9.A2.6b}$$

- Long-term annually chain-linked quarterly Paasche deflator:

For measuring the overall change from the average of year 0 (the reference year) to quarter q of year 2:

$$CPP_{(\overline{0}) \to (q,2)} = \frac{V_{q,2}}{V_0} \bigg/ CLQ_{(\overline{0}) \to (q,2)} \tag{9.A2.7a}$$

$$= \frac{\sum_i p_{i,q,2} \cdot q_{i,q,2}}{\sum_i \overline{p}_{i,0} \cdot \overline{q}_{i,0}} \bigg/ \frac{\sum_i \overline{p}_{i,0} \cdot \overline{q}_{i,1}}{\sum_i \overline{p}_{i,0} \cdot \overline{q}_{i,0}} \cdot \frac{\sum_i \overline{p}_{i,1} \cdot q_{i,q,2}}{\sum_i \overline{p}_{i,1} \cdot \overline{q}_{i,1}}$$

$$= \frac{\sum_i p_{i,q,2} \cdot q_{i,q,2}}{\sum_i \overline{p}_{i,1} \cdot q_{i,q,2}} \cdot \frac{\sum_i \overline{p}_{i,1} \cdot \overline{q}_{i,1}}{\sum_i \overline{p}_{i,0} \cdot \overline{q}_{i,1}}$$

For measuring overall change from the average of year 0 (the reference year) to quarter q of year Y:

$$CPP_{(\overline{0}) \to (q,Y)} = \left[\prod_{y=1}^{Y-1} \frac{\sum_i \overline{p}_{i,y} \cdot \overline{q}_{i,y}}{\sum_i \overline{p}_{i,y-1} \cdot \overline{q}_{i,y}} \right] \cdot s \frac{\sum_i p_{i,q,Y} \cdot q_{i,q,Y}}{\sum_i \overline{p}_{i,Y-1} \cdot q_{i,q,Y}} \tag{9.A2.7b}$$

9.A2.5. The corresponding monetary term chain-volume measure for quarter q of year Y with the average of year 0 as reference base can be constructed as the following:

$$MCQ_{q,Y_{\overline{0}}} = CLQ_{(\overline{0}) \to (q,Y)} \cdot \sum_i \overline{p}_{i,0} \cdot \overline{q}_{i,0} \tag{9.A2.8}$$

$$= CLQ_{(\overline{0}) \to (q,Y)} \cdot \tfrac{1}{4} V_0$$

9.A2.6. The monetary term chain-volume measure in equation (9.A2.8) can alternatively be derived by rescaling the constant price levels directly using the corresponding implicit annual Paasche deflator index (annually chain-linked). This follows from the following elaboration of equation (9.A2.8), for simplicity only shown in a three-period context, and Example 9.A2.1 below:

(9.A2.9)

$$MCQ_{q,2_{\bar{0}}} = CLQ_{\overline{(\bar{0})}\rightarrow(q,2)} \cdot \sum_i \bar{p}_{i,0} \cdot \bar{q}_{i,0}$$

$$\equiv \sum_i \bar{p}_{i,0} \cdot \bar{q}_{i,0} \cdot \frac{\sum_i \bar{p}_{i,0} \cdot \bar{q}_{i,1}}{\sum_i \bar{p}_{i,0} \cdot \bar{q}_{i,0}} \cdot \frac{\sum_i \bar{p}_{i,1} \cdot q_{i,q,2}}{\sum_i \bar{p}_{i,1} \cdot \bar{q}_{i,1}}$$

$$\equiv \frac{\sum_i \bar{p}_{i,0} \cdot \bar{q}_{i,1}}{\sum_i \bar{p}_{i,1} \cdot \bar{q}_{i,1}} \cdot \sum_i \bar{p}_{i,1} \cdot q_{i,q,2}$$

$$\equiv \sum_i \bar{p}_{i,1} \cdot q_{i,q,2} \left/ \frac{\sum_i \bar{p}_{i,1} \cdot \bar{q}_{i,1}}{\sum_i \bar{p}_{i,0} \cdot \bar{q}_{i,1}} \right.$$

where

$\dfrac{\sum_i \bar{p}_{i,1} \cdot \bar{q}_{i,1}}{\sum_i \bar{p}_{i,0} \cdot \bar{q}_{i,1}}$ is the corresponding implicit annual Paasche deflator index with period 0 as base and reference period.

B.   The One-Quarter Overlap Technique

9.A2.7. The short-term Laspeyres volume index series in (9.A2.2) can be re-referenced to be expressed with the fourth quarter of the previous year as reference period as follows:

(9.A2.10)

$$LQ_{(4,y-1)\rightarrow(q,y)_{\overline{(y-1)}}} = \frac{\sum_i \bar{p}_{i,y-1} \cdot q_{i,q,y}}{\sum_i \bar{p}_{i,y-1} \cdot q_{i,q,y-1}} \left/ \frac{\sum_i \bar{p}_{i,y-1} \cdot q_{i,q,y}}{\sum_i \bar{p}_{i,y-1} \cdot \bar{q}_{i,q,y-1}} \right.$$

$$\equiv \frac{\sum_i \bar{p}_{i,y-1} \cdot q_{i,q,y}}{\sum_i \bar{p}_{i,y-1} \cdot q_{i,4,y-1}}$$

where

$LQ_{(4,y-1)\rightarrow(q,y)_{\overline{(y-1)}}}$ is a Laspeyres volume index for quarter q of year y with average year $y-1$ as base period and the fourth quarter of the previous year as reference period.

9.A2.8. Thus, the corresponding long-term chain-linked volume index measuring the overall change from the average of year 0 (the reference year) to quarter q of year 2 can be constructed as

$$CLQ_{\overline{(0)}\rightarrow(q,2)} = \frac{\sum_i \bar{p}_{i,0} \cdot q_{i,4,1}}{\sum_i \bar{p}_{i,0} \cdot q_{i,0}} \cdot \frac{\sum_i \bar{p}_{i,1} \cdot q_{i,4,2}}{\sum_i \bar{p}_{i,1} \cdot q_{i,4,1}} \quad (9.A2.11)$$

9.A2.9 And the long-term chain-linked volume index measuring the overall change from the average of year 0 (the reference year) to quarter q of year Y can be constructed as

$$CLQ_{\overline{(0)}\rightarrow(q,Y)} \quad\quad\quad\quad (9.A2.12)$$

$$= \frac{\sum_i \bar{p}_{i,0} \cdot q_{i,4,1}}{\sum_i \bar{p}_{i,0} \cdot q_{i,0}} \cdot \left[\prod_{y=2}^{Y-1} \frac{\sum_i \bar{p}_{i,y-1} \cdot q_{i,4,y}}{\sum_i \bar{p}_{i,y-1} \cdot q_{i,4},y-1} \right] \cdot \frac{\sum_i \bar{p}_{i,1} \cdot q_{i,q,Y}}{\sum_i \bar{p}_{i,1} \cdot q_{i,4,Y-1}}$$

9.A2.10. The corresponding monetary term chain volume measure with the average of year 0 as reference base can be constructed as

$$MCQ_{q,Y_{\bar{0}}} = CLQ_{\overline{(0)}\rightarrow(q,Y)} \cdot \sum_i \bar{p}_{i,0} \cdot q_{i,0} \quad (9.A2.13)$$

$$= CLQ_{\overline{(0)}\rightarrow(q,Y)} \cdot {}^1\!/_4\, V_0$$

9.A2.11. The monetary term chain volume measure in (9.A2.13) can alternatively be derived by re-scaling the constant price levels directly using the corresponding implicit fourth quarter weighted annual Paasche deflator. This follows from the following elaboration of equation (9.A2.13), which for simplicity is only shown in a three period context:

$$MCQ_{q,2_{\bar{0}}} = CLQ_{\overline{(0)}\rightarrow(q,2)} \cdot \sum_i \bar{p}_{i,0} \cdot q_{i,0} \quad (9.A2.14)$$

$$= \sum_i \bar{p}_{i,0} \cdot q_{i,0} \cdot \frac{\sum_i \bar{p}_{i,0} \cdot q_{i,4,1}}{\sum_i \bar{p}_{i,0} \cdot q_{i,0}} \cdot \frac{\sum_i \bar{p}_{i,1} \cdot q_{i,q,2}}{\sum_i \bar{p}_{i,1} \cdot q_{i,4,1}}$$

$$\equiv \frac{\sum_i \bar{p}_{i,0} \cdot q_{i,4,1}}{\sum_i \bar{p}_{i,0} \cdot q_{i,4,1}} \cdot \sum_i \bar{p}_{i,1} \cdot q_{i,q,2}$$

$$\equiv \sum_i \bar{p}_{i,1} \cdot q_{i,q,2} \left/ \frac{\sum_i \bar{p}_{i,1} \cdot q_{i,4,1}}{\sum_i \bar{p}_{i,0} \cdot q_{i,q,2}} \right.$$

where

$\dfrac{\sum_i \bar{p}_{i,1} \cdot q_{i,4,1}}{\sum_i \bar{p}_{i,0} \cdot q_{i,4,1}}$ is the corresponding implicit fourth-quarter-weighted annual Paasche deflator index with period 0 as base and reference period.

Example 9.A2.1. Quarterly Data and Annual Chain-Linking
An Alternative "Annual Price Scaling" Version of the Annual Overlap Technique

Annual sums and averages in bold.

The basic data are the same as in Example 9.4.

This example provides an alternative presentation of the annual overlap chain-linking technique presented in Example 9.4. The final results are the same, but the procedure of obtaining the linked time series differs.

	Total at Current Prices	At 1997 Constant Prices 1998 = 100	Implicit Paasche Deflator 1997 = 100	At 1998 Constant Prices	Implicit Paasche Deflator	At 1999 Constant Prices	Chain Volume Measures for the Total in Monetary Terms Referenced to its Average Current Price Level in 1997
1997	**3,173.00**	**3,173.00**	100.00				**3,173.00**
q1 1998	871.94	817.40	106.67				817.40
q2 1998	885.51	828.40	106.89				828.40
q3 1998	910.05	839.60	108.40				839.60
q4 1998	926.50	850.70	108.91				850.70
1998	**3,594.00**	**3,336.00**	107.73		3,594.00	**100.00**	**3,336.00**
q1 1999	934.78			916.60	101.98		850.80
q2 1999	963.07			923.85	104.25	857.53	
q3 1999	940.42			931.10	101.00	864.26	
q4 1999	940.73			939.45	100.14	872.01	
1999	**3,779.00**			**3,711.00**	101.83	**3,779.00**	**3,444.60**
q1 2000	955.70					953.80	869.40
q2 2000	961.70					958.85	874.00
q3 2000	973.22					962.35	877.19
q4 2000	1018.36					972.00	885.99
2000	**3,908.97**					**3,847.00**	**3,777.78**

Step 1: As in Example 9.4, compile estimates for each quarter at the annual average prices of the previous year; the annual data being the sum of the four quarters.

Step2: Derive the corresponding annual implicit Paasche deflators with the previous year as base and reference period.
1998   [3594.0/3336.0] · 100 = 107.73
1999   [3779.0/3711.0] · 100 = 101.83

Step 3: Scale down the quarterly constant price estimates to measures at previous year's average prices, to the average price level of 1997.
e.g.:   q1 1999   916.60/ 1.0773 = 850.80
     q4 1999   939.45/ 1.0773 = 872.01
     q1 2000   953.80/ (1.0773 · 1.0183) = 869.40

Observe that the resulting monetary termed chain-linked volume measures are identical to the ones derived in Example 9.5.a.

X Work-in-Progress

A. Introduction

10.1. Work-in-progress concerns production that goes beyond one period. Measurement of such production poses the problem that a single process has to be split into separate periods. Because of the shorter accounting period, these difficulties are relatively more significant for quarterly national accounts (QNA) than for annual national accounts (ANA).

10.2. The general national accounting principle is that production should be measured at the time it takes place and be valued at the prices of that time. In most cases, this treatment presents no problems, because the production process is short and thus output can be measured from the value of the finished product. When the production process transcends a single accounting period, however, production needs to be shown in two or more periods. This production results in output of unfinished products, which is called work-in-progress in both business and national accounting. As stated in the *1993 SNA*, "it would distort economic reality to treat output as if it were all produced at the moment of time when the process of production happens to terminate" (paragraph 6.39). Also, where prices have changed during the production process, the price paid at the end will include holding gains (or possibly losses) that need to be excluded in order to have a correct measure of production.

10.3. There are many activities in which production cycles go outside a single period. Even with very short processes, there can be work-in-progress. Some activities have quite long production cycles and so work-in-progress is particularly important. These activities include the following:
- Agriculture, animal husbandry, forestry, and fishing. In agriculture, crops may grow over several seasons. Similarly, growing livestock, cultivating timber, cultivating fruit, viticulture, and fish

farming are all cases where production occurs over more than one period before the final output is marketed. Also, wool is usually collected only once a year.
- Manufacturing. Ships, submarines, airplanes, and some heavy equipment have long production cycles.
- Construction. The production cycle is often quite lengthy, varying from a few months for a house to many years in the case of a civil engineering project.
- Services. Examples in this category are movies, architectural services, and large sport events.

10.4. This chapter first explores the general reasons why work on unfinished products is considered output. Subsequently, the principles of measurement and some practical solutions are discussed. Briefly, the solution for measuring of work-in-progress is to use output measures based on quarterly input costs in conjunction with values or markups for the whole process. Where such costs are not available, proxies such as fixed proportions can be used.[1]

10.5. Recording work-in-progress poses special difficulties for agriculture and related industries because of the uncertainties intrinsic to the dependence of the production process on forces of nature and because of the volatility of prices. Also, because the concept of work-in-progress is not generally applied in these industries, its application in national accounts is exposed to criticism denouncing it as artificial.[2] It has been suggested that most of the problems involved in applying work-in-progress concepts to agriculture could be solved through the application of seasonal

---
[1]As well as its direct effect on measuring output, work-in-progress also has consequential effects on income accounts, capital accounts, and balance sheets. These effects are discussed in the annex.
[2]Although examples can be mentioned in which prices do reflect the value of work-in-progress. One such example is keeping sheep for wool, where the price of sheep reflects the harvestable amount of wool (prices plunge immediately after harvesting).

adjustment, but it should be emphasized that recording work-in-progress and seasonal adjustments are unrelated issues and that recording work-in-progress affects the unadjusted estimates. These issues are discussed in Section D.

10.6. Inclusion of work-in-progress affects many components of the accounts, but in a consistent way, so that it does not create discrepancies. In addition to the effect on output, there is an equal effect on operating surplus/mixed income and other income aggregates. On the expenditure side, output in the form of work on unfinished products is classified either as fixed capital formation or as changes in inventories of work-in-progress. It is part of fixed capital formation if it consists of construction work done on contract and put in place in stages or if it consists of capital goods produced on own account by their eventual final user. In all other cases, including speculative construction (that is, without a contract and not for own final use) and most agricultural production, work-in-progress is included in changes in inventories. Financial transactions are unaffected, except in the case of construction work on contract, because resulting changes in estimates on saving are fully absorbed in the estimates on fixed capital formation or changes in inventories for the same institutional unit. In the case of production of a capital good under contract, however, the full effect on savings for the producer will be carried over to the financial account in the form of payments received from installments and other accounts receivable accrued.

10.7. Proper recording of work-in-progress has the added advantage of removing production-related holding gains and losses from the estimates, which should also be done in ANA. The potential danger of leaving holding gains and losses in the estimates can be large, especially if inflation is substantial. If production processes do not exceed the accounting period for the ANA, the holding gains and losses involved in work-in-progress risk being ignored in the compilation of these accounts. An important message to the compilers of ANA is that they should also remove holding gains and losses from their estimates on subannual production processes, not only to ensure consistency between ANA and QNA, but also to achieve correct ANA estimates.

B. Why Should Work-in-Progress Be Treated as Output?

10.8. Production is "an *activity* in which an enterprise uses inputs to produce outputs" (*1993 SNA*

paragraph 6.6, italics added). Thus, production is a process that leads to a distinct product, but the recording of inputs and outputs in the accounts is not determined by the time that the finished product becomes available for use. Paragraph 6.39 of the *1993 SNA* explains this further as follows:

> For simplicity, the output of most goods or services is usually recorded when their production is finished. However, when it takes a long time to produce a unit of output, it becomes necessary to recognize that output is being produced continuously and to record it as work-in-progress.

10.9. While it is useful to emphasize that production is a process rather than the resulting product, the definitions are circular to the extent that the recognition and measurement of production depend on the meaning of output. In the *1993 SNA*, output does not mean finished products but can be any goods or services that "can be sold on markets or at least be capable of being provided by one unit to another ..." (*1993 SNA* paragraph 1.20). For instance, an unfinished construction project or a crop growing in the field both have the quality of having value that can, at least potentially, be provided to another unit, and, hence, output can be recognized and measured.

10.10. In the absence of recognition of work on unfinished products as output, inputs would appear in different periods from the corresponding output. As a result, value added could be negative in some periods and disproportionally large in other periods. Thus, the meaning of value added for the affected periods would be open for debate.[3]

10.11. An objection is sometimes made that recording work on unfinished products as output brings intransparency to the accounts. That is, it involves unnecessary complexity and artificiality and distorts the view of income generation and saving, because output does not generate money inflows before it is sold. Two arguments counter this view. First, transactions in the national accounts need not necessarily involve actual money flows; well-known examples are barter transactions and wages in kind. Second, one could also argue

---

[3]Note that negative value added can legitimately occur (where no marketable product appears at the end—for instance, an internal research project that failed—or where the marketable product is small in relation to inputs—for instance, the start-up phase of a business or other loss-making situations). However, it is not desirable that negative value added appears simply because of failure to recognize that a productive process was occurring.

that disregard of work-in-progress results in artificiality because outlays on production would show up without any apparent link to output.

10.12. It is sometimes suggested that recording work-in-progress is relevant on the level of individual units, but for the total economy, or even specific industries, aggregation would cancel out the effects of not recording work-in-progress. This would only apply in the situation of very stable period-to-period production processes, however, which is highly unlikely to reflect real conditions, particularly in the context of QNA.

C. Measurement of Work-in-Progress

1. Economic Concepts

10.13. The starting point for the theoretical and practical issues in measurement of production is economic theory. The general principle of valuation in economics is use of the transaction price. In a very few cases, an incomplete project may be marketed, such as when an unfinished building project or a farm with crops in the field changes hands. It is far more common, however, that products are not sold until finished, so transaction prices are not available for the unfinished product. It is, therefore, necessary to adopt a convention to value the production in each period.

10.14. The usual principle to value an item when there is no transaction is the market-equivalent price. The market equivalent is what buyers would be prepared to pay if they wished to obtain the unfinished product or what suppliers would need to be paid to produce it. This value is equivalent to the total input costs for each period plus a markup. Because there is no separate markup for each quarter, the markup must be the ratio of output to costs for the whole production cycle. In other words, the net operating surplus is estimated as earned over the production cycle in proportion to costs in each period.

10.15. In the rest of this section, the application of the convention of valuing work-in-progress carried out in a certain quarter as input costs plus a markup is discussed in a business and national accounting context. The section also discusses methods to use when data are incomplete and how to account for the effects of changes in prices during the production period.

2. Business Accounting Treatment of Work-in-Progress

10.16. Business accountants face the same problem of splitting incomplete production cycles into accounting periods. Estimation of the value of work put in place is part of an accrual accounting system. Businesses seeking to measure their own performance need to value the work put in place to match output with expenses and avoid lumpiness in their accounts. In the absence of observable prices, business accounts must also depend on input costs, with or without some markup.

10.17. However, there are two areas of difference between business accounting practice and economic concepts. First, business measures of income do not distinguish between holding gains and production, whereas this difference is fundamental in economic analysis. Second, because of the doctrine of prudence in business accounting, work may be valued at less than the expected price (i.e., without a markup or with an underestimated markup), so that profits are not counted fully or at all until they are realized. This delay in recognition of profits causes lumpiness at the completion of the work, but time-series consistency is less important to business accounting.

10.18. There are three alternative arrangements for work on products with long production cycles:
- own final use,
- contract, and
- speculative basis (i.e., the final client is not known).

10.19. For work for own final use, the producer is the final user; for example, an electricity company builds its own generating plant or distribution network. In this situation, there is no transaction price, even on completion. Accordingly, output is measured by the enterprise itself, ideally at a market-equivalent price or, more typically, on the basis of input costs, including capital costs and overhead. If measured from costs, the data are already recorded on an ongoing basis by the producer, and there is no more difficulty in measuring production in each period than there is in measuring the total project.

10.20. For contract work, there are different possible payment arrangements. A price may be fixed in advance or variable; or paid by installments or at the end of the job. Progress payments are installments that relate to the amount of work done. To the extent that progress payments closely match work done, they already measure output on an ongoing basis.

However, if payments are infrequent, delayed, or have a substantial bonus component at the end, they give a misleading time series, and a cost-based measure would provide a better measure of production.

10.21. For work done on a speculative basis, there are no ongoing receipts, and usually the final value of the product is unknown until after completion. This situation is common in manufacturing and construction. In addition, many agricultural products resemble speculative manufacturing or construction in that there is no sale or identified buyer until after the product is completed. In contrast to manufacturing and construction, however, estimates of work-in-progress are not normally made by farmers in their own accounts.

10.22. Measures of work-in-progress are often available, particularly from larger and more sophisticated producers. Such estimates have the advantage that the data are transparent and estimation is done at a detailed level with specific information. However, such data are not automatically suitable. For example, progress payments or installments may not match work done because of long lags or because there is a large component of bonus for the completion of the job. Or it may also be too costly to collect business data quarterly, for example, if building work is done by many small operators who are reluctant to complete statistical questionnaires. Or the quarterly data may be too lumpy if the profit is only included at the time of sale. In these circumstances, it is necessary to derive estimates for national accounts by making adjustments to business estimates.

3. Measurement in a National Accounts Context

10.23. The *1993 SNA*'s recommendations on the valuation of incomplete products follow from the economic concepts discussed in Subsection 1 of this section and are partly compatible with the business practices discussed in Subsection 2. The *1993 SNA* recommends following the businesses' own estimates if they approximate production, mentioning progress payments on a contract (paragraph 6.74) and capital goods for own final use (paragraph 6.85). When no acceptable quarterly output data are available from businesses, the *1993 SNA* principle is to measure production of incomplete products from costs for each period, raised by a markup that relates to the whole production cycle. The *1993 SNA* considers two situations for markup data: whether an estimate of the value of the finished product is available (paragraph 6.77) or not (paragraph 6.78).

10.24. Changes in prices during the production cycle affect the measurement of production. When prices are changing, the eventual value at the time of completion will differ from the sum of the value of work-in-progress carried out in the production quarters, because the prices of that kind of product have changed between the time of production and the time of completion. The difference represents holding gains or losses. In order to measure production, price changes between the time of production and the time of sale must be removed from selling prices. These problems can be avoided by compiling constant price estimates first (to put all the flows on a consistent basis) and subsequently deriving the current price estimates on the basis of the constant price estimates. (This deflate-then-reflate method is found in related areas of inventory valuation and capital stock measurement where valuation also includes prices from different periods.)

10.25. The measure of input costs should be as complete as possible. The input costs should include compensation of employees, intermediate consumption, taxes on production, and costs of using land and capital (rent, consumption of fixed capital, and interest). In cases where owners and unpaid family members are an important source of labor, it is desirable to derive a value for these inputs as well. In practice, the data on costs may be incomplete, and so the markup needs to be adjusted accordingly. Obviously, parts of these input costs are part of value added (for instance, compensation of employees) and some are included in operating surplus/mixed income (for instance rent and interest). This does not preclude them, however, from being costs of production that must be taken into account when estimating output from the cost side.

10.26. Allocation of output on the basis of costs does not always apply in full. From the rationale for work-in-progress—namely, allocating output to periods in which production is occurring—it logically follows that no output should be allocated to periods in which there is no ongoing production process, even if there are ongoing costs. This applies in particular to the cost of using land and capital, which may not correspond to the actual production process. For instance, interest on a loan financing a piece of equipment accrues over the period of the loan, no matter whether the equipment is used. An example of a situation in which this may apply is agriculture, where production may stop completely during certain periods. Food-processing

Example 10.1. Ex Post Estimation of Work-in-Progress with
(a) Total Value of Project
(b) Quarterly Costs

Objectives of example:
(a) To illustrate the allocation of a total on the basis of costs.
(b) To illustrate the inclusion of holding gains in the total value.

Consider a speculative construction project taking place between January and December 1999. It is completed and sold at the end of December 1999 for 5800. The objective is to produce output estimates for each quarter and exclude holding gains from the output estimates. A high rate of price increases is assumed in order to highlight the effect of holding gains.

Primary Data

	q1 1999	q2 1999	q3 1999	q4 1999	q1 2000
Output/input price index (average 1998 = 100)	110.0	120.0	130.0	140.0	150.0
Production costs at current prices:					
Intermediate consumption	160	340	530	300	
+ Compensation of employees	300	310	340	400	
+ User-costs for use of land and capital, etc.	200	250	300	350	
=Total production costs at current prices	660	900	1170	1050	

To simplify the calculations, the same price index is used for inputs and outputs; in principle, separate price measures should be used.

Step 1. Derive value of the project at average 1998 prices

Deflator value at the end of q4 1999	1/2(q4 1999 +q1 2000) =145.0
Value at average 1998 prices	5800/1.45=4000

The value of the project at average 1998 prices is estimated by deflating the sales value with a price deflator that reflects changes in prices of similar projects from average 1998 to the end of q4 1999. The price index given measures the average price level in each period of similar construction products relative to their average price in 1998. Assuming a smooth change in prices over time, the deflator value at the end of q4 1999 can be estimated as approximately (140+150)/2=145.

industries that are dependent on harvests coming in are also an example. In these cases, it is important to clearly define the production periods (for instance, in Nordic climates the agricultural production periods may include fall when land preparation takes place, exclude winter when no activities take place, and commence again in spring with seeding, fertilizing, etc.).

10.27. Example 10.1 brings together the measurement issues discussed so far. It covers an ex post situation, that is, after the completion of the product when the final price is known. Data on input costs are also available. In the example, the final price and cost data are used to derive a markup ratio for the whole project. The example shows the derivation of output estimates and, from that, the calculation of holding gains.[4]

---
[4]This example is designed to show concepts and may not be realistic from the point of view of data availability.

10.28. From the example, it is important to note that holding gains are excluded from production measures. Hence, the output is 5040 in the example, not 5800. A substantial rate of price increases is assumed, so the holding gains are quite large in the example. It should also be noted that the cost/markup ratio is derived at constant prices (i.e., 4000/3000) and not at transaction prices (i.e., 5800/3780), because the latter include holding gains. It is also worth noting that the quarterly estimates of output, by definition, follow the same quarterly pattern as the costs. It can be seen that the recognition of work-in-progress results in a less lumpy series for output. It is not a substitute for seasonal adjustment or calculation of a trend-cycle series, however, because the series will still be subject to any seasonality or irregularity in the cost series.

10.29. Having established the general principles of measurement, we will now consider some of the permutations arising from different data situations. The situations covered include deriving the markup when

Example 10.1 *(continued)*

Step 2. Derive costs at constant prices

	q1 1999	q2 1999	q3 1999	q4 1999	Total
Production costs at 1998 prices	600	750	900	750	3000

In step 2, input estimates at constant prices are derived by deflating the current price values.

Step 3. Derive the output/cost ratio
Output to cost ratio at average 1998 prices—the markup ratio—(1.333) is derived as the value of the project (4000)/total costs (3000). The output/cost markup ratio is calculated for the project. It has to be derived at constant prices to exclude holding gains.

Step 4. Derive output at constant and current prices

	q1 1999	q2 1999	q3 1999	q4 1999	Total
Output at average 1998 prices	800	1000	1200	1000	4000
Output at current prices	880	1200	1560	1400	5040

Quarterly output at 1998 prices is derived by raising the value of costs at 1998 prices by the output/cost ratio. Quarterly output at current prices is derived by reflating the estimates of output at 1998 prices.

Step 5. Derive value of the stock of work-in-progress at current prices

	Value of work put in place current prices	Holding gains in subsequent quarters				Value at time of sale
		q1 1999	q2 1999	q3 1999	q4 1999	Dec . 1999
q1 1999	880	40	80	80	80	1,160
q2 1999	1,200		50	100	100	1,450
q3 1999	1,560			60	120	1,740
q4 1999	1,400				50	1,450
Total	5,040	40	130	240	350	5,800
		<---------------------------------760 -------------------------------->				

The derivation of holding gains is shown in this step. In this example, the output price index shows that the prices of similar construction projects increased continuously during 1999. Thus, the prices are higher at the end of each quarter than in the beginning or middle of the quarter. As a result, the total cumulated value of work put in place (5040) differs from the project sales value (5800), because prices have risen between the time of construction and time of sale; that is, the sales price includes both output and holding gains.

For example, the work put in place in q1 is worth 800 at 1998 prices, but 880 at average q1 prices (i.e., 800·1.1); 920 at the end of q1 (i.e., 800·(1.1+1.2)/2); 1000 at the end of q2 (i.e., 800·(1.2+1.3)/2); 1080 at the end of q3 (i.e., 800·(1.3+1.4)/2); and 1160 at the end of q4 (i.e., 800·(1.4+1.5)/2).

there are (a) other payment times; (b) quantities available but not values; and (c) forecasts available instead of actual prices for the final product. When markups for a particular period are not available, other sources of markups are considered. Where cost data are not available, the use of a cost profile is proposed.

10.30. In some cases, payment is not made at the completion of the product. It may be made at the beginning of work or in several installments. An advance payment reflects prices of the beginning of the period. If the price is paid in installments, such as progress payments for construction work, the payments are from several different periods and, hence, different price levels. In each case, by converting the payments to constant prices (using the price index of the time of payment), the measurement can be put on a consistent basis, and the calculations can be made accordingly. (As discussed earlier in this section, if progress payments closely match production costs and timing, they should be used directly to estimate output.)

10.31. In some cases, the data available on the final product are in quantity terms, for instance, a house measured in square meters or a crop in tons. The principles of measurement are the same as in Example 10.1, except that the constant price values are derived by multiplying the volume measure by a price per unit in the base year. Current price values can be derived by multiplying the volume measure by a price per unit in the current period. In the case of some crops, there are special problems in measuring prices in periods between harvests; these issues are discussed in Section D of this chapter.

10.32. Forecasts may need to be used for incomplete work if the value of the final product is not yet known. While national accountants do not normally use forecasts, unfinished production may require forecasts, and such forecasts are often available. For example, builders often forecast a value of a project at the time of seeking building approval. Also, in many countries the ministry of agriculture (or another government agency)

Example 10.2. Ex Ante Estimation of Work-in-Progress with
(a) Quarterly Costs
(b) Markup Ratio

Objective of example: To illustrate the calculation of work on the basis of costs and markup.

Primary Data

	q1 1999	q2 1999	q3 1999	q4 1999
Output/input price index (average 1998 = 100)	110.0	120.0	..	..
Production costs at current prices	660	900	..	..
(wages and salaries, raw materials, etc.)			..	..
Industry standard average markup over costs, 33.3% after excluding holding gains		1.333 (in ratio form)		

Step 1. Derive output at current and constant prices

	q1 1999	q2 1999	q3 1999	q4 1999
Production costs at average 1998 prices	600	750	..	..
Output at average 1998 prices	800	1,000	..	..
Output at current prices	880	1,200	..	..

The data are the same as for the first two quarters in Example 10.1.
Production costs at constant prices are derived by deflating the current price value (e.g., for 1999 q1, 660/110*100).
Output at average 1998 prices is derived by multiplying the production costs at 1998 prices by the markup ratio (e.g., for 1999 q1, 600*1.333=800).
Output at current prices is derived by reflating the constant price value (e.g., for 1999 q1, 800*110/100).

makes crop forecasts based on an estimate of the output of a certain crop. (These usually are in volume terms, but sometimes also in value terms.) These crop estimates are typically based on an estimate of the acreage under cultivation combined with yield estimates. Estimates of acreage under cultivation could be based on surveys or on aerial and satellite photography; yield estimates could be based on average crop yields and revised on the basis of expert views and trends. It may be surmised that in many agricultural countries, this kind of information is available. In some cases, it may be necessary for the national accounts compilers to make forecasts themselves. While forecast values differ in being more uncertain and more subject to revision, the method for calculation of quarterly output is the same as the ex post situation. Of course, when actual data become available, the data should be revised and the difference between the forecast and actual value assessed for accuracy and signs of bias.

10.33. When there is no actual or forecast estimate of the finished value, the *1993 SNA* recommends estimation of output on the basis of costs plus an estimate of a markup from another source. The *1993 SNA* does not elaborate how this markup is to be derived; possible sources are studies on standard margins used in a particular industry, a previous year's data, or comparable recently completed projects. Example 10.2 demonstrates how such methods could work in practice.

10.34. The concept and measurement of quarterly production are the same in Examples 10.1 and 10.2. Only the source of the markup ratio is different; in Example 10.1, a markup ratio for the particular project is derived in steps 1 to 3; in Example 10.2, it is taken from previous data. The estimates made ex ante, as in Example 10.2, would need to be revised when actual prices and volumes became available.[5] The technique shown in Example 10.1 could then be used, so that the markup ratio assumed in advance could be replaced by the actual one. If markup ratios vary substantially from year to year, as is often the case for agriculture, the revisions may be quite large. This danger looms large in situations in which output depends on exogenous factors, as is the case for agriculture and related industries (for instance, if a locust plague necessitates an extraordinary use of pesticides for a certain crop). In such cases, a markup based on a forecast of the annual crop should be preferred to markups based on previous data.

10.35. Another common data situation is that quarterly cost data are unavailable; in that case, a cost profile can be used instead. Actual data on input costs may not be available because of collection costs or because businesses do not keep separate records of costs for each project. An alternative in

---

[5]In some cases, such as the production of movies, no actual market price is available at the end of the production process, and the value has to be derived through an estimate of discounted future receipts.

such situations is to make an estimate for each quarter's share of total costs, that is, a cost profile. It could be based on statistical observations on input intensities in recent periods or on expert views. Statistical observations could be obtained through small-scale surveys, because cost patterns in industries of concern are often fairly standard between units and also fairly stable. For instance, in agriculture the cost pattern is strongly dependent on the growth phases of crops, and in construction the pace of production is strongly dictated by an inherent sequence of activities. If a production process is strongly dictated by physical or biological factors, expert opinions may suffice to establish a cost profile. If stable, the same profile could be used for all periods. If all of this is not available, a very simple production profile, such as an equal distribution over time, could be used as a default. The cost profile should be calculated from the constant price data on production costs.

10.36. Use of a cost/production profile is shown in Example 10.3. A cost profile is derived from the data in Example 10.1—the production cycle lasts four quarters, with 20 percent in q1 (i.e., 600/3000), 25 percent in q2, 30 percent in q3, and 25 percent in q4. By definition, the cost profile has the same pattern as the resulting production estimate at constant prices.

10.37. The cost profile method is often used for construction in conjunction with data on building permits. In cases where only volume indicators such as square meters are available, the values are derived by average prices per unit obtained from a benchmark survey or expert assessment. If value data are available, the value concept needs to be identified—current prices or forecast end-of-period prices. The cost profile should take into account the lags between approval, commencement, and completion. It may also account for low work periods such as monsoons and holiday/vacation periods. The expected value should be adjusted for projects that are approved but not implemented. Also, it might be desirable to estimate work-in-progress on individual large projects on a case-by-case basis; compilers of source statistics might be best placed to do this.

Example 10.3. Estimation of Work-in-Progress with
(a) Estimate of Output Quantities
(b) Cost Profile

Consider a crop that takes four quarters to grow, from preparation of the cultivation area beginning in the first quarter of 1999 to harvesting in the fourth quarter of 1999.

Primary Data

	q1 1999	q2 1999	q3 1999	q4 1999	q1 2000
Output price index (average 1998 = 100)	110.00	112.00	114.00	116.00	118.00
Cost profile	0.20	0.25	0.30	0.25	

Total estimated crop	1000 tons
Average value per ton for similar crops in 1998	5.0

Step 1. Derive total output at constant prices
Value at average 1998 prices   1000*5.0=5000

Step 2. Derive quarterly output at current and constant prices

	q1 1999	q2 1999	q3 1999	q4 1999	Total
Output at average 1998 prices	1,000	1,250	1,500	1,250	5,000
Output at current prices	1,100	1,400	1,710	1,450	5,660

First, the value of the crop at average 1998 prices is estimated by multiplying the physical data on the volume of the crop by the obtained data on average value per ton in 1998, that is, 1000 · 5 = 5000.

Second, output estimates at constant prices are derived by distributing the estimated value of the crop at average 1998 prices over the quarters in proportion to the assumed production intensity. For instance, the constant price estimate for q1 1999 is derived as 0.2 · 5000 = 1000.

Third, output estimates at current prices are derived by inflating with the output price index. For instance, the estimate for q1 1999 is derived as 1000 · 1.1 = 1100.

Note that the harvest value (at end-of-production prices) could be derived as 1000 · 5 · (1.16+1.18)/2=5850. The difference between the harvest value and the estimate of output at current prices is holding gains (5850−5660 = 190). (One of the difficulties surrounding the inclusion of agricultural work-in-progress is that output differs from harvest value, which may seem counterintuitive to many users.)

D. Special Issues for Agriculture

10.38. The general principles of recording production on an ongoing basis also apply to agriculture. Usually, it would be feasible to use one of the methods discussed in the previous section, typically a cost profile in conjunction with actual totals (for previous years) or forecasts (for the current year).

10.39. However, the degree of uncertainty about the eventual output makes the treatment somewhat more problematic for agriculture and related industries, both for practical and conceptual reasons. This has caused many countries not to apply the work-in-progress concepts in the case of agriculture. While supporting the allocation of agricultural output to nonharvest periods in principle, the *1993 SNA* recognizes the specific problems involved. It states the following in paragraph 6.100:

> There may be circumstances in which the uncertainties attached to the estimation of the value of work-in-progress in advance of the harvest are so great that no useful analytical or policy purpose is served by compiling such estimates.

10.40. Weather is obviously the major component of uncertainty in agriculture. There are variations in temperature, rainfall, and sunlight, with droughts, hurricanes, and floods being the extremes. Also, in some cases, insect or other animal plagues may be important. The degree of uncertainty varies significantly among countries.

10.41. One aspect of uncertainty is that estimates made before the harvest need to be based on forecasts. This is particularly the case in the QNA, where the emphasis on timeliness implies that the estimates for preharvest quarters will have to be made well in advance of harvest time. If the value is uncertain, there are concerns about potentially large revisions in the national accounts.

10.42. Another aspect of uncertainty concerns catastrophic events. The treatment of output losses in the national accounts is quite different between normal events and catastrophes. For normal events, the losses are reflected in reduced output because only the output that materialized is recorded. For catastrophes, output is measured as if nothing happened and the losses are recorded on the other changes in volume of assets account. Recording a crop that never materialized in output because it was hit by a catastrophe is counterintuitive.

10.43. The *1993 SNA* restricts catastrophic events to singular events of a general nature, for example, major earthquakes, volcanic eruptions, tidal waves, exceptionally severe hurricanes, drought, and other natural disasters (paragraph 12.36). Limitation of catastrophic events to singular events of a general nature means, among other things, that losses of crops through frequent floods and droughts should not be regarded as catastrophic losses, no matter how devastating they are for crops under cultivation. The *1993 SNA*'s definition of catastrophic events leaves room for interpretation, however, which may hamper international comparability.

10.44. A further aspect of uncertainty concerns the prices to assign production in nonharvest periods. This issue of price uncertainty arises in both ex post and, even more, ex ante data. There may be no or only a very limited market for crops in the nonharvest periods, so that the prices are more uncertain and have to be extrapolated (ex ante) or interpolated (ex post). The prices of crops[6] in nonharvest periods may be available but may be misleading to the extent that they also include storage and holding costs or the off-season scarcity of fresh produce. In such cases, the observed prices would not be relevant for valuing the harvest. As a solution, some downward adjustment based on past years' off-season patterns may be derived, or the observed prices could be replaced by interpolation or extrapolation of harvest prices. In addition, prices of subsequent years' crops may be quite unrelated, so estimation of the work-in-progress on the new harvest with prices of the old may be misleading. The supply-and-demand situation often differs considerably among crops, so that the prices may be completely different. For instance, if an abundant crop is followed by a meager one, the price of the second crop at harvest time may jump compared with the price of the first crop. Obviously, in such a case, the current price estimates need to be revised, but the price development of the first crop is not valid for the revision of the quarterly estimates. A relatively simple solution to this problem would be to derive new indices relevant for the production quarters of the new crop by an interpolation between the price of the previous crop at harvest time and the price of the present crop at harvest time.

---

[6]If no local prices are available, world-market prices could be considered; however, these prices may not be indicative for local supply in a particular country.

10.45. Consideration of behavioral aspects is relevant to the inclusion of agricultural work-in-progress in national accounts estimates. If the economic agents themselves react to the uncertainty of prices and volumes by behaving as if the work-in-progress carried out were not output (and thus not generating income), then the estimates will not help in understanding economic developments. For instance, the imputations needed to record subsistence farming may impede the usefulness of QNA data for monetary policies.[7]

10.46. By measuring production before the producers do, statisticians may be exposed to the accusation of counting the chickens before they hatch. Unlike many other producers, farmers do not normally record their own work-in-progress. One singular aspect of this would be the imputation of income flows before they are realized, and possibly even in cases in which they are not realized. As a result, the concerns about artificiality and complexity of methods made in the Section B of this chapter are particularly strong in the case of agriculture. For that reason, in the case of agriculture, recording production simply as the harvest value may be considered.[8]

10.47. Whether a harvest or work-in-progress approach is used for agriculture, the resulting output series will often be lumpy. In the case of the harvest approach, the output will often be concentrated in one or two quarters while the others may have little or no output. In the case of the work-in-progress approach, discontinuities will occur between crop years, effectively because of the change in the output/cost markup ratio. With either approach, the lumpiness is the valid and necessary result of the production concept adopted in conjunction with the intrinsic limitations of presenting an annual process in a quarterly form. It would be feasible to smooth out the lumpiness in the series by mathematical techniques, but, in the context

of non-seasonally adjusted data, this would not be justified by the economic concept of production and would just cover up the issue. Users, however, may prefer the seasonally adjusted or trend-cycle series for some purposes.

10.48. Because of their special features, quarterly data on agricultural production need to be interpreted carefully. The data are necessarily artificial when a yearly or multiquarter process is split into quarters. The quarter-to-quarter movements are driven by the cost profile used rather than by new information on output. Because the cost profile is a seasonal pattern, it will be removed by the seasonal adjustment process.[9]

10.49. Techniques of presentation of the data may help users deal with the difficulties associated with measurement of quarterly output from agriculture. In view of the multiple uses of quarterly accounts, there may be alternative solutions to the conceptual and practical problems. In this respect, three recommendations can be made. First, document the methodology carefully so users are able to form their own opinions. Although this will not enhance the quality of the figures, it will at least enable a view on whether they are suitable for particular purposes. Second, to serve users who deem the allocations unsuitable or do not care for allocations anyway, specify and quantify the allocations. Third, present the data with sufficient details to allow users to exclude the work in progress if they wish.

10.50. In conclusion, as a general principle, the *1993 SNA* states that agricultural work-in-progress should be included in output. As mentioned in paragraph 6.100 of that manual, however, the uncertainty and data issues associated with agricultural work-in-progress are often more severe than in other cases, so the decision on whether to include it needs to take into account the circumstances and analytical benefits in each country.

[7]In the revision process in preparation of the *1993 SNA*, the case was made for presenting a version of the accounts excluding *all* nonmonetary imputations. This case seems particularly relevant for imputations relating to the allocating of output from agriculture to nonharvest quarters.
[8]An alternative treatment that has been proposed is to measure output for nonharvest quarters as equal to cost without any markup and for the harvest quarter as equal to the difference between cumulated costs and harvest value. While this would have the advantage of avoiding the need to revise the back series at the time the crop is harvested, it would also imply that all operating surplus/mixed income would be allocated to the harvest quarter. The latter has no economic rationale (it is difficult to see why operating surplus/mixed income would be generated only in the harvest quarter). Also, if output is lower than costs, this method would imply recording positive output in preharvest quarters and negative output in the harvest quarter. Such an outcome seems artificial.

[9]If there are zero-production periods, a nonmultiplicative method of seasonal adjustment must be used. See Chapter VII for a discussion of seasonal adjustment techniques.

Annex 10.1. Recording Work-in-Progress in the *1993 SNA* Sequence of Accounts

10.A1.1. Although estimation of work-in-progress primarily concerns output, in the context of a consistent system such as the national accounts we will also have to consider other transactions that relate to work-in-progress, as well as balances (such as value added). In this annex we will explain which other transactions and balances are affected. A numerical illustration of the effects of work-in-progress on main aggregates in the *1993 SNA*'s sequence of accounts and balance sheets is provided in Example 10.A.1. The example demonstrates that significant effects can be found throughout the full sequence of accounts.

10.A1.2. In the general case, where work-in-progress is not sold until the product is finished, the two initial entries in the accounts are (a) output and (b) changes in inventories (increases) in the case of agriculture, manufacturing, services, and speculative construction, and capital formation in the case of own-account capital formation. After the product is finished and sold, two further transactions are (a) changes in inventories (decreases) and (b) changes in financial assets. In the case of production of a capital good under contract, four entries have to be recorded: (a) output for the producer, (b) fixed capital formation for the user, (c) increase in financial assets for the producer, and (d) decrease in financial assets for the user.

10.A1.3. In the production account of the producer, besides output, the only entry that is affected by work-in-progress is value added; the other entries—intermediate consumption, taxes and subsidies on production, and consumption of fixed capital—are not. Because inputs are actually made, there is no conceptual problem in allocating them to relevant periods. Value added is derived as a balance and, thus, estimates will result automatically once the problem of measuring output is resolved. Consumption of fixed capital is not an issue in this context because, per axiom, it is assumed to take place on a continuous basis (for a discussion of consumption of fixed capital in a QNA context, see Chapter IV). Taxes and subsidies on production are not affected because these are to be recorded at the time the output is sold, transferred, or used (see *1993 SNA*, paragraph 8.49).

10.A1.4. In the generation of income account of the producer, the effect on value added in the production account will be carried over to operating surplus/mixed income, because wages as such are not affected by work-in-progress. Similarly, in the allocation of primary income account, the impact on operating surplus/mixed income will directly carry over to the closing balance, primary income, because none of the transactions on this account are affected by work-in-progress. The same applies to transactions on the secondary distribution of income account in that, again, only the closing balance of this account, disposable income, will be affected.

10.A1.5. On the use of income account of the producer, the changes in disposable income would be fully absorbed by savings because consumption is not affected. The effect on saving for the producer would, in the case of work undertaken on own-account, not carry over to the financial account because increased savings would be absorbed by offsetting changes in inventories or capital formation on the capital account for the same institutional unit. In the case of production of a capital good under contract, however, the full effect on savings for the producer will be carried over to the financial account in the form of payments received from installments and other accounts receivable accrued.

10.A1.6. The other changes in assets accounts can be affected in two ways. First, because prices of the goods in inventories change over time, the resulting holding gains or losses have to be recorded on the revaluation account. second, if work-in-progress is lost because of catastrophic events, this has to be recorded on the other changes in volume of assets account.

10.A1.7. Finally, the balance sheets of the system show the stocks resulting from the changes on the current and accumulation accounts. The output of unfinished products is recorded as inventories of work-in-progress unless it is sold. At the time the product is finished, a reclassification has to be made from inventories of work-in-progress to inventories of finished goods, and at the time the product is eventually sold, this sale will be reflected on the balance sheets through lower inventories, with a concomitant effect on financial assets and liabilities.

Example 10.A.1 Effects of Work-in-Progress on Main Aggregates in the *1993 SNA* Sequence of Accounts and Balance Sheets

(Data in bold refer to treatment *with* work-in-progress)

In this Example, the results obtained in Example 10.1 are presented in the format of *1993 SNA* sequence of accounts. The accounts show how, with work-in-progress recorded, each quarter would have had a positive value added; whereas, without work-in-progress recorded, the first three quarters would have had a negative value added and only the fourth would have had a positive value added. The accounts also show that without recording work-in-progress, a holding gain (caused by inflation) would have been included in output and value added. Furthermore, the example demonstrates that the increased saving is fully absorbed by increased inventories, so that the financial transactions (in this example, loans) are unaffected. (This example concerns an economic activity for which no installment payments are made that would affect the financial accounts.)

Current Accounts

	Intermediate Consumption		Output	
q1	160	**160**	0	**880**
q2	340	**340**	0	**1,200**
q3	530	**530**	0	**1,560**
q4	300	**300**	5,800	**1,400**
The year	1,330	**1,330**	5,800	**5,040**

	Value Added	
q1	−160	**720**
q2	−340	**860**
q3	−530	**1,030**
q4	5,500	**1,100**
The year	4,470	**3,710**

	Compensation of Employees	
q1	300	**300**
q2	310	**310**
q3	340	**340**
q4	400	**400**
The year	1,350	**1,350**

	Saving	
q1	−460	**420**
q2	−650	**550**
q3	−870	**690**
q4	5,100	**700**
The year	3,120	**2,360**

Capital Transactions, Financial Transactions and Balance Sheets

	Opening Balance Sheet		Additions		Withdrawals		Holding Gains		Closing Balance Sheet	
Nonfinancial Assets (Inventories)										
Quarterly Data										
q1	0	**0**	0	**880**	0	**0**	0	**40**	0	**920**
q2	0	**920**	0	**1,200**	0	**0**	0	**130**	0	**2,250**
q3	0	**2,250**	0	**1,560**	0	**0**	0	**240**	0	**4,050**
q4	0	**4,050**	5800	**1,400**	0	**0**	0	**350**	5,800	**5,800**
Annual Data	0	**0**	5800	**5,040**	0	**0**	0	**760**	5,800	**5,800**
Financial Liabilities (Loans)										
Quarterly Data										
q1	0	**0**	460	**460**	0	**0**	0	**0**	460	**460**
q2	460	**460**	650	**650**	0	**0**	0	**0**	1,110	**1,110**
q3	1,110	**1,110**	870	**870**	0	**0**	0	**0**	1,980	**1,980**
q4	1,980	**1,980**	700	**700**	0	**0**	0	**0**	2,680	**2,680**
Annual Data	0	**0**	2,680	**2,680**	0	**0**	0	**0**	2,680	**2,680**
Net worth										
q1	0	**0**	−460	**420**	0	**0**	0	**40**	−460	**460**
q2	−460	**460**	−650	**550**	0	**0**	0	**130**	−1,110	**1,140**
q3	−1,110	**1,140**	−870	**690**	0	**0**	0	**240**	−1,980	**2,070**
q4	−1,980	**2,070**	5,100	**700**	0	**0**	0	**350**	3,120	**3,120**
Annual Data	0	**0**	3,120	**2,360**	0	**0**	0	**760**	3,120	**3,120**

XI Revision Policy and the Compilation and Release Schedule

A. Introduction

11.1. Revisions are an essential part of good quarterly national accounts (QNA) compilation practice because they provide users with data that are as timely and accurate as possible. Resource constraints, in combination with user needs, cause tension between the timeliness of published data on the one hand and reliability, accuracy, and comprehensiveness on the other hand. To reduce this tension, typically, preliminary data are compiled that later are revised when more and better source data become available. Good management of the process of revisions requires the existence of a well-established and transparent revision policy.

11.2. It is important to emphasize that revisions are conducted for the benefit of users, namely, to provide users with data that are as timely and accurate as possible. Revisions provide the possibility to incorporate new and more accurate information, and thus to improve the accuracy of the estimates, without introducing breaks in the time series. Although repeated revisions may be perceived as reflecting negatively on the trustworthiness of official statistics, delaying the incorporation of new data in the published estimates may increase the magnitude of later revisions (in particular, if these go in the same direction). Furthermore, not passing on known revisions reduces the actual trustworthiness of data even more because the data do not reflect the best available information, and the public may know this or find this out (for instance, the public may wonder why a revision in the monthly production index is not reflected in the QNA). Moreover, series that are revised frequently are not necessarily less accurate, even initially, than those subject to little or no revision. The absence of revisions may indicate that no better information became available to improve poor first estimates. Finally, attempting to avoid revisions by producing accurate but very untimely, and thus less useful, data may result in not making the best use of the information available. If the official QNA compilers fail to serve users' needs, other organizations may compile their own estimates, resulting in confusion from conflicting estimates to the point that many users may consider the official data irrelevant. Obviously, that will result in reduced prestige and respect for the official QNA compilers.

11.3. Revisions to past data are not without potential problems and may draw criticism if not properly handled. Revisions to past data are inconvenient to users because they entail revisions to their databases and applications. More important, frequent revisions—particularly to data for the most recent periods–may cause users to feel uncertain about the current economic situation and thus uncertain about what policy actions should be taken. Some of this uncertainty may be unavoidable and merely reveal the fact that the information base for the estimates for the most recent periods is limited and thus that the data should be used with care. Some of the uncertainty, however, may be caused unnecessarily by the way the revisions are carried out or presented. On the other hand, the temptation to suppress needed revisions may lead to deserved criticism from users and severely reduce the usefulness and trustworthiness of the data. Unjustified differences between national accounts estimates and their source data may cause users to doubt the competence of the national accounts compilers with serious—and justified—criticism of the national accounts data as a result.

11.4. To deal with the issues surrounding revisions and to avoid unnecessary criticism, a well-designed and carefully managed revision policy is needed. Essential features of a well-designed revision policy are predictability and openness, advance notice of causes and effects, and explanation, as well as easy access to sufficiently long time series of revised data. This chapter elaborates on the elements that make for a well-established revision policy.

B. User Requirements and Resource Constraints

11.5. The trade-off between timeliness on the one hand and accuracy and reliability on the other is caused by a conflict between different user requirements in combination with limitations in statistical resources. National accounts data are used for multiple purposes that have partly conflicting requirements. To allow corrective policy actions to be taken in time, policymakers and other users need a coherent, comprehensive, and reasonably accurate picture of the current economic situation that is as up-to-date as possible. For other purposes, such as time series and structural analysis of past events, users require long time series of very detailed annual, or quarterly, national accounts data. Finally, users are interested in both the period-to-period rates of change in the series and their levels. The resources available for statistical purposes, however, are limited. Collection of sufficiently accurate and detailed source statistics is time-consuming and expensive both for the statistical office and for the respondents, and compilation of comprehensive, accurate, and detailed national accounts is in itself time-consuming and expensive. Also, frequent collection of comprehensive and detailed data may impose an unwarranted burden on respondents, who themselves may not even have such data on a timely and short-term basis.

11.6. As a result, only a limited set of monthly or quarterly source data typically is available on a very timely basis. More detailed and more comprehensive monthly or quarterly source statistics typically become available on a less timely basis, while the most detailed, comprehensive, and reliable source data may be annual or less frequent data that become available with varying delays long after the reference year. And to provide sufficiently reliable benchmark data, many countries conduct periodic "benchmark censuses," collecting very detailed and reliable annual data every 5 or 10 years. These are often linked to periodic compilation of supply and use tables. The monthly and quarterly data commonly are based on smaller samples and less complete sample frames than the corresponding annual data. Finally, the annual data may be based on audited business accounts through comprehensive questionnaires that facilitate a thorough checking and editing of the reported data, while the quarterly data may be collected using simpler questionnaires that allow less extensive checking and editing.

C. Waves of Source Data and Related Revision Cycles

11.7. As explained above, national accountants may experience three "waves" of statistical source data that become available. Each of these waves may lead to revisions of earlier estimates and the incorporation of more details in the published accounts. In accordance, three revision cycles may be distinguished. A quarterly revision cycle is determined by the evolution of the short-term statistics as used in the QNA, and an annual revision cycle is caused by incorporation of annual source data or annual national accounts (ANA) estimates based on a separate ANA compilation system into the QNA through benchmarking. Finally, a periodic major revision cycle originates from incorporating data from periodic benchmark censuses, revised international guidelines, and other changes that cannot be incorporated on a continuous basis because of resource constraints. Revisions may, of course, also be caused by compilation errors, which need to be corrected when found.

11.8. The evolution of short-term statistics used in the QNA may cause revisions for two reasons: (a) corrections or changes in specific short-term source data and (b) incorporation of additional, somewhat less timely, short-term data. Changes in short-term source data can be caused by late responses received after initial publication of source statistics and by the use of prepublished data that are still open to change. To increase the timeliness of the QNA, the first estimates may have to be based on an incomplete set of short-term source data. Monthly and quarterly source data commonly become available with varying delays. Thus, when preparing the first estimates, only data for two months of the last quarter may be available for some series, while data may be missing altogether for other series. To fill these source data gaps, provisional estimates must be made based on simple trend extrapolation or on alternative indicators that are more timely but less reliable. During the course of the current year, these provisional estimates must be revised to incorporate more and better data as the less timely short-term source statistics become available.

11.9. Incorporation of more reliable annual data into the quarterly estimates implies several revisions to the QNA estimates over time for two reasons. First, the annual data themselves may be revised. Second, for technical reasons, the benchmarking procedure will result in revisions to quarterly data for earlier years in addition to the year(s) with new annual data.

As explained in Chapter VI, these additional revisions to past estimates are needed to avoid introducing breaks (the "step problem") in the QNA time series between successive pairs of years. Benchmarking of QNA on more reliable annual data has the advantage of conveying the accuracy and reliability of the annual data to the QNA and allows for a degree of comprehensiveness that the short-term source data by themselves do not admit. Annual source data may become available throughout the year or clustered around a few times of the year. The annual data can either be incorporated into the QNA estimates series by series—when the new annual source data for a series become available—or simultaneously for all series, depending among other things on the design of the ANA and QNA compilation systems (see also paragraph 11.19 below as well as Chapter II, paragraphs 2.5 and 2.6).

11.10. Periodic major revisions may be needed to the complete quarterly and annual time series or to a large part of the time series. Over time, periodic benchmark censuses may be conducted, new types of annual source data may become available, and improved compilation methods may be developed, all indicating a need for level adjustments. In addition, international guidelines are periodically revised. To introduce these improvements without creating breaks in the quarterly and annual time series, the complete time series—or a large part of the time series—must be revised at the same time. Ideally, this should be done on a continuous basis, series by series; however, resource constraints often do not permit such a frequent backcasting approach. Simplified ratio-based backcasting techniques may help in dealing with this problem.

D. The Compilation and Release Schedule

11.11. A crucial part of a well-established and transparent revision policy is devising an appropriate compilation and release schedule. When establishing a compilation and release schedule, it is important to decide (a) how timely the initial quarterly estimates should be; (b) how frequent new quarterly source data should be incorporated; (3) how early and how frequent annual source data should be incorporated; and (4) how frequent regular major revisions should be conducted.

11.12. Major elements in determining the compilation and release schedule are (a) timing of arrival of major data sources, and the source data revision policy; (b) timing of preparation of important economic political documents; (c) attitudes toward the trade-off between timeliness and accuracy, as well as toward size and frequency of revisions; (d) dissemination modes; and, finally, (e) workloads and the design of the national accounts compilation system.

11.13. To minimize the number of revisions needed without suppressing information, it is advisable to coordinate statistical activities. The revision schedule is, or should be, largely driven by the arrival of source data, and coordinating their arrival would substantially help reduce the number of revisions needed. Tying introduction of new concepts and methods, or new international guidelines such as the *1993 SNA*, to the time of other planned revisions would also help reduce the number of revisions. Although the timing of censuses and new surveys may not be at the discretion of national accountants, they may have a strong say in this, and they are well advised to use their influence to achieve maximum consistency with their revision policy.

11.14. Account needs to be taken of the coordination of QNA with related economic policy documents, such as the general government budget and other important documents related to the parliament's or legislature's budget discussions. To provide timely inputs to the preparation of these documents, the release of the estimates may have to be brought forward or, if this is deemed impossible, delayed. Release of new estimates shortly after the government budget has been presented or in the midst of a budget debate may cause problems (although this should not change the release schedule once it has been fixed).

11.15. The initial estimates for a quarter could be prepared and released too early. Improved timeliness could require use of a higher proportion of incomplete source data, resulting in unacceptable reduction in the accuracy of the estimates and larger revisions. The information content of estimates based on very incomplete source data may be limited and, in some cases, more misleading than informative. In those cases, the users would be better served by less timely initial estimates for a quarter.

11.16. Finally, the design of the national accounts compilation system has important implications for how frequently it is possible and appropriate to incorporate new source data. Large and complicated compilation systems with detailed and extensive balancing and reconciliation procedures (e.g., based on quarterly or annual compilation of integrated supply and use tables and a complete set of integrated sectoral accounts) make it costly to incorporate new source data very frequently.

11.17. Timeliness of release of the initial estimates for a quarter varies greatly from country to country, mainly reflecting different perspectives on the timeliness-accuracy-revision trade-off. The earliest releases of QNA data in some countries come within the first month after the reference quarter. A more common release time for the initial estimates among statistically advanced countries is around two to three months after the end of the quarter.[1,2] To provide very early annual estimates, some countries release their initial estimates earlier after the end of the fourth quarter than for other quarters. Correspondingly, there is typically a shift of focus in the presentation from the estimates of the quarters to the estimates for the full year. While the main focus may be on the estimates for the full year, the fourth-quarter data need to be published in their own right because failing to do so will cause users who need integrated annual and quarterly data to wrongly derive the fourth quarter as the difference between the annual total and the sum of the three previously published quarters. If the initial estimates for the fourth quarter are released earlier than for other quarters, it is preferable to highlight the lower quality of the fourth-quarter estimate, for example, by noting its revisions in previous years and the specific shortcomings in the data used.

11.18. How frequently new quarterly source data are incorporated varies. Countries that release their initial estimates within the first month of the reference quarter typically release revised and more detailed estimates shortly thereafter. These early estimates are often revised once or twice in the first quarter after the reference quarter. The estimates may be open to quarterly revisions thereafter. A more common practice, followed by countries that are less timely in releasing their initial estimates, is to revise the estimates quarterly linked to the preparation and release of the initial estimates for the following quarters. To reduce the number of revisions, it may be tempting to allow the estimates to be revised only once during the ongoing

year. However, temporarily suppressing information may result in larger revisions later. Suppression of information may also sometimes be technically difficult to implement and thus may result in compilation errors. The common practice is to let all estimates be open to revision during the ongoing year.

11.19. Annual source data can be incorporated into the QNA estimates either series by series, when the new annual source data for a series become available, or simultaneously for all series. The first approach has the advantage of allowing new annual information to be incorporated in as timely a manner as possible. Some countries compile their quarterly and annual estimates using basically the same time-series-oriented compilation system—typically without detailed and extensive balancing and reconciliation procedures—making this approach the natural choice. Most countries use a separate system for compiling their annual estimates, however, which makes it natural to filter the annual source data through the annual accounting system before incorporating the information into the QNA estimates. In those circumstances, to avoid inconsistencies between quarterly and annual accounts, the second approach may be the natural choice. Some countries use a combination of the two approaches.

11.20. Countries with an independent ANA compilation process typically revise their annual estimates from two to four times before the books are closed until a major revision is undertaken. These regular revisions to the annual estimates are normally undertaken once a year, although a few countries conduct them more frequently. The timing within the year of these annual revisions varies widely. The emphasis is typically on providing accurate and detailed data for structural analysis, with less emphasis on timeliness. They are nearly always more detailed than the QNA and may encompass a more complete set of the integrated economic accounts, including supply and use tables. All these features make backcasting a demanding task and thus restrict the frequency with which level adjustment originating from new data sources and new methods can be incorporated.

11.21. Box 11.1 gives an illustration of a possible compilation and release schedule followed by countries with independent ANA compilation systems. In this example, the annual accounts are revised only once, but in many countries the annual accounts are revised several times before they are declared final. These subsequent revisions of the ANA should also

---

[1]These issues are dealt with and international practices are compared in Smith, Philip, (1993).
[2]The Special Data Dissemination Standard (SDDS) specifies timeliness for the initial QNA estimates at three months after the end of the quarter.

be put through in the QNA so that the number of revisions of QNA eventually depends on the number of revisions of the ANA. If a major overhaul of the ANA system is performed later, it should also be put through in the QNA time series. It should be noted that in the benchmarking procedures recommended in this manual, revisions of past years will also necessitate revisions in the quarters of later years, including the quarters of the current year. Revisions to the quarters of the current year (in Box 11.1, data for q1 through q3 of year y+1) would not be necessary if the annual data for the past years were incorporated before release of the initial estimates for the first quarter of the current year (in Box 11.1, 5 to 6 months instead of 10 to 12 months after the end of year *y*).

E. Other Aspects of Revision Policy

11.22. In addition to developing a compilation and release schedule, the following are other important elements of a well-established revision policy:

- A balance between timeliness and accuracy of the initial estimates.
- Well known release dates published through an advance release calendar, as prescribed by the IMF's Special Data Dissemination Standard (SDDS) and General Data Dissemination System (GDDS).
- Candid and easily available documentation of sources and methods showing the main flows of source data leading to revisions.
- Provision of Available information on the accuracy of the estimates and the degree of potential future revisions (e.g., through records of past revisions).
- Provision of sufficiently long, consistent time series.
- Provision of detailed data in an easily accessible format (e.g., electronic).
- Published tables showing the revisions to the data with accompanying text explaining their causes.
- Advance notice to users of the national accounts data.

11.23. To inform users and avoid unmerited criticism, a well-established revision policy requires

---

Box 11.1. Compilation and Revision Schedule, An Illustration

Current Estimates for a Year y
- Initial estimate: 2 to 3 months after the end of the quarter
- Revised estimate: 5 to 6 months after the end of the quarter
- All estimates may be open to revisions during the current year

First Annual Round of Revisions:

		Annual Data for:	Quarterly Accounts
10–12 months after the end of year y	year y	Preliminary annual estimates based on a separate annual accounting system	Revised estimates for q1 – q3 of year y + 1 + Revised quarterly estimates
	year y – 1	"Final" annual estimates based on a separate annual accounting system	for year y, and y – 1 + Slightly revised quarterly pattern through year y – 2 to y – 4 to avoid steps between year y – 1 and y – 2

Subsequent Annual Rounds of Revisions:

22–24 months after the end of year y	Incorporation of "final" annual estimates for year y and preliminary estimates for year y + 1 based on a separate annual accounting system
32–36 months after the end	Incorporation of "final" annual estimates for year y + 1, of year y and preliminary annual estimates for year y + 2
46–48 months after the end	Incorporation of "final" annual estimates for year y + 2, of year y and preliminary annual estimates for year y + 3

The last two rounds of revisions are caused by technical properties of the recommended benchmarking methods (more rounds with minor revisions may in some cases be needed).

The "final" annual estimates may be revised later as needed, if new data become available or improved methods are developed.

Box 11.2. Presentation of Revisions, An Illustration[1]

Changes in This Issue

Data for the mining and manufacturing industries have been revised as a result of the incorporation of new annual census results for the previous year. As a result, value added for most industries has been revised upward in the previous and current years.

Retail output and household consumption have been revised for the most recent two quarters following the processing of late questionnaires. The most recent quarter has been revised down slightly as a result.

Changes in the Next Issue

Release date: xxxxx.

The methodology for estimating financial services will be revised in line with new international standards. The conceptual issues and quantitative effects are discussed in a research paper available on request.

Summary Tables of Revisions

Table 1: Revisions to Domestic Production Account in Currency Units: Eight Most Recent Quarters

Table 2: Revisions to Percentage Changes in Domestic Production Account: Eight Most Recent Quarters

---

[1]Based on actual country practices.

---

candid communication with users and easy access to the revised time series on a sufficiently detailed level.

11.24. Users should be properly informed of the quality of the estimates and the degree of revisions to expect on predetermined dates in the future. Properly informing users of the quality of the estimates involves giving them candid and easily available documentation of sources and methods for the different versions of the quarterly estimates, clearly showing the main flows of source data leading to revisions. When releasing revised estimates, best practice is to simultaneously publish articles summarizing the main revisions and their causes since the previous release. (See Box 11.2 for an illustration.) Best practice also involves periodically conducting and publishing studies of long-term trends in the revision patterns. Summaries of these studies may accompany the regular quarterly release of data to remind users that data are subject to revisions.

11.25. It is particularly important to inform users properly of the quality of the estimates when releasing QNA estimates for the first time. For a good indication of the degree of future revisions of the main

aggregates to expect, the complete compilation process should be simulated based on historic data before releasing the new estimates. That is, the proposed QNA compilation system should be used to produce QNA estimates for the past years as if one were back in time and were producing the initial preliminary estimates for those years (see the discussion of the "tracking exercise" in Chapter II).

11.26. Finally, providing easy access to the revised time series on a sufficiently detailed level should substantially ease the inconvenience for users of frequent revisions. This involves electronic release of the complete, detailed time series, not only the aggregated data for the most recent periods, which will make it easier for users to keep track of the revisions and update their databases. It should be emphasized that release of complete time series for all revised periods is needed because users often use QNA data in a time-series format and need to be alerted to any changes in data for past periods. Not providing them with revised historic data will create breaks in the time series they use, which will seriously hamper the serviceability of the data.

Bibliography

This bibliography lists material bearing on quarterly national accounts that came to the authors' notice as well as country sources and method publications found on the IMF *Dissemination Standards Bulletin Board,* http://dsbb.imf.org.

I. Introduction

Commission of the European Communities, International Monetary Fund, Organization for Economic Cooperation and Development, United Nations, and World Bank, 1993, *System of National Accounts 1993 (1993 SNA)* (New York: United Nations).

Eurostat, 1999, *Handbook on Quarterly National Accounts* (Luxembourg: Office for Official Publications of the European Communities).

Giovannini, E., 1988, "A Methodology for an Early Estimate of Quarterly National Accounts," *Economia Internazionale,* Vol. 41 (August–November), pp. 197–215.

Hyllenberg, S., 1998, "Comment," *Journal of Business and Economic Statistics,* Vol. 16 (April), pp. 167–68.

International Monetary Fund, *Dissemination Standards Bulletin Board.* Available via the Internet: http://dsbb.imf.org

Lääkäri, E., 1994, "The Monthly GDP Indicator," paper presented at INSEE-Eurostat Quarterly National Accounts Workshop, Paris, December.

Organization for Economic Cooperation and Development, 1968, *Quarterly National Accounts as Data for Economic Policy: A Report on Progress in OECD Countries,* prepared with the assistance of T.P. Hill (Paris).

———, 1979, *Quarterly National Accounts: A Report on Sources and Methods in OECD Countries* (Paris).

———, 1996, *Quarterly National Accounts: Sources and Methods Used by OECD Member Countries* (Paris).

———, 1998, *Quarterly National Accounts: Central and Eastern Europe* (Paris).

———, 2000, *System of National Accounts, 1993: Glossary* (Paris).

Reed, G., 2000, "How the Preliminary Estimate of GDP Is Produced," *Economic Trends,* No. 556 (March), pp. 53–61.

Salazar, E., R. Smith, M. Weale, and S. Wright, 1994, "Indicators of Monthly National Accounts," paper presented at INSEE-Eurostat Quarterly National Accounts Workshop, Paris, December.

Yeend, C., and A. Pottier, 1996, "A Monthly Indicator of GDP," *Economic Trends,* No. 509 (March), pp. 28–33.

II. Strategic Issues in Quarterly National Accounts

Cainelli, G., and C. Lupi, 1999, "The Choice of the Aggregation Level in the Estimation of Quarterly National Accounts," *Review of Income and Wealth,* Series 45 (December), pp. 483–92.

Caplan, D., and S. Lambert, 1995, "Quarterly GDP – Process and Issues," *Economic Trends,* No. 504 (October), pp. 40–43.

Cope, I., 1995, "Quarterly National Accounts in the United Kingdom: Overview of UK Approach," *Economic Trends,* No. 498 (April), pp. 22–25.

Janssen, R., and S. Algera, 1988, Methodology of the Dutch System of Quarterly Accounts, Occasional Paper No. NA-025 (Voorburg: Netherlands Central Bureau of Statistics).

Janssen, R., P. Oomens, and N. van Stokrom, 1994, "Data Flows in the Dutch Quarterly National Accounts," paper presented at the INSEE-Eurostat Workshop on Quarterly National Accounts, Paris, December.

III. Sources for GDP and Its Components

General and Multicountry:

Daniel, D., 1996, "The Use of Quarterly Current Price Output Data in National Accounts," *Economic Trends,* No. 516 (October), pp. 16–23.

Eurostat, 1998a, *Methodology of Industrial Short Term Indicators–Rules and Recommendations* (Luxembourg: Office for Official Publications of the European Communities).

————, 1998b, *Handbook on the Design and Implementation of Business Surveys* (Luxembourg: Office for Official Publications of the European Communities).

Pike, R., and G. Reed, 2000, "Introducing the Experimental Monthly Index of Services," *Economic Trends,* No. 565 (December), pp. 51–63.

United Nations, 1986, "Handbook of National Accounting. Accounting for Production: Sources and Methods," Studies in Methods, Series F, No. 39 (New York).

Country publications:

The following list of country publications is derived from information on the SDDS website http://dsbb.imf.org; the SDDS website also contains summary methodologies:

- Argentina: *Sistema de Cuentas Nacionales Argentina Año Base 1993, Estimaciones trimestrales y anuales: años 1993–1997,* Ministerio de Económia y Obras y Servicios Públicos, Spanish.
- Australia: *Australian National Accounts: Concepts, Sources and Methods,* ABS Catalogue Number 5216.0, and Statistical Concepts Reference Library on CD-ROM, Australian Bureau of Statistics.
- Austria: *Annex B of the regulation (EG) Nr. 2223/96 of the European Council.*
- Canada: *Guide to the Income and Expenditure Accounts,* Catalogue No. 13-603E-F; *A Guide to the Financial Flow and National Balance Sheet Accounts,* Catalogue No. 13-585E-F; *A User Guide to the Canadian System of National Accounts,* Catalogue No. 13-589E-F; and *The Input-Output Structure of the Canadian Economy,* Catalogue No. 15-511, Statistics Canada.
- Chile: *Cuentas Nacionales de Chile 1985–1992,* Central Bank of Chile.
- Colombia: *Metodología de Cuentas Nacionales, Departamento Administrativo Nacional de Estadísticas.*
- Croatia: *Quarterly Gross Domestic Product, Monthly Statistical Report, and Statistical Yearbook,* Central Bureau of Statistics.
- Czech Republic: *National Accounts for the Czech Republic and Annual National Accounts of the Czech Republic 1997,* Czech Statistical Office.
- Denmark: *Konjunkturstatistik: Supplement,* Statistics Danmark.
- Ecuador: *Cuentas Nacionales Trimestrales del Ecuador 1980.II-1991.I and Cuentas Nacionales Trimestrales del Ecuador 1965.I–1992.II,* Banco Central del Ecuador.
- El Salvador: *El Salvador: Metodologia del Producto Interno Bruto Trimestral,* Central Reserve Bank of El Salvador.
- Estonia: *National Accounts of Estonia,* Statistical Office of Estonia.
- Finland: *Statistics Finland Statistical Studies, No. 62 (1980),* Uotila, Leppä, Katajala, Statistics Finland.
- France: *INSEE. Méthodes n°13: Comptes nationaux trimestriels,* Institut National de la Statistique et des Etudes Economiques.

- Germany: *Selected Working Documents on Federal Statistics in number 7 Survey of National Product Calculations of the Federal Statistical Office,* number 19 *Housing Rentals,* number 21 *Input-Output Tables as the Basis of National Product Calculation,* number 22 *Construction Investments,* number 23 *Production Approach,* number 24 *Equipment Investments,* and number 25 *Subsidies,* and the working paper *Private Consumption, State Consumption, Net Exports,* Federal Statistical Office.
- Hong Kong SAR, China: *Gross Domestic Product 1961 to 1999,* Census and Statistics Department.
- Hungary: 1999 issue of *National Accounts Hungary,* Hungarian Central Statistical Office.
- Iceland: *Compiling Icelandic National Accounts, Documentation of Methods Applied, Output and Expenditure Approaches,* National Economic Institute.
- India: 1999 edition of the annual *National Accounts Statistics,* Central Statistical Organisation.
- Indonesia: *Pendapala Nasional Indonesia, Triwulanan,* 1991–93, Badan Pusat Statistik.
- Ireland: *National Income and Expenditure,* Central Statistics Office.
- Israel: *Current Briefings in Statistics* (March of each year), Central Bureau of Statistics.
- Italy: *Statistica in Breve* (May 26, 1999 and August 4, 1999), *Comunicato Stampa* (June 30, 1999), *Note Rapide* (April 30, 1999), Istituto Nazionale di Statistica.
- Japan, *The System of National Accounts in Japan,* Economic Planning Agency.
- Korea: *Estimation Methods of National Income Accounts in Korea,* Bank of Korea.
- Latvia: *National Accounts of Latvia,* Central Statistical Bureau of Latvia.
- Lithuania: *Lithuanian National Accounts,* Statistics Lithuania.
- Malaysia: *Quarterly National Product and Expenditure Account, xxx Quarter xxxx,* Departments of Statistics, Malaysia.
- Mexico: *Producto Interno Bruto Trimestral, Oferta y Demanda Global Trimestral a Precios Corrientes, and Oferta y Utilización Trimestral a Precios Constantes de 1993,* Instituto Nacional de Estadística, Geografía e Informática.
- Netherlands: *Fast GDP-growth Estimates, Data Flows in QNA, The Methodology of the Dutch System of Quarterly National Accounts, and A Provisional Time Series of 1977 – 1994 Quarterly National Accounts data linking up with the 1995 –1999 ESA 1995 figures: method and results,* Statistics Netherlands.
- Norway: *Quarterly National Accounts 1978–1998. Production, Uses and Employment,* Statistics Norway.
- Peru: *Cómo Leer la Nota Semanal,* Central Reserve Bank of Peru.
- Philippines: *Sources and Methods,* National Statistical Coordination Board.
- Poland: *Gross Domestic Product by Quarters for the Year 1995–1998,* Central Statistical Office.
- Singapore: *Singapore National Accounts 1987* and *Singapore System of National Accounts, 1995,* Department of Statistics.
- Slovak Republic: *Macroeconomic Indicators of Quarterly National Accounts and Value Added* and *CESTAT Statistical Bulletin,* Statistical Office of the Slovak Republic.
- Slovenia: *National Accounts of the Republic of Slovenia. Sources, Methods and Estimates,* Statistical Office of the Republic of Slovenia.
- South Africa: *Statistical Release P0441 of June 1999,* Statistics South Africa.
- Spain: *Contabilidad Nacional Trimestral de España. Metodología y serie Trimestral 1970–1992,* Instituto Nacional de Estadística.
- Switzerland: *Die Quartalsschätzungen des Bruttoinlandproduktes, Mitteilungsblatt für Konjunkturfragen, Heft 1,* State Secretariat for Economic Affairs.
- Turkey: *Gross National Product; Concepts, Methods and Sources,* State Institute of Statistics.
- United Kingdom: *Concepts, Sources and Methods* and *The UK National Accounts,* Office for National Statistics.
- United States: "A Guide to the NIPA's," *Survey of Current Business,* March 1998, Bureau of Economic Analysis.

IV. Sources for Other Components of the *1993 SNA*

Jenkinson, G., 1997, "Quarterly Integrated Economic Accounts – the United Kingdom Approach," Economic Trends, No. 520 (March), pp. 60–65.

V. Editing and Reconciliation

Arkhipoff, O., 1990, "Importance et diversité des problèmes d'agrégation en comptabilité national: esquise d'une théorie générale de l'agrégation," in *La Comptabilité National Face au Defi International,* ed. by E. Archambault and O. Arkhipoff (Paris: Economica).

Aspden, C., 1990, "Which Is the Best Short-Term Measure of Gross Domestic Product?" in *Australian National Accounts: National Income, Expenditure and Product,* Catalogue 5206.0 (Canberra: Australian Bureau of Statistics).

Bloem A., F. Maitland-Smith, R. Dippelsman, and P. Armknecht, 1997, "Discrepancies between Quarterly GDP Estimates," IMF Working Paper 97/123 (Washington: International Monetary Fund).

Kim, C., G. Salou, and P. Rossiter, 1994, "Balanced Australian National Accounts," Australian Bureau of Statistics Working Papers in Econometrics No. 94/2 (Canberra: Australian Bureau of Statistics).

Snowdon, T, 1997, "Quarterly Alignment Adjustments in the UK National Accounts," *Economic Trends,* No. 528 (November), pp. 23–27.

Stone, R., D.G. Champernowne, and J.E. Meade, 1942, "The Precision of National Income Estimates," *Review of Economic Studies,* Vol. 9, No. 2, pp. 111–25.

Stone, J.R.N., 1975, "Direct and Indirect Constraints in the Adjustment of Observations," in *National Accounts Models and Analysis. To Odd Aukrust in Honor of His Sixtieth Birthday,* Samfunnsøkonomiske Studier no. 26 (Social Economic Studies No. 26) (Oslo: Statistics Norway).

VI. Benchmarking

Alba, E. de, 1979, "Temporal Dissaggregation of Time Series: A Unified Approach," in *Proceedings of the Business and Economic Statistics Section,* American Statistical Association (Washington: American Statistical Association), pp. 359–70.

Barcellan, R., 1994, "ECOTRIM: A Program for Temporal Disaggregation of Time Series," paper presented at INSEE-Eurostat Quarterly National Accounts Workshop, Paris, December.

Bassi, V.L., 1939, "Interpolation Formula for the Adjustment of Index Numbers," in *Proceedings of the Annual Meeting of the American Statistical Association* (Washington: American Statistical Association).

———, 1958, "Appendix A," in *Economic Forecasting,* ed. by V.L. Bassi (New York: McGraw-Hill).

Bournay, J., and G. Laroque, 1979, "Réflexions sur la methode d'élaboration des comptes trimestriels," *Annales de l'Insee,* Vol. 36 (October–December), pp. 3–30.

Chen, Z.-G., P.A. Cholette, and E.B. Dagum, 1997, "A Nonparametric Method for Benchmarking Survey Data via Signal Extraction," *Journal of the American Statistical Association,* Vol. 92 (December), pp. 1563–71.

Cholette, P.A., 1978, "A Comparison and Assessment of Various Adjustment Methods of Sub-Annual Series to Yearly Benchmarks," Research Paper No. 78-03-001B (Ottawa: Statistics Canada).

———, 1984, "Adjusting Sub-Annual Series to Yearly Benchmarks," *Survey Methodology,* Vol. 10 (December), pp. 35–49.

———, 1988a, "Concepts, Definitions and Principles of Benchmarking and Interpolation of Time Series," Working Paper No. TSRA-87-014e (Ottawa: Statistics Canada).

———, 1988b, "Benchmarking System of Socio-Economic Time Series," Working Paper No. TSRA-88-017e (Ottawa: Statistics Canada).

———, 1994, "Users' Manual of Programme BENCH to Benchmark, Interpolate, and Calendarize Time Series Data," Working Paper No. TSRA-90-008 (Ottawa: Statistics Canada).

———, and A. Baldwin, 1988, "Converting Fiscal Year Data into Calendar Values," Working Paper No. TSRA-88-012e (Ottawa: Statistics Canada).

Cholette, P.A., and N. Chhab, 1991, "Converting Aggregates of Weekly Data into Monthly Values," *Applied Statistics,* Vol. 40, No. 3, pp. 411–22.

Cholette, P.A., and E.B. Dagum, 1994, "Benchmarking Time Series with Autocorrelated Survey Errors," *International Statistical Review,* Vol. 62 (December), pp. 365–77.

Chow, G. C., and An-loh Lin, 1971, "Best Linear Unbiased Interpolation, Distribution and Extrapolation of Time Series by Related Series," *Review of Economic and Statistics,* Vol. 53 (November), pp. 372–75.

Dagum, E.B., Cholette, P.A., and Z.G. Chen, 1998, "A Unified View of Signal Extraction, Benchmarking, Interpolation and Extrapolation of Time Series," *International Statistical Review,* Vol. 66, No. 3, pp. 245–69.

Denton, F.T., 1971, "Adjustment of Monthly or Quarterly Series to Annual Totals: An Approach Based on Quadratic Minimization," *Journal of the American Statistical Association,* Vol. 66 (March), pp. 92–102.

Di Fonzo, T., 1994, "Temporal Disaggregation of System of Time Series When Aggregate Is Known. Optimal Versus Adjustment Methods," paper presented at INSEE-Eurostat Quarterly National Accounts Workshop, Paris, December.

Durbin, J., and B. Quenneville, 1997, "Benchmarking by State Space Models," *International Statistical Review,* Vol. 65, No. 1, pp. 23–48.

Dureau, G., 1995, "Methodology of French Quarterly National Accounts," INSEE Methods No. 13 (Paris: INSEE).

Fernandez, R.B., 1981, "A Methodological Note on the Estimation of Time Series," *Review of Economic and Statistics,* Vol. 63 (August), pp. 471–76.

Friedman, M., 1962, "The Interpolation of Time Series by Related Series," *Journal of the American Statistical Association,* Vol. 57 (December), pp. 729–57.

Ginsburgh, V.A., 1973, "A Further Note on the Derivation of Quarterly Figures Consistent with Annual Data," *Applied Statistics,* Vol. 22, No. 3, pp. 368–74.

Helfand, S.D., N.J. Monsour, and M.L. Trager, 1977, "Historical Revision of Current Business Survey Estimates," in *Proceedings of the Business and Economic Statistics Section, American Statistical Association* (Washington: American Statistical Association), pp. 246–50.

Hillmer, S.C., and A. Trabelsi, 1987, "Benchmarking of Economic Time Series," *Journal of the American Statistical Association,* Vol. 82 (December), pp. 1064–71.

Laniel, N., and K. Fyfe, 1990, "Benchmarking of Economic Time Series," *Survey Methodology,* Vol. 16 (December), pp. 271–77.

Lanning, S.G., 1986, "Missing Observations: A Simultaneous Approach versus Interpolation by Related Series," *Journal of Economic and Social Measurement,* Vol. 14 (July), pp. 155–63.

Mian, I.U.H., and N. Laniel, 1993, "Maximum Likelihood Estimation of Constant Multiplicative Bias Benchmark Model with Application," *Survey Methodology,* Vol. 19 (December), pp. 165–72.

Monsour, N.J., and M.L. Trager, 1979, "Revision and Benchmarking of Business Time Series," *in Proceedings of the Business and Economic Statistics Section, American Statistical Association* (Washington: American Statistical Association), pp. 333–37.

Nasse, P., 1973, "Le Système des Comptes Nationaux Trimestriels," *Annales de l'Insee,* No. 14 (September–December), pp. 119–61.

Pinheiro, M., and C. Coimbra, 1993, "Distribution and Extrapolation of Time Series by Related Series Using Logarithms and Smoothing Penalties," *Economia,* Vol. 17 (October), pp. 359–74.

Sanz, R., 1981, "Metodos de Desagregacion Temporal de Series Economicas," Banco de Espana, Servicio de Estudios, Seri de estudios economicos no. 22 (Madrid: Banco de Espana).

(Also available in English under the title *Temporal Disaggregation Methods of Economic Time Series.*)

Schmidt, J. R., 1986, "A General Framework for Interpolation, Distribution, and Extrapolation of Time Series by Related Series," in *Regional Econometric Modeling,* ed. by R. Perryman and J.R. Schmidt (Boston: Kluwer/ Nijhoff), pp. 181–94.

Sjöberg, L., 1982, *Jämförelse av Uppräkningsmetoder för Nationalräkenskapsdata* (Comparison of Adjustment Methods for National Accounts Data), Memorandum (Stockholm: Statistics Sweden).

Skjæveland, A., 1985, *Avstemming av Kvartalsvise Nasjonalregnskapsdata mot Årlige Nasjonalregnskap* (Reconciliation of Quarterly National Accounts Data Against Annual National Accounts), Interne notater 85/22 (Oslo: Statistics Norway).

Somermeyer, W.H., R. Jansen, and A.S. Louter, 1976, "Estimating Quarterly Values of Annually Known Variables in Quarterly Relationships," *Journal of the American Statistical Association,* Vol. 71 (September), pp. 588–95.

Trabelsi, A., and S.C. Hillmer, 1990, "Benchmarking Time Series with Reliable Benchmarks," *Applied Statistics,* Vol. 39, No. 3, pp. 367–79.

VII. Mechanical Projections

Al-Osh, M., 1989, "A Dynamic Linear Model Approach for Disaggregating Time Series Data," *Journal of Forecasting,* Vol. 8 (June), pp. 85–96.

Boot, J.C.G., W. Feibes, and J.H.C. Lisman, 1967, "Further Methods of Derivation of Quarterly Figures from Annual Data," *Applied Statistics,* Vol. 16, No. 1, pp. 65–75.

Lisman, J.H.C., and J. Sandee, 1964, "Derivation of Quarterly Figures from Annual Data," *Applied Statistics,* Vol. 13, No. 2, pp. 87–90.

Stram, D.O., and W.W.S. Wei, 1986, "A Methodological Note on the Disaggregation of Time Series Totals," *Journal of Time Series Analysis,* Vol. 7, No. 4, pp. 293–302.

Wei, W.W.S., and D.O. Stram, 1990, "Disaggregation of Time Series Models," *Journal of Royal Statistical Society,* Series B, Vol. 52, No. 3, pp. 453–67.

VIII. Seasonal Adjustment and Estimation of Trend-Cycles

Alterman. W.F., E. Diewert, and R. Feenestra, 1999, "Time Series Approaches to the Problem of Seasonal Commodities," in *International Trade Price Indexes and Seasonal Commodities,* ed. by W.F. Alterman, E. Diewert, and R. Feenestra (Washington: U.S. Bureau of Labor Statistics).

Australian Bureau of Statistics, 1987, *A Guide to Smoothing Time Series—Estimation of "Trend,"* Information Paper 1316.0 (Canberra: Australian Bureau of Statistics).

————, 1993, *A Guide to Interpreting Time Series–Monitoring "Trends,"* Information Paper 1348.0 (Canberra: Australian Bureau of Statistics.).

Baxter, M., 1999, "Seasonal Adjustment of RPIY," *Economic Trends,* No. 546 (May), pp. 35–38.

Bell, W.R., and S.C. Hillmer, 1984, "Issues Involved With the Seasonal Adjustment of Time Series," *Journal of Business and Economic Statistics,* Vol. 2 (October), pp. 291–349. With comments by H. Akaike, C. Ansley and W.E. Wecker, P. Burman, E.B. Dagum and N. Laniel, M.M.G. Fase, C. Granger, A. Maravall, and D.A. Pierce.

Butter, F.A.G. den, and M.M.G. Fase, 1991, *Seasonal Adjustment as a Practical Problem* (Amsterdam; New York: North-Holland).

Cleveland, W.S., and S.J. Devlin, 1980, "Calendar Effects in Monthly Time Series: Detection by Spectrum Analysis and Graphical Methods," *Journal of the American Statistical Association,* Vol. 75 (September), pp. 487–96.

Compton, S., 1998, "Estimating and Presenting Short-Term Trend," *Economic Trends,* No. 538 (September), pp. 33–44.

————, 2000, "Presentation of Trend Estimates in Official UK and International Practice," paper presented at the Second International Conference on Establishment Surveys, Buffalo, New York, June.

Cristadoro, R., and R. Sabbatini, 2000, "The Seasonal Adjustment of the Harmonised Index of Consumer Prices for the Euro Area: A Comparison of Direct and Indirect Methods," Banca d'Italia temi di discussione No. 371 (Rome: Banca d'Italia). Available via the Internet: http://www.bancaditalia.it/pubblicazioni/temidi; internal&action=contenuti.action

Dagum, E.B., 1982, "Revisions of Time Varying Seasonal Filters," *Journal of Forecasting,* Vol. 1 (April–June), pp. 173–87.

————, 1987, "Monthly Versus Annual Revisions of Concurrent Seasonally Adjusted Series," in *Time Series and Economic Modeling,* ed. by I.B. MacNeill and G. J. Umphrey (Dordrecht: D. Reidel), pp. 131–46.

————, 1988, *The X-11-ARIMA/88 Seasonal Adjustment Method – Foundations and User's Manual* (Ottawa: Statistics Canada).

————, and M. Morry, 1984, "Basic Issues on the Seasonal Adjustment of the Canadian Consumer Price Index," *Journal of Business & Economic Statistics,* Vol. 2 (July), pp. 250–59.

Dagum, E.B., and N. Laniel, 1987, "Revisions of Trend-Cycle Estimators of Moving Average Seasonal Adjustment Methods," *Journal of Business & Economic Statistics,* Vol. 5 (April), pp. 177–89.

Deutsche Bundesbank, 1987, "Seasonal Adjustment as a Tool for Analysing Economic Activity," *Deutsche Bundesbank Monthly Report,* Vol. 39 (October), pp. 30–39.

————, 1991, "Data Adjusted for Seasonal and Working-Day Variations, on the Expenditure Component of GNP," *Monthly Report,* Vol. 43 (April), pp. 35–40.

————, 1999, "The Changeover from Seasonal Adjustment Method Census X-11 to Census X-12-ARIMA," *Monthly Report,* Vol. 51 (September), pp. 39–51.

European Central Bank, 2000, *Task Force on Seasonal Adjustment; Final Report* (Frankfurt).

Eurostat, 1998, *Seasonal Adjustment Methods – A Comparison for Industry Statistics* (Luxembourg: Office for Official Publications of the European Communities).

Findley, D.F., B.C. Monsell, H.B. Shulman, and M.G. Pugh, 1990, "Sliding-Spans Diagnostics for Seasonal and Related Adjustments," *Journal of the American Statistical Association,* Vol. 85 (June), pp. 345–55.

Findley, D. F., B.C. Monsell, W.R. Bell, M.C. Otto, and B.-C. Chen, 1996, "New Capabilities and Methods of the X-12-ARIMA Seasonal Adjustment Program," *Journal of Business and Economic Statistics,* Vol. 16 (April), pp. 127–77. With comments by W. Cleveland, S. Hyllenberg, A. Maravall, M. Morry and N. Chhab, K. Wallis, and E. Ghysels.

Findley, D.F., and C. C. Hood, undated, X-12-*ARIMA and Its Application to Some Italian Indicator Series.* Available via the Internet: http://www.census.gov/srd/www/x12istat_abs.html

Ghysels, E., 1997, "Seasonal Adjustment and Other Data Transformations," *Journal of Business & Economic Statistics,* Vol. 15 (October), pp. 410–18.

Hecq, A., 1998, "Does Seasonal Adjustment Induce Common Cycles?" *Economic Letters,* Vol. 59 (June), pp. 289–97.

Hylleberg, S., ed., 1992, *Modelling Seasonality* (Oxford: Oxford University Press).

Jain, R.K., 1989, "The Seasonal Procedure for the Consumer Price Indexes: Some Empirical Results," *Journal of Business & Economic Statistics,* Vol. 7 (October), pp. 461–74.

Kenny, P.B., and J. Durbin, 1982, "Local Trend Estimation and Seasonal Adjustment of Economic and Social Time Series," *Journal of the Royal Statistical Society,* Series A, Vol. 145, No. 1, pp. 1–41.

Knowles, J., 1997, *Trend Estimation Practices of National Statistical Institutes,* United Kingdom Office for National Statistics Methods and Quality Paper Number 44 (London: Office for National Statistics).

———, and P. Kenny, 1997, *An Investigation of Trend Estimation Methods,* United Kingdom Office for National Statistics Methods and Quality, Paper Number 43 (London: Office for National Statistics).

Ladiray, D., and B. Quenneville, 2001, *Seasonal Adjustment with the X11 Method* (New York: Springer-Verlag).

Lothian, J., and M. Morry, 1977, *The Problem of Aggregation: Direct and Indirect Seasonal Adjustment,* Time Series Research and Analysis Division Research Paper No. 77-08-001 (Ottawa: Statistics Canada).

McKenzie, S., 1984, "Concurrent Seasonal Adjustment with Census X-11," *Journal of Business & Economic Statistics,* Vol. 2 (July), pp. 235–49.

Organization for Economic Cooperation and Development, 1997, *Seasonal Adjustment of Industrial Production Series in Transition Countries in Central and Eastern Europe and the Russian Federation* (Paris).

Pierce, D.A., 1980, "Data Revision With Moving Average Seasonal Adjustment Procedures," *Journal of Econometrics,* Vol. 14 (September), pp. 95–114.

———, and S. McKenzie, 1987, "On Concurrent Seasonal Adjustment," *Journal of the American Statistical Association,* Vol. 82 (September), pp. 720–32.

Shiskin, J., A.H. Young, and J.C. Musgrave, 1967, *The X-11 Variant of the Census Method II Seasonal Adjustment Program,* Technical Paper 15 (Washington: Bureau of the Census, U.S. Department of Commerce).

Soukup, R., and D.F. Findley, undated, *On the Spectrum Diagnostics Used by X-12-ARIMA to Indicate the Presence of Trading Day Effects after Modeling or Adjustment.* Available via the Internet: http://www.census.gov/srd/www/rr9903_abs.html

U.S. Bureau of the Census, undated, *X-12-ARIMA Reference Manual.* Available via the Internet: http://www.census.gov/srd/www/x12a/x12down_pc.html#x12doc

———, undated, *Manufacturing and Construction Division Frequently Asked Questions on Seasonal Adjustment.* Available via the Internet: http://www.census.gov/const/www/faq2.html

Wallis, K.F., 1982, "Seasonal Adjustment and Revision of Current Data: Linear Filters for the X-11 Method," *Journal of the Royal Statistical Society,* Series A, Vol. 145, No. 1, pp. 74–85.

IX. Price and Volume Measures: Specific QNA-ANA Issues

Al, P.G., B. Balk, S. de Boer, and G.P. den Bakker., 1985, "The Use of Chain Indices for Deflating the National Accounts," National Accounts Occasional Papers No. 5, (Voorburg: Netherlands Central Bureau of Statistics). Also in *Statistical Journal of the United Nations Economic Commission for Europe,* Vol. 4 (July 1987), pp. 347–68.

Allan, R.G.D., 1975, *Index Numbers in Theory and Practice* (Chicago: Aldine Publishing Co.)

Australian Bureau of Statistics, 1998, "Introduction of Chain Volume Measures in the Australian National Accounts," Information Paper 5248.0 (Canberra: Australian Bureau of Statistics).

Brueton, A., 1999, "The Development of Chain-Linked and Harmonised Estimates of GDP at Constant Prices," *Economic Trends,* No. 552 (November), pp. 39–45.

Dalgaard, E., 1997, "Implementing the Revised SNA: Recommendations on Price and Volume Measures," *Review of Income and Wealth,* Series 43 (December), pp. 487–503.

de Boer, S., J. van Dalen, and P. Verbiest, 1997, "The Use of Chain Indices in the Netherlands," paper presented at the Conference on Measurement Problems in Econometric Modeling, Istituto Nazionale di Statistica, Rome, January. Also presented at the joint UNECE/Eurostat/OECD meeting on national accounts, Paris, June.

Diewert, W.E., 1976, "Exact and Superlative Index Numbers," *Journal of Econometrics,* Vol. 4 (May), pp. 114–45.

————, 1978, "Superlative Index Numbers and Consistency in Aggregation," *Econometrica,* Vol. 46 (July), pp. 883–900.

————, 1996a, "Price and Volume Measures in the System of National Accounts," in *The New System of National Economic Accounts,* ed. by J. Kendrick (Boston: Kluwer Academic Publisher), pp. 237–85.

————, 1996b, "Seasonal Commodities, High Inflation and Index Number Theory," Discussion Paper No. 96-06 (Vancouver: Department of Economics, University of British Columbia, Canada). Available via the Internet: http://web.arts.ubc.ca/econ/diewert/Disc.htm

————, 1998, "High Inflation, Seasonal Commodities, and Annual Index Numbers," *Macroeconomic Dynamics,* Vol. 43 (December), pp. 456–71.

————, 2000, "Index Numbers," in draft *Manual on Consumer Price Indices,* ed. by the ECE, EEC, ILO, IMF, OECD, UNSD, and World Bank (forthcoming). Available via the Internet: http://www.ilo.org/public/english/bureau/stat/guides/cpi/ index.htm

Ehemann, C., 1997, *Analyzing the Chain-Dollar Measures of Output: Contribution of Components to Level and Change* (unpublished; Washington: U.S. Bureau of Economic Analysis).

————, A.J. Katz, and B. Moulton, 2000, "How the Chain-Additivity Issue Is Treated in the U.S. Economic Accounts," paper presented at the 2000 Annual OECD Meeting of National Accounts Experts, Paris, September.

Forsyth, F.G., and R.F. Fowler, 1981, "The Theory and Practice of Chain Price Index Numbers," *Journal of the Royal Statistical Society,* Series A, Vol. 144, No. 1, pp. 224–46.

Fuà, G., and M. Gallegati, 1996, "An Annual Chain Index of Italy's 'Real' Product, 1861–1989," *Review of Income and Wealth,* Series 42 (June), pp. 207–24.

Hill, T.P., 1971, *The Measurement of Real Product: A Theoretical and Empirical Analysis of the Growth Rates for Different Industries and Countries* (Paris: OECD).

————, 1988, "Recent Developments in Index Number Theory and Practice," *OECD Economic Studies,* No. 10 (Spring), pp. 123–48.

————, 1996, "Price and Quantity Measures," in *Inflation Accounting: A Manual on National Accounting Under Conditions of High Inflation,* ed. by T.P. Hill (Paris: OECD), pp. 43–56.

Jackson, C., 1996, "The Effect of Rebasing GDP," in *National Economic and Financial Accounts, Second Quarter 1996,* Statistics Canada Cat. No. 13-001-XPB (Ottawa: Statistics Canada).

Janssen, R., and P. Oomens, 1998, "Quarterly Chain Series," paper presented at the Annual OECD Meeting of National Accounts Experts, Paris, December.

Landefeld, S., and R. Parker, 1995, "Preview of the Comprehensive Revision of the National Income and Product Accounts: BEA's New Featured Measures of Output and Prices," *Survey of Current Business,* Vol. 75 (July), pp. 31–38.

————, 1997, "BEA's Chain Indexes, Time Series, and Measures of Long-Term Economic Growth," *Survey of Current Business,* Vol. 77 (May), pp. 58–68.

Lasky, M.J., 1998, "Chain-Type Data and Macro Modeling Properties: The DRI/McGraw-Hill Experience," *Journal of Economic and Social Measurement,* Vol. 24 (Summer), pp. 83–108.

Lynch, R., 1996, "Measuring Real Growth – Index Numbers and Chain-Linking," *Economic Trends,* No. 512 (June), pp. 22–23.

Moulton, B.R., and E.P. Seskin, 1999, "A Preview of the 1999 Comprehensive Revision of the National Income and Product Accounts," *Survey of Current Business,* Vol. 79 (October), 6–17.

Parker, R.P., and J.E. Triplett, 1996, "Chain-Type Measures of Real Output and Prices in the U.S. National Income and Product Accounts: An Update," *Business Economics,* Vol. 31 (October), pp. 37–43.

Reinsdorf, M., E. Diewert, and C. Ehemann, 2000, "Additivity Decompositions of the Change of Fisher, Törnquist and Geometric Mean Indexes," Discussion Paper No. 01-01 (Vancouver: Department of Economics, University of British Columbia, Canada). Available via the Internet: http://web.arts.ubc.ca/econ/diewert/Disc.htm

Ribe, M., 1999, "Effect of Subcomponents on Chained Price Indices Like the HICP and the MUICP," paper presented at the Eurostat meeting of the working party of consumer price indices, Luxembourg, September.

Szultc, B., 1983, "Linking Price Index Numbers," in *Price Level Measurement: Proceedings of a Conference Sponsored by Statistics Canada,* ed. by W.E. Diewert and C. Montmarquette (Ottawa: Statistics Canada), pp. 537–66.

Triplett, E., 1992, "Economic Theory and BEA's Alternative Quantity and Price Indexes," *Survey of Current Business,* Vol. 72 (April), pp. 49–52.

United Nations, Department of International Economic and Social Affairs, 1979, *Manual on National Accounts at Constant Prices,* Statistical Papers, Series M, No. 64 (New York).

Varvares, C., J. Prakken, and L. Guirl, 1998, "Macro Modeling with Chain-Type GDP," *Journal of Economic and Social Measurement,* Vol. 24, (Summer), pp. 123–42.

Young, A., 1992, "Alternative Measures of Change in Real Output and Prices," *Survey of Current Business,* Vol. 72 (April), pp. 32–43.

———, 1993, "Alternative Measures of Change in Real Output and Prices, Quarterly Estimates for 1959–92," *Survey of Current Business,* Vol. 73 (March), pp. 31–37.

X. Work-in-Progress

XI. Revision Policy and the Compilation and Release Schedule

Barklem, A.J., 2000, "Revision Analysis of Initial Estimates of Key Economic Indicators and GDP Components," *Economic Trends,* No. 556 (March), pp. 31–52.

Di Fonzo, T., S. Pisani, and G. Savio, 1994, "Revisions to Italian Quarterly National Accounts Aggregates: Some Empirical Results," paper presented at INSEE-Eurostat Quarterly National Accounts Workshop, Paris, December.

Grimm, B.T., and R.P. Parker, 1998, "Reliability of the Quarterly and Annual Estimates of GDP and Gross Domestic Income," *Survey of Current Business,* Vol. 78 (December), pp. 12–21.

Johnson, A.G., 1982, "The Accuracy and Reliability of the Quarterly Australian National Accounts," Australian Bureau of Statistics Occasional Paper No. 1982/2 (Canberra: Australian Bureau of Statistics).

Kenny, P.B., and U.M. Rizki, 1992, "Testing for Bias in Initial Estimates of Key Economic Indicators," *Economic Trends,* No. 463 (May), pp. 77–86.

Lal, K., 1998, "National Accounts Revision Practice: Canada," paper presented at the Annual OECD Meeting of National Accounts Experts, Paris, December.

Mork, K.A., 1987, "Ain't behavin': Forecast Errors and Measurement Errors in Early GNP Estimates," *Journal of Business & Economic Statistics,* Vol. 5 (April), pp. 165–75.

Penneck, S., 1998, "National Accounts Revision Policy," paper presented at the Annual OECD Meeting of National Accounts Experts, Paris, December.

—————, 1998, "The UK Approach to Educating Users," paper presented at the Annual OECD Meeting of National Accounts Experts, Paris, December.

Rizki, U.M., 1996a, "Testing for Bias in Initial Estimates of Key Economic Indicators," *Economic Trends,* No. 510 (April), pp. 28–35.

—————, 1996b, "Testing for Bias in Initial Estimates of the Components of GDP," *Economic Trends,* No. 514 (August), pp. 72–82.

Seskin, E., and D. Sullivan, 2000, "Annual Revision of the National Income and Product Accounts," Survey of Current Business, Vol. 80 (August), pp. 6–33.

Smith, P., 1993, "The Timeliness of Quarterly Income and Expenditure Accounts: An International Comparison," *Australian Economic Indicators* (September), pp. xi–xvi.

Statistics Norway, 1998, "National Accounts Revision Policy in Norway," paper presented at the Annual OECD Meeting of National Accounts Experts, Paris, December.

U.S. Bureau of Economic Analysis, 1998, "U.S. National Income and Product Accounts: Release Schedule and Revision Practice," paper presented at the Annual OECD Meeting of National Accounts Experts, Paris, December.

Wroe, D., 1993, "Handling Revisions in the National Accounts," *Economic Trends,* No. 480 (October), pp. 121–23.

York, R., and P. Atkinson, 1997, "The Reliability of Quarterly National Accounts in Seven Major Countries: A User's Perspective," OECD Economics Department Working Paper No. 171 (Paris: OECD).

Young, A.H., 1993, "Reliability and Accuracy of the Quarterly Estimates of GDP," *Survey of Current Business,* Vol. 73 (October), pp. 29–43.

Index